Living More Human(e)ly?

Living More Human(e)ly?

Towards Better Approaches to Dating and Couple Relationships in Contemporary Anglo-American Contexts

Rebecca Leong

☙PICKWICK *Publications* · Eugene, Oregon

LIVING MORE HUMAN(E)LY?
Towards Better Approaches to Dating and Couple Relationships in Contemporary Anglo-American Contexts

Copyright © 2025 Rebecca Leong. All rights reserved. Except for brief quotations in critical publications or reviews, no part of this book may be reproduced in any manner without prior written permission from the publisher. Write: Permissions, Wipf and Stock Publishers, 199 W. 8th Ave., Suite 3, Eugene, OR 97401.

Pickwick Publications
An Imprint of Wipf and Stock Publishers
199 W. 8th Ave., Suite 3
Eugene, OR 97401

www.wipfandstock.com

PAPERBACK ISBN: 979-8-3852-0193-8
HARDCOVER ISBN: 979-8-3852-0194-5
EBOOK ISBN: 979-8-3852-0195-2

Cataloguing-in-Publication data:

Names: Leong, Rebecca, author.

Title: Living more human(e)ly? : towards better approaches to dating and couple relationships in contemporary anglo-american contexts / by Rebecca Leong.

Description: Eugene, OR : Pickwick Publications, 2025 | **Includes bibliographical references.**

Identifiers: ISBN 979-8-3852-0193-8 (paperback) | ISBN 979-8-3852-0194-5 (hardcover) | ISBN 979-8-3852-0195-2 (ebook)

Subjects: LCSH: Sex—Religious aspects—Christianity. | Sexuality—ethics. | Man-woman relationships—Religious aspects—Christianity. | Dating (Social custom)—Religious aspects—Christianity. | Marriage—Religious aspects—Christianity.

Classification: BT705.8 .L46 2025 (paperback) | BT705.8 .L46 (ebook)

VERSION NUMBER 04/21/25

Scripture quotations marked ESV are from the ESV® Bible (The Holy Bible, English Standard Version®), © 2001 by Crossway, a publishing ministry of Good News Publishers. Used by permission. All rights reserved.

Scripture quotations marked KJV are from the King James or Authorized Version.

Scripture quotations marked NIV are taken from the Holy Bible, New International Version®, NIV®. Copyright © 2011 by Biblica, Inc.® Used by permission of Zondervan. All rights reserved worldwide.

Scripture quotations marked NKJV are from the New King James Version, copyright © 1982 by Thomas Nelson, Inc. Used by permission. All rights reserved.

Scripture quotations marked NRSV are from the New Revised Standard Version, copyright © 1989, Division of Christian Education of the National Council of the Churches of Christ in the United States of America. Used by permission. All rights reserved.

*For my children, E and C,
and all my family, especially my parents, CL and KT,
celebrating their fifty-fifth wedding anniversary at the time of writing*

CONTENTS

Acknowledgments | xiii
Introduction | xvii
List of Abbreviations | xxiv

Chapter 1: Assumptions and Intellectual Context | 1
1.1 Introduction   1
1.2 Parameters of This Study and Clarifications   4
1.3 Grounding a Christian Version of "Lifelong Monogamy" on Interpretations of Scripture and Tradition   11
1.4 Christianity as, in Some Ways, Countercultural   22
1.5 On a Theology of Dating   24
1.6 Conclusion   36

Chapter 2: Learning from the Past: Historical and Cross-Cultural Aspects | 38
2.1 Introducing Four "Types"   38
2.2 Further Discussion of Each Type in Historical Perspective   46
2.3 Further Evaluation and Arguments   81

Chapter 3: Contemporary Anglo-American Contexts: Sociological Aspects | 85
3.1 Introduction   85
3.2 Continuing Shift Towards the "Pure Relationship"   89
3.3 Continuing "Culture Wars"   102

3.4   Increased Sexualization of Everyday Culture   105
3.5   Technology, the Internet, and Online dating   107
3.6   More Prevalent Economic Insecurity   114
3.7   Medical Advances Transforming Approaches Towards Sex   118
3.8   Conclusion   122

Chapter 4: Complexities of Being Human in Relationship: Psychological Aspects | 124

4.1   Introduction   124
4.2   Discussing Psychological Research Relating to the Five Recommended Approaches   137
4.3   Summary   177

Chapter 5: Saints Among Us (an Empirical Study): Learning from the Lived Experiences of Ten Long-Term Happily Married Couples Embodying Virtues | 179

5.1   Overview   179
5.2   Interview Findings   185
5.3   Discussing Data in Response to Four Follow-Up Questions   193
5.4   Further Analysis of Findings   197
5.5   Summary of Findings and Conclusions   199

Chapter 6: Living More Human(e)ly? Towards Better Approaches | 204

6.1   Introduction: Pushing Back Against Neoliberal Currents   204
6.2   On Christian Virtue Ethics   209
6.3   Developing a Multifaceted Integrated Model of Interpretation of the *Imago Dei* in Connection with Christian Virtue Ethics   219
6.4   On the Cardinal Virtues, Judeo-Christian Scripture, and Christian Virtue Ethics   230
6.5   A Fivefold Ethic   243
6.6   Further on this Fivefold Ethic   258
6.7   Conclusion   261

Chapter 7: Living More Human(e)ly? Further Application and Concluding Thoughts | 263

7.1 Drawing Together Findings from the Preceding Chapters   263

7.2 Further Applying This Christian Virtue-Ethical Approach to Contemporary Dating   267

7.3 Further Discussion of "You Always Marry the Wrong Person"   272

7.4 Further Observations in Connection with a Discussion of Compatibility   274

7.5 Further Drawing Together the Findings of the Preceding Chapters   278

7.6 Limitations of This Study and Suggested Areas for Future Research   282

7.7 Concluding Thoughts   283

Appendix A: Sample Interview Questionnaire | 285
Appendix B: Compilation of Interviewees' Responses | 291
Bibliography | 311

ACKNOWLEDGMENTS

I AM VERY GRATEFUL to God and to the following people who helped make the completion of this book a reality:

First, my doctoral supervisors Professor Robert Song and Professor Christopher Cook for their wisdom, fortitude, kindness, and more besides. I could not have asked for a better supervisory team for the daunting work which formed the basis for this book. They have inspired me, challenged me, patiently guided and encouraged me through various turbulent seas in the course of this wide-ranging interdisciplinary project. To them I say again thank you so much for steadfastly believing in me and this work.

Also, Professor Jason King and Professor Pete Ward for their very kind encouragement of this work and generous and insightful thoughts on my doctoral thesis, from which this book has grown.

The very brilliant faculty and my superb fellow students at Durham's Theology and Religion Department, particularly fellow attendees at departmental seminars with whom I have enjoyed and been inspired by many stimulating conversations through the years.

Dr. Jocelyn Bryan for very generously spending time with me in two helpful discussions and sharing insights from her wonderful book.

From St. Andrews, my lovely fellow students and fabulous faculty, including Dr. John Perry, Dr. Steve Holmes, Dr. Eric Stoddart, Dr. Michael Burdett, and especially Dr. Elizabeth Shively—from whom I have also learned much that is valuable which in one way or another have helped form material in this book.

Professor N. T. Wright for his kindness and an unforgettable discussion during coffee in St. Andrews and for inspiring a key argument in this book. I hope my work does his justice.

Professor Robin Gill of the journal *Theology* for so kindly giving my humble paper a hearing and motivating me to keep writing.

Past and current leaders and committee members of the very wonderful community of persons that the SSCE is (especially Andrew, Brian, David, Esther, Helen, Jackie, Jennifer, Joel, John, Josh, Medi, Neil, Nicholas, Phil, Richard, Rob, Sam, Susan, and other esteemed colleagues, past and present, with whom I have had the privilege to serve), and postgraduate convenors through the years (certainly not least: Annie, Ed, Johnny, Kaz, Michael, Wan-Yin, and Will) along with members and delegates whose conversations and insights at many a conference have helped inspire, illuminate and encourage my work.

Attendees of two seminars at the Department of Theology and Religion, Durham University, in 2023 and a short paper presentation at SSCE Conference 2024, at which various versions of chapters of this book were read and discussed, for their very kind, lively and helpful feedback.

My incomparable interviewees in my empirical study, who surprised me and inspired me with their life stories and practical wisdom. My work is so much enriched because of time spent with each of you. Thank you so much again.

Brilliant and dedicated teachers through the years–including Miss C. Lim, Ms. George, Mrs. Yap, and so many more from Newnham College Cambridge, NUS, RJC, RGS, and St. Margaret's Primary, Singapore. Thank you so much, teachers, for first inspiring in me a genuine love for learning, reading and persevering with writing. This book is a testament to your care too.

Wonderful friends both here in the UK and overseas, especially KG and W, H and WL, CH and PE, M and S, C and N, and all (not least, in Singapore) who have supported, prayed, encouraged, and cheered me on through these challenging years of endeavoring to balance home responsibilities and theological study/academic work. Thank you so much to you all.

Church friends from Singapore and members of the congregations of St. Mary's and St. Sebastian's, Lincolnshire, fellow pilgrims who have also in myriad ways inspired and illuminated my work through these years. Thank you so much.

The brilliant and dedicated team at Wipf and Stock who have so wonderfully brought this book to publication—including Chelsea, Charlie, Calvin, Rebecca A, Kyle, Matt, George, Karlie, and all the team. Many grateful thanks to each of you.

My family across the world (extended and immediate), for their love and prayers through the years, and especially: My parents CL and KT, siblings (VL and JL) and family (LH and J, J, J and J), and my children, who have tirelessly supported my many endeavors and traveled stoically with me on this long and winding road. Heartfelt thank you so much to all of you. As said to my children on completion of my doctoral thesis, I say again here (though in a moderately different context): E and C, Mummy is finally finishing this very, very long essay!

INTRODUCTION

In March 2016, the decree absolute came through for my divorce. The problems, increasingly intractable, had been rumbling on for years, even though not always apparent to those looking from the outside. Finally, by some miracle, I found the courage to get divorced after over thirteen years of what was often a mirage of a marriage, and face the stigma of being a "divorcee" till this day, more than eight years later. Like many others, I had soldiered on with the marriage for the sake of my children, determined to make things work, so that my children would not have to grow up in a broken home. I had read plenty of Christian counseling books on marriage, as far as I could gather, and endeavored to apply all the advice—*Five Languages of Love*; *His Needs, Her Needs*; *The Marriage Book*, the list goes on—but to no avail.

Separately, I have friends whose first marriages were abusive. One left the marital home, when her husband intentionally harmed her and her life was at risk, but her church told her "go back to your husband." I am glad she did not follow that advice. She remarried some years later, and remains happily remarried today, with a flourishing family that walks the way of Christ.

Whatever the causes (often convoluted) that led to divorce, I ask myself: Is there anything any of us could have done differently? Is there something we could have read or heard that could have helped us to make different choices when we were young?[1] Would we have listened? Would I have listened?

In a way, this book (and the thesis from which it grew) is like a long letter, a very long letter to my younger self. I ask myself what or

---

1. Primarily of whom to date, how to date, and whom to marry.

who I would have listened to in my younger years. When in our twenties, we tend to assume we've got it all figured out. Who would I have listened to? Perhaps only good, reliable, trustworthy scholarly sources, scientific sources. Perhaps those who had lived through similar experiences and come through the other side. Perhaps those who had somehow found a way to genuinely happy lifelong monogamy—not the idealized over-romanticized "and they lived happily ever after" head-in-the-clouds Disney-inspired version of marriage, but gritty, down-to-earth yet flourishing committed monogamy, that has managed to survive, even thrive, through the challenging times.

On the premise that a happy flourishing lasting monogamous marriage is a human good that is worth promoting and protecting,[2] I ask: Are there any forms of dating or approaches to dating that can help humans to realize this good?[3] And if so, what do they consist of? Stemming perhaps from my personal experience of intractable problems that could not be solved by merely "continuing to work" (which I did, very much) at marriage, in my research I am particularly interested[4] in whether dating approaches affect marital outcomes—engaging, for example, with questions such as whether it is always true that "you always marry the wrong person."

This book does not comprise a "magic formula" to "guarantee that you find your happily ever after." Rather, it is the fruit of more than eight years of labor and ceaseless searching, in as much as practicable of the relevant key fields of scholarly inquiry, to find answers to my questions.

Having persevered through and reflected on extensive research on these questions for all of these years now, I am convinced that substantial parts of the material that I offer in this book could have helped me, and perhaps my friends, even those years ago. It is my hope now that, written for our twenty-first century context, it can help others too.

As I mentioned to a fellow conference participant at a Society for the Study of Christian Ethics conference a few years ago, when explaining my project, the topic of dating has its particular challenges for study, as everybody appears to have something to say about it, or has

---

2. That is, in "everyday speak," I still believe in good loving marriages that last a lifetime.

3. Or are some people just plain "lucky"?

4. Without denigrating the importance of what one does within marriage (including continued fidelity, perseverance in love, personal and mutual growth, recourse to marital counseling and other forms of support) for the survival of a marriage.

an opinion about it one way or another, often quite assertively—from the very young to the very old, and everyone in between. Even my then ten-year-old child, for example, observing with some exasperation that many schoolmates from primary school had been dating and forming couples for quite a few years already, exclaimed: "Five-year-olds shouldn't be allowed to date! They're way too young!" (Question: Should they be allowed to? If so, what form should that take?)

And then, of course, there are the millions (or should that be billions by now?) of popular songs churning around everyday in our mainstream (and alternative) media, describing to us (and sometimes preaching or promoting their particular philosophy concerning) various aspects of the experiences of romantic love found and lost, and all the multifaceted encounters along the way. Further, in our internet-driven age, we not only have popular self-help books and the familiar "agony aunt" sections in various forms of media; we now also have online dating coaches and virtual "relationship experts," whether self-styled or with more impressive credentials, all accessible at the click of a button.

Questions that one might ask include the following . . .

> Is there such a thing as "true love"? Or is that a hopelessly over-romantic notion in the reality of daily life?
>
> Does it matter who makes the first move?
>
> Should women (and men) follow *the rules*?
>
> Is offline dating preferable to online dating?
>
> Is it better to date lots of people before reaching any decision for long-term commitment or marriage? Or should one "kiss dating goodbye" and approach a romantic partner only in terms of "courtship," as a prospect for marriage?
>
> Are dating apps any good? Does online dating help or hinder the formation of long-term committed relationships?
>
> Is there an optimum or minimum time a couple should date for before contemplating marriage?
>
> Can long-distance relationships work?
>
> Does it matter what couples do on dates, as long as they stay legal?

> Is friendship a prerequisite for a good marriage? Does "the one" exist? How about soulmates?
>
> Does cohabitation actually help make marriages better or does it increase the chances of a subsequent marriage failing?
>
> Should couples just cohabitate and not marry at all?
>
> How young is "too young" to start dating? Can one be too old to date?

And the list goes on.

> Does it really matter who one chooses to marry and how one makes a choice as to who to marry, or is it basically true that "you always marry the wrong person"?
>
> Does it matter whether one focusses on romantic criteria ("falling in love") or on more practical considerations? Was Jane Austen right in her portrayals of couples marrying for "love," for "comfort," or for both?
>
> What about arranged marriages?
>
> Will getting involved in casual sex or "hookup culture" affect one's chances of eventually realizing "happy lifelong monogamy"? Are promoters of "purity culture" basically right that their approach will help lead to happy lasting marriages? Can there be a way forward through the culture wars?

In the course of this book, I will be endeavoring to answer in particular substantial parts of the latter four questions[5] (and, in the process, hopefully offer answers for at least some of the others as well), primarily by studying aspects of five key fields (in addition to theology) which I suggest are particularly relevant in this context. The long-term intention (though, for practical purposes, not the immediate aim) of my project is therefore to promote stronger marriages (happy, flourishing, lifelong monogamy, which I describe in ch. 1) through attention to better approaches to dating and courtship in contemporary Anglo-American contexts (studying in particular heterosexual dating practices, due to space and time constraints, though I do not rule out the applicability of these approaches to nonheterosexual relationships).

Thus my central research questions in this book are:

---

5. These are condensed into two main questions set out below.

1. Assuming a Christian version of happy, flourishing, lifelong monogamous marriage is a good, are there any approaches to heterosexual dating in contemporary Anglo-American contexts that help realize or promote this good?
2. And if so, what do they consist of?

In chapter 1, I will set out my assumptions and the intellectual context for exploring answers to these questions. This will include outlining a Christian version of long-term marriage which I describe in terms of "happy, flourishing, lifelong monogamy."

Methods

To answer my research questions, and eventually to construct a Christian ethical framework for heterosexual dating in contemporary Anglo-American contexts, I will ultimately turn to Christian theology and Christian virtue ethics, particularly to take into account relevant themes pertaining to human nature and behavior and human relationships. These will be discussed in chapter 6.

At the same time, I suggest theology and virtue ethics may be enriched by learning from other disciplines, particularly on questions of human nature, behavior and intimate relationships. Hence I propose an interdisciplinary exploration for a richer discussion and have selected the following fields as among the most relevant to be key conversation partners with theology and Christian virtue ethics for addressing my research questions:

1. History: To consider what approaches to dating and courtship have already been adopted in the course of over two millennia of human experience and civilization, particularly in Western contexts, and to analyze their features (ch. 2)
2. Sociology: To consider what key themes of contemporary Anglo-American contexts are to be taken into account when constructing an ethical framework for heterosexual dating in these contexts (ch. 3)
3. Psychology: To investigate aspects of human nature and human behavior to be taken into account particularly when navigating human intimate relationships and to identify relevant findings that may be helpful (ch. 4)

4. The field of ordinary human experience, specifically the lived experiences of ordinary married couples: To consider what particular dating approaches have been taken within recent decades by happily married couples and to explore aspects of their married lives that may be relevant to marital longevity, through empirical research comprising semi-structured interviews of ten long-term happily married couples (ch. 5)

Summary

THIS BOOK IS THUS an interdisciplinary endeavor, a journey that involves, in the chapters that follow, engaging with and learning from history, sociology, psychology, people's lived experiences, theology and Christian virtue ethics.

In chapter 1, I set out assumptions, definitions, parameters and an overview of the field, including a discussion of the thought of Augustine, Thomas Aquinas and Martin Luther on a theology of marriage, as well as contemporary texts on a theology of dating. I also discuss theological perspectives on compatibility and "Hauerwas's law" ("you always marry the wrong person").

In chapter 2, on historical and cross-cultural aspects, I survey dating and courtship practices and approaches across different cultures over the past two thousand five hundred years or so, and propose and advance a fourfold typology, based on: (1) criteria for selection of one's marriage partner (functional to nonfunctional approaches) and (2) degree of openness to physical intimacy prior to or without monogamous marriage (nonpermissive to permissive approaches).

In chapter 3, on sociological aspects, I consider and assess six features or themes I propose are particularly distinctive of heterosexual dating culture in contemporary Anglo-American contexts, including in view of developments related to and after the sexual revolution of the 1960s and early 1970s in Western societies, considering the period of about fifty years since then to the present day.

In chapter 4, on relevant psychological research, I discuss the psychology-theology interface and aspects of and key research from social psychology, evolutionary psychology, developmental and personality psychology, relevant to this topic, and advance five recommended approaches that I offer as a practical outworking of my proposed fivefold ethic (discussed in ch. 6), including in particular the virtue of prudence/practical wisdom.

In chapter 5, I discuss findings from my empirical study, involving ten semi-structured interviews, seeking to learn from the lived experiences of ten long-term happily married couples, and suggest how this provides supportive evidence and supportive data for my thesis.

In chapter 6, partly as a pushback against neoliberal currents in contemporary contexts which I suggest are antithetical to authentic Christian thought and practice, I build and advance my proposed Christian virtue-ethical approach (connected to a multifaceted integrated model of interpretation of the *imago Dei*), which I argue may be expressed in terms of a fivefold ethic (comprising cardinal virtues of prudence, justice, courage, temperance, and a fifth overarching virtue of love and care) applicable for contemporary sexual ethics. This will develop (partly) on views expressed by N. T. Wright in a 2008 essay, and also engage with existing (particularly Thomistic) versions of virtue ethics.

In chapter 7, I include further suggestions for application of this proposed fivefold ethic in contemporary contexts and draw together various strands advanced in the preceding chapters to offer some concluding thoughts and a possible way forward.

As I would like to think much academic work is, this is a work in progress. I am finalizing this manuscript during a time of holding (and juggling) substantial responsibilities in various forms. I hope there can be forbearance from my readers on aspects of this work (of which there are likely many) which will be less than perfect. I also apologize in advance to readers who may at times be puzzled by the two different (sometimes alternating) registers in which I write this work, which (rather ambitiously, or unrealistically, some may say) due to space and time constraints, also comprises an attempt to speak to both academic and general audiences in the same book.

With this, I offer here my imperfect and small, yet hopefully somewhat helpful, contribution to the fields of Christian sexual ethics, virtue ethics, and theologies of dating.

ABBREVIATIONS

Hor	*Horizons*
IBC	Interpretation: A Bible Commentary for Teaching and Preaching
JRE	*Journal of Religious Ethics*
NAC	*New American Commentary*
ONS	Office for National Statistics
SJT	*Scottish Journal of Theology*
STI	Studies in Theological Interpretation
TynBul	*Tyndale Bulletin*
WBC	Word Biblical Commentary

CHAPTER 1: ASSUMPTIONS AND INTELLECTUAL CONTEXT

1.1 Introduction

1.1.1 First Things

LET ME SAY AT the outset that the following are caveats to the assumptions that I set out in this chapter (particularly regarding the assumption that happy, flourishing, lifelong monogamy is a good, elaborated on below):

Dating itself can be, and very often is, a formative experience—for better or for worse.

It need not end in marriage. And yet it can be good. Whether it is good—or otherwise—is not determined by whether or not a particular dating relationship ends in marriage (or civil partnership), whatever form that marriage may take. One of my main arguments in this book is that my proposed fivefold ethic (elaborated on in chs. 6 and 7) should be held central throughout the process of dating, and that if dating is approached with this fivefold ethic (which is intentionally formative in itself) and prioritized, then one's lived experience of dating can be viewed as good, even if it does not end in marriage (for whatever reason).

As I will also elaborate in chapter 6, I am also suggesting that we need to venture beyond neoliberal/market-oriented/consumer-driven approaches to dating, so prevalent in contemporary Anglo-American contexts—albeit in many different forms—and instead prioritize growth in the character virtues of prudence/wisdom, justice, courage/fortitude, temperance, and love and care.

Whatever the outcome of dating may be, developing on themes in the core areas of virtue ethics and sexual ethics (which I elaborate on in chs. 6 and 7), I also argue against manipulative, deceptive, abusive and/or exploitative (and other reductionistic and dehumanizing) practices in contemporary dating—and hence for living more human(e)ly, including in the contexts of contemporary Anglo-American dating.

1.1.2 "Happy, Flourishing, Lifelong Monogamy" as a Good

One may ask whether there are any substantial links between behavior, choices or approaches in dating (or courtship) and marital outcomes. For the purposes of my research questions, I am assuming that a Christian version of happy, flourishing, lifelong, monogamous marriage is a good. I will be elaborating later on each of the aspects, "happy," "flourishing," and "lifelong monogamy" that I am assuming. When I say I assume this version of marriage is "a good," I mean primarily that it brings good to society and the individuals within it—for example, by being associated with marriages less likely to end in divorce, and arguably also in couples being less likely to intend harm, or be indifferent to causing harm, to each other. However, I am not saying that this version of marriage is "the good" or "the only good." Nor am I setting this version in stone as a theology for marriage.

I am therefore assuming that it is good that human intimate relationships take place within the context of long-term (ideally lifelong) mutual commitment (lifelong monogamy) between two people who love and cherish each other for life (for example, as set out in various forms of Christian marriage vows), and who are exclusive sexual partners for each other. I will define "happy" in terms of each partner answering in the affirmative when asked if they would marry each other again. I will also argue that such a Christian version of happy, lifelong marriage should be outward-looking, that the couple involved should be concerned both with their mutual flourishing and the flourishing of society around them—hence my inclusion of the word "flourishing" in my definition and understanding of happy, lifelong marriage. Overall, I refer to this form of couple relationship as "happy, flourishing, lifelong, monogamous marriage." Having made the assumption that this is a good, I am asking if there are any approaches to dating in contemporary Anglo-American contexts that help realize or promote this good.

That there may be such approaches cannot be taken for granted, of course. For example, if one follows strictly what is sometimes known as "Hauerwas's law" (described later in this chapter), that "you always marry the wrong person," one may well take the position that virtually any approach or dating practice will do, and one may marry almost anyone at all who is available, and still have a successful marriage, as long as one works hard enough at "making it work." Following this approach, it almost does not matter at all who one chooses to marry, or how one makes that choice. I will discuss this issue in detail later in this chapter.

As a further clarification, when I refer to sexual partnership within happy, flourishing, lifelong monogamy, I am not assuming that married people will always have or always should have sexual intercourse with each other, although the evidence may indicate that many do. I do assume, however, that those in a happy, lifelong marriage will live in a state of sexual fidelity to each other—that is, by sexual partnership with each other, I mean sexual exclusivity, that they are sexually committed to each other, with the intention that if they do have sexual intercourse, that will be with each other and not anyone else. In this sense, by including the concept of sexual partnership, I also assume that "happy, lifelong monogamy" goes beyond "happy, lifelong, platonic friendship" (a type of relationship that one can enjoy with many others, is not mutually exclusive, and does not involve the prospect of sexual intercourse).

Of course (as stated earlier), it may be observed that not all dating ends in nor is directed at ending in marriage. Many practices of dating, particularly in contemporary contexts, are often "casual" in nature, or merely exploratory, a "getting to know you" process. All such practices are also included within my study, and I do not assume that dating does or should end in marriage. Indeed, I argue that some dating relationships are likely best concluded without ending in marriage—for example, if there is evidence of abuse or exploitation in the relationship, or if there are clear indicators pointing towards the likelihood that one or both parties will find a lifelong commitment to the other a burdensome challenge that they will experience as a misery rather than a joy.

Further, I am not assuming that divorces do not occur or should not occur. Indeed, I have argued elsewhere that in the context of abuse, for example, divorce may well be the best recourse.[1] I do assume, however, that where divorce occurs, there is a recognition that there is something

---

1. Leong, "Divorce and Remarriage."

less than ideal in this outcome for marriage (and that perhaps it may have been better if the parties had never married at all), and also that any subsequent marital relationship should be entered into with the intention that that marriage—viewed perhaps as a "second chance" at happy, lifelong marriage—should as far as possible be permanent.

I also do not assume that marriage in itself is the sole ideal state for human flourishing. Indeed, I am in accord with voices from Christian tradition that singleness is at least as much (if not more) a desirable state as marriage. I elaborate on this later in my discussion of celibacy.

This chapter will be composed of two parts. In the first part, alongside discussing some parameters, I will set out and elaborate on my assumptions regarding "happy, flourishing, lifelong monogamy." In the second part of this chapter I will discuss existing literature from key Christian scholars who have published work relating to a theology of dating, thereby forming the intellectual context for my subsequent explorations in this field. This latter part will also include a discussion of "Hauerwas's law."

1.2 Parameters of This Study and Clarifications

1.2.1 Universalizability

It may be noted that in my book—while recognizing elements that set apart Christian marriage as in some significant ways unique and held to somewhat tougher standards—I am seeking to identify universalizable norms for the practice of heterosexual dating that apply both in Christian and non-Christian contexts in Anglo-American society.

While I assume, in seeking to develop such norms, that happy, flourishing, lifelong monogamy is a God-given good for the well-being[2] of humanity, I am not seeking in this book to impose norms—particularly on non-Christians—to enable the achievement of the tougher standards expected of Christians in matters of sexual ethics, due to the particular nature of the calling and vocation which is held to be an integral part of Christian marriage (as distinguished from marriage in general).

On balance, I seek to set out in this chapter a Christian version of marriage that is universalizable, that I suggest is not just for Christians, but may also be applicable to and is also conducive to the flourishing of

---

2. I define well-being in general terms and note it may be measured in various ways. See, for example, Mental Health Foundation, "What Is Wellbeing."

non-Christian marriages and society in general. I suggest that this Christian version of "happy, flourishing, lifelong monogamy" that I set out in this chapter is a good that can benefit society in general.

Therefore, to clarify:

i. I will not be arguing in detail that the Christian version of marriage set out in this chapter is superior to other forms of marriage (such as polygamy, or open marriages, for example), as that discussion is beyond the scope of this book.

ii. For the purposes of my book (including the detailed discussions on history, sociology, psychology, my empirical study and virtue ethics that will follow), I will assume that the Christian version of marriage described and set out in this chapter is normatively what should apply for the flourishing of society—and I will then proceed to explore answers to my research questions as to whether there are any forms of dating that help promote or enable the realization of this version of marriage ("happy, flourishing, lifelong monogamy"), and if so what they consist of.

1.2.2 On Dating

My definition of "dating" in this book is an expansive one, extending to all intimate relations and couple relationships prior to or without marriage—including hookups and other casual sexual encounters, online dating, "offline" dating, courtship, cohabitation, and so on—other than sex work, as well as all acts intended to be preparatory to or exploratory of marriage (even if nonsexual in nature), such as meetings and activities as part of arranged marriage processes.

As mentioned, I will not be discussing nonheterosexual relationships in this book, as, due to space constraints, my study is limited to heterosexual relationships. However, I do not rule out the possibility that some of my findings may also be applicable to same-sex relationships.

Two key aspects of dating approaches that I will consider in detail in chapter 2 are:

i. The basis for one's choice of marriage partner/life partner (not necessarily the same as for temporary dalliances): ranging from functional to nonfunctional approaches

ii. Degrees of permissiveness in physical intimacy (combining theory and practice) during courtship/dating/prior to marriage: ranging from nonpermissive to permissive approaches.

1.2.3 On "Flourishing"

I suggest that a concept of human flourishing that is particularly applicable in the context of my book is that advanced by Nicholas Wolterstorff in his evocative idea of shalom. Wolterstorff writes:

> There can be no shalom without justice. Justice is the ground floor of shalom. In shalom each person enjoys justice . . . what is due them. . . .
>
> Shalom goes beyond justice, however. Shalom incorporates right relationships in general . . . right relationships to God, to one's fellow human beings, to nature, and to oneself. The shalom community is not merely the *just* community but is the *responsible* community, in which God's laws for our multifaceted existence are obeyed.
>
> It is more even than that . . . Shalom incorporates *delight* in one's relationships. To dwell in shalom is to find delight in living rightly before God . . . in living rightly in one's physical surroundings . . . in living rightly with one's fellow human beings . . . even in living rightly with oneself. . . .
>
> The vision of shalom comes to us . . . as a two-part command: We are to pray and struggle for the release of the captives, and we are to pray and struggle for the release of the enriching potentials of God's creation.[3]

Consistent with this vision of shalom for human flourishing, I argue in chapter 6 for a fivefold ethic (of prudence, justice, courage, temperance, and love and care) for application to heterosexual dating in contemporary Anglo-American contexts.

Further, it is important to observe that this Christian version of happy, lifelong marriage is meant to be outward-looking, rather than turned inward mainly for the indulgent or self-centered benefit of the two in the relationship. In line with a vision of flourishing that follows

---

3. "Teaching for Shalom," in Wolterstorff, *Educating for Shalom*, locs. 480–492 of 4705; emphasis in original.

Wolterstorff's version of shalom described above, I assume a Christian version of happy, lifelong monogamy that—while bearing fruit in the personal flourishing of the lives of the couple involved—should also be directed at advancing the flourishing of society around them. This may be contrasted, say (to give an extreme example) with a "happy, lifelong marriage" of two partners in crime, who successfully support each other throughout a life of criminal exploitation and tyranny. Many other negative examples of "happy marriage" can probably be noted in the course of pondering further on this matter.

Hence, rather than a narrow requirement of "procreation" in terms of physical offspring as a core aspect of marriage, I advocate a more expansive understanding of fruitfulness, in terms of being directed outwardly towards the flourishing of society around them.

To distinguish this version of happy marriage from "happy marriages" that are not directed at the flourishing of society in the sense that I have described above, I will use the term "happy, flourishing, lifelong monogamy" in the course of this book to refer to this Christian version of happy marriage that I advocate. It is also this version of happy marriage that I am assuming as normative when I ask my research questions set out above and seek to answer these questions in the course of the next five chapters.

Wherever I use the term "happy, flourishing, lifelong monogamy" in this book, it should be understood as a term of art referring specifically to the Christian version of happy, lifelong, monogamous marriage that I discuss and describe in this chapter.

1.2.4 Distinguishing Theological Perspectives of Marriage from Legal/Sociological Perspectives

It is important to distinguish between a theological model of marriage—which I would argue is centered on covenant commitment and oneness/intimacy in its various aspects—and the societal/legal institution of marriage which takes various forms—with different rules and conventions in different societies/cultures around the world. From a virtue-ethical perspective, I would argue in favor of legislation on marriage amounting to virtuous regulation of intimate relations between humans, including to discourage or address injustices or abuse.[4] It may

---

4. For example, Rivers argues for effective regulation (including addressing the

be observed that compared to cohabitation (which offers little or no protection if the relationship breaks down), couple relationships which are registered, such as marriage or civil partnership allow for some legal regulation of aspects of intimate relations/domestic relations which offer a level of protection (though not necessarily adequate) against injustices, or at least provide some possibly helpful recourse in the event of breakdown of the relationship.[5]

1.2.5 Aspects of Marriage

Considering the key constituents of this model of marriage that I assume is a good, it is important to distinguish between what is essential and what is contingent.

I suggest that the essence of marriage is oneness, and the following core elements are essential:

i. Mutual commitment with the clear intention for permanence/lifelong monogamy—lifelong commitment, which may be described in terms of "covenant commitment," and

ii. Sexual exclusivity. As mentioned above, sexual activity is not essential (for example, it may be hampered by external circumstances), but sexual exclusivity is integral to the bond—that is, if either does engage in sexual activity, it will be with each other and not anyone else.

iii. Sexual intimacy[6] in the marriage should ideally be experienced as the culmination of intimacy in other aspects of the couple relationship, including emotional, intellectual, and spiritual intimacy—although, as stated earlier, this does not imply that sexual intercourse is a necessary part of marriage.

---

sometimes weighty and messy repercussions) of intimate relations between humans, in the interests of justice ("Could Marriage Be Disestablished?").

5. Even so, as I will suggest in this book, it would be better to exercise due diligence during the period of dating and/or courtship, so as to minimize, to the extent possible, the likelihood of occurrences of injustice or abuse in the relationship, so that recourse to legal remedies becomes unnecessary.

6. It is beyond the scope of this book as to whether this includes only heterosexual intimacy, or may extend to homosexual intimacy, but as stated at the start of this chapter, the present discussion is limited to the study of heterosexual relationships.

Overall therefore I assume that "lifelong monogamy" consists essentially of a lifelong pair bond with sexual exclusivity.

I would argue that the following elements are contingent (nonessential), but I will not be elaborating on these here:

i. Whether there is an active sexual relationship
ii. Traditional gender roles—for example, the male as head of the household, complementarian versus egalitarian structures
iii. Whether marriage is related to procreation,
iv. Sharing bed and board/living under the same roof
v. Whether marriage is dissoluble/whether divorce is allowed

I assume that procreation, such as argued by Augustine (and Aquinas) as being integral to marriage, and pleasure (for example, as argued by Hollinger in the context of the meaning of sex)—while being very often natural offshoots of sexual intimacy—should not stand independently as essential elements for marriage, but as being often a natural part of sexual intimacy in the marriage. I suggest therefore that a couple should be open to these aspects of their marital relationship, procreation and pleasure— in accordance with the flourishing of their relationship lived to the full, but if these aspects are absent for particular reasons such as illness or extraneous circumstances, or for other reasons, that should not disqualify the relationship from being viewed as being essentially marriage.[7]

1.2.6 Defining "Love" and Being "Happy"

I should also clarify that by "happy" lifelong marriage, I do not mean a state of constant marital bliss, through all the different seasons of life. Indeed, conflicts are inevitable in any long-term marital relationship— as researchers such as John Gottman have pointed out.[8] A "happy" marital relationship, as I define it here, is not one that is free of moments or seasons of disagreement, nor necessarily one where the parties are constantly feeling euphoric about their relationship. Instead, I define

---

7. It may also be noted that the Church of England's *Living in Love and Faith* indicates the development of a model of marriage—from the Book of Common Prayer to Common Worship—in which children/procreation gradually become less central to the concept of marriage (*Living in Love and Faith*, 28–29).

8. Gottman and Silver, *Why Marriages Succeed or Fail*, 28.

"happy" to mean that each person in the marriage would answer an affirmative yes when asked, "If given the chance now to marry anyone you choose, would you marry your current partner again?" This is a similar question to the one I asked each of the interviewees in my empirical study of ten long-term happily married couples in Lincolnshire, which I discuss in chapter 5.

From a theological standpoint and leading to the next section discussing the nature of love, I should also point out that in this matter (while disagreeing with key aspects of his views on sexuality, as I discuss in detail in sec. 1.3.2) I am mostly in agreement with Augustine in his perspective regarding the difference between "using" (*uti*) and "enjoying" (*frui*). Augustine contrasts these two versions of love, concluding that "this world must be used, not enjoyed, that so the invisible things of God may be clearly seen."[9]

Van Nieuwenhove explains that this is an "often misunderstood distinction," and that what Augustine[10] is seeking to emphasize in the contrasting of *frui* and *uti* is that "God should be our ultimate concern in all our activities (intellectual or practical)," that "no created being should be considered as the ultimate."[11] He further clarifies that, contrary to some contemporary misconceptions of the issue, such a perspective does not lead to an instrumentalizing view of persons:

> Everything we "use" needs to be referred back to our ultimate concern: God as the object of our fruition. Other human beings are not really to be enjoyed . . . or, if we are willing to concede that they can be enjoyed, they should only be enjoyed "in God." . . .
>
> It may seem to modern commentators that the notion that only God is to be enjoyed, necessarily implies an instrumentalization of creation, including human persons. I would argue with Augustine and the medieval tradition after him, that the opposite is the case: Augustine's radical theocentric focus—only God is to be enjoyed—is exactly what keeps us from either idolizing creation, or contemptuously disregarding it. For only when our desire is immediately focused on God, and only indirectly on created beings, can we attribute intrinsic meaning to created beings.[12]

---

9. Augustine, "On Christian Doctrine" 3–4.
10. Further on this, see also Williams, *On Augustine*, ch. 11, "Augustinian Love."
11. Van Nieuwenhove, *Introduction to Medieval Theology*, 24.
12. Van Nieuwenhove, *Introduction to Medieval Theology*, 25.

CHAPTER 1: ASSUMPTIONS AND INTELLECTUAL CONTEXT

Following Van Nieuwenhove's interpretation of Augustine's thought regarding this matter, I argue for a similar approach towards intimate relationships and seeking happiness, that in these, we should seek our ultimate happiness in God, and we ought to love our neighbor "in God," rather than idolize our neighbor or any earthly relationship, and in so doing, love them aright.

Eleonore Stump helpfully surveys and describes different possible accounts of the nature of love and presents a compelling interpretation of Aquinas's account of the nature of love,[13] consisting of two interconnected but different desires:

i. First, wanting the best for the other ("desiring the good for the beloved"):[14] this aspect is not connected to qualities of the beloved, and may be generically applied to many.

ii. Second, desiring union with the beloved: the level of union in question (which may primarily be in terms of communion, rather than in necessarily sexual terms) varies between relationships, and is closely connected with qualities of the beloved, "both the intrinsic and relational characteristics."[15]

In the context of romantic relationships, I argue that Stump's interpretation of Aquinas's account of love, as set out above, is particularly relevant and applicable.

I will discuss the nature of love further in the context of an ethic of love and care, as part of the fivefold ethic that I propose in chapter 6.

1.3 Grounding a Christian Version of "Lifelong Monogamy" on Interpretations of Scripture and Tradition

1.3.1 On Scripture

Passages in Judeo-Christian Scripture often referred to for a Christian theology of marriage include the creation narrative in Gen 2, Jesus's teaching on marriage and divorce in the Gospels, 1 Cor 7, and Eph 5:21–33. Adrian Thatcher argues that there is no single "biblical picture

---

13. Stump, *Wandering in Darkness*, 91–100.
14. Stump, *Wandering in Darkness*, 96.
15. Stump, *Wandering in Darkness*, 96.

of marriage" and that diversity of teaching in Scripture about marriage should be acknowledged more widely.[16]

1.3.2 On Monogamy in Scripture

One will likely be aware that polygamous practices were not unusual among the Jews in the millennia before the time of Christ, as can be observed in the Old Testament accounts of the lives of the patriarchs and others, including notably Jacob, David, and Solomon. Almost invariably, though, their polygamous lives were associated with long-running incidents of rivalry, jealousy, and deep unhappiness of one form or another.

Among several other well-regarded New Testament scholars, both Craig Blomberg and Grant Osborne emphasize that since creation God has intended human marriage to be permanent and between two people (one man and one woman) joining together to form a one-flesh union.[17]

Further on polygamy being quite apparent in the Old Testament, and why monogamy is normative for Christians as clearly reflected in the New Testament and the overall biblical story, N. T. Wright argues that "despite the centuries of apparently unrebuked polygamy in the Old Testament, the New Testament assumes on every page that monogamy is now mandatory for the followers of Jesus" and that this is because "in Jesus of Nazareth the creator of the world—the whole world . . . is being rescued and renewed."[18]

1.3.3 On Tradition

The fourth-century church father Saint Augustine laid out, for the first time, a theology of marriage—in terms of the three goods of marriage: "sexual fidelity" (*fides*), "offspring" (*proles*), and "the indissoluble bond" (*sacramentum*)[19]—for the Western church, which became authoritative for the next millennium, and authoritative even among many in the Christian church till this day. It may be observed that this Augustinian theology of marriage based on the three goods of marriage has been

---

16. Thatcher, "Marriage, the New Testament."
17. Blomberg, *Matthew*, 290; Osborne, *Matthew*, 1008.
18. N. T. Wright, *Scripture and the Authority*, 191–93.
19. See, for example, Cahill, *Sex, Gender, and Christian Ethics*, 188.

accepted pretty much in its entirety through to the twentieth century in many parts of the worldwide church.

I will start by outlining Augustine's three goods of marriage which hold authoritative position. Further to this, it should also be observed that:

   i. The important contribution that Aquinas brings to a Christian theology of marriage is the value of the friendship between husband and wife (I will refer to Lisa Cahill's thought on this).

   ii. The key innovation that Luther brings to a Christian understanding of marriage is his emphasis on marriage, rather than on celibacy.

   iii. Twentieth- and twenty-first-century writers have tended to discuss the third good in terms of "fruitfulness," rather than "procreation" in the narrow sense.[20]

Hence a current revisionist view of the three goods of marriage may be understood as composed of: two people for life, to the exclusion of all others, with the intention of fruitfulness.[21]

1.3.4 Augustine

While recognizing the immense weight and authoritative nature of the church father Augustine's writings on sexuality and marriage, I will seek here to connect Augustine's thought with his life, reflecting on how theology may be connected with biography, particularly as Augustine does this too in *Confessions*.[22] In "On the Good of Marriage," Augustine sets out authoritatively three goods of marriage, namely: procreation, fidelity to one's partner (faith), and sacrament:

> Therefore the good of marriage throughout all nations and all men stands in the occasion of begetting, and faith of chastity:

---

20. An example of this is Robert Song. On Song's revisionist view on the theology of marriage, it may be noted that Song's account "of fruitfulness within marriage is not intended as an account of Augustine, who very clearly talks about *proles*, i.e., children/procreation, but rather an account of marriage in the light of Christ" (as stated by Song in email to author on Mar. 9, 2021).

21. There is a significant divide between adherents of "fruitfulness" thought and those of "procreation" thought, although not always apparent.

22. As Cahill observes, "Augustine invites biographical references in interpreting his theology, for he himself ties personal history, religious experience, and theological insight closely together in his *Confessions*" (*Sex, Gender, and Christian Ethics*, 175).

> but, so far as pertains unto the People of God, also in the sanctity of the Sacrament. . . .
>
> All these are goods, on account of which marriage is a good; offspring, faith, sacrament.[23]

It may be observed that even in "On the Good of Marriage," Augustine appears to have an ambivalent attitude towards sex (which appears to be in continuity with the teaching of church fathers before him).[24] He clearly sets celibacy, in terms of "continence" as a higher and more desirable state than marriage, while allowing for sexual intercourse within marriage for the sake of gaining progeny, and also—even while accepting that marital sex is acceptable for bringing lust within legal bounds—disapproves of any sexual activity, even within marriage, which is unrelated to procreating and which therefore in his view is motivated by lust (and hence considered to be a "venial" sin).[25] Going further than considering Augustine's position as ambivalent, Timothy Chappell comes out strongly in his assertion that "Augustine's own account of sexuality comes dangerously close, not just to treating sex as special in a hard-to-define way, but to demonizing it."[26]

With respect, I suggest that Augustine's sexual ethics and theology of marriage, while certainly formed by his predecessors in church tradition, may also have been deeply colored by his personal experiences of sex, including the profoundly traumatic experience—that he describes in his spiritual autobiography *Confessions*—of having to send away his concubine (his sexual partner to whom he had been deeply attached and to whom he was sexually faithful for some fifteen years), and then subsequently taking on another mistress while waiting for the girl to whom he had been betrothed (for the sake of contracting a lucrative marriage) to come of age, because he had felt unable at that stage in his life to temper his sexual desire. One can possibly only imagine the degree of guilt that tormented him. In *Confessions*, he describes the putting away of his concubine graphically in terms of a deep wounding, including in the memorable words: "My heart which was deeply attached was cut and wounded, and left a trail of blood" and "But my wound,

---

23. Augustine, "On the Good of Marriage," para. 32.
24. See also Cahill, *Sex, Gender, and Christian Ethics*, 172–75.
25. Augustine, "On the Good of Marriage," paras. 3–6.
26. Timothy Chappell, "Augustine's Ethics," in Meconi and Stump, *Cambridge Companion to Augustine*, 198.

inflicted by the earlier parting, was not healed. After inflammation and sharp pain, it festered."[27]

Earlier in *Confessions*, he describes his connection with her in terms of a faithful loving sexual relationship, based on mutual consent (but not directed at having children): "Nevertheless, she was the only girl for me, and I was faithful to her."[28] Considering the detail of his life with some sensitivity and care, James Wetzel describes Augustine's concubine as being in effect (though not legally) "his wife":

> Augustine did have a wife, not by law, but certainly in affection, and he tells us that he remained sexually faithful to her, his one woman . . . during the years they were together.[29]

Wetzel goes on to argue that Augustine's account of losing his concubine is a significant key to understanding his eventual turn from a life driven by sexual desire to one of celibacy:

> His description of his separation from his partner, written to echo Genesis . . . is an important passageway into the depths of his conversion, superficially his turn-about from pacts of lust to a stably celibate life of Christian service.[30]

Lisa Cahill includes a critique of Augustine's views on sexuality and marriage in *Sex, Gender, and Christian Ethics*, while noting that Thomas Aquinas (though still holding a position of male superiority, and seeing virginity as preferable to marriage, for not hindering the contemplative life) draws out the importance of the close friendship between husband and wife and does not downgrade marriage.[31] Drawing together influences from Augustine's upbringing, his family of origin and his own experiences of sexual relationship and the prospect of marriage, Cahill observes:

> When one adds to all this the fact that Augustine's own prospect of marriage began with a political arrangement that promised perfectly to imitate the circumstances of his upbringing, one can hardly blame him for failing to perceive in the marital bond much potential for spiritual companionship and love. . . .

---

27. Augustine, *Confessions* 6.25.
28. Augustine, *Confessions* 4.2.
29. Wetzel, *Augustine*, 99.
30. Wetzel, *Augustine*, 100.
31. Cahill, *Sex, Gender, and Christian Ethics*, 176–79.

Augustine came to see celibacy as his only hope for an integrated life.³²

Further, Margaret Whipp observes the perplexing legacy from "Augustinian" attitudes towards sexuality, although there is also undoubtedly much that is rich and valuable in Augustine's thought.³³

1.3.5 Thomas Aquinas

Thomas Aquinas's views on sexual ethics generally followed Augustine's, but saw some improvement for the position of women, in that, for example, according to Cahill's interpretation he "describes the love between husband and wife as the greatest sort of friendship, and as characterized by the highest intensity of all loves, because of their union "in the flesh."³⁴

Thus, it may be perceived from the following statements that Aquinas advocated committed monogamy and equality between the spouses in marriage based on mutual friendship, good moral order and male-female oneness described in Scripture's creation account:

> Besides, friendship consists in an equality. So, if it is not lawful for the wife to have several husbands, since this is contrary to certainty as to offspring, it would not be lawful, on the other hand, for a man to have several wives, for the friendship of wife for husband would not be free, but somewhat servile. . . .
>
> If a wife has but one husband, but the husband has several wives, the friendship will not be equal on both sides. So, the friendship will not be free, but servile in some way.³⁵

Cahill also interprets Aquinas's writing to mean that he somewhat softens the strict negative Augustinian view concerning sexual pleasure in marriage, and places the emphasis on love within marriage:

> Although Aquinas retains the Augustinian teaching that sex for pleasure's sake is a sin, he does not see the enjoyment of pleasure itself as wrong, as long as it is properly contained within the marital and procreative union. Aquinas has achieved a link

---

32. Cahill, *Sex, Gender, and Christian Ethics*, 177.
33. Whipp, *Pastoral Theology*, locs. 1027–1043 of 3556.
34. Cahill, *Sex, Gender, and Christian Ethics*, 193.
35. Aquinas, *Providence* 124.4–124.7.

between sexual intimacy, even sexual pleasure, and the intense love of spouses.³⁶

Overall, I am in sympathy with a "reconstructed" Thomistic view of marriage, which has been cleansed of elements which promote male superiority, and highlights the emphasis on equity and friendship which may be discerned in Aquinas's thought on marriage including in *Summa Contra Gentiles*—for example, as advanced by Don Browning.³⁷ Following this argument, I advocate the view that lifelong faithful monogamous marriage is a gift of God, discernible in creation, for the flourishing and well-being of humankind.

1.3.6 Martin Luther

In contrast perhaps to many patristic and medieval thinkers (particularly in their emphasis on celibacy as a state preferable to marriage), and certainly in contrast to Augustine, the reformer Martin Luther is notable (among many other things, of course) for his very high esteem of marriage.

For example, in *The Large Catechism* of 1530, in the process of explaining the sixth commandment, Luther enthusiastically promotes the institution of marriage, writing at length about "how gloriously God honors and extols" the estate of marriage, and noting that with the sixth commandment (against adultery) God has "hedged [the state of matrimony] about and protected it."³⁸ Strongly defending this position and advocating marriage (in terms of lifelong committed heterosexual monogamy) as a desirable state, he continues:

> Therefore [God] also wishes us to honor it, and to maintain and conduct it as a divine and blessed estate; because, in the first place, He has instituted it before all others, and therefore created man and woman separately (as is evident), not for lewdness, but that they should [legitimately] live together, be fruitful, beget children, and nourish and train them to the honor of God.
>
> Therefore God has also most richly blessed this estate above others, and, in addition, has bestowed on it and wrapped up in

---

36. Cahill, *Sex, Gender, and Christian Ethics*, 193.

37. Don Browning, "World Family Trends," in Gill, *Cambridge Companion to Christian Ethics*, 265–67.

38. Luther, *Large Catechism*, 1461. "The Sixth Commandment".

it everything in the world, to the end that this estate might be well and richly provided for.[39]

Further and notably, he goes on to state very clearly his view that in God's eyes (which he expounds in terms of God's command) the married state is preferable to celibacy for the large majority of people, and that marriage is in fact a necessary state for most, as a preventative measure against sin, because of the embodied fleshly nature of men and women.

In his characteristically unabashedly forthright fashion, Luther thus challenged the prevailing priestly wisdom of the day which privileged the celibate state above matrimony, and (particularly heinous in his view) the mandatory state of celibacy for monks and nuns which sometimes (or often) resulted in sexual immorality in his day. Luther thus appears to strongly advance the position that the apostle Paul's injunction, "better to marry than to burn" of 1 Cor 7:9, applies to the vast majority of people, including priests, monks and nuns, and ordinary folk, and that those with the "gift" of celibacy should be viewed as being very much the exception rather than the norm.

While I am not necessarily in agreement with all aspects of Luther's extensive theology and writings, it should be noted that a highly significant turning point in history and key social development as part of the Protestant Reformation was Luther's challenging and overturning of the institution of clerical celibacy, and his championing of the good of clerical marriage, and the desirability of marriage in general—through his writing, and through his own match-making activities, including of several nuns whom he had helped to rescue, and through the example of his own happy marriage to a former nun.

It is likely that Luther's views on marriage (and that of other Reformers along similar lines) significantly influenced developing views on love and marriage in Western societies in subsequent years, helping to form the trajectory of the gradual development and eventual prevalence of "companionate marriage" as a societal norm.

1.3.7 Further Discussion of Tradition

In traditional Catholic thought, there is an integral and "inseparable connection" between the unitive and procreative aspects of marriage, with a basis in natural law, as expressed notably in *Humanae Vitae*:

---

39. Luther, *Large Catechism*, 1461. "The Sixth Commandment."

> This teaching, set forth by the Magisterium on numerous occasions, is founded upon the inseparable connection, willed by God and which man may not break on his own initiative, between the two significances of the conjugal act: the unitive significance and the procreative significance.[40]

Further, in *Issues in Human Sexuality*, the House of Bishops of the Church of England set out their view of the "Christian Vision for Human Sexuality," including an emphasis on a directly proportionate relationship between the degree of commitment in a relationship and the degree of physical intimacy.[41]

1.3.8 Considering Reason and Experience Following Christian Ethicists Interacting with Scripture and Tradition

In this section I will discuss the perspectives and insights of a few Christian ethicists on a theology of marriage as they interact with Scripture and tradition. Hence, I will be considering reason and experience on a limited basis, from a Christian viewpoint, regarding lifelong monogamy as a good.

Affirming the permanent character of the sacrament of marriage, Cloutier quips about the proper place of romance: "Put simply, romance is lovely so long as it is not understood to be the foundation of marriage and family."[42]

Hollinger argues that the purposes of the God-created gift of sex are fourfold: consummation of the marriage covenant, procreation, love, and pleasure.[43] He contends that sex is a good, though fallen, gift from God, a gift which needs to be redeemed and enjoyed in right contexts.[44] Hence, he argues that "to experience the goodness and to withstand the fallen, sinful perils, we must know and incorporate the ends or purposes of the gift," thereby concluding that:

---

40. Paul VI, *Humanae Vitae*, para. 12.

41. House of Bishops, *Issues in Human Sexuality*, 3.1–3.2. It should also be noted, however, that in accordance with recent discussions at synod, it is anticipated that *Issues in Human Sexuality* will be replaced fairly soon, in due course, with new guidance by the Church of England regarding Christian sexual ethics.

42. Cloutier, "Marriage and Sexuality," 323.

43. Hollinger, *Meaning of Sex*, 94.

44. Hollinger, *Meaning of Sex*, 93.

> A morally legitimate sexual act is one that is in the context of [the four purposes above]. When we isolate only one or several of the purposes, we distort God's intentions and fall short of his designs and hence his joy.[45]

Adrian Thatcher argues that it is important that clergy and church leaders (and consequently also the couples that they minister to) be equipped with a theologically rich understanding of marriage,[46] including in terms of the following seven "pictures of marriage" that Thatcher advances, based on interpretation of sources from Scripture and (particularly Anglican and Catholic) tradition, along with his observations and insights:

  i. "A communion of persons that involves deep physical intimacy"—which Thatcher describes as "a powerful and perhaps supreme instance of communion among or between persons."

  ii. "A gift of bodies"—in the sense that "marriage mimes the love of Christ for the church," whereby the mutual giving and receiving of the bodies and persons of each partner in marriage deeply represents or imitates "the self-giving of God for us in love and in death."

  iii. "A covenant"—quoting both Catholic (from the Second Vatican Council) and Protestant authorities (particularly the thought of John Calvin), this is contrasted with mere "contracts," in that the concept of marriage as a covenant conveys a deeper and more permanent level of human relationship, which is not based on economic or commercial value.

  iv. "An image of the New Covenant"—quoting Pope John Paul II, this is understood in terms of marital love being a symbol of (and something of a signpost to) the "communion of love between God and [His] people."

  v. "A mutual ministry"—in the sense that marriage, as a sacrament, is "the only sacrament that does not . . . need to be administered by a priest," although it often involves a pronouncement and blessing by a priest, as "the couple minister the sacrament [of marriage] to each other" so that "everything they do for one another is a ministry, an administering of their sacrament."

---

45. Hollinger, *Meaning of Sex*, 116.
46. Thatcher, *Making Sense of Sex*, 75.

CHAPTER 1: ASSUMPTIONS AND INTELLECTUAL CONTEXT

vi. "A unity of heart, body and mind"—this conveys a profound sense of oneness in marriage, referring to Jesus's clear statements on marriage in Mark 10:8–9 and Matt 19:5–6, pointing directly back to Gen 2:24 where marriage is described in terms of "one flesh," as reflected, for example, in the Church of England's Common Worship marriage service (2000) in which marriage is described as "a gift of God in creation . . . that as man and woman grow together in love and trust, they shall be united with one another in heart, body and mind."

vii. "An anticipation of the end"—referring to "nuptial mysticism," involving "the use of imagery drawn from marriage to express deeper truths about God," Thatcher argues that "the union of husband and wife in a common life becomes the material out of which the union of God with the estranged world is envisaged," so that "as the Church awaits the culmination of the ages and the restitution of all things through Christ [that is, the triumph of divine love at the end of time] . . . marital imagery [such as images in Scripture of wedding receptions and marriage feasts] lies at the base of the expression of this hope," and therefore "the mutual love of partners for each other provides the inductive basis for discovery of that deeper, divine love that already embraces them."[47]

Thatcher thus declares that "the doctrinal heart of marital theology is God, nothing else but God, revealed in Incarnation, Trinity and Eucharist," giving rise to the above deeply significant pictures of marriage, which Thatcher argues ought to be communicated effectively to couples considering marriage, so that they "can see their own marriage as the good news of who God is and what God does."[48] Overall, I advocate advancing couple relationships characterized by happy, flourishing, lifelong monogamy along lines similar to the above, as described by Thatcher for Christian marriages.

---

47. Thatcher, *Making Sense of Sex*, 69–75.
48. Thatcher, *Making Sense of Sex*, 75.

1.4 Christianity as, in Some Ways, Countercultural

1.4.1 Countercultural Marriage

While long-term monogamous marriage was promoted in the Greco-Roman contexts in which early Christianity grew,[49] Christian marriage may be understood as being distinctive in terms of being a:

i. Sacrament (in traditional Catholic thought) or a covenant (in Calvinist thought)

ii. Signpost to God's new creation and sign/symbol of the relationship between Christ and the church

The covenant model may be understood as being distinctively characterized by the elements of irrevocable promise, exclusivity and permanence, going beyond a "mere contract," as "God [is viewed as] a third party to every marriage covenant, and God set its basic terms in the order and law of creation."[50]

While, due to space constraint, I will not be discussing further nor advancing in detail a Christian theology of marriage in the above terms, I will focus (in the discussion below) on a further key aspect of the countercultural character of Christianity, that is, the emphasis in early Christianity on celibacy.

1.4.2 Celibacy

The apostle Paul is at times associated with advice that appears to favor celibacy over marriage—notably, for example, in 1 Cor 7:25–31. My assumption here is that celibacy should be held in as high regard[51] as marriage (understood in terms of happy, flourishing, lifelong

---

49. See, for example, Witte, *From Sacrament to Contract*. Witte observes: "Foundational to the Western Christian tradition were Aristotle's insights that monogamous marriage is a natural institution for most men and women, that it is at once 'useful,' 'pleasant' and 'moral' for their lives, that it provides efficient pooling and division of specialized labor and resources within the household, and that it serves for the fulfilment, happiness, and lasting friendship of husbands and wives, parents and children" (3).

50. Witte, *From Sacrament to Contract*, 8.

51. I suggest there is a particular need to emphasize this in Protestant Christian circles, where singles have sometimes been sidelined, denigrated, or viewed with pity or suspicion.

monogamy)—that is, neither superior nor inferior to marriage, but held in equal esteem, as a viable alternative and fruitful way of life. This should be understood particularly in terms of Christianity's countercultural character.

Peter Brown argues that celibate early Christians "[renounced] all sexual activity [so that] the human body could join in Christ's victory."[52] Rosemary Radford Ruether also observes the countercultural character of such decisions:

> By such practices as sexual continence, fasting, and vigils, Christians anticipated the definitive transformation of the bodily in a redeemed cosmos whose imminent arrival they expected . . .

> The renunciation of sex was seen as a key expression of world renunciation, but not necessarily because sex was the most urgent need of the body. . . . Rather, sex tied a person to marriage and family, to the pride and avarice of the kinship group that desired to reproduce the large houses, the great landholdings with their crowds of slaves and clients, the demand for power and status in the civil and imperial world. Through sex and marriage, "the world" as a social system of power and possessions was reproduced. To renounce marriage was to renounce that "world" in all its social, economic, and political implications.[53]

Such observations are particularly pertinent, bearing in mind that in antiquity, the time period when the apostle Paul wrote 1 Cor 7, marriage was almost always spoken of in relation to offspring, reproduction and future generations.[54] As Cahill notes, "For early Christians, permanent vocational celibacy was a stand against the civic-minded, and often kin-manipulated, procreation of standard hierarchies through one's children."[55]

Thus it may be said that celibacy practiced by the early Christians, in countercultural mode, was also primarily in resistance to the prevailing pagan/Greco-Roman priorities of the time—particularly in their emphasis on progeny/future generations (including, perhaps, in their dependence on progeny as a "solution" to the problem of human mortality).

---

52. Brown, *Body and Society*, 32.
53. Ruether, *Making of Modern Family*, 37–38.
54. My thanks to John Barclay for highlighting this.
55. Cahill, *Sex, Gender, and Christian Ethics*, 153.

Along with assuming that singleness and celibacy are to be held in as high regard as marriage in contemporary Christian circles, I suggest a fresh contemporary approach of regarding the real meaning of sex as not necessarily tied to procreation—nor to be instrumentalized for the acquisition or maintenance of status, power, or influence—but as an expression of oneness between two people in covenant commitment, that may lead to a conclusion that sex and marriage in the right contexts can also form part of "world renunciation" and discipleship, following Christ.

1.5 On a Theology of Dating

1.5.1 Current Intellectual Context on a Theology of Dating

In the first edition of their book, Stassen and Gushee articulate a helpful question for decision-making in dating regarding choosing a prospective partner: "Whom can I trust to live my life with, to be faithful to and to be faithful to me?"[56]

Donna Freitas and Jason King, authors of *Save the Date*, which promotes dating as a meaningful path to growth, set out a theology of dating in a 2003 article in which they define dating by distinguishing it both from friendship (as dating includes a sexual dimension) and from marriage (as dating is temporary in nature rather than permanent).[57] Among various other observations, they point out, based on a survey of the literature at the time, that typically, a Christian perspective on dating tends to "[equate] dating with sex" (seeing dating primarily in terms of the issue of premarital sex)[58] and views dating as a rival against God for our affections, with young people being "led to believe that the only acceptable outcome of dating is marriage, and if marriage is not the result, dating is at best a failure and at worst a sin."[59] King and Freitas sound a solemn warning of the detrimental effects of a negative and narrow view of dating in such terms:

> By condemning dating and offering celibacy or married life as the *only* religiously and spiritually sound options for relationships, a serious and terrible danger is created and perpetuated

---

56. Stassen and Gushee, *Kingdom Ethics*, ch. 14, loc. 6099 of 12445.
57. J. King and Freitas, *Sex, Time, and Meaning*, 25–40.
58. J. King and Freitas, *Sex, Time, and Meaning*, 27.
59. J. King and Freitas, *Sex, Time, and Meaning*, 27.

for the younger generations: alienation from religion. To offer only the single life, to present dating as something to fear and protect oneself against is unrealistic in a society where individuals no longer marry at age fifteen.[60]

King and Freitas go on to advance a theology of dating in terms of meaning-making, as two individuals encounter and help each other in their life goals, and emphasizing the value of dating in and of itself (even with its finitude and temporal nature) for human flourishing in the context of a life journey (and for Christians in terms of discipleship), asserting that "dating is a component of redemption valuable in and of itself regardless of whether it leads to marriage."[61]

Compared to the volumes of theological literature on marriage, there has been a relative paucity of serious theological literature on dating—while, of course, there has been no lack of popular literature on the market offering advice in various forms on Christian dating. It is regrettable that the subject of dating has not been given more serious and extensive attention among Christian theologians. Notable exceptions include Kari-Shane Zimmerman, Jennifer Beste, and Jason King, while Adrian Thatcher in the UK has contributed substantial theological discussion on cohabitation.[62] The subject has also been discussed as part of general volumes on Christian sexual ethics, notably Margaret Farley's *Just Love* and Dennis Hollinger's *The Meaning of Sex*, which I will consider further below, and in the Church of England's updated resources on marriage and relationships.[63] Lawler and Salzman have also engaged with the subject.[64]

I suggest that substantial engagement with the various aspects of contemporary dating practice is much-needed and overdue particularly among Protestant scholars—especially as dating and cohabitation are increasingly widely practiced in contemporary Anglo-American contexts, and marriage less so, as young people are choosing to marry later, if at all.

Overall, while there has been a significant amount of focus on marriage in the theological literature—and while among Catholic

---

60. J. King and Freitas, *Sex, Time, and Meaning*, 28; emphasis in original.
61. J. King and Freitas, *Sex, Time, and Meaning*, 38.
62. Thatcher, *Living Together and Christian Ethics*.
63. Church of England, *Living in Love and Faith*.
64. See, for example, Lawler and Salzman, "People Beginning Sexual Experience,"

scholars[65] (including Jason King, Jennifer Beste, James Keenan, Megan McCabe, Karen Peterson-Iyer, and Kari-Shane Zimmerman in recent years) there has been substantial writing on premarital relationships—on hookup culture, along with other aspects of contemporary dating culture—among Protestant scholars there has generally been a lack of substantial engagement with dating and premarital relationships in the theological literature, apart from the emphasis on chastity and overall discouragement of premarital sexual activity[66] (exemplified perhaps by "purity culture"—though there has been some pushback against this, as described below). As mentioned, Anglican theologian Adrian Thatcher may perhaps be considered an exception to this, with his published work on cohabitation.

Thatcher draws a distinction between cohabitation with a view towards marriage and cohabitation with no intention of marriage. For example, in *Living Together*, along with upholding the "marital norm," he advances what he terms a "basic distinction" between prenuptial cohabitation and non-nuptial cohabitation[67] and advocates the "betrothal solution," that is, to revive the ancient practice of betrothal (which Thatcher argues has strong biblical and theological grounding, but which has been largely forgotten in Catholic and Protestant theologies of marriage, due in part to significant developments in the church's regulation of marriage which have led to "betrothal [falling] out of use" particularly in "the last quarter of the history of Christianity."[68]

Also as mentioned, there has been some pushback against purity culture (at the other end of the spectrum from hookup culture). This pushback is epitomized well by *Talking Back to Purity Culture*. In this book, Rachel Joy Welcher offers a concise overview, description, and discussion of the main features of evangelical "purity culture." Key concerns she discusses regarding purity culture include:

i. The "idolization of virginity"

ii. Mixed messages from purity culture about sex and lust

---

65. See also substantial writing by Jack Dominian in earlier years.

66. See, for example, Smedes, *Sex for Christians*; Winner, *Real Sex*; Hollinger, *Meaning of Sex*.

67. Thatcher, *Living Together and Christian Ethics*, ch. 2, s.vv. "Basic Distinction."

68. See, for example, Thatcher, *Living Together and Christian Ethics*, ch. 3; ch. 6, s.vv. "Hardwicke Marriage Act and Its Legacy" and "'Tridentinism' and 'Engagement Drift.'"

iii. The transactional approach to blessings from God (staying chaste before marriage in exchange for "great sex in marriage")

Joshua Harris, famed author of *I Kissed Dating Goodbye* and related books which advanced purity culture, has issued a public statement that he no longer holds the views expressed in the book.[69] A documentary directed by Jessica Van Der Wyngaard, *I Survived "I Kissed Dating Goodbye,"* is also accessible online, with detailed coverage of Harris's change of views, in conversation with others.

Dennis Hollinger argues strongly against the practice of premarital sex. Arguing from his model for the meaning of sex in terms of the fourfold purposes outlined above (consummation of the marriage covenant, procreation, love, and pleasure), Hollinger cautions against arguments permitting premarital sex (such as "we are going to get married anyway" or "we love each other and it feels right" in our contemporary context), as they "overlook the essential meaning of sex as a one-flesh union that consummates a marriage."[70] He asserts: "God designed that sex consummate the marriage, not initiate it."[71]

Hollinger also argues against practicing premarital sex or cohabitation as a "test for compatibility," stating, "Marriage and sex are about commitment that is for keeps. Compatibility in sex arises from the give-and-take process of a committed, covenant relationship in which we fully trust and accept the other."[72]

Further, Hollinger reminds of the "inherently procreative" dimension of sexual intimacy. He argues that two people engaging in sex need to be ready and "willing to bear the potential result that comes from this inherently procreative act." He notes that people engaging in sex outside of marriage are generally not bearing this in mind, but that instead "they are usually looking inward to their own fulfilment, rather than outward to the generative dimension that is part of sex."[73] He concludes:

> Despite the statistical norm that says premarital sex is nearly universal in our society, God's transcendent norm takes us back to his original designs for this good gift—a one-flesh union in a loving covenant marriage, capable of bearing the procreative

69. Harris, "Statement."
70. Hollinger, *Meaning of Sex*, 129.
71. Hollinger, *Meaning of Sex*, 129.
72. Hollinger, *Meaning of Sex*, 131.
73. Hollinger, *Meaning of Sex*, 135.

> fruit in the midst of God-given pleasure . . . keeping the two together will bring greater personal and marital rewards, for then our lives will fit with the way God intended us to be."[74]

In *Just Love*, Margaret Farley develops and proposes seven norms for a just sexual ethic, that is: do no unjust harm, free consent, mutuality, equality, commitment, fruitfulness, and social justice.[75] She derives these norms from "the concrete reality of persons" and these are "focused on respect for their autonomy and relationality," thus "[respecting] persons as ends in themselves."[76]

Jennifer Beste, in her analysis of college hookup culture, applies the norms proposed by Margaret Farley in *Just Love*, alongside helpful insights drawn from the work of Johann Baptist Metz.[77]

1.5.2 "You Always Marry the Wrong Person"

As a further key aspect of the theological context surrounding my research questions, I turn now to considering an influential saying associated with the renowned theological ethicist Stanley Hauerwas and popularly known as "Hauerwas's law." I should clarify first that there are many aspects of Hauerwas's work that I admire—not least his ability to provoke fresh thought over an issue, challenging conventional assumptions.

Discussion of "Hauerwas's Law"

In *A Community of Character* (1981), Hauerwas wrote memorably:

> Equally destructive is the self-fulfillment ethic that often goes hand in hand with the autonomous ideal. We are encouraged to assume that marriage and the family are primarily institutions of personal fulfilment that are necessary for us to be "whole" people. The assumption is that there is someone right for us to marry and that if we look closely enough we will find the right person.
>
> This moral assumption overlooks two crucial aspects to marriage. First, it fails to appreciate the fact that we always marry

---

74. Hollinger, *Meaning of Sex*, 142.
75. Farley, *Just Love*, 216–32.
76. Farley, *Just Love*, 231.
77. Beste, *College Hookup Culture*.

the wrong person. We never know whom we marry; we just think we do. Or even if we first marry the right person, just give it a while and he or she will change. For marriage, being what it is, means we are not the same person after we have entered it. The primary problem morally is learning how to love and care for this stranger to whom you find yourself married.[78]

In 1978, Hauerwas wrote along similar lines, albeit in a different article, adding the description "Hauerwas's law" to his memorable phrase.[79]

While I appreciate the deliberately provocative effect of Hauerwas's hyperbolic statement "you always marry the wrong person" ("Hauerwas's law"), working directly against an overly romanticizing and self-centered approach to intimate relationships, I am concerned about how easily this statement may be misinterpreted or misused to mean that "it doesn't matter who you marry (or how you go about choosing who to marry), all that matters is what you do within marriage to make it work." Particularly among young people, emerging adults who are still in the process of finding their way in life, and perhaps easily driven by the working of hormones and societal pressures, it may be particularly dangerous to send them off on the dating scene with advice to the effect that "it doesn't matter who you marry, really."

The spirit of Hauerwas's law, whether specifically named and attributed as such or not, may be seen to be quite prevalent particularly in conservative Christian circles. For example, in the popular and widely-read marital advice book, *The Meaning of Marriage*, in a section titled "You Never Marry the Right Person" the Kellers write:

> The Christian answer to this is that *no* two people are compatible. Duke University ethics professor Stanley Hauerwas has famously made this point....
>
> Hauerwas shows that the quest for a perfectly compatible soul mate is an impossibility. Marriage brings you into more intense proximity to another human being than any other relationship can. Therefore, the moment you marry someone, you and your spouse begin to change in profound ways, and you can't know ahead of time what those changes will be....
>
> Many people have bristled at Hauerwas's statement, and that is to be expected, because he intentionally is looking for a head-on

---

78. "Family," in Hauerwas, *Community of Character*, 268–69.
79. Hauerwas, "Sex and Politics."

> collision with the spirit of the age. To create this collision, he generalizes.
>
> Of course there are good reasons not to marry someone who is a great deal older or younger, or someone with whom you do not share a common language, and so on. Marriage is hard enough, so why add the burden of bridging those gaps? There are gradations, then, in Hauerwas's Law. Some people are really, *really* the wrong people to marry. But everyone else is still incompatible. All who win through to a good, long-term marriage know what Hauerwas is talking about.[80]

While I appreciate the Kellers' robust defence of Hauerwas's position in terms of his generalizing strategy as part of an intended "collision with the spirit of the age" and their clear advocacy of an important approach to marriage that perseveres through difficult times, with respect I suggest that their discussion of the issue of "compatibility" in intimate relationships hardly scratches the surface of this complex issue. I suggest that this is an area where careful engagement with psychological research relevant to interpersonal relationships may help to inform and sharpen perspectives. This is what I will endeavor to advance in chapter 4.

Complicating things further is the fact that Hauerwas wrote the above two pieces (in 1978 and 1981) while married to his first wife, Anne, who he describes in his 2010 memoir, *Hannah's Child*, as suffering from serious mental illness and who, according to his account, eventually deserted him.[81] He went on to marry his second wife, Paula, in 1989. In his memoir he describes his relationship with Paula, mentioning several similarities in their interests, values, and direction in life.[82]

It is not entirely clear whether by the time of his marriage to Paula, in 1989, whether Hauerwas still held the same view as before (Hauerwas's law). On the one hand, he does describe the substantial similarities and friendship that he has with Paula. But he also says:

> We often think of marriage as quintessential friendship. But in fact marriage depends not upon friendship but upon an unconditional promise two people make to one another and to God that they will remain together to the end. Such a promise does not depend upon friendship. Rather, it enables the risks that make friendship possible. Of course, in good marriages

---

80. Keller and Keller, *Meaning of Marriage*, loc. 426 of 3838.
81. Hauerwas, *Hannah's Child*, 219–21.
82. Hauerwas, *Hannah's Child*, 237, 242–44.

two people do become friends with one another, but such marriages also thrive on the changes in the relationship that other friends can bring.[83]

It would seem that this sets out clearly the spirit of Hauerwas's theology of marriage, though it does not appear to go so far as to reassert "Hauerwas's law."

Gilbert Meilaender observes that "you always marry the wrong person" is about patiently making the wrong person the right person over time, as "it is the task of faithfulness to make the wrong person into the right person."[84] He thus appears to hold (with Hauerwas) to the position that it is what one does within marriage (rather than any practices or choices before marriage) that matter most for the survival and thriving of the marital relationship.

However, two related critiques (with which I am generally in agreement) that Meilaender advances of Hauerwas's approach to sexuality and marriage are that it:

i. (Particularly in "demystifying" marital love) has an insufficiently developed sense of the unitive good of marriage[85] (one might refer here to traditional Catholic teaching on the unitive and procreative goods of marriage)

ii. Is insufficiently "anti-Manichean," with an insufficient sense of the embodied nature of our existence this side of the eschaton,[86] including of our creaturely human need for love that marriage as a "created gift" can help to meet[87]

Discussing the Saying in General

It may be noted that the phrase "you always marry the wrong person" does not emanate merely from Hauerwas's writing. It may be encountered circulating widely in popular thought. It may also be seen promoted by famous faces such as Alain de Botton.[88]

83. Hauerwas, *Hannah's Child*, 244–45.
84. Meilaender, "Time for Love," 252.
85. Meilaender, "Time for Love," 254.
86. Meilaender, "Time for Love," 255.
87. Meilaender, "Time for Love," 253.
88. See, for example, De Botton, "Why You Will Marry the Wrong Person."

To what extent is such a view valid? While acknowledging the possible pitfalls such views endeavor to address[89] and the importance of the reminder that one needs to take care to avoid a perfectionist and "throwaway" mentality in approaching intimate relationships and marriage, I argue that it carries significant potential for overgeneralization that may be dangerously misleading. It is helpful to note, certainly, that marriage should not be expected to be always a bed of roses, and that two people in a relationship who want it to last will—in spite of many other elements of "fit" or compatibility—always find aspects that still need to be adjusted to or adapted to, and will always have to keep making the effort to nurture the relationship and keep growing together in the same direction ("working at it," as referred to in everyday parlance).

This does not mean, however, that any partner will be as good as another—a view which, unfortunately, an overgeneralized take on "you always marry the wrong person" will likely lead to. It will also not mean that a careful process of getting to know the other person for real, and carefully ascertaining compatibility, as far as practicable, during the dating or courtship stages of a relationship, are unnecessary. Indeed, I argue that these processes are entirely necessary as part of a good approach to choosing a partner to spend one's life with.

It will also not mean that there is no such thing as a "good fit" (in everyday parlance) or genuine substantial compatibility in a relationship. Particularly for intimate relationships, I argue that genuine substantial compatibility is very helpful, and indeed often necessary, for the relationship to thrive and the individuals involved to flourish. By "genuine substantial compatibility," I am referring to key aspects including substantial shared goals or concerns, values and worldview, and often matching levels of spiritual, intellectual and emotional depth. Though every couple will have differences between them—many of which likely add color and diversity to the character of their relationship—I argue that core areas of compatibility, enabling sustainable and enduring mutual support and companionship, remain necessary to hold a relationship together for the long term. Supporting evidence for this may also be found in empirical research, aspects of which will be discussed in chapters 4 and 5.

To give an analogy, consider that the process of good dating or courtship is like building a foundation for a house that one hopes can

---

89. For example, Zahl argues that "De Botton put his finger on the extent to which we have, often without realizing it, made potential mates into potential saviors and the fallout that pressure creates in our hearts and lives" (*Seculosity*, 32).

weather the storms of life. If a strong foundation is built, the likelihood that a strong house can be built upon it is also stronger. Of course, the house itself (marriage) will still need to be built well and with good materials in order to withstand the storms of life, but having a strong foundation to build it on goes a significant way in enabling the building of a strong house overall. If there is no foundation or a weak one, then even if the best materials are harnessed to build a house thereafter, it is likely that such a house will be unable to last when there is stormy weather—and most marriages, however idyllic in features, will likely have to face stormy weather, challenges of one kind or another, at some time in the course of life.

Part of my task here is to consider what the elements are which form a good foundation for a strong, lasting, happy marriage where both partners flourish and are enabled to grow and be their best selves. Part of my argument is that there are good or "better" approaches to dating or courtship which help to form such a helpful foundation. While these can be no guarantee of a strong and "successful" marriage for the long term—as a couple will always need to keep "working at," building, maintaining, nurturing their relationship through the years in order for it to weather the long term, just as a house will still need to be built well and with good materials in order to weather difficult weather—starting with a good, strong foundation will surely help the process.

Of course, it is also a matter of degrees of support/companionship, and of thresholds beyond which one considers that there is an insufficient level of support/companionship. Such thresholds, and what are considered to be substantial or sufficient levels of support will likely also depend on a multitude of factors, conditions and circumstances. For example, in times of scarce resources and when life expectancy is low, one may well be less "choosy" in criteria for a mate, and may well consider a mate suitable, even if not obviously well matched in terms of age or interests, if he/she brings to the partnership significant resources considered valuable for those times. No doubt, many marriages in history have been forged on such terms. What is considered sufficient or substantial support and companionship thus tends to be relative to the times, circumstances and conditions one lives in.

For contemporary Anglo-American contexts—with typical conditions of increased life expectancy amid the comforts and conveniences brought about by scientific and technological advances through the centuries, and with the significantly increased availability of often a bewildering array of choices made possible by the internet and other modern technological advances—I suggest that the threshold of suitability for support/companionship one would typically seek in a mate, at a level that may well be considered sensible/wise in the circumstances, is higher than it has been at any other time in Western history.

On Arranged Marriages

The example is sometimes referred to of arranged marriages (which were the dominant mode for premarriage practices for much of history, particularly prior to the nineteenth century, and across different cultures, and still practiced among various cultures today, often resulting in stable long-term marriages—which, though not necessarily characterized by euphoria or passion, may nevertheless be found often to be content). I argue that this does not necessarily support the proposition that "it does not matter whom you marry; it only matters what you do after marriage to make it work." It is of course helpful for the longevity of the relationship to enter into marriage with a mindset that the relationship is meant to last, even through difficult times, and I recognize that this may be a positive feature of arranged marriages in cultures where marital stability is prized. I suggest that a further feature of the practice of arranged marriages that may have contributed (or may be continuing to contribute in the present age) to stable content marriages is the fact that usually a fair amount of thought and care is applied to the process of choosing a marriage partner.

Though the criteria and reliability of checks may vary widely, decisions as to the suitability of a prospective marriage partner are often made on the basis of rigorous criteria, usually with careful background checks, rather than based on whim or fancy. In this sense, to the extent that arranged marriage practices may be characterized by processes of careful due diligence and assessment of prospective candidates—rather than based on emotion or passion—resulting in stable content long-term partnerships, I suggest that they provide another example of how it does matter who one marries and how one makes that choice. At the same time, of course, one should not discount the incidence of unhappy pairings that occur in cultures where arranged marriages are the dominant practice, resulting in a perception that continuing in such practices may be perpetuating a form of tyranny. I will discuss arranged marriages further in chapter 2, where I set out a typology of dating/courtship practices across different periods of history and different cultures.

Concluding Thoughts on "You Always Marry the Wrong Person"

Discussing the above is relevant for my book, as it contributes part of the basis for my research questions as to whether there are, in dating practice, "recommended approaches" that promote happy, flourishing, lifelong monogamy/marriage (this might contrast, say, with a position that holds that a successful marriage is all about working at it after one is married, and has very little or nothing to do with how or what is done before marriage—such as how one chooses a partner, or who one chooses).

To clarify, the focus of my book is not primarily on "Hauerwas's law," although I consider it in some detail. From reading the material discussed above, it is uncertain to me whether Hauerwas himself has changed position over the years from his original "law," what the extent of the hyperbole in "Hauerwas's law" may be, what exactly the associated implications are, and so on. Nor have I asked the interviewees in my empirical study (findings of which are discussed in ch. 5) what they think about the proposition "you always marry the wrong person." My research questions extend wider (though aspects of answering them do overlap with addressing "Hauerwas's law"):

i. Assuming a Christian version of happy, flourishing, lifelong, monogamous marriage is a good, are there any approaches to heterosexual dating in contemporary Anglo-American contexts that help realize or promote this good?

ii. And if so, what do they consist of?

Further, it should be emphasized that I am not advocating an approach that is based on some kind of irrational romanticism or over-idealistic preoccupation with finding "the One." Rather, I am seeking to encourage an approach that is indeed rational and level-headed, while not denying the place of emotions—particularly in matters of the heart—in which one thinks carefully about who one is relating to and considering to be one's romantic partner. Instead of dismissing one's attempts at due diligence in making one's choices while dating (such as by saying, "You only think you know the person, but actually you don't really," implying that there is not much point in trying to get to know a person well over time), I contend that there needs to be a renewed focus on encouraging carefully considered and well-informed choices in the practice of dating in contemporary contexts—particularly in the midst of influences that may fuel a dismissal of rational thought in dating practice, or an over-preoccupation with physical attributes or surface personality traits. Overall, I advocate a fivefold ethic (developed and discussed further in ch. 6)—comprised of an ethic of prudence, temperance, courage, justice, and love and care—and which engages with the relevant empirical findings (including psychological research on romantic relationships and personality, discussed in ch. 4, and other lessons from history, sociology, and people's lived experiences, discussed in chs. 2, 3, and 5), as part of "better approaches" to dating, to help enable the realizing of more instances of happy, lifelong, monogamous marriages in contemporary Anglo-American contexts.

1.6 Conclusion

I am not arguing that marriage is ontologically, by its very nature, indissoluble. Rather, I contend for an interpretation of Jesus's words in Mark 10:9 to the effect that two people joined together in marriage, although they can (ontologically) be separated, should not be separated (the emphasis being on "should").[90]

Given that there are such weighty implications of entering into a committed marital relationship, based on promises to be with the other "for better, for worse," I suggest this calls all the more for due diligence and particular care on the part of individuals and couples before entering into such an obligation. Here, I refer by analogy to the duty of utmost good faith (*uberrimae fidei*) in the field of insurance contracts, which carries a heavier obligation for honesty and substantial disclosure, because of the particularly weighty obligations that come with an agreement to insure. This well-established principle of the duty of utmost good faith applicable in insurance contracts is set out, for example, in the authoritative case of *Carter v. Boehm* in which Lord Mansfield emphasized the duty of the insured to disclose material facts and not to mislead.[91]

---

90. William A. Heth, "Response to Craig S. Keener," in Strauss and Engels, *Remarriage After Divorce*. Heth notes his agreement with Keener that "Jesus' statement, "What God has joined together, let no one separate" (Mark 10:9 TNIV), does not mean that the marriage covenant *cannot* be broken but that it *should not* be" (loc. 2022 of 2548; emphasis in original).

91. Carter v. Boehm (1766) 3 Burr. 1905. See also Birds, *Birds' Modern Insurance Law*, 121–28.

Hence I argue that dating and courtship practices should be characterized by particular due diligence, in view of the particularly weighty implications of a lifelong marital commitment (while assuming—as set out in this chapter—that such a lifelong commitment is a good).

I refer again to Wolterstorff's vision of shalom described at the beginning of this chapter. In somewhat similar vein, Stassen and Gushee's observation, albeit in the first edition of their book, is still very relevant today regarding the blessings and divine purpose of well-directed sexuality in advancing God's kingdom for the flourishing of the world:

> Human beings require stable, rightly ordered sexual relationships in order to flourish. . . . Christians, as people devoted to the kingdom, want all aspects of their personhood rightly ordered. . . . Believers who enjoy the blessing of sound, stable, covenantal sexual/family relationships and are characterized by sexual integrity are in the best position to advance God's reign with energy and focus. Undistracted by frustrated or misdirected sexuality, they can turn their attention to the advance of God's cause in a broken world.[92]

I will proceed in the next chapter to discuss dating and courtship practices in the past and through history.

---

92. Stassen and Gushee, *Kingdom Ethics*, ch. 14, loc. 6554 of 12445.

CHAPTER 2: **LEARNING FROM THE PAST**

Historical and Cross-Cultural Aspects

2.1 Introducing Four "Types"

IN VIEW OF THE significant diversity in expressions of and approaches towards sexuality and marriage over more than two millennia and across different cultures, it is not possible within the limited space of this chapter to give exhaustive treatment to each of these. Hence, I will consider the rest of this chapter in terms of Weberian "ideal types."

The concept of ideal types, associated notably with the sociologist Max Weber, is based on the argument that reality itself is too complex to be grasped in all its detailed entirety. Hence, "it is only by simplifying reality that thought can comprehend it." Weber was "not . . . content to leave [what he perceived in reality] as different, unrelated phenomena but [sought], rather, to achieve a level of generalisation which shows what they have in common."[1] In advancing ideal types, Weber reasoned that this "[imposes] order on reality through introducing order and discipline into our intellectual life, and the role of the 'ideal type' is to focus inquiry by providing coherence and direction."[2]

Therefore, the ideal type cannot be expected to accurately reflect reality in all its detail, as it "explicitly distorts reality, giving a logically extreme . . . depiction of the things it covers," rather than providing a

---

1. Hughes et al., *Understanding Classical Sociology*, 129.
2. Hughes et al., *Understanding Classical Sociology*, 130.

CHAPTER 2: LEARNING FROM THE PAST 39

particularly precise explanation of it.³ Yet, this method may be useful for efforts to make sense of reality, as its purpose is to point towards possibly helpful directions as one seeks to understand actual human behavior.⁴ It has been applied in both secular and religious contexts.⁵

In *Methodology of the Social Sciences*, Weber observes:

> From the logical point of view . . . the normative "correctness" of these types is not essential. For the purpose of characterizing a specific type of attitude, the investigator may construct either an ideal-type which is identical with his own personal ethical norms, and in this sense objectively "correct," or one which ethically is thoroughly in conflict with his own normative attitudes, and he may then compare the behavior of the people being investigated with it. Or else he may construct an ideal-typical attitude of which he has neither positive nor negative evaluations. . . . Whatever the content of the ideal-type . . . it has only one function in an empirical investigation. Its function is the comparison with empirical reality in order to establish its divergences or similarities, to describe them with the *most unambiguously intelligible concepts*, and to understand and explain them causally.⁶

In this chapter, I discuss four "ideal types" of approaches to heterosexual dating, courtship and/or intimate relations prior to (or without) marriage, as seen through the course of various centuries and across various cultures around the world. I advance these as four "ideal types" of approaches, encompassing elements of both theory and practice, bearing in mind that theory (what individuals/couples think about dating, courtship and intimate relations—particularly in terms of criteria for choice of partner, and level of permissiveness in norms, primarily regarding physical intimacy) and practice (what they actually do) relate to and may affect each other.

---

3. Hughes et al., *Understanding Classical Sociology*, 131.
4. Hughes et al., *Understanding Classical Sociology*, 130.
5. An example of application of this method in a Christian context of study may perhaps be seen in H. Richard Niebuhr's *Christ and Culture*, although it is arguable whether Niebuhr's method is best construed as "Weberian." See, for example, where Witte offers his five models of marriage "not as Weberian ideal types but as Niebuhrian conceptual constructs"—ways of "stopping the endless Western dialogue" on marriage "at certain points" (quoting Niebuhr) (*From Sacrament to Contract*, 3).
6. Weber, *Methodology of Social Sciences*, 42; emphasis in original.

The key distinguishing features of each type in this typology are focused around:

i. The means of and criteria for choice of partner for marriage, if the person marries (not necessarily the same as criteria for dating or nonmarital relationships), ranging from "functional" to "nonfunctional"

ii. The norms, practices, and behavior between the couple during the period of dating/courtship/intimate relationship, particularly concerning physical intimacy, and other relevant aspects, prior to marriage (with or without progressing to marriage), ranging from "nonpermissive" to "permissive"

I argue that most examples from history, and across various cultures, may be divided among the following four "ideal types":

Type (1): "Functional" (or pragmatic) considerations above all, for choice of marriage partner

Type (2): "Conservative," inflexible norms particularly regarding physical intimacy, alongside romantic or companionate considerations in choice of marriage partner

Type (3): "Moderate," often balancing both romantic and practical considerations for choice of marriage partner, and typified by proportionality in norms regarding physical intimacy prior to marriage

Type (4): "Permissive," sometimes lax, in norms and approaches

Various distinguishing features are discussed further below.

It will likely be apparent there are one or two types that may be more dominant than others during each historical period or among particular cultures.

Of course, it may be noted that one's reasons for marriage (entering into, and then remaining in the marriage) and choice of partner may well vary over the course of time, and through different seasons of life. At different times or ages of life, for example, an individual or couple may be minded to marry or stay in a marriage for reasons of passion, romance, raising children, companionship, or for pragmatic reasons, such as finances or social considerations. The typology proposed here focuses mainly on approaches in dating or courtship, and hence will concentrate on approaches, reasons or behavior of individuals and couples during the stages of dating, courtship and entering into marriage, rather than during later stages of marriage.

By way of introduction:

For type (1), the distinguishing feature is embarking on marriage based on "functional" or "pragmatic" considerations above all. The essential characteristic is courtship, choice of marriage partner and entering into marriage based almost wholly on functional or pragmatic considerations (rather than, say, being based on emotion). Such functional or pragmatic considerations may include the begetting of progeny (with desirable "breeding" and so on), acquisition of property, societal status, political alliances, wealth, "trophy spouses," and so on. The aims of marriage in such contexts may also be perceived in more noble terms, such as to advance the particular community, family or nation's interests. This might be thought to be coterminous with arranged marriages, but I will argue that arranged marriages—with the key feature being a lack of individual choice—are a subcategory, but not the only example or expression of this type (as individuals may sometimes freely choose to marry for functional/pragmatic reasons). Besides the key characteristic of functional criteria for choice of partner, this type—being dominant in many historical contexts, including Greco-Roman society in antiquity (discussed below)—is also typically expressed in terms of nonpermissive (or more rarely, flexible) norms regarding courtship practices prior to marriage, particularly concerning physical intimacy between the couple prior to marriage.

For type (2), the essential characteristic is courtship and marriage based on "conservative," inflexible norms, particularly with an emphasis on sexual purity—no sex—before marriage, and other relevant aspects. This may be seen particularly among various conservative cultures, both in the past and in modern times—including among conservative Christians, Jews, Muslims, and also several other Asian cultures. While in past centuries the standard practice may have been arranged marriages based on "functional" criteria for spouse selection—expressing type (1)—in more recent times and in contemporary context, young people, in particular, from such cultures may choose instead to "marry for love" (that is, with at least a significant proportion of nonfunctional or "romantic" criteria), while still following strict moral norms particularly regarding physical intimacy prior to marriage.

For type (3), the distinguishing feature is choice of partner based on a "moderate" companionate or romantic model, balancing both romantic (or emotional) and practical considerations, along with a flexible and proportionate approach to moral norms. I will argue that this type has roots in developments from around the time of the Protestant Reformation of the sixteenth century and events thereafter—although there may be earlier examples—and that the high point of this type may be seen in dating and courtship practices (and marriages) of the 1920–70 era, particularly before the "sexual revolution" of the late 1960s. Some expressions of type (3)—particularly those with Christian roots—may sometimes be seen as overlapping somewhat with type (2), but (as also emphasized below) type (3) is distinguished from type (2) in its significantly more flexible approach towards norms prior to marriage, concerning physical intimacy and other relevant aspects.

This model is typified by a moderate approach towards premarital physical intimacy, which is neither overly permissive nor particularly strict. Each couple's level of physical involvement prior to marriage will typically be strongly connected to their level of commitment to each other, with sexual intimacy sometimes established when the couple are engaged. Further, this model often involves a balance of head and heart in approaching dating/courtship, in that both rational and affective elements feature significantly, while recognizing that the two, the rational and the affective, often interact and each likely influences the other. Couples may tend to recognise that both facts and feelings matter, while bearing in mind that feelings may be affected by a wide range of factors, including one's environment, circumstances and various conditions, hormones/bodily chemicals, and so on.

For type (4), the distinguishing feature is "permissive," at times lax, approaches towards dating, courtship, choice of marriage partner and marriage. This may be characterized by an "anything goes, as long as you like it" (primarily based on "consent", usually free consent, alone) philosophy towards intimate and sexual relationships, perhaps calling to mind moral relativism. Sexual intimacy prior to (or without) marriage may be considered almost as a matter of course for approaches in this type. Expressions may be typified by Giddens's description of the "pure relationship" developed in Western society in recent decades (discussed further below). It may be observed that even within type (4)—perhaps most often seen in contemporary Anglo-American and Western European context—there can be widely varied approaches to dating, some more based on emotional satisfaction and others more functional in approach.⁷

As mentioned, the main difference between type (2) and type (3) can be seen practically in the degree of physical intimacy prior to marriage, alongside other norms. Overall, type (2) has absolute, inflexible norms, particularly that sexual activity should be confined strictly within marriage (usually traditionally defined in terms of being initiated by a formal wedding ceremony). Contrasting with this, a type (3) approach is distinctly more flexible. Practices within type (3) may include a range of expressions of physical or sexual intimacy—including kissing, cuddling and petting during the dating/courtship stage—although the degree of intimacy may vary from "light petting" to "heavy petting," and so on. Some—though not all—couples of this type may go "all the way" to full sexual intercourse prior to marriage, but this level of physical involvement—differing from type (4)—is almost always strongly connected to a significant level of commitment between the individuals, such as engagement. This may extend to cohabitation prior to marriage, with the clear intention on the part of the couple to marry. In other words, rather than absolute norms, there is flexibility and proportionality in the levels of physical intimacy, directly connected to the level of commitment of the couple to each other. Underpinning this—and similar to type (2), but contrasting with type (1) in this sense—there is almost always a strong companionate or romantic basis to the relationship and choice of partner.

Type (2), historically and in modern times, may be seen most strongly (in the Western context) in Puritan and/or conservative Christian (including Catholic) approaches to courtship and marriage, but also in approaches to marriage in other conservative cultures, such as conservative Asian or Jewish cultures, as mentioned earlier. In contrast to type (3), type (2) involves strict norms—including little (perhaps a chaste kiss, holding hands, and nothing much else) or no physical intimacy prior to marriage, hence the clear situating of this type at the "nonpermissive" end of the scale. In this, type (2)—although it may be companionate in basis and often in modern times will involve the free choice of partner by the individuals involved—shares similarities with type (1), including the category

---

7. Indeed, there may be some approaches within type (4) that are not fundamentally based on emotional satisfaction, and which may appear similar to type (1) in terms of approximating consumerist or instrumentalizing approaches. It should also be noted that there are diverse versions of what may amount to emotional satisfaction for different individuals.

of arranged marriages, where couples may sometimes not even be permitted to spend any time alone together prior to marriage. The motivations for such strict norms may vary, and may include, for example, a concern to maintain purity of bloodlines, with particularly female virginity being prized in various traditional cultures, a concern to maintain sexual purity as an expression of obedience to God, or simply as part of a cultural norm or in response to societal or community pressures.

It is helpful to illustrate the key features of these four types by means of a graph, comprised of the following two key characteristics forming the graph's two axes, as mentioned above:

i. Vertical axis: ranging from functional to nonfunctional approaches—regarding criteria for choice of one's marriage partner

ii. Horizontal axis: ranging from nonpermissive to permissive approaches—concerning norms or practices in dating or courtship prior to (or without) marriage, particularly relating to the degree of physical or sexual intimacy, and other relevant matters. This illustrates the level of interpersonal interaction between the relationship partners outside of monogamous marriage, correlated to the level of exclusive commitment to the relationship—with arranged marriages at the low end of the scale, being typically strictly nonpermissive (with low levels of interaction before marriage, and high levels of commitment accompanying physical intimacy) and hookup culture at the high end of the scale, being highly permissive (with high levels of sexual activity, alongside low levels of commitment).

In using the following terms in this chapter, I also define them as follows:

i. "Moderate" meaning a proportionate approach to physical intimacy, connected to the level of commitment/engagement, a balance between nonpermissive (absolute/conservative) and permissive approaches

ii. "Companionate" meaning an approach which integrates both romantic (nonfunctional) and practical considerations in choice of partner, and fundamentally based on companionship

iii. "Romantic" meaning a highly non-pragmatic approach to choice of partner in dating/courtship—such as being based primarily on emotions, friendship, and so on

CHAPTER 2: LEARNING FROM THE PAST

With the two axes of "functional" to "nonfunctional" (vertical) and "nonpermissive" to "permissive" (horizontal) respectively, and considering nine possible general locations on the graph, I suggest that:

> Type (1)—"Functional"—occupies a spectrum across the lower section of the graph.
>
> Type (2)—"Conservative"—occupies a spectrum at the upper left and center left of the graph.
>
> Type (3)—"Moderate"—occupies a spectrum at the upper middle and center of the graph.
>
> Type (4)—"Permissive"—occupies a spectrum across the right of the graph.

One may find an overlap at the lower right of the graph between type (1) and type (4), characterized by both a "permissive" and "functional" approach to dating.

The nine possible general locations on the graph may be visualized as follows:

<u>Nonfunctional</u>

<u>Nonpermissive</u>		<u>Permissive</u>
3	6	9
2	5	8
1	4	7

<u>Functional</u>

Type (1) ("Functional") occupies locations 1, 4, and 7.

Type (2) ("Conservative") occupies locations 2 and 3.

Type (3) ("Moderate") occupies locations 5 and 6.

Type (4) ("Permissive") occupies locations 7, 8, and 9.

The approaches encapsulated by these possible locations on the graph may be further described as follows:

> Approach 1: "Functional-absolute"
>
> Approach 2: "Conservative-companionate"
>
> Approach 3: "Conservative-romantic"
>
> Approach 4: "Functional-moderate"

Approach 5: "Moderate-companionate"

Approach 6: "Moderate-romantic"

Approach 7: "Permissive-functional"

Approach 8: "Permissive-companionate"

Approach 9: "Permissive-romantic"

The graph may also be composed of data from my empirical study, involving interviews of ten long-term happily married couples—discussed in detail in chapter 5—as follows:

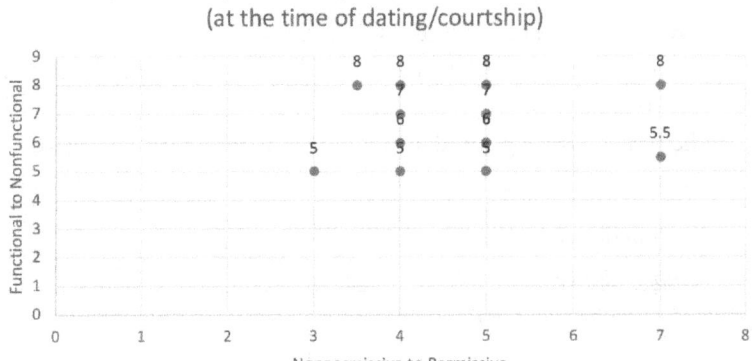

2.2 Further Discussion of Each Type in Historical Perspective

Let us turn now to a detailed description of each type.

2.2.1 Type (1): "Functional" Above All

Gaius is a mature man in his early thirties living in the second century AD in a thriving city in the Roman empire, of some standing in his community, having a promising career in politics ahead of him particularly if he makes the right match in his marriage. He has a history, in his youth, of pederasty with an eminent male philosopher (although that had to be kept private, considering that sexual violation of a freeborn male was illegal under Roman law),[8] but those days are behind him now. He is

---

8. K. Harper points out the illegal yet still persistent occurrence of pederasty with

in the process of preparing for his marriage, which has been arranged for him by his family with a young teenage girl (sixteen years of age) whom he has met only once and knows little about personally, beyond the formal knowledge about her family connections and assets. She is, however, from a well-regarded family, and her hand in marriage is considered particularly desirable, in view of the substantial property and connections she will bring to the match. It is expected that she will have had no prior sexual experience, of course. This is particularly important for the marriage, considering her indispensable role as the producer of progeny for his family line. He, in contrast, has had a rather colorful, but not unusual sexual past, considering societal norms for men of his stature—having substantial experience both with pederasty in his youth, and with prostitutes who initiated him to the pleasures and skills of heterosexual intimate relations. He expects to bring some of this experience to his marriage, and hopes the match will be a happy one, and in time they may even grow to love each other, though he will not be entirely disappointed if theirs is a marriage of mere mutual contentment, as are the vast majority of marriages in his community. If the marriage turns out unhappy, particularly if it does not satisfy him sexually, he is aware that various options will remain available to him, including extramarital liaisons and the presence of household slaves.[9]

Different versions of this type, in terms of the emphasis on functional and pragmatic approaches to marriage—though not necessarily with features of pederasty in the manner of Greco-Roman society—may be found particularly in numerous ancient societies, including among the ancient civilizations of the Middle East (around the Tigris-Euphrates Valley), Africa (around the Nile Valley), India, China, Central America (such as the Mayan empire and the Aztecs) and South America (such as the Incas). Of these, Coontz observes:

> These societies were separated from one another by thousands of years and a myriad of distinctive cultural practices. But in all of them, kings, pharaohs, emperors, and nobles relied on personal and family ties to recruit and reward followers, make

---

freeborn boys in Roman society (*From Shame to Sin*, 29).

9. "The sexual use of slaves is prominent from the very beginnings of Roman literature, and it is simply pervasive across the long tradition of amorous poetry at Rome.... Slave ownership was not just the preserve of ... super-rich aristocrats.... One in ten families in the empire owned slaves; the number in the towns was probably twice that. The ubiquity of slaves meant pervasive sexual availability" (K. Harper, *From Shame to Sin*, 26).

alliances, and establish their legitimacy. Marriage was one of the key mechanisms through which such ties were forged.[10]

Further, this permeated to all levels of society, as she notes:

> In the millennia before the development of banks and free markets, marriage was the surest way for people lower down the social scale to acquire new sources of wealth, add workers to family enterprises, recruit business partners, and preserve or pass on what they already had. People who aspired to even the lowest rungs of government office often found it crucial to contract a marriage with the "right" set of in-laws....
>
> But the stakes of marriage were much higher for the ruling and upper classes. For them, marriage was crucial to establishing and expanding political power.[11]

Key Features

The essential characteristics of this type are choice of marriage partner based primarily on functional or pragmatic considerations—such as maintaining or gaining of status, property, and so on, or for progeny—rather than primarily for the emotional satisfaction of the individuals—often accompanied by strict, nonpermissive norms (or at most with some limited flexibility) particularly regarding physical intimacy prior to marriage. Other features found in some, particularly ancient, societies, such as practices of pederasty, concubinage and slavery, are contingent (rather than essential) features of this type.

Before the availability of reliable contraception, this type would often involve no sex before marriage, particularly for "honorable women," with virginity at marriage being expected for women of "respectable" classes—including to be able to identify progeny and maintain purity of bloodlines. This type could involve variable sexual standards for men—for example, in Greco-Roman society in antiquity, it was widely expected that men would marry significantly later in life than women, and would often have sexual experience before marriage.[12] In Jewish

---

10. Coontz, *Marriage*, 53.
11. Coontz, *Marriage*, 54.
12. K. Harper, *From Shame to Sin*, 54–55.

CHAPTER 2: LEARNING FROM THE PAST 49

culture the primary expectation was likely virginity for both men and women prior to marriage.

In the case of arranged marriages (a subcategory of this type), choice of partner (predominantly based on functional or pragmatic considerations) would usually be determined by the family or community, rather than by individual preference/choice, with little or no contact between the couple prior to marriage.

This type also includes cases which may not be strictly viewed as arranged marriages—particularly where the individuals do have a choice as to who they marry—but where the criteria for choice of marriage partner are still primarily functional or pragmatic (such as political or economic considerations).

The strengths of this type, with functional criteria and nonpermissive norms, are usually relative stability and order—particularly for the community or society—with the practical needs of the community, and sometimes also of the marriage partners, being met.

A key weakness or drawback of this type is that it may give rise to a dehumanizing approach to marriage, dating and courtship, with the process sometimes degenerating into a "meat market" culture. Arranged marriages have the additional drawback of lack of freedom and little regard for individual preferences.

As mentioned, I argue that arranged marriages—defined in terms of marriages based on decisions of the family or community, rather than primarily individual choice, and usually with very little contact between the couple prior to marriage—are a dominant form of this type in various cultures, including Greco-Roman culture in antiquity, much of Western culture in the medieval period, many Asian cultures through the centuries, and so on, but they are not the only form of type (1). Therefore, while arranged marriages are a common example of type (1), they are not the only example, and their characteristic feature of lack of individual choice may be regarded as a contingent/nonessential feature, rather than essential feature.

2.2.2 Examples and Further Observations

Arranged Marriages

As stated above, I argue that arranged marriages—where mate selection is primarily the decision of others (family, elders in the community, and so on) rather than of the marriage partners involved—is a subset and primary example of type (1), but not the only possible manifestation of type (1).

The prevalence of functional or pragmatic considerations is apparent from the following summary of the practice of arranged marriage across different cultures, notwithstanding the diversity in expressions of the practice:

> Throughout history, cultures have varied markedly in who possessed the power to select romantic, sexual, and marital partners. In the distant past, in most societies, parents, kin, and the community usually had the power to arrange things as they chose. . . . When contemplating a union, parents, kin, and their advisors were generally concerned with a number of background questions: What was the young person's caste, status, family background, religion, and economic position? Did their family possess any property? How big was their dowry? Would they fit in with the entire family?[13]

Further, pointing out the main drawback of arranged marriages, namely the lack of individual freedom to choose one's own mate, Hatfield and Rapson observe: "Some miserable young people commit suicide rather than marry against their will."[14]

Hatfield and Rapson go on to discuss the advantages and disadvantages of arranged marriages, particularly compared with "love matches," and trends going forward. Referring to various studies in the latter half of the twentieth century, including among couples in India, China, and Japan, they observe the following:

1. Arranged marriages may sometimes lead to love and mutual liking growing between a couple, over the years, although generally it is found that more men than women eventually feel satisfied in arranged marriages.

2. Worldwide, there is a clear momentum among young people away from arranged marriages and parental control towards "marrying for love."

3. This "social revolution" is not, however, a straightforward one. As Hatfield and Rapson note, it is true, overall, that "arranged

---

13. Hatfield and Rapson, *Love and Sex*, 45–46.
14. Hatfield and Rapson, *Love and Sex*, 52.

marriages are yielding to marriages for love," but "the process of change is not a direct, linear one," as "arranged marriages come in a variety of shapes and forms" and "many compromises, confusions, and inconsistencies are encountered along the way."[15]

In *An Uncommon Correspondence*, Ivy George discusses her reservations and frustrations, as she describes in at times humorous detail her experiences of the culture of arranged marriages in her home country of India.[16] Her response was to leave.[17]

Indeed, a notable recurrent element in many expressions of type (1) courtship culture appears to be the significant weight or influence of societal pressures—for example, in the "arranged marriages" culture to have a son or daughter married off to a "good match" at an early age, rather than to be "left on the shelf." Such pressures may also be perceived in contemporary Western societies, even in a "romantic culture," in terms of the pressure to be paired off in intimate relationships, or to show oneself to be desirable and attractive by being able to attract a mate viewed as being of significant social status, and so on. From a theological perspective, this may well be a reflection of human finitude and the superficiality of human judgments, rather than being tied to a particular time period, place, or a particular culture such as an "arranged marriage" culture or "romantic" culture. The dangers of such external pressures should be borne in mind, as they may often result in hasty pairings or unwise choices of mates, influenced by the desire to appear desirable and attractive, rather than "left on the shelf."

Further on Pragmatic Considerations

On the criteria often considered important for mate selection across different cultures, David Buss conducted an extensive study involving more than ten thousand men and women from thirty-seven countries, and found that while both men and women generally desired similar things in a mate such as "someone they could love, who was dependable, emotionally stable, and mature . . . had a pleasing disposition, and so forth,"[18] there were also some key differences between male and female preferences

---

15. Hatfield and Rapson, *Love and Sex*, 55–58.
16. George and Masson, *Uncommon Correspondence*, 22–24.
17. George and Masson, *Uncommon Correspondence*, 24–25.
18. Hatfield and Rapson, *Love and Sex*, 40.

when choosing a mate, particularly that "men seemed to care more about traits that signalled *reproductive capacity* . . . [and] about good looks than women did," while "women seemed to care more about cues to *resource acquisition* than did men," tending to value "mates who possessed status, who had good financial prospects, and who were ambitious and industrious."[19] Hatfield and Rapson also observe that "other researchers, who have studied societies ranging from the most individualistic to the most collectivist have secured similar results."[20]

Whether resulting from social conditioning or universal biological instincts (discussion of which is outside the scope of this book), I suggest that such preferences as outlined above (particularly male preoccupation with traits associated with "reproductive capacity" and female preoccupation with traits associated with "resource acquisition") reflect primarily pragmatic approaches to mate selection, possibly connected with evolutionary concerns with survival and reproduction. Simply put, in much of human history, men sought women who could bear babies and rear them well, while women sought men who could protect and provide for them, particularly during the vulnerable stages of pregnancy, childbirth, and child-rearing.

I argue that where such considerations form the primary criteria for mate selection, that is an expression of type (1) (the tendency to place pragmatic considerations above all), regardless of whether there is individual freedom in choice of mate or not.

Practices in Greco-Roman Society in Late Antiquity

Kyle Harper observes that among key themes of sexuality during the Greco-Roman age are the "routine sexual exploitation of slaves [as] an integral part of the sexual economy" in the "slave society of the Roman empire,"[21] and the "dichotomisation" of women in society into:

i. Those viewed with honor, such as virgins and matrons

---

19. Hatfield and Rapson, *Love and Sex*, 41; emphasis in original. See also Buss, "Sex Differences."
20. Hatfield and Rapson, *Love and Sex*, 40.
21. K. Harper, *From Shame to Sin*, 19.

ii. Those viewed without honor and often being subject to various degrees of mistreatment, exploitation, and abuse, including slaves and prostitutes—those who earned their income from sexual activity[22]

As he observes:

> That there were two fates for women was a fundamental and unchanging tenet of ancient sexual ideologies. Down one path lay promiscuity and shame, personified in the prostitute; down the other lay chastity and honor, personified in the virgin and the matron. These two fates were deeply embedded in patterns of social reproduction, loosely codified in public law, and actively reinforced by the social technology of honor and shame.[23]

Most marriages during this period, under the conditions described above, thus tended to be expressions of type (1), with "honorable women"—virgins from families considered respectable in society—being viewed as most eligible for marriage.

Also related to this discussion is the ancient practice of concubinage, particularly where the female was viewed as unsuitable for marriage (with its legal, social and practical implications)—usually in terms of family origin, class, or wealth. For example, as discussed in chapter 1, we know from *Confessions* that Augustine of Hippo had a concubine whom he was deeply attached to, who bore him a son, with whom he cohabited faithfully for some fifteen years, but whom he eventually was compelled to send away in order to make way for an arranged marriage. This usually reflects a worldview that regards marriage in "functional" terms (type (1)), in which the choice of a marriage partner is made primarily on the basis of pragmatic considerations—wealth, status, and so on—with little or no weight given to emotion. Sexual partners (usually female) who were deemed unsuitable for marriage in pragmatic terms would thus have to settle for the role of concubine, although such relationships could sometimes be characterized by a strong emotional bond and may not necessarily be short lived.

---

22. K. Harper, *From Shame to Sin*, 37–38.
23. K. Harper, *From Shame to Sin*, 37.

Practices in the Middle Ages

Mazo Karras argues that there were two key preoccupations in the Middle Ages concerning sexuality, particularly propagated by church teaching: reproduction and celibacy. Noting that the church promoted celibacy as being superior to marriage, she observes that this resulted in a stance towards reproduction that was not entirely straightforward.[24] She points out:

> By the central and later Middle Ages this idea of reproduction as the only acceptable justification for sexual intercourse, and even that reproductive sex outside of marriage was less sinful than non-reproductive sex within it, was expressed in terms of "nature."[25]

Mazo Karras observes the pervasive influence of Augustinian thought on medieval attitudes toward marriage and sexuality, noting that "for many Christian writers . . . there were other reasons for marriage, but reproduction was the only thing that justified sexual activity within it" and "most medieval texts participated to a greater or lesser extent in the Augustinian tradition, placing reproduction as the main justification for sexual intercourse."[26]

On marriage and the prevalence of various long-term heterosexual quasi-marital arrangements in the Middle Ages, Mazo Karras observes the pragmatic factors, particularly concerning social status, governing such unions as well, concluding "this was true at any level of society . . . a woman of lower rank was not respectable enough to marry."[27]

She further explains:

> Given the nature of the sources, it is not always possible to tell just how casual or committed a given union was, but there was a rich variety of arrangements that were assimilated or analogized to marriage or contrasted with it to various degrees. . . .

---

24. Ruth Mazo Karras, "Reproducing Medieval Christianity," in Thatcher, *Oxford Handbook*, 271–75.

25. Ruth Mazo Karras, "Reproducing Medieval Christianity," in Thatcher, *Oxford Handbook*, 273.

26. Ruth Mazo Karras, "Reproducing Medieval Christianity," in Thatcher, *Oxford Handbook*, 273.

27. Mazo Karras, *Unmarriages*, 6.

> Many couples in the Middle Ages could not marry or chose not to marry when they could have.[28]

Mazo Karras points out further key features during medieval times, including:

i. The sexual "double standard" for men and women

ii. Class divisions being a key factor/influence on whom men/women chose to form relationships with and (more stringently) whom they chose/were able to marry

iii. Entrenched dependence of women on men across all social classes[29]

Under the conditions described above, the most common approach towards marriage and courtship in Europe during the Middle Ages was, again, most likely type (1). Men and women may have formed relationships akin to types (2), (3), or (4), but in most cases, as explained above, such relationships—if not grounded on prevailing pragmatic considerations, particularly regarding the social status of the partners—would not progress to marriage.

Stephanie Coontz also observes that marriage in a primarily functional form, particularly as a political and economic institution, was the dominant mode for most of Western society for thousands of years. She notes:

> Certainly, people fell in love during those thousands of years, sometimes even with their own spouses. But marriage was not fundamentally about love. It was too vital an economic and political institution to be entered into solely on the basis of something as irrational as love.[30]

There may, however, have been some early forms of departure from strictly type (1) marriages particularly before significant changes in Western practice during the eleventh century. Coontz points out varied practices among couples regarding courtship and marriage prior to the eleventh century, and that prior to the eleventh century the church recognized as marriage any exchange of vows or promises made by a couple, even if these were privately made without any formal ceremony and without

---

28. Mazo Karras, *Unmarriages*, 7–8.
29. Mazo Karras, *Unmarriages*, 68–70.
30. Coontz, *Marriage*, 7.

family or community approval.[31] Although one may only speculate here given the limited evidence, it is possible that this relative laxity before the eleventh century may have allowed for the development of some type (2) or type (3) relationships leading to marriage.

Practices after the Reformation and Enlightenment Differing Among Social Classes

Lawrence Stone points out that "in the eighteenth century, there developed in England several types of marriage, each most characteristic of a particular sector of society and each definable by a series of different variables."[32]

Five main variables of the times that Stone points out are:

i. "Inter-generational conflict about the selection of a particular spouse"
ii. "The mixture of motives for . . . selection of the particular spouse, the basic options being lineage 'interest,' companionship, romantic love, sexual attraction, or need for an economic assistant"
iii. "Distribution of authority within the family, which could range all the way from patriarchal despotism through egalitarian joint decision-making to de facto matriarchal dominance"
iv. "Character of the marital relationship"
v. "Sexual satisfaction"[33]

Stone observes different types of marriage prevailing for the different classes, based on the above variables, including:

i. The aristocracy: "In which parents retained considerable influence over the choice of spouse and in which economic, social or political considerations were often still paramount."

---

31. Coontz, *Marriage*, 106. On marriage formalities, Lombard's ruling that exchange of consent in the present constituted a marriage was authoritative in the Middle Ages. The Lateran Council of 1215 set out three requirements for a marriage to be valid: a bridal dowry, publishing of banns prior to the wedding, and the wedding taking place in church (106).
32. Stone, *Family, Sex and Marriage*, 518.
33. Stone, *Family, Sex and Marriage*, 518–20.

ii. Lesser nobility/squirarchy/gentry and the professional and upper middle classes: "Choice of spouse was increasingly left in the hands of the children themselves and was based mainly on temperamental compatibility with the aim of lasting companionship."

iii. Lower middle classes and "labor aristocracy": Mainly economic considerations dominating marriage choices, "since a little capital was so important in the establishment of a secure niche in this socially precarious class."

iv. The propertyless poor: "Since neither had any capital to contribute to the union, parental direction was minimal, pre-nuptial sexual relations were common, and freedom of choice was the norm. . . . After marriage, fairly brutal treatment of wives by husbands was normal, and the subordination of the former was almost as great as it had been centuries earlier in the higher ranks of society."[34]

It thus appears that some classes, notably the lesser nobility/gentry and the "propertyless poor," had significantly more freedom in choice of marriage partner—approaching type (2), type (3), or type (4)—than other classes, particularly the aristocracy and "labor aristocracy" who were still largely governed by functional or pragmatic, type (1) considerations.

2.2.2 Type (2): "Conservative" Inflexible Norms

Vincent, a young minister living in John Calvin's Geneva, is eagerly anticipating his marriage to Amelie, whom he considers an eminently suitable companion for himself. The process of finding a suitable match for him was not entirely straightforward, as one of his good friends, a rather overenthusiastic matchmaker had expended tireless efforts to locate and recommend various "eligible" young women to him.[35] All these women were considered in terms of the prevailing criteria of their community, that is, to be of "ample piety, modesty, and virtue especially, [and] of comparable social, economic, and educational status as well," with "spiritual beauty" in particular, although physical beauty could also be considered

---

34. Stone, *Family, Sex and Marriage*, 520–22.

35. This account is based in part on the true story of Pierre Viret, a close friend of John Calvin, as described in Witte and Kingdon, *Courtship, Engagement, and Marriage*, ch. 3, locs. 1638–1682 of 7990.

helpful.[36] A few of them he did not have the opportunity to meet at all, and he did insist to his friend that he certainly could not agree to a match without first meeting the woman. In the end, none of the prospective matches came to fruition, and he considered himself most fortunate to have made the acquaintance himself of Amelie during a gathering at a mutual friend's house. They each took some time to get to know the other, without rushing into talk of a match, although he must admit that for him, it was quite close to falling in love at their first meeting. Over the course of several months, and with the support of interested friends, he was able to ascertain that Amelie embodied all the substance, character, and personal qualities he considered essential in a lifelong companion. They seldom spent much time alone in the course of their courtship. Most of their getting acquainted with each other was in the company of mutual friends, family or acquaintances, with perhaps just occasional short walks together when they could speak more in private. Any physical contact other than a chaste kiss was of course considered quite inappropriate prior to engagement, and even after they were engaged, they continued to maintain strict limits on their physical interaction, with nothing more than occasional kisses until their eagerly anticipated wedding day.

Key Features

This type differs from type (3) in terms of being significantly stricter, more rigid and absolute in approach, particularly concerning norms on physical intimacy prior to marriage and other relevant aspects.

Essential characteristics of this type are:

i. Strict emphasis on sexual purity before marriage, no sex outside of marriage

ii. Emphasis on marriage as a couple's lifelong commitment to each other

iii. Some variation in bases for choice of partner—some based on individual preference, some may be more guided by family, community, or even the church's preferences. While the basis of most choices will likely be companionate, this "type" may well lend itself to choice of partner for a myriad of other reasons, not always romantic nor companionate, and

36. Witte and Kingdon, *Courtship, Engagement, and Marriage*, loc. 1708 of 7990.

iv. Generally a "rules"-based approach, with less flexibility in terms of moral expectations

Strengths of this type include relative stability and order, and protection of the vulnerable, in its emphasis on commitment and minimal sexual involvement before marriage. There may also be significant potential for growing companionship in the marriage, and there are no lack of examples of happy or at least content marriages for this type, particularly between couples well suited for each other.

Weaknesses of this type may include inflexibility which may lead to hardship for individuals/couples whose circumstances do not fit the ideal reflected in the absolute norms. There is also often a tendency in this type to emphasize commitment above compatibility (which taken to extreme creates the idea that "any marriage can work, with enough commitment"), along with a tendency to encourage couples to get married sooner rather than later—in order to maintain sexual purity. This may, directly or indirectly, cause unwise marriage decisions, and a resulting proliferation of unhappy marriages, including where couples or individuals may suffer in silence. A typical critique of type (2) may often characterize such an approach as being "repressed" and/or "ignorant," reflected, for example, in works such as Ian McEwan's *On Chesil Beach*.

A further possible weakness of this type is a lack of proportionality in approach, as it is based on strict absolute norms, particularly on physical intimacy prior to marriage. Couples may thus find themselves ill equipped for sexual intimacy within marriage when they have not had sufficient space to acquire a level of physical comfort with each other before marriage.

Protestant Model of Marriage Giving Rise to Some Versions of Type (2)

I suggest that the Protestant Reformation—and various social, religious and political changes thereafter in the sixteenth and seventeenth centuries—laid key foundations for the trajectory of developments towards establishing companionate marriage. This was sometimes expressed in terms of type (3), a popular approach by the 1920s–70s in Anglo-American society.

I observe here that Protestant theologies of marriage also sometimes formed the basis for strict models of courtship and marriage (alongside other strict norms possibly passed on in some manifestations from classical or medieval times), in the form of type (2)—characterized by inflexible and more absolute norms than type (3). As Witte observes, concerning Puritan sexual norms deriving from the Calvinist model of marriage:

> This covenantal model of marriage came to dominate numerous Calvinist communities in Switzerland, Germany, Hungary, France, the Netherlands, Scotland, England, and later North America. . . . They also set stern codes of sexual ethics for Calvinist communities designed to curb fornication, adultery, sodomy, pornography, prostitution, dancing, and other sexual expression. These firm moral codes formed the backbone of Puritan sexual ethics in early America and also animated the chastity and modesty ethics of nineteenth-century Victorians.[37]

Examples and Further Observations

The essential characteristic of type (2) is non-permissiveness, in its emphasis on strict, conservative moral norms particularly during courtship/dating, most typically the expectation of no sex (and often very little physical intimacy) between the partners before marriage. This type may sometimes be seen (along with type (1)) as being particularly associated with patriarchal societies—characterized by strict norms, such as male headship, submission of wife to husband, no sex before marriage, and so on.

As evidence of this approach, one may consider, as Lawrence Stone points out, the harsh societal attitudes and public punishments for "fornication," particularly in England in the late sixteenth and early seventeenth centuries, including as set out in legislation and meted out by justices of the peace.[38] There was some "extraordinary obsession with flogging in the sixteenth and seventeenth centuries" for various perceived sins and disobedience, including sexual sins.[39] There was, however, in the course of time, gradual change in attitudes in the late seventeenth century "which eventually distinguished private sin from public law."[40]

---

37. Witte, "Sex and Marriage," 309.
38. Stone, *Family, Sex and Marriage*, 821–24.
39. Stone, *Family, Sex and Marriage*, 299.
40. Stone, *Family, Sex and Marriage*, 822–23.

There appears to have been a gradual move away from such overly harsh approaches towards sexual behavior, from around the latter part of the seventeenth century, as noted, for example, by Gowing:

> From 1660, the formal regulation of sex was harder to enforce. . . . In the late seventeenth and early eighteenth centuries in London and major cities, the campaigns of the Societies for the Reformation of Manners pressed for brief, draconian clampdowns on fornication and sodomy, resulting in thousands of prosecutions annually; but the viability of sexual policing was being dramatically reduced.[41]

There may be variations in approach, and some adherents to this "type" may have a more balanced approach, with some helpful advice on ascertaining compatibility in key aspects—particularly in terms of character and values—prior to marriage. Contrary to stereotypes (of an overly harsh and repressed approach to intimacy), one may discern, for example, a particularly strong companionate theme in Puritan concepts of the marital relationship. Thomas Hooker wrote the following evocative and memorable lines:

> The man whose heart is endeared to the woman he loves . . . dreams of her in the night, hath her in his eye and apprehension when he awakes, museth on her as he sits at the table, walks with her when he travels. . . . She lies in his bosom, and his heart trusts in her, which forceth all to confess that the stream of his affection, like a mighty current, runs with full tide and strength.[42]

Twentieth-century expressions of this type among conservative Christians are exemplified perhaps by Josh Harris's book, *I Kissed Dating Goodbye*,[43] and other similar work. While these may include relevant and helpful advice, including on practical aspects of courtship in contemporary contexts, they still generally adopt a type (2) approach, particularly in terms of strict and absolute nonpermissive norms on physical intimacy prior to marriage. These then also carry the strengths of the approach, in terms of providing safeguards and clear boundaries in intimate relationships—which may be particularly helpful to those who may be vulnerable to exploitation in relationships—and also the weaknesses

41. Gowing, *Gender Relations*, 17.
42. As quoted in Ryken, *Worldly Saints*, 39.
43. As mentioned in ch. 1, Harris has in recent years publicly renounced the views expressed in his book.

(particularly the usual criticisms concerning possible ignorance, repression, inflexibility, and so on).

An example of this type still prevailing in parts of Europe during the 1940s may be discerned from the writings of Chris Barker, a British soldier serving in Italy during the Second World War, in correspondence with his fiancée as follows:

> I have been hearing more of the customs of these folk in this village, and it is probably the same all over this part. There is no "courting" before marriage. The young man writes his prospective wife's parents. They consent to him coming to tea. They are never left alone, and the first time he holds her hand is when they are man and wife. . . . None of the girls dare be seen talking to men (let alone soldiers), lest they be the subject of gossip.[44]

In more recent times, an expression of type (2) may also be seen in the sexual purity/purity culture/"True Love Waits" movement spearheaded by conservative/evangelical Christians in America in the 1990s–2000s, as described, for example, by Hodgson.[45] Further, it should be noted that in various conservative non-Christian contexts—including conservative Jewish, Muslim and several other Asian cultures—prevalent models of marriage are also often governed by strict moral norms. Thus, type (2) may also be seen in such cultures, including in today's context, where modern couples may choose to "marry for love," but may still follow strict norms particularly on physical intimacy—including by practicing "no sex before marriage."

2.2.3 Type (3): "Moderate," Balancing the Romantic and Practical

Chris Barker and Bessie Moore are in a passionate romantic relationship during the Second World War. Although thousands of miles apart for most of their courtship, due to Barker's postings overseas during the war, they correspond with each other regularly by letter.[46] He dreams often of her, sometimes visualizing her in vividly physical terms, and their letters are peppered with intimate references and endearment. In the precious few occasions when they have been able to spend time physically together during Barker's home leave, they have engaged in some

---

44. Barker and Moore, *My Dear Bessie*, 107.
45. See Hodgson, *Curious History of Dating*, locs. 2753–2769 of 3846.
46. As described in Barker and Moore, *My Dear Bessie*.

heavy petting, which they have no qualms in referring to and recalling fondly in their letters to each other, although they have not yet had full sexual intercourse. They are eagerly preparing for marriage, with Moore attending to many of the practicalities of setting up home together. They expect that they may start a family fairly soon after marriage, especially as whatever contraception that is available in their day is not particularly reliable, and most married couples of their generation understand that marriage involves, unless there are any physical difficulties, having children of their own fairly soon after the wedding. In their letters, Barker and Moore emphasize in endearing terms their mental and emotional compatibility, their deep feelings of suited-ness for each other, and also their clear devotion and commitment to each other.

Key Features

At the heart of this type is often a vision of marriage as the closest relationship one may have on earth, particularly in terms of support and companionship, along with a proportionate approach towards physical intimacy—with physical and/or sexual activity perceived as a natural expression of the couple's love and devotion to each other. This type (along with some less absolute expressions of type (2)) is probably what most often springs to mind when one talks of "marrying for love." Yet, when one refers to various real-life examples, what becomes clear is that the longevity of such relationships is often premised on both romantic and practical considerations, with the criteria for choice of partner occupying a center ground between functional and nonfunctional approaches. Individuals may vary, of course, in the degree to which romantic and practical considerations interact. (For example, some may be more romantically inclined than others who may have more pragmatic temperaments). Hence their approaches to choice of partner form a short spectrum from "companionate" to "romantic" approaches. Pragmatic considerations which may feature significantly include home-making concerns, such as in the example of Barker and Moore above, and social aspects such as the joining together of two families and the formation of a stable basis for social reproduction.

As mentioned, while being companionate or romantic in nature (features shared with type (2)), this type is characterized by flexibility in norms particularly concerning physical intimacy prior to marriage and other related practices, hence occupying the center ground in the spectrum from nonpermissive to permissive approaches. Rather than strict nonpermissive norms, or outright permissive norms, the approach here is most often one of proportionality, with levels of physical and emotional intimacy expressed in proportion to levels of commitment.

This type has various strengths, including flexibility, proportionality and balance in approaches, space for expressions of individuality and personal preferences, and romance, while also being grounded in practical considerations. Of the four types considered here, this type likely holds greatest potential for emotional satisfaction in the relationship, characterized by fidelity and companionship (although it may be argued that some expressions of type (2) may also possibly offer these advantages).

In terms of weaknesses/drawbacks, this type (being often associated with what is sometimes considered the high point of marriage before the sexual revolution of the late 1960s) may at times be superficially dismissed as an outdated "1950s" ideal that bears no relevance to contemporary contexts, particularly when this type is conflated with type (2). Some adaptation and variation may be required if this type is to be applicable in twenty-first-century Western contexts, including with the widespread availability of contraception, the internet and other scientific, technological and social developments.

A further possible drawback of this type—in its more flexible and proportionate approach towards physical intimacy between couples prior to marriage, for example—is that this poses a less clear-cut model for couples and may give rise to a "slippery slope" of physical involvement towards permissiveness. There is sometimes a difficulty of knowing where or how to draw the line on physical intimacy, and there may be a particular risk to vulnerable individuals who could be taken advantage of in a flexible system without definite norms.

It may also be noted that while type (3) approaches typically involve individual choice and preference—in ways that are quite diametrically opposed to arranged marriages—practical considerations are still relevant and important for type (3). Hence the opinions, guidance, and wisdom of parents, family and/or community will often still be relevant and helpful to take account of for couples following this type.

Further, this type is not necessarily tied to a nuclear family structure, although it is often associated with such a structure (recalling, for example, the familiar 1950s image of family comprising a mother, father and children). It should be emphasized that type (3) approaches (as do the other types) may vary considerably in expression, and are not restricted to a "1950s" version of courtship and marriage. This is the case, although it may most often be associated with the "1950s" model, which, as mentioned, has been generally acknowledged as a "high point" for marriage based on measures such as high rates of marriage and low rates of divorce,[47] as Hera Cook, for example, points out:

> In the 1950s, there was a high rate of marriage, a low divorce rate, and a reduced possibility of death on the part of one of the partners. This produced what the demographer Michael Anderson has described as a moment of marital stability without known historical precedent.[48]

It is worth reminding again that type (3) is not limited to a male breadwinner nuclear household model (most often associated with the "1950s" image), but may be expressed in various other forms—as long as the key features of flexibility and proportionality (in levels of physical intimacy, in relation to commitment), and companionate basis with a balancing of both romantic and practical considerations (rather than predominantly functional criteria) are evident.

Examples and Further Observations

I argue that this type—along with some expressions of type (2)—was developed with significant Christian influence, though not entirely conforming to a strict conservative Christian model. One may particularly note a model of marriage based on Eph 5:21-33, often held up as a key model for Christian marriage, based on the example of Christ and the church—the husband's self-sacrificial love and the wife's responsive love, with each submitting to the other out of reverence for Christ (v. 21).

In this approach to dating/courtship, there appears significant leeway given to individual preferences and expressions of romantic love/passion, while at the same time there is also an emphasis on commitment—that is, dating/courtship with an understanding that the individuals are seeking to discern compatibility for marriage and lifelong commitment, rather than, say, "aimless dating for the sake of it."

---

47. One may note, of course, that marital stability may not necessarily be equated with high rates of emotional satisfaction.

48. H. Cook, *Long Sexual Revolution*, ch. 15, locs. 4197 of 5278.

There is usually, for this type, a significant level of strong positive emotion, passion or bond between the partners (though this may be expressed in different ways depending on personalities)—what is usually identified as "love"—although this may not be the sole governing factor for the relationship, as practical matters are also considered significant for this type, particularly for long-term sustainability of the relationship.

Type (3)'s approach may be contrasted with type (2)—discussed earlier, which emphasizes strict moral norms. Type (3) is distinct in adopting a more proportionate and flexible approach to intimate relations, while not extending to the permissive nature of type (4). For type (3), there appear a much wider range/variation of expressions of physical intimacy allowed during the period before marriage, but usually in the context of a growing bond, companionship and commitment between the couple. Often for this type, physical intimacy between the courting individuals before marriage is recognized as occurring quite naturally—as part of the expression of genuine emotion and attraction between the partners—and with some regularity, and is accepted as long as the level of physical intimacy is proportionate to the level of commitment to the relationship between the partners. Engaged couples may therefore be often quite sexually intimate even before the actual wedding ceremony.

The roots for the development of a more personal approach to marriage may sometimes be traced further back, into Christian thought and practice prior to the Reformation. It may perhaps be argued by some that companionate marriage developed partly from the courtly love tradition during the medieval period, but as an expression of romantic love within marriage rather than extra-marital romantic love (as was the case for courtly love). Richardson makes the case that the practice of courtly love among the medieval aristocracy paved the way for a transformation in perceptions of interpersonal sexual relations and a gradually increasing societal interest in the potential depths of romantic love, intimacy and communion between sexual partners, as distinct from the mere interaction of bodies.[49] Also tracing links for the development of a more companionate approach to marriage to developments during the medieval period, Lisa Sowle Cahill argues that Christian thought and practice in the Middle Ages regarding marriage helped lay foundations for more personal (and hence nonfunctional) approaches to marriage.[50]

---

49. Richardson, *Nun, Witch, Playmate*, 49–56.
50. Cahill, *Sex, Gender, and Christian Ethics*, 167.

Overall Trajectory Towards Companionate Marriage from the 1500s to the 1800s

Drawing a clear link between the religious developments of the Protestant Reformation and significant movements in the sixteenth century towards companionate marriage, John Witte observes:

> Political leaders rapidly translated [the] new Protestant gospel into new civil laws in place of the Catholic Church's canon laws. Viewed together, these new state laws:
>
> 1. shifted marital jurisdiction from the church to the state;
>
> 2. abolished monasteries and convents;
>
> 3. commended, if not commanded, the marriage of clergy;
>
> 4. rejected the sacramentality of marriage and the religious tests traditionally required for valid unions;
>
> 5. banned secret marriages and required the participation of parents, peers, priests, and political officials in marriage formation;
>
> 6. sharply curtailed the number of impediments used to annul engagements and marriages; and
>
> 7. introduced fault-based complete divorce with a subsequent right for divorcees to remarry.[51]

To nuance this further, it should also be noted that, particularly in the course of the past five centuries or so, there have been different concepts of marriage in the West. John Witte presents five models of marriage which he argues have prevailed in the Christian-influenced West historically among different groups and are relevant for consideration today. He argues that these models are the fruit of efforts by each group to answer key questions, giving priority to one or more of the following four perspectives on marriage: spiritual (regarding marriage as "sacramental"), social (regarding marriage as a "social estate," subject to community norms and state laws), contractual (regarding marriage as a "voluntary association") and naturalist (regarding marriage as a created institution, subject to the natural laws of reason, conscience, and the Bible").[52] He observes:

---

51. Witte, "Sex and Marriage," 304.
52. Witte, *From Sacrament to Contract*, 2.

> Historically, Catholics, Lutherans, Calvinists, Anglicans, and Enlightenment thinkers constructed systematic models of marriage to address those cardinal questions. Each group recognized multiple perspectives on marriage but gave priority to one perspective in order to achieve an integrated understanding. Their efforts have yielded five models of marriage for the modern West. These I have labelled (1) the Catholic sacramental model, (2) the Lutheran social model, (3) the Calvinist covenantal model, (4) the Anglican commonwealth model, and (5) the Enlightenment contractarian model.[53]

I mention this to illustrate the significant variation in models of marriage and different concepts of marital relations that should be borne in mind when referring to dating or courtship behavior prior to "marriage" in historical and contemporary Anglo-American contexts. There is not one singular or uniform concept of "marriage" for all individuals of different philosophical or religious persuasions who contemplate marriage in the present or the past—though secular law may of course lay the boundaries that couples are bound by for the ordering of society, and societal norms will tend to affect commonly held expectations concerning what "marriage" entails.

Stone discusses the complex, varying picture between different social classes in their approaches towards marriage during the 1500s–1800s, and also observes the gradual trajectory towards companionate marriage in England, accelerating through various developments from the seventeenth century onwards. He discusses this phenomenon of the rise of the "companionate" model for marriage, including due to several significant legal, political, and educational changes in the late seventeenth and eighteenth centuries, which he describes as "largely consequences of changes in the ideas about the nature of marital relations." He observes:

> Once it was doubted that affection could and would naturally develop after marriage, decision-making power had to be transferred to the future spouses themselves, and more and more of them in the eighteenth century began to put the prospects of emotional satisfaction before the ambition for increased income or status.[54]

Overall, it may be observed that there is a distinct, though by no means straightforward, trajectory of development, particularly from

---

53. Witte, *From Sacrament to Contract*, 3.
54. Stone, *Family, Sex and Marriage*, 427.

Reformation times through to the seventeenth, eighteenth, and nineteenth centuries, comprising: a gradual movement away from regarding marriage as primarily a family/community decision—often for political, business, status, property, economic or other pragmatic reasons (that is, very often type (1) in nature)—towards marriage as a matter for personal choice (including development of love matches, companionate marriages, and so on (more type (2) and type (3) in nature). As Coontz notes:

> The new norms of the love-based, intimate marriage did not fall into place all at once but were adopted at different rates in various regions and social groups. In England, the celebration of the love match reached a fever pitch as early as the 1760s and 1770s, while the French were still commenting on the novelty of "marriage by fascination" in the mid-1800s.[55]

"Golden Age" for Marriage: 1920s–Early 1970s

Despite the great tragedies and immeasurable personal losses experienced during each of the world wars, the period around 1920–70, peaking in the 1950s, has generally been identified by some scholars as a "golden age" for marriage, particularly in terms of marital stability (though one might argue that this cannot be equated with high rates of emotional satisfaction in marriages). For example, Claire Langhamer, partly quoting Pat Thane, observes:

> In many ways this period looks like a golden age of marriage: "the only age, of the near universal, stable, long-lasting marriage, often considered the normality from which we have since departed." More people were marrying than ever before in the demographic history of modern Britain. Those born in 1946 were less likely than any other cohort to remain single.[56]

Perhaps there is something to be said for the qualities of resilience, perseverance, courage, love and sacrifice honed in times of war that enabled marriages to survive longer. Perhaps also there were strong cultural pressures to stay in marriages—maintaining societal stability—even if some were not happy marriages. Whatever the case, the data appear quite clear that the period of around 1920–70 was characterized by high

---

55. Coontz, *Marriage*, 146.
56. Langhamer, *English in Love*, 4.

rates of marriages and low rates of divorces, contrasting quite markedly with subsequent decades. Szreter and Fisher observe that "the current orthodox general interpretation of the history of gender relations as pertaining to marriage and sexuality in modern Britain envisages the period 1918–63 as encompassing the rise of 'companionate marriage,'" thought to be "a major transformation."[57]

Coontz also refers to "the long decade of the 1950s, stretching from 1947 to the early 1960s in the United States and from 1952 to the late 1960s in Western Europe" as "a unique moment in the history of marriage" in terms of unprecedented freedom in courting and choice of marriage partner, setting up of households independent of extended family/home communities, popularity of marriage and the perception that nuclear families built around marriage were the norm.[58]

One may also consider developments leading up to such a perceived "golden age" for marriage. Of the first decade of the twentieth century, Hall observes the "contradictory ways" in which this era has been represented, juxtaposing the "nostalgic image of Edwardian England [including as a 'long garden party']" and "characteristically modern developments technological (aircraft, radiotelegraphy, cinema) and cultural (psychoanalysis, literary modernism, 'modern art')."[59] A lack of reliable contraception may have contributed to the relative restraint shown by couples, even amid a growing openness towards romantic and passionate motivations for marriage. Hall observes the dismal state of contraception throughout the period leading up to the early 1900s,[60] which would likely have influenced attitudes towards sex and marital intimacy. She points out further key themes of the period, including a continuing culture of censorship of "indecent or obscene materials," particularly promoted by "various bodies concerned with public morality," despite objections from some parts of the literary world.[61] Overall, Hall reports, concerning the relatively sanitized condition of British society of that era, that "the number of divorces was very low . . . partly due to the state of the law, and

---

57. Szreter and Fisher, *Sex Before the Sexual Revolution*, introduction, s.vv. "Gender Relations and Companionate Marriage."
58. Coontz, *Marriage*, 229–30.
59. Hall, *Sex, Gender and Social Change*, 57.
60. Hall, *Sex, Gender and Social Change*, 54.
61. Hall, *Sex, Gender and Social Change*, 67–68.

partly to social stigma" and that "illegitimate births had declined since the mid-nineteenth century, for reasons which were debated."[62]

Of the 1940s, Hall observes that "by 1950 . . . licit sex remained closely allied with marriage" and that "premarital sex was more likely to occur between engaged or courting couples than between young men and prostitutes," while "individuals were growing less inclined to put up with sexual disharmony and, perhaps, less ashamed of seeking sexual pleasure," particularly as "one of the great fears overhanging sexuality, that of venereal disease, seemed to have been abolished by modern science."[63]

Tension Between Sense of Duty/Self-Regulation and Self-Expression

Langhamer asserts that:

> The royal crisis [of 1955 when Princess Margaret Windsor announced the end of her relationship to Peter Townsend] occurred at a time when the emotional landscape was changing. Margaret's battle between love and duty was one manifestation of a wider conflict between self-discipline and self-expression.[64]

There appear to have been remnants of type (1) approaches in marriages involving the royal family even in the twentieth century—most notably in the examples of Princess Margaret (where her intended marriage to Peter Townsend for love was thwarted by family and societal expectations) and Prince Charles and Lady Diana Spencer, with deeply unhappy consequences. One may observe a continuing tension between type (1) and type (3) (or type (2)) considerations in marriages involving royals through relatively recent history (including with the abdication crisis involving Edward VIII, and other royals), although with the arrival of the twenty-first century, and particularly as seen most recently in the examples of Prince William and Prince Harry's marriages, type (3) appears to have finally prevailed.

Szreter and Fisher give a lively account of interviews and testimonies from eighty-nine individuals in England, from geographically and socially diverse backgrounds, mostly born in the twenty-year period 1905–24, with most of their testimony "[relating] to their lives and their marriages in the era after the Great War but before the cultural impact of 'the

62. Hall, *Sex, Gender and Social Change*, 69.
63. Hall, *Sex, Gender and Social Change*, 131.
64. Langhamer, *English in Love*, 3.

sixties' ... spanning [the] interwar and immediately post-war decades."[65] They challenge stereotypes that characterize this period as a time of sexual repression, and provide a more detailed and balanced picture of premarital and marital relationships during this period.

They point out that the generations getting married between the 1920s and 1950s were not necessarily merely bound by "traditional codes of virginity."[66] Although there was evidence of quite widespread abstinence from sexual relations before marriage, and "although many were fearful, often with justification, of becoming pregnant, those who had premarital sex did not necessarily see themselves as having transgressed."[67] They remind that "there were a range of circumstances in which men and women saw sex during courtship as acceptable or desirable, as a means of securing the future of a relationship or for demonstrating commitment."[68]

Concerning class differences, Szreter and Fisher also observe it is necessary to be careful not to jump to unsupported views, while concluding that "gendered and class-based codes surrounding sexual knowledge and communication shaped different communities' premarital intimate behaviors."[69] They note that "although [they] found that more working-class respondents had intercourse before marriage, this was not indicative of its greater acceptability."[70] They observe that middle-class respondents generally came across as having been more knowledgeable about sexual matters prior to marriage, giving them a greater confidence in their approach to sexuality in dating and courtship.[71]

Szreter and Fisher also observe the emphasis during this period on discerning long-term sustainability in a prospective romantic partner:

> Respondents did not, in rejecting the idea of romance, seek to emphasize the rationality of their decision-making but mainly sought to demonstrate their commitment to a workable version of love, in contrast with heady passion or fleeting infatuation. The desire for a marriage based on a relationship to a partner which promised material security, domestic harmony

---

65. Szreter and Fisher, *Sex Before the Sexual Revolution*, introduction, s.vv. "The Interviewees and Their Historical Contexts."

66. Szreter and Fisher, *Sex Before the Sexual Revolution*, ch. 3, s.vv. "Conclusion."

67. Szreter and Fisher, *Sex Before the Sexual Revolution*, ch. 3, s.vv. "Conclusion."

68. Szreter and Fisher, *Sex Before the Sexual Revolution*, ch. 3, s.vv. "Conclusion."

69. Szreter and Fisher, *Sex Before the Sexual Revolution*, ch. 3, s.vv. "Conclusion."

70. Szreter and Fisher, *Sex Before the Sexual Revolution*, ch. 3, s.vv. "Conclusion."

71. Szreter and Fisher, *Sex Before the Sexual Revolution*, ch. 3, s.vv. "Conclusion."

and family acceptance was in itself conducive to romantic love and tenderness. This was fuelled by a vision of married love which emphasized the need for a marital bond that was sustainable in the long-term.[72]

Their research provides further evidence of the prevalence of type (3) approaches (alongside some type (2) practices) to courtship and dating during the 1920s to early 1970s, prior to the "sexual revolution."

Reinforcing this view of type (3) approaches among British couples before the 1960s are the writings of Chris Barker (mentioned earlier), a British soldier serving during the Second World War, and his fiancée, Bessie Moore. In the course of their correspondence, it is evident that both romantic and practical considerations feature in their courtship, along with a proportionate approach to physical intimacy. In one letter, for example, Barker writes effusively of their "mental suitability" in describing their compatibility discerned over the course of time:

> In the last six months . . . we have seen much of what is in the other's mind. I see you more clearly. I love you more dearly. From having a hazy idea, I have a clearer outline. I have learnt to respect you. I think a little more, because, although there are things to be straightened, there is so much evidence of our mental suitability, and that, whether it is my mind or not that is the clearer, we are nearer each other than we thought.[73]

On the extensive practice of cohabitation in contemporary Western contexts, it is important to distinguish between contexts where cohabitation is initiated and continued substantially with no genuine commitment between the couple and those where cohabitation is an expression of stable commitment between a couple for the long term. Lawler and Salzman argue that sexual intercourse between a cohabiting couple who have the definite intention to marry (but whose progressing to a formal wedding ceremony may have been delayed, for example, for socioeconomic reasons) is morally legitimate, as it "meets the legitimate moral requirement that any sexual activity, including a first, ought to take place within a stable marital relationship."[74] They consider that "the mutually committed nuptial cohabiting couple are already, if

---

72. Szreter and Fisher, *Sex Before the Sexual Revolution*, ch. 4, s.vv. "She Was on the Same Wavelength."

73. Barker and Moore, *My Dear Bessie*, 104.

74. Lawler and Salzman, "People Beginning Sexual Experience," 570.

inchoately, married, and their intercourse, therefore, is not premarital but inchoately marital."[75] To this end, they describe marriage in terms not of an instantaneous event occurring in a formal ceremony, but in terms of "a step-by-step process that is initiated by mutual commitment and consent, is lived in mutual love, justice, charity, and fulfilment in a nuptial cohabitation progressing to a wedding."[76]

With fairly similar sentiments, Adrian Thatcher refers to the "important distinction between pre-nuptial and non-nuptial cohabitation" and observes that while "non-nuptial cohabitation cannot be commended [particularly as commitment levels, especially of men, are generally lower]":

> Those couples who intend to marry and live together first, enjoy relationship quality equal to married couples who were formally non-cohabitors. Their marriages last as long.[77]

Adopting Thatcher's terms, and along similar lines as described by Lawler and Salzman, I would argue that "pre-nuptial cohabitation" is an example of a type (3) approach, while "non-nuptial cohabitation" is an expression of a type (4) approach.

2.2.4 Type (4): "Permissive," Sometimes Lax

Tina is a female student in an American secular college, immersed in "hookup culture" in its full swing—while some of her acquaintances are enjoying the "benefits" of the experience, others (including herself) quietly find the experience leaves them feeling hollow and empty.[78] Most recently, she has hooked up with a young man at a party with whom she had had a couple of lines of conversation on Tinder and whom she found physically reasonably attractive. It was not the most enjoyable experience for her—quite unsatisfying, if she was absolutely honest—but she did enjoy chatting about it in casual conversation with some of her college mates after the event, with a dose of exaggeration about the enthusiasm the guy had communicated to her about their encounter and herself emphasizing the "meaninglessness" of the encounter for her, of course—lest

75. Lawler and Salzman, "People Beginning Sexual Experience," 570.
76. Lawler and Salzman, "People Beginning Sexual Experience," 570.
77. Thatcher, *God, Sex, and Gender*, 235.
78. Parts of this story are based on descriptions from Freitas, *Sex and the Soul*; and Wade, *American Hookup*.

anyone think of her as "desperate," which would be one of the worst impressions to have to carry around on campus.

She was always careful to use protection, of course, and some of the encounters could be quite pleasurable from time to time, but she had to remember not to get too attached to any particular guy. That is just one of the unwritten rules she had to live by in the social circles she was part of. She sometimes worried about the lingering sense of emptiness she felt after some of her sexual encounters, but life being the way it was for her on campus, she simply could not allow herself to think too much about that.

Key Features

As described earlier, type (4) is essentially characterized by relative permissiveness towards the sexual behavior of both sexes. There may be a wide variation of criteria for choice of partner, with, overall, an "anything goes, as long as you like it" approach (primarily based on "consent", usually free consent, alone).

Notable for this type, sexual intimacy is usually not directly connected to each party's level of commitment to the relationship, and is not restricted, for example, to only when the couple are engaged or living together. Significantly more permissive norms distinguish this type, such as "sex on the third date," or earlier, or as and when the parties feel they prefer to be sexually intimate, and so on.

Strengths of this approach are freedom and a maximum scope for individual choices and preferences. There are very few restrictions on sexual behavior for this type, apart from criminal law.

Weaknesses of this type include:

i. Danger of "slippery slope" and leading to an "anything goes" attitude

ii. Significant potential for harm (physical or psychological) in relationships which may be abusive, and/or if a relationship does not work out, due to the highly emotive nature of sexual matters. Also potentially detrimental to individuals' self-esteem and personal well-being, when attitudes towards their sexuality are too casual.

iii. Instability in society and various social problems, due to relationship breakdowns and transience of relationships

iv. Increased risk of sexually transmitted diseases where this type, particularly with the practice of casual sex, dominates

Further, while type (4) may have the advantages of freedom of choice and an emphasis on individuality, it may be observed that, without the help of humanizing principles, this type may too easily degenerate into a version where dating culture becomes a dehumanizing "modern meat market."

One may also observe scenarios from contemporary contexts of women and men approaching dating in terms of sex/money/status exchange—with echoes of "meat market" approaches/commercial transactions rather than respecting the dignity and unique personhood of each individual. The dehumanizing effects of neoliberal approaches to sex and relationships (though these may be manifested in a variety of different ways) remain an ongoing concern and will be discussed further in chapter 6.

Examples and Further Observations

Developments in Western society leading to liberalizing of sexual norms

Of the liberalizing of norms, Witte observes that, following the long trajectory of social and political developments from the Protestant Reformation to the Enlightenment and after:

> The key move made by the liberal philosophers in the twentieth and early twenty-first century was to gradually remove the necessary natural and social dimensions of marriage as well. This liberalized the institution of marriage even more, reducing it to a private contract between a man and a woman who had reached the age of consent. . . . They were free to renegotiate the terms of their marital contract. And they were free to live in various intimate relationships without any contracts at all.[79]

It appears there were various expressions of such liberalization in approaches towards sexual relationships even well before the twentieth century, though perhaps confined to particular areas or contexts, rather than widespread in Western society as a whole. For example, of London in 1750, Jesse Norman writes:

> Britain was then undergoing what has been called the first sexual revolution, as public and official attitudes softened towards such matters as premarital sex, adultery and prostitution, and new

---

79. Witte, "Sex and Marriage," 318.

norms of behavior emerged. In the 1650s barely 1 per cent of births had been outside marriage. By 1800, however, a quarter of first-born children were illegitimate. It was an age of remarkable sexual freedom, and London in 1750 was at the center of it.[80]

Late twentieth century: Sexual revolution of the late 1960s, 1970s, 1980s, and beyond

Propelled also by scientific and societal developments, including the increasingly widespread availability of reliable contraception from the late 1960s onwards—along, perhaps, with medical advances, including in treatment of sexually transmitted diseases and so on—type (4) appears to have developed substantially both partly as a reaction against type (2) and type (1) approaches (particularly overly strict moral norms and arranged marriages with little freedom of choice for individuals) and also as an expression of the freedom, afforded by scientific and medical advances, from traditional anxieties about pregnancy and sexually transmitted diseases.

On the gradual sexual revolution, Hera Cook argues that "young women's reproductive careers continued to be governed by the constraints that made up the north-west European marriage system right up until the late 1960s," but that "this world has been turned upside down," as "sexual intercourse is no longer directly linked to family formation and marriage is now optional."[81]

Cook argues that there was a particularly radical "transformation of sexual mores" during the period 1965–69, spurred on significantly by a reforming Labour government at the time.[82] She also notes a quite dramatic shift in government policy towards contraception, from virtually no government provision to free availability to all, regardless of single or married status, in the space of just about twenty years from 1955 to 1975 (with significant increase in government provision particularly from 1966).[83] This would most likely have further enabled a change from type (3) to type (4) approaches among many individuals.

---

80. Norman, *Edmund Burke*, 21.
81. H. Cook, *Long Sexual Revolution*, loc. 4157 of 5278.
82. H. Cook, *Long Sexual Revolution*, loc. 3856 of 5278.
83. H. Cook, *Long Sexual Revolution*, locs. 3794, 3867, 3949 of 5278.

Further evidencing a significant movement from type (3) to type (4) approaches, Cook discusses a shift in attitudes towards sex in the late 1960s, largely reflected in a shift from a "Laurentian" view (based on D. H. Lawrence's thought, reflected particularly in *Lady Chatterley's Lover*) of sex being clearly connected to committed love, to views reflecting influences such as Alex Comfort's *Sex in Society* that sex should essentially be for pleasure and need not be tied to love.[84]

Coontz lists the following as being among the significant changes in the 1960s that posed formidable challenges to the stability of the nuclear family structure of the 1950s and helped propel the sexual revolution of the late 1960s:

> When sustained prosperity turned people's attention from gratitude for survival to a desire for greater personal satisfaction . .
>
> When the expanding economy of the 1960s needed women enough to offer them a living wage . . .
>
> When the prepared foods and drip-dry shirts that had eased the work of homemakers also made it possible for men to live comfortable, if sloppy, bachelor lives . . .
>
> When the invention of the birth control pill allowed the sexualization of love to spill over the walls of marriage . . .
>
> When the inflation of the 1970s made it harder for a man to be the sole breadwinner for a family . . .[85]

Giddens describes the emergence in society in recent decades of "plastic sexuality" (defined by Giddens as "decentered sexuality, freed from the needs of reproduction")[86]—not least due to the development of contraception, along with other societal changes—and the "pure relationship" (described by Giddens as "a relationship of sexual and emotional equality.")[87] On "plastic sexuality," Giddens observes:

> The creation of *plastic sexuality*, severed from its age-old integration with reproduction, kinship and the generations, was the precondition of the sexual revolution of the past several decades.[88]

---

84. H. Cook, *Long Sexual Revolution*, locs. 3743, 3752 of 5278.
85. Coontz, *Marriage*, 243.
86. Giddens, *Transformation of Intimacy*, 2.
87. Giddens, *Transformation of Intimacy*, 1; see also 58.
88. Giddens, *Transformation of Intimacy*, 27; emphasis in original.

On the "sexual revolution of the past several decades," Giddens points out that this revolution includes the phenomenon of increasing equality between the sexes, along with some unease about such changes—including (at times) among males regarding changes in control/power dynamics.[89] Giddens also observes that a study by Lillian Rubin in 1989 on the sexual histories of a thousand heterosexual people in the US aged between eighteen and forty-eight in 1989 revealed that "the early sexual lives of respondents over forty contrasted dramatically with those reported by younger age-groups," including with significantly higher levels of attitudes of sexual permissiveness particularly among teenage girls.[90] Rubin's research also showed a significant expansion over time in the "variety of sexual activities in which most people either engage or deem it appropriate for other to participate in if they so wish."[91] Giddens concludes that "it is beyond dispute that, broadly speaking, developments of the sort charted by Rubin are happening throughout most Western societies—and to some extent in other parts of the world as well [though] of course, there are significant divergencies between different countries, subcultures and socio-economic strata."[92]

Further, Giddens draws parallels between "pure relationship" and "confluent love," contrasting this with "romantic love"—which he asserts is dependent on "projective identification," whereby the emphasis is on a "special person" to whom one is attracted and bound, and "is strengthened by established differences between masculinity and femininity." "Confluent love," on the other hand, as described by Giddens, marks a shift in emphasis from a "special person" to a "special relationship" and is characterized by intimacy and mutual sexual fulfilment, but not necessarily permanence nor exclusivity.[93] As he says: "Confluent love is active, contingent love, and therefore jars with the 'for-ever,' 'one-and-only' qualities of the romantic love complex."[94]

Giddens notes contradictions in the nature of "pure relationship," including that "it is a feature of the pure relationship that it can be terminated, more or less at will, by either partner at any particular point,"[95]

89. Giddens, *Transformation of Intimacy*, 7–11.
90. Giddens, *Transformation of Intimacy*, 9.
91. Giddens, *Transformation of Intimacy*, 11.
92. Giddens, *Transformation of Intimacy*, 12.
93. Giddens, *Transformation of Intimacy*, 60–62.
94. Giddens, *Transformation of Intimacy*, 61.
95. Giddens, *Transformation of Intimacy*, 137.

and yet commitment is somehow necessary to sustain the relationship. Overall, he draws a contrast between "pure relationship"/"confluent love"—most closely identified with type (4)—and "romantic love," which I suggest is most closely identified with type (3).

Further examples

Examples of type (4) may also be observed from antiquity/the Greco-Roman era, particularly including those women who were viewed as "without honor" such as slaves and prostitutes—those who earned their income from sexual activity—and were most vulnerable to exploitation.[96]

Examples more prevalent in contemporary Anglo-American contexts, particularly with the widespread availability of reliable contraception, include various transitory encounters or arrangements usually involving casual sex, such as "one-night stands," "hookup" culture, "friends with benefits," and so on. I will discuss hookup culture in chapter 3.

Polyamory, open relationships, and/or consensual nonmonogamous relationships are another expression of this type, and will also be discussed in chapter 3.

One may also note the prevalence of polygamy, particularly polygyny, in history. Reiterating the definition of the horizontal axis of my typology-based graph in terms of the level of physical intimacy and sexual involvement correlated to the level of exclusive commitment to the couple relationship, such that "nonpermissive" refers to exclusive pair-bonding and sexual relations only within monogamous marriage, and "permissive" refers to sexual relations outside of an exclusive pair-bond (that is, outside of monogamous marriage), I argue that polyamory and polygamy both fall within type (4) of my typology. There are various manifestations of polygamy in different cultures throughout history, most prominently in the practice of polygyny—often seen in examples of wealthy and/or powerful men keeping several wives (possibly alongside mistresses or concubines).[97] Less common is polyandry, though the Mosuo people, a matrilineal society, appear to maintain practices approximating this.[98]

---

96. K. Harper, *From Shame to Sin*, 37.

97. Polygamous marriages through history which are largely associated with arranged marriages and/or pragmatic considerations are closer to type (1) than type (4).

98. Ryan and Jetha, *Sex at Dawn*, 142–45.

CHAPTER 2: LEARNING FROM THE PAST

Writers Christopher Ryan and Cacilda Jetha argue that monogamy is an unnatural state for humans, and seductively advance their case for openness towards polyamorous relations in keeping with humankind's "ancient appetites,"[99] demonstrated by an apparently more liberated prehistoric past and examples they cite from various cultures, past and present. They point to increasing discontent with traditional forms of marriage, sex scandals and breakdown in nuclear family structures as further evidence that "vehement denial, inflexible religious or legislative dictate, and medieval stoning rituals in the desert have all proved powerless against [human] prehistoric predilections."[100]

Recognizing the prevalence of permissive attitudes in contemporary Western society, yet pointing out that such modes of relating belie a hollowness that leaves many wanting, sociologist Mark Regnerus observes from his extensive research on sexual behavior of Americans in contemporary contexts:

> The relationship histories that young Americans tell us about are growing increasingly predictable: plenty of sex, starting early (before expressions of love but not necessarily before feelings of and hopes about it), underdeveloped interest in sacrificing on behalf of the other (especially but not exclusively discernible in men), accounts of "overlapping" partners, much drama, and in the end nothing but mixed memories and expired time.[101]

I suggest that in so far as type (4) may be viewed as a reaction against strict type (2) approaches, while the correction (liberalization away from overly strict approaches to intimate relations) has been necessary, the pendulum has perhaps in some ways swung too far, resulting in an overly permissive, sometimes lax, approach to intimate relations which overall poses significant risks to human well-being.

2.3 Further Evaluation and Arguments

It appears that throughout most of the millennia of human history preceding the past 250 years or so, type (1)—and at times type (4)—have been the prevailing modes of approaching human heterosexual intimate relations. I argue that type (3) and some companionate expressions of

---

99. Ryan and Jetha, *Sex at Dawn*, 325.
100. Ryan and Jetha, *Sex at Dawn*, 326.
101. Regnerus, *Cheap Sex*, 5.

type (2) grew with Christian influence, including with teaching from Scripture such as Eph 5:21–33, and gathered pace particularly with the Protestant Reformation (and the various social, cultural and political changes thereafter).

Type (2)—often seen as quite representative of dating/courtship practices before the sexual revolution—is typically denigrated as "repressed" and/or "ignorant." Without necessarily agreeing with such criticisms (which may themselves be poorly informed), I argue it is important to distinguish type (2) from type (3), which is related yet may be substantially different in its various expressions, as I have described above. Szreter and Fisher's (among others') research indicates a significantly more varied picture of dating/courtship in the 1920s–60s. Many of their observations are pertinent, pointing to a need for more nuance in perspectives on the past.

Overall I suggest that there is a trajectory of development—from antiquity to modern times—of movement towards companionate marriage (that is, marriage not necessarily tied to pragmatic considerations such as progeny and status), made possible by scientific, social and political advances. I suggest that this development reached a peak in expression during the period 1920–70, and particularly the 1950s, on which historians have observed an unprecedented level of stability in marriage and family relationships in Western society—with high levels of marriage, low levels of divorce, and low levels of mortality of marriage partners (although, of course, one may not necessarily equate such indicators with high levels of marital happiness; societal norms likely exert significant influence in many cases).

However, I suggest that particularly with the "sexual revolution" of the late 1960s and 1970s—including with the increasingly widespread availability of the pill and other reliable forms of contraception—along with ongoing scientific, social and political developments in subsequent decades, including with the advent of computer technology and the internet, mass long-distance transportation, and so on, the progression of improvement in well-being of individuals in intimate relationships is not safeguarded. While there likely have been some improvements in human well-being in intimate relationships through the changes of recent decades, including in terms of more personal freedoms—including with "liberation" of societal attitudes towards sexual behavior prior to marriage—and in emphasis on authenticity (being one's true self, rather than a false persona trying to live up to societal expectations),

CHAPTER 2: LEARNING FROM THE PAST

there are other aspects where the potential for well-being of individuals in intimate relationship has been eroded. In particular, the trend of widespread "fluidity" (including as observed by Giddens in *The Transformation of Intimacy*)—rather than stability in intimate relationships—has given rise to attitudes approaching "anything goes as long as you like it," with no safeguard for the long-term emotional, mental, and physical health of the individuals involved.

At the same time, I suggest that with ongoing scientific, technological, social, and political advances, individuals actually have unprecedented means to maximize their well-being and flourishing in interpersonal and intimate relationships, including in companionate committed relationships—if able to learn lessons from the past, and not collapse back into a "cattle-market" approach to human intimate relationships.

Reflecting the ongoing developments of the times in views towards marriage, James Wood describes well the celebrated eighteenth-century novelist Jane Austen's brilliant yet subtle critique of the order of the marriage service in the Book of Common Prayer (which lists three reasons for marriage as: first, for the "procreation of children" and their Christian upbringing, second, as "a remedy against sin, and to avoid fornication," and third, "for the mutual society, help, and comfort" of the partners) through her portrayal of Mr. Collins and his outrageous marriage proposal to Elizabeth Bennet in *Pride and Prejudice* (where Mr. Collins states his first reason in terms of his duty as a clergyman, his second reason in terms of his personal happiness, and the third reason—with emphasis on the weightiness of the reason—being the "particular advice and recommendation" of his patroness):

> Not until the priest reaches reason number three does he begin to get around to what most people would imagine to be the first and best reason to marry: "for the mutual society, help, and comfort, that the one ought to have of the other." Surely it struck the canny and satiric Jane Austen as intolerably pompous and tedious that the Church apparently prized the production of Christian children and the avoidance of fornication above the mutual happiness of its congregants? And so she thought of Mr. Collins as the suitable vessel of that tediousness and pomposity, and gave him a narcissistically exaggerated version of the Prayer Book's liturgy. Thomas Cranmer's indelible words live on in Jane Austen's, even if not in quite the form he would have desired.[102]

---

102. Wood, "Introduction," xxi–xxii.

I suggest that type (3), along with companionate expressions of type (2) that are close to type (3)—or a blend of type (2) and type (3)—though not perfect, is probably closest to the *telos* for human marriage, and flourishing of humanity, as reflected in Gen 2:18–24 and elsewhere, discussed above.

Further, I suggest that in contemporary Western context—particularly with the various medical, scientific, technological, social and political advances of the past centuries—there is now more scope and capacity than ever before for long-term fulfilling relationships/marriages on the companionate basis—particularly type (3), or less absolute expressions of type (2). Unlike various times in the past, most men and women in twenty-first-century Western society are not under significant pressure—economic, political, societal or otherwise—to marry/commit to a long-term relationship, unless they desire to, and often have the means to live meaningful and fulfilling lives as singles. There are also more tools and resources (online and offline) than ever before to assist all who are desirous of finding their "soulmate," or long-term/life companion with shared interests, shared values and so on.

Overall, and as I will reiterate in chapters 6 and 7, I advocate a type (3) approach—or an expression of type (2) that is close to type (3)[103]—which prioritizes criteria for choice of partner which are internal and specific to the individual—including features such as: character traits, goals/motivations/concerns, and personal narrative—and a companionate approach, rather than instrumentalizing or predominantly functional approaches, with level of physical intimacy correlated to level of commitment. At the same time, such an approach should not be based on "blind emotion" (as reflected, for example, in the saying "love is blind"), but should be cognizant of and responsive to the actual qualities, both strengths and weaknesses, of the particular individual.

Hence, I contend that with the right focus—following a Christian virtue-ethical approach advocated later in this book—there is more scope than ever before in twenty-first-century Western contexts for individuals to have long-term fulfilling/flourishing relationships—with features of type (3), or a blend of type (2) and type (3).

---

103. Bearing in mind that not all expressions of type (2) are close to type (3).

CHAPTER 3: CONTEMPORARY ANGLO-AMERICAN CONTEXTS
Sociological Aspects

3.1 Introduction

THIS CHAPTER CONSIDERS SEVERAL significant themes or features of heterosexual dating culture in contemporary Anglo-American contexts, including in view of developments related to and after the sexual revolution of the 1960s and 1970s in Western societies (considering the period of about fifty years since the 1960s and 1970s to the present day). Overall, I seek to describe and provide, based on authoritative sources, a reasonably accurate picture of the contemporary contexts in which I contend for the applicability of the virtue-ethical approach (discussed in ch. 6) that I advocate for approaches to dating. Developing in the wake of the sexual revolution of the 1960s and 1970s, this context is pluralistic in nature.

I identify the following six features or themes as being particularly distinctive of heterosexual dating culture in contemporary Anglo-American contexts:

i. *A continuing shift towards the form of "pure relationship"* (referring to Giddens's definition of the term),[1] partly as a trajectory of development from the sexual revolution of the 1960s and 1970s

ii. *Culture wars*: Continuing culture wars, including on matters concerning sexuality, with often polarized positions between

---

1. For example, Giddens, *Transformation of Intimacy*.

conservatives and progressives/liberals. Such wars are especially pronounced in America but may also be apparent in other Western societies.

iii. *Economic insecurity*: Heightened economic concerns, especially after the global economic crisis of 2008 but with roots and developments occurring decades before 2008, characterized by the decline of financial and social safety nets, and likely leading to young adults preferring to settle down (or marry) later than the generations before them

iv. *Medical advances* significantly lowering the traditional risks or costs of sexual interactions and enabling the normalization of casual sexual interactions: particularly the widespread availability of reliable contraception and improved treatments for sexually transmitted infections (STIs)

v. *Increased sexualization of everyday culture*: Including with the ubiquity of sexualized images in the vast majority of people's everyday experiences, and widespread availability of high-quality pornography, fueled by technology, including the internet and other media

vi. *Fast-improving technology and the internet*: Leading to the phenomenon, unprecedented in previous generations, of the ubiquity of social media, online dating and dating apps, with their accompanying advantages, risks, opportunities and pitfalls

Of the above features or themes, it is helpful to distinguish between:

- Those which are particular developments directly relevant to the practice of dating
- Those which are circumstances or conditions affecting dating, although not forming a direct part of dating practice

Features (iii) and (iv), "economic insecurity" and "medical advances" may be described in terms of the second bullet point, that is, they comprise developments, circumstances, or conditions which affect dating practice, although not forming a direct part of dating practice. Features (i), (ii), (v), and (vi) are more in the nature of the first bullet point, that is, they may be understood in terms of particular developments which are a direct part of or directly relevant to dating practice. For ease of discussion, I will consider features in the nature of the first bullet point first, discussing features (i), (ii), (v), and (vi) first in the sections below. I will then follow up that discussion by considering themes in the nature of the second bullet point, that is themes (iii) and (iv), "economic insecurity" and "medical advances." I will then conclude this chapter with a further discussion of "hookup culture," particularly discernible in university campuses in parts of Anglo-American society, considering significant studies and perspectives from key scholars in the field.

Dating at different ages or life stages will likely involve different priorities and concerns. Teenagers and young adults may be preoccupied with "youthful passion," while also seeking to advance in their studies or careers. Those in their late twenties or thirties may be more ready to think about "settling down," with mortgages or possibly starting a family likely to be pressing concerns. Middle-aged and older adults may prioritize stable companionship more than those of younger age groups, while there may also be more focus on care, with good health no longer taken for granted among older age groups. Still, there may also be individuals and couples who combine different concerns and interests, not necessarily confined to those typically associated with their age group.

Skolnick and Skolnick identify a "triple revolution" that has occurred over the past few decades, namely "the move towards a postindustrial service and information economy," "a life course revolution brought about by reductions in mortality and fertility" and a "psychological [revolution, that is, a psychological] transformation rooted mainly in rising educational levels." They also point out that women have been key agents in this change, noting:

> Most women's lives and expectations over the past three decades, inside and outside the family, have departed drastically from those of their own mothers. Men's lives today are also different from their fathers' generation, but to a much lesser extent.[2]

Describing what they refer to as a "life course revolution" exerting a significant effect on how marital relationships are perceived, they observe that:

> Declining mortality rates have had a profound effect on women's lives. Women today are living longer and having fewer children.
> ...
>
> One of the most important changes in contemporary marriage is the potential length of marriage and the number of years

2. Skolnick and Skolnick, *Family in Transition*, 7.

spent without children in the home.... By the 1970s, the statistically average couple spent only 18 percent of their married lives raising young children, compared with 54 percent a century ago.... As a result, marriage is becoming defined less as a union between parents raising a brood of children and more as a personal relationship between two individuals.[3]

Furthermore, the internet, technology and social media have wrought significant changes in the landscape of dating in contemporary Anglo-American contexts. This will be elaborated on later. I will also discuss the particular phenomenon of "hookup culture" towards the end of this chapter.

Similarities and Differences Between American and British Dating Culture

Cherlin describes what he considers distinctive about American dating and marital culture in terms of an "emblematic American pattern of high marriage and divorce rates, cohabiting unions of short duration, and childbearing among unpartnered women and men."[4] He notes a significantly "greater attachment to marriage" in American culture, across different social groups, classes, and ethnicities, though the actual rates of marriage vary significantly among different classes and ethnicities.[5] Finkel reinforces this view, pointing to Cherlin's observation of the "marriage-go-round" arising as a result of how "Americans are unique among Westerners in how strongly we value *both* marital commitment and self-expression [and therefore] tend to both marry and divorce at elevated rates."[6]

In some contrast, Cherlin points out that British attitudes towards marriage/cohabitation appear to be somewhere in-between American culture and mainstream European culture which is characterized by significantly lower rates of "marriage metabolism," that is, "transitions into and out of marriage [and cohabitation]," such as marriage and divorce, than American culture.[7]

---

3. Skolnick and Skolnick, *Family in Transition*, 8.
4. Cherlin, "American Marriage," 136.
5. Cherlin, "American Marriage," 129, 134.
6. Finkel, *All-or-Nothing Marriage*, 152; emphasis in original.
7. Cherlin, "American Marriage," 131.

Further on the American context, Finkel observes that rates of socioeconomic inequality in America (based on differences in social class, in terms of factors such as "income, education, and occupation") have increased significantly in recent decades, noting that these rates "started rising in the 1970s and, by the 2010s had reached levels rivaling those from the Roaring Twenties." In particular, he points out the phenomenon of the "hourglass economy":

> A central cause of this rising inequality is the decline in working-class jobs—especially manufacturing jobs—that pay a decent wage, largely due to a combination of automation and outsourcing/offshoring. . . . Collectively, these forces have hollowed out the middle of the American labor market, creating an "hourglass economy" in which Americans with college and postgraduate degrees are getting wealthier, while those without a college education are getting poorer.[8]

Observing that this rising inequality is a particular cause for concern, including in terms of marital outcomes for working-class families, Finkel also points out that:

i. "Wealthier Americans are more likely to marry than poorer Americans are . . . and people who do marry are increasingly doing so within their own socioeconomic stratum."[9]
ii. "The link between social class and marital outcomes is strong," referring to data "[revealing] greater disruption rates among lower-income than among higher-income Americans, a difference that emerges in the first year of marriage and gets stronger over time."[10]

3.2 Continuing Shift Towards the "Pure Relationship"

3.2.1 Increasing Individualization of Marriage and Relationships

Cherlin refers to sociologist Ernest Burgess's identification of a transition in marriage during the twentieth century "from institution to companionship," that is, from "institutional marriage" to "companionate

---

8. Finkel, *All-or-Nothing Marriage*, 153.
9. Finkel, *All-or-Nothing Marriage*, 154.
10. Finkel, *All-or-Nothing Marriage*, 155.

marriage."[11] Cherlin goes on to describe a further transition in the latter part of the twentieth century from "companionate marriage" to "individualized marriage."[12]

Giddens also describes a significant ongoing worldwide transformation of the family and relationships. He describes the "traditional family" (sometimes associated with images of 1950s marriages) in his terms, and argues there is a distinct shift away from it globally, resisted only by "authoritarian governments and fundamentalist groups."[13] Defining the traditional family quite specifically, he asserts:

> The traditional family was above all an economic unit. Agricultural production normally involved the whole family group, while among the gentry and aristocracy, transmission of property was the main basis of marriage.[14]

Giddens argues that there is a worldwide shift—though occurring in uneven ways and at varying pace across different cultures and countries—an overall movement away from the "traditional family" towards "an emotional democracy" or "democracy of the emotions," as he terms it. He connects this emotional democracy to the "pure relationship" he has described in other writings, characterized by the centrality of emotional communication and intimacy.[15] This "pure relationship" he defines as "a relationship based upon emotional communication, where the rewards derived from such communication are the main basis for the relationship to continue,"[16] with "self-disclosure" and "active trust" being key elements of intimacy in such a relationship.[17] He is rather disparaging of the "traditional family," associating its preservation in some parts with, as mentioned, authoritarianism and "fundamentalist groups," arguing that the "emerging democracy of emotions" he identifies is "on the front line in the struggle between cosmopolitanism and fundamentalism" and predicting the eventual decline of that "traditional

---

11. As quoted in Cherlin, "American Marriage," 125, 138. It should also be noted that use of the terms "companionate marriage" or "companionship [in marriage]" in this context is not necessarily the same as my use of the terms elsewhere in this book.
12. Cherlin, "American Marriage," 126.
13. Giddens, "Global Revolution," 27.
14. Giddens, "Global Revolution," 28.
15. Giddens, "Global Revolution," 30–31.
16. Giddens, "Global Revolution," 30.
17. Giddens, "Global Revolution," 31.

family" form.[18] He appears not to make any room for emotionally satisfying and companionate 'old-fashioned' marriages.

Giddens also observes how the above trends may correlate with an increasing acceptance of homosexuality in some societies, as "a logical outcome of the severance of sexuality from reproduction."[19] On marriage and relationships, he asserts that "the idea of a relationship is . . . surprisingly recent" and declares that:

> Only 30 or so years ago, no one spoke of "relationships." They didn't need to, nor did they need to speak in terms of intimacy and commitment. Marriage at that time was the commitment, as the existence of shotgun marriages bore witness. While statistically marriage is still the normal condition, for most people its meaning has more or less completely changed . . . marriage is no longer the chief defining basis of coupledom.[20]

Elaborating on the emphasis on emotional satisfaction, Eli Finkel observes how marriage has evolved over the years from functional marriages to companionate models to today's Western context in which there appears to be a paradox: marriage seems to be needed less than ever before for human fulfilment, and yet more is expected of it than ever before, in terms of delivering meaning and happiness, requiring higher standards and levels of investment in relationship than previous generations.[21]

Arlene Skolnick refers to key longitudinal studies of married couples, some conducted in the 1960s and 1970s, and observes from these "the great potential for change in intimate relationships." She also describes "a great deal of variation" in the forms of happy marriages, based on her own longitudinal study of couples, concluding:

> Apart from the deep friendship that typified all the happy couples they differed in many other ways . . . if the emotional core of marriage is good, it seems to matter very little what kind of lifestyle the couple chooses to follow.[22]

---

18. Giddens, "Global Revolution," 32.
19. Giddens, "Global Revolution," 29.
20. Giddens, "Global Revolution," 30.
21. Finkel, *All-or-Nothing Marriage*.
22. Arlene Skolnick, "Grounds for Marriage," in Skolnick and Skolnick, *Family in Transition*, 145.

3.2.2 Discussing Developments Following the Sexual Revolution of the 1960s and 1970s

Giddens describes our contemporary world, particularly Western society after the sexual revolution of the 1960s and 1970s as a "new world... of sexual negotiation, of 'relationships,' in which new terminologies of 'commitment' and 'intimacy' have come to the fore."[23] He also notes that in today's world, men and women typically come to marriage with significantly higher levels of "sexual experience and knowledge" than in past recent generations, and "far more is anticipated sexually of marriage... by both women and men.... Women expect to receive, as well as provide, sexual pleasure, and many have come to see a rewarding sex life as a key requirement for a satisfactory marriage."[24]

Noting the profound effects of the sexual revolution of the 1960s—the pill and accompanying societal changes—Mark Regnerus observes, based on substantial empirical research, the phenomenon in contemporary Western society of "cheap sex" (easily available access to sex, with a much lower cost to pay for sexual encounters). Regnerus argues that heterosexual sexual relationships typically take the form of an exchange or market, in which women provide sex in exchange for the male supply of resources. He observes with concern that "sexual access today... has gotten easier or "cheaper," including as a result of the widespread availability of reliable hormonal contraception, significantly reducing or eliminating the risk of pregnancy.[25] As he notes: "[Cheaper sex] is the cognitive and behavioral norm today.... The Pill's injection into the mating market altered much about modern life and relationships, reducing women's dependence on men's resources while dropping the price of sexual access for men."[26]

He further argues that this phenomenon has resulted in a "split [in] the mating market [into] two," giving rise to a market for sex and a market for marriage "laying bare men's long-standing hopes for sex with fewer strings alongside women's stable interests in stronger signals of commitment first."[27] He observes the resulting "relationship frustrations," as:

---

23. Giddens, *Transformation of Intimacy*, 8.
24. Giddens, *Transformation of Intimacy*, 11–12.
25. Regnerus, *Cheap Sex*. See, for example, ch. 2 where he argues this.
26. Regnerus, *Cheap Sex*, 60.
27. Regnerus, *Cheap Sex*, 60.

Women want men but don't need them while men want sex but have more options now.... It's not that love is dead, but the sexual incentives for men to sacrifice and commit have largely dissolved, spelling a more confusing and circuitous path to commitment and marriage than earlier eras.[28]

Regnerus discusses key parts of Giddens's *Transformation of Intimacy*, including Giddens's observations concerning the "malleability of human sexuality" (using Giddens's term, the creation of "plastic sexuality") which Regnerus observes Giddens "linked to our dramatic advancement in fertility control." He notes that in Giddens's conception this "sexual revolution . . . was not "gender-neutral" . . . [but rather] prompted "the flourishing of homosexuality, male and female."[29]

In sum, advancements such as the contraceptive pill may be viewed as a double-edged sword. On the one hand, they enable the further liberation of women from "bondage" to seemingly continuous cycles of pregnancies and childbirth. Yet at the same time, they also enable men to be less responsible in their sexual choices—and more demanding in their expectations of sexual favors without the possible repercussions and responsibilities of pregnancy and fatherhood.

Polyamory and Consensual Nonmonogamous Relationships

Further, polyamory, open relationships, and/or consensual nonmonogamous relationships appear to be gradually gaining more acceptance, or at least tolerance, in public discourse, particularly with the increasing emphasis on authenticity and self-expression as prized values in recent decades. Recent publications such as Ryan and Jetha's *Sex at Dawn* argue that monogamy is not natural for humans, and that polyamory is a more desirable state that solves the problems associated with traditional forms of marriage. Yet, while polyamory and/or open relationships may appear to solve some issues, they may give rise to other (possibly more complex) problems or dilemmas. A realistic assessment of the variety of considerations involved, and a more nuanced evaluation of the matter is necessary. Renowned therapist Esther Perel identifies some of the key issues involved and frames the discussion thus:

28. Regnerus, *Cheap Sex*, 61.
29. Regnerus, *Cheap Sex*, 54.

> Cheating and lying aside, I see the conversation about ethical nonmonogamy as a valiant attempt to tackle the core existential paradoxes that every couple wrestles with—security and adventure, togetherness and autonomy, stability and novelty.[30]

> [Couples who consider non-monogamy] are trying to wrap their arms around the imponderables: Can love be plural? Is possessiveness intrinsic to love or is it merely a vestige of patriarchy? Can jealousy be transcended? Can commitment and freedom coexist?[31]

Most couples desire the stability and security that commitment brings, but most individuals also value autonomy and freedom from monotonous routines. Perel notes the practical complications that may often be involved when considering open relationships, pointing out key concerns: "Inequality, gender, power, and a solid foundation are all considerations that need to be addressed before broaching how to open up a relationship."[32]

It may well be that given the demands of everyday life in much of contemporary Anglo-American contexts, a majority of modern couples, while at times entertaining notions of the appeal of open relationships, may find such practices unsustainable in reality. There may be others, however, even if in the minority, who find they are able to negotiate a more satisfying way forward based on consensual non-monogamy. To clarify terminology, Perel also reminds that polyamory is a relatively recent concept, that the term was included in *The Oxford English Dictionary* in 2006, and that it is to be distinguished from mere casual flings.[33]

Discussing a 2016 YouGov survey of Americans containing the question: "On a scale where 0 is completely monogamous and 6 is completely nonmonogamous, what would your ideal relationship be?," Finkel notes that regardless of age, a majority of respondents replied that 0 (completely monogamous) was ideal for them, but that, significantly, this majority decreased very markedly as participants got younger (from 70 percent for those aged sixty-five and older, to 63 percent for those aged forty-five to sixty-four, to 58 percent for those aged thirty to forty-four,

---

30. Perel, *State of Affairs*, 259.
31. Perel, *State of Affairs*, 262.
32. Perel, *State of Affairs*, 273.
33. Perel, *State of Affairs*, 276.

and a mere 51 percent for those under thirty).[34] He concludes with a possible prediction about future years:

> If these results represent generational shifts more than aging processes, which seems plausible, a larger and larger proportion of American adults will, in the coming decades, view consensually nonmonogamous relationships as ideal.[35]

Whether that last line will turn out to be a prophetic utterance only time can tell. What does appear evident from the current data is that the past few decades have seen an increasing emphasis on sexual attractiveness and sexual performance, rather than on virtues perhaps more prized in earlier generations such as fidelity and resilience.

David Zahl observes:

> In the wake of the sexual revolution of the late 1960s and '70s, sexual expression came to be held as virtually synonymous with self-expression, an unquestioned good and therefore measure of enoughness. We are no longer justified by our sexual purity so much as our sexual *appeal*.[36]

That does appear to describe fairly accurately contemporary Anglo-American dating culture.

3.2.3 The American Context

Along lines referred to above, Andrew Cherlin argues that contemporary American culture uniquely prioritizes both: (i) the value of marriage and (ii) individualism, choice, and personal satisfaction—leading to earlier marriages and cohabiting relationships, and higher rates of marriages, divorces, remarriages, and overall transitions than in other developed countries.[37]

On premarital or nonmarital relationships, as mentioned above, Regnerus points to the existence of an active market for sex, observed in contemporary American contexts,[38] but also applicable in other Western societies. Going through history, Beth Bailey described "the

---

34. Finkel, *All-or-Nothing Marriage*, 249.
35. Finkel, *All-or-Nothing Marriage*, 249.
36. Zahl, *Seculosity*, 24.
37. Cherlin, *Marriage-Go-Round*, 9–16, 23–26.
38. Regnerus, *Cheap Sex*.

transition from calling to dating" as "complete" (by around the 1930s) and "fundamental,"[39] arguing that although "through much of Western history, courtship was firmly based in the reality of the economy,"[40] in the course of the twentieth century, "youth increasingly moved their courtship from the private to the public sphere"[41] and "gradually, a new cultural construct metaphorically substituted the marketplace for the home as the controlling context for courtship rituals," such that "courtship largely was construed and understood in models and metaphors of modern industrial capitalism."[42] She observed that "the new system of courtship privileged competition . . . valued consumption" and "it presented an economic model of scarcity and abundance as a guide to personal affairs."[43] Further, she noted that as "dating moved courtship into the public world, relocating it from family parlors and community events to restaurants, theaters, and dance halls," it also "removed couples from the implied supervision of the private sphere—from the watchful eyes of family and local community—to the anonymity of the public sphere."[44] In addition, this new dating system "shifted power from women to men."[45] In this system, while "before the war, American youth prized a promiscuous popularity," after the war "youth turned to 'going steady' for 'a measure of security and escape from the pressures of the postwar world.'"[46]

Regnerus notes the development, in the course of the twentieth century, of perceptions of virginity as a "neutral or negative attribute" first among young men and then among young women, such that by now "it has become unusual for adolescent boys and girls to retain and respect virginity."[47] In 2011, Regnerus and Uecker estimated, based on their extensive empirical work, that around 84 percent of unmarried young adults (aged eighteen to twenty-three) in America had already had sex.[48]

Of the contemporary American dating scene generally, Regnerus and Uecker observe that:

39. Bailey, *From Front Porch*, 13.
40. Bailey, *From Front Porch*, 5.
41. Bailey, *From Front Porch*, 3.
42. Bailey, *From Front Porch*, 4–5.
43. Bailey, *From Front Porch*, 5.
44. Bailey, *From Front Porch*, 13.
45. Bailey, *From Front Porch*, 19.
46. Bailey, *From Front Porch*, 25.
47. Regnerus, *Forbidden Fruit*, ch. 5, loc. 1598 of 3747.
48. Regnerus and Uecker, *Premarital Sex in America*, 1.

CHAPTER 3: CONTEMPORARY ANGLO-AMERICAN CONTEXTS 97

> A distinctive fissure exists in the minds of young Americans between the carefree single life and the married life of economic pressures and family responsibilities.... In the minds of many, sex is for the young and single, while marriage is for the old. Marriage is quaint, adorable.[49]

Meanwhile, the estimated median age of Americans at first marriage in America rose from 26.7 for men and 25 for women in 1998, to 30.5 for men and 28.6 for women in 2022.[50] Further, "a higher proportion of men than women were never married but both sexes experienced an increase in the proportion never married across age groups from 2006 to 2016."[51]

3.2.4 The British Context

Of the start of a new millennium, the twenty-first century, Hall observes that "it becomes increasingly difficult to write a coherent account of sex, gender, and social change," as "very little historical work has been done." Referring to the second National Sexual Attitudes and Lifestyles Survey (NATSAL), which "provides a snapshot of sexual attitudes and behavior at the turn into the 2000s," she notes that it "found some significant differences since 1990." She notes that "for both men and women there were increased reported numbers of heterosexual partners and of homosexual partnerships," "concurrent partnerships," "consistent condom use" and "a higher rate of cohabitation without marriage."[52]

She also notes "there was wide variability, but an increase in numbers of partners, particularly among the younger age-group ... with an increase in risk factors for sexually transmitted infections (STI) in spite of the apparently greater consistent condom use: trends consistent with rises in STIs and attendance at genitourinary medicine clinics over the same period."[53]

Gabb and Fink argue that relationship practices (including routine "acts of love" or "loving gestures," such as "preparing a meal")[54] provide an important window into the reality of couple relationships, that is, "what

49. Mark Regnerus and Jeremy Uecker, "Sex and Marriage," in Skolnick and Skolnick, *Family in Transition*, 111.
50. Statista, "Estimated Median Age."
51. United States Census Bureau, "Number, Timing and Duration."
52. Hall, *Sex, Gender and Social Change*, 175.
53. Hall, *Sex, Gender and Social Change*, 175.
54. Gabb and Fink, *Couple Relationships*, 220.

love might mean in practice for couples in long-term relationships."[55] Referring to one of their interviewees, "Zoe," describing her long-term relationship with her partner, they observe the fluid and multifaceted nature of the relationship, reflecting both romantic and companionate elements and no clear division between the two:

> It demands multiple terms to describe its depth and extent; the couple are simultaneously lovers, friends and partners. . . . Her account is a synthesis of romantic feeling and fond affection, which is woven into the fabric of her life and, like other couples' accounts in the study, is expressed and enacted through diverse relationship practices.[56]

Of the *Enduring Love?* study,[57] Gabb concludes that "in the end, what's important is that all these different people are finding their own ways towards long-lasting love, and that there are no right or wrong ways. As long as it works for you and your partner—then it works."[58] This appears to adopt a utilitarian or consequentialist approach to relationships (with no objective value judgments).

Findings of the British sex survey 2014 may also be relevant. Key differences from 2008 findings were noted in the 2014 results, including an apparent increase in positive attitudes towards monogamy (regarding it as natural and desirable). There was also apparently a decline in perception of the importance of sex in long-term relationships/marriages.[59]

A 2021 study conducted by Relate and eHarmony found evidence of adverse effects of the COVID-19 pandemic on participants' intimate relationships, and observed its impact is still being assessed.[60]

ONS Data

Data from the Office for National Statistics (ONS) show the average age at marriage for opposite-sex couples in England and Wales from 1968 to

---

55. Gabb and Fink, *Couple Relationships*, 222.
56. Gabb and Fink, *Couple Relationships*, 140.
57. This is a study led by Jacqui Gabb (Open University) involving over five thousand participants in couple relationships. For an overview, see Gabb, "About *Enduring Love?*"
58. Gabb, "About *Enduring Love?*"
59. Mann, "British Sex Survey 2014."
60. Relate, *Way We Are Now 2021*.

CHAPTER 3: CONTEMPORARY ANGLO-AMERICAN CONTEXTS 99

2018 steadily increasing since the early 1970s, and indicate that "in 2018 the average (mean) age at marriage for opposite-sex couples was 38.1 years for men and 35.8 years for women," while in 2022 "the median age for an opposite-sex marriage (and first legal partnership) was 32.7 years for men and 31.2 years for women."[61]

Further data from the ONS indicate (perhaps unsurprisingly) that the percentage of men and women who had ever married by age twenty-five years and thirty years in England and Wales declined steadily over the decades from 1967 to 1993, and "reflect the increasing proportion of men and women delaying marriage to later in life or not getting married at all."[62]

3.2.5 Further Matters of Concern in the Contemporary Dating Landscape

There is also the issue of transactional relationships, including "sugar daddy" relationships. In these contexts, there are often blurred lines between such transactional relationships and sex work. There is also a significant risk of STDs. The influence of social media and a surrounding culture driven by "get rich quick" mentalities may further fuel the incidence of such relationships. It may be observed that this is not just a phenomenon in developing countries, but may also be found in "First World countries," including involving, for example, young female students on university campuses, seeking funding for their studies or further lifestyle perks, and wealthy older men. For example, a 2018 BBC News article discusses "sugar babies" in the UK, including university students using dating apps to find relationships with "sugar daddies" to fund their studies, due to financial pressures.[63]

Further significant features to consider in this context include: the easy availability of pornography, including of particularly addictive "high-quality" varieties with developments in technology/the internet, sexual harassment, stalking, the #MeToo movement, and the increasing

---

61. Ghosh, "Marriages in England and Wales: 2018," fig. 3 and sec. 4, s.vv. "Average Age at Marriage." See also Demography Team, "Marriages in England and Wales: 2021 and 2022," para. 1, s.vv. "Main Points."

62. Ghosh, "Marriages in England and Wales: 2017," fig. 8 and sec. 7, s.vv. "Proportion of Men and Women Who Have Ever Married." See also Demography Team, "Marriages in England and Wales: 2021 and 2022."

63. Smith, "'Sugar Baby' Students."

normalization of practices of casual sex, including as promoted by the media, celebrity culture, and so on. In addition to these, domestic abuse is a significant cause for concern, particularly in view of incidents often arising in the context of intimate relationships.

One may also observe the pervasive influence of celebrity culture—particularly fueled by mass media, including the internet—and how this has likely significantly influenced perceptions of what is acceptable or desirable in dating culture and couple relationships.

3.2.6 Cohabitation

There are many forms of cohabitation, which may range, for example, from "students living together in a flat-share," to "a boyfriend and girlfriend living together while contemplating marriage," to "a couple who have deliberately decided to avoid marriage,"[64] with relationships that "may vary from quasi-marital to ephemeral."[65]

Susan Golombok observes that "cohabitation has become commonplace" across America and Europe,[66] reflecting the significant changes in Western societies in sexual behavior, family and relationship structures and attitudes towards cohabitation and other nonmarital relationships since the sexual revolution of the 1960s and 1970s. In Britain "the number of unmarried couples living together has more than doubled from 1.5 million in 1996 to 3.3 million in 2017,"[67] reaching 13.1 percent of the population in 2020[68] and 22.7 percent of couples living together and aged above sixteen in 2022.[69] As of 2021, while "the number of families that include a couple in a legally registered partnership in the UK has increased by 3.7% in the past decade, to 12.7 million," "by comparison, the number of cohabiting couples families saw an increase of 22.9% over the same period, to 3.6 million."[70] Cohabiting couple families comprised 18 percent of families

---

64. Herring, *Family Law*, 119.
65. Hoffman, *Re P* (2008) UKHL 38, sec. 12.
66. Golombok, *Modern Families*, 2.
67. BBC, "Cohabiting Couples Warned," para. 2.
68. Hill, "Population Estimates: 2020."
69. Sharfman and Cobb, "Population Estimates: 2022."
70. Sharfman and Cobb, "Families and Households: 2021," sec. 1, s.vv. "Main Points."

CHAPTER 3: CONTEMPORARY ANGLO-AMERICAN CONTEXTS 101

in the UK in 2023.[71] In America, as of 2019, "the number of unmarried partners living together ... nearly tripled in two decades from 6 million to 17 million," 7 percent of the total adult population,[72] and as of 2018, among young people aged eighteen to twenty-four, "cohabitation [9 percent] is now more prevalent than living with a spouse [7 percent]."[73]

On this extensive practice of cohabitation, a key question arising is whether premarital cohabitation leads to better or worse marital outcomes (if couples marry thereafter). Answers to this question may depend on who is asked. A 2019 survey in America by the Pew Research Center found that adults younger than thirty "are more likely than older adults to see cohabitation as a path to a successful marriage."[74] Interestingly, there is research indicating that women who marry in their twenties without cohabiting first are among the least likely to divorce.[75]

Overall, it is a vexed question, and the complexity of the decades-long discussion of the "cohabitation effect" (associating cohabitation with a higher risk of divorce) should be recognized. There is continuing debate over the major study by Rosenfeld and Roesler (which they continue to defend) where they conclude (contrary to popular views) that premarital cohabitation does lead to an increased risk of divorce.[76] As Scott Stanley observes, "There is no simple answer for questions about premarital cohabitation."[77]

Drawing on empirical research, sociologist Linda Waite and journalist Maggie Gallagher argue vigorously in favor of marriage as being significantly more beneficial to society and individuals than alternative lifestyles including singleness and cohabitation. Based primarily on research in contemporary American context, Waite and Gallagher observe:

> What some social scientists predicted—a virtual blurring of the social boundaries between marriage and cohabitation—has not taken place. Both the general public and cohabitors themselves typically make a sharp distinction between marriage and living together. Cohabitation is not "just like marriage" but rather an

71. Demography Team, "Families and Households: 2023."
72. Gurrentz, "Cohabiting Partners Older," para. 1.
73. Gurrentz, "Living with an Unmarried Partner," para. 3.
74. Horowitz et al., "Marriage and Cohabitation in the U.S.," para. 21, s.vv. "Younger Adults Are More Likely to See Cohabitation as a Path to a Successful Marriage."
75. Wilcox and Stone, "Too Risky to Wed."
76. Stanley, "Is Cohabitation Still Linked."
77. Stanley, "Is Cohabitation Still Linked," final para.

emerging social lifestyle with a different set of social meanings, which generally serves different purposes.[78]

However, Waite and Gallagher do make the distinction (quite similar to Thatcher's "basic distinction" described in ch. 1) between:

i. Cohabitors "with definite plans to marry"—whom they point out do "act and behave in ways that are similar to married couples" (and they also note that many cohabitors are preparing for marriage)

ii. Cohabitors "without plans to marry"—whom they note "look very different from married couples—in their health habits, in the way they spend money, in their attitudes toward divorce and marriage, leisure and money, and in their fertility patterns"[79]

Citing empirical studies, they also observe that in America "the majority of cohabitors either break up or marry within two years."[80]

These observations by Waite and Gallagher are consistent with Andrew Cherlin's findings, discussed earlier in this chapter, regarding the possibly more distinctive preference for marriage, and shorter duration of cohabiting relationships, in American culture, in contrast, say, to European cultures.[81]

3.3 Continuing "Culture Wars"

3.3.1 Contrasts in Lived Experiences

Cultural differences may still be evident across the various sections of society. One may find, for example, at one end of the spectrum, purity culture,[82] an approach akin to that advocated in *I Kissed Dating Good-*

---

78. Waite and Gallagher, *Case for Marriage*, 36.
79. Waite and Gallagher, *Case for Marriage*, 37.
80. Waite and Gallagher, *Case for Marriage*, 36.
81. Cherlin, *Marriage-Go-Round*, 23–26.
82. The discussion here on purity culture is primarily based on American contexts and research carried out in America, but it is also reasonable to assume that there may be some similar features encountered in British contexts, particularly among conservative evangelical churches that may be influenced by similar literature and role models as their American counterparts. However, further exploration of this (to what extent "purity culture" may be encountered in British contexts and how it may differ from that found in American contexts) is beyond the scope of this book.

CHAPTER 3: CONTEMPORARY ANGLO-AMERICAN CONTEXTS

bye[83] and at the other end, all-out "hookup culture"[84] (discussed later in this chapter), and perhaps, somewhere along the way, "sex on the third date" or "friends with benefits" arrangements, or other expressions of casual sexual encounters. One might find in many contexts teenagers and young adults keen to experiment with their increasing sense of sexuality, while one might also find those of a similar age group deciding that they prefer celibacy, at least for a season, whether for reasons of work, studies, to avoid pregnancy, sexually transmitted diseases, or for religious or other reasons.

Those who adhere to a strict "purity culture" may view with some disdain or distress those who embrace casual sexual encounters or "hookup culture," while those who champion the "merits" of campus "hookup" culture may consider conservative "purity culture" inauthentic or simply unworkable. Still others, substantial numbers in between, may be enamoured neither with "hookup culture" nor a strict "purity culture," but may face their own challenges navigating the complex issues embedded in the potentially hazardous (even if outwardly enticing) landscape of contemporary Anglo-American dating or courtship culture.

I discuss "hookup culture" further in section 3.7.2. In this section I will therefore focus the discussion on the contrasting culture at the other end of the spectrum, conservative or evangelical dating or courtship culture.

3.3.2 Different Culture, and Different Sets of Problems, Among Some Conservative Groups

One cannot assume, of course, that the prevalence of casual sex in many contemporary contexts equates to the practice being regarded as a norm

---

83. See the popular book on Christian dating: Harris, *I Kissed Dating Goodbye*. Harris has written further books, including *Boy Meets Girl* and *Sex Is Not the Problem (Lust Is)*, which some may argue reflect perhaps a more tempered view towards the subject. As mentioned in ch. 1, he has since publicly renounced his views in *I Kissed Dating Goodbye*.

84. The discussion in this chapter on hookup culture is primarily based on American contexts and research conducted in America, but it is reasonable to assume that there may be some similar features encountered in British contexts, particularly in university and college campuses that are run along similar lines as their American counterparts, and possibly in other settings such as nightclubs or discotheques. However, space constraint does not allow for further exploration of this question (to what extent "hookup culture" exists in British contexts and how it may differ from that found in American contexts).

among all, or even most, groups in Anglo-American society. Conservative groups, in particular, may operate with quite different norms.

For example, Samuel Brebner observes the following, sometimes amusingly, concerning approaches towards dating among conservative Christian men: "Young Christian men, we have a problem. . . . It's a problem that's disappointing many of the young Christian women in our lives. . . . We aren't dating them."[85]

His observations appear to reflect Donna Freitas's findings, as described in her 2008 book discussing American campus culture, of the phenomenon of "ring by spring" pressures (pressures to get engaged or committed to marry) among students in some evangelical Christian campuses, at the opposite end of the spectrum from the "hookup culture" found in many other college campuses (secular and also some Catholic) across America. Freitas describes how on evangelical college campuses, there is an emphatic preoccupation with maintaining a culture of "purity"—the emphasis in purity culture being typically on abstinence until marriage, alongside promoting female passivity and male initiative, and exemplified by "promise rings," "purity balls," and programs such as "Silver Ring Thing" and "True Love Waits."[86]

As she observes:

> Hookup culture may dominate the student social scene of spiritual colleges, but students at evangelical schools face unique pressures of their own. They are preoccupied with finding a spouse for life, not with finding a sexual partner for the evening.[87]

She quotes from her memorable interview with a young man at an evangelical university, describing the relationship culture on campus in a pithy line:

> "You know what they say," he tells me with a wry smile. . . . "Ring by spring or your money back!"[88]

A further interview she describes discloses a darker undercurrent to this culture, as a young woman caught up in that dating climate shares:

> There's this big pressure to find somebody, and if you haven't found somebody, then there's something wrong with you. . . .

---

85. Brebner, "Are Christian Guys," paras. 1, 2, 3.
86. Freitas, *Sex and the Soul*, 79–86.
87. Freitas, *Sex and the Soul*, 113.
88. Freitas, *Sex and the Soul*, 114.

> Girls are expected to *not* make the first move—the guys are expected to.... But then the girls get frustrated with guys for not wanting to make the first move, so there's that tension.[89]

Describing the situation for men based on her empirical research, which is somewhat reminiscent of what Samuel Brebner expresses above, Freitas notes:

> One was rather smug about his privileged position as the man—the person with the power to decide, to choose, to do the asking. ... But many other young men were afraid to even ask someone out because, if they do, the relationship automatically becomes serious. You can't really date, in other words, without dealing with the marriage question from the start. This makes some guys afraid, so afraid that it stops them from asking women out altogether. So the culture creates a formidable impasse.[90]

I suggest that neither of these observed cultures ("ring by spring"/purity culture or "hookup culture") are healthy, in terms of the long-term flourishing and well-being of the young people involved. In my book I advocate a balanced virtues-based approach, described in chapter 6, that neither encourages individuals to rush too quickly into marriage without adequate time and discernment nor promotes a casual attitude towards sexual relationships characterized by early intimacy and physical involvement without actual commitment.

3.4 Increased Sexualization of Everyday Culture

Overall, it may be observed that there has been increased sexualization of Anglo-American culture in the course of recent decades, including (by now) with the ubiquity of sexualized images in the vast majority of people's everyday experiences, and widespread availability of "high-quality" pornography, substantially fueled by technology, including the internet and other media. Of this phenomenon, particularly in the twenty-first century, Linda Papadopoulos observes astutely:

> The world is saturated by more images today than at any other time in our modern history. ... The predominant message that is perpetuated to girls is that their value depends on their desirability and to boys that they need to be hypermasculine, strong

---

89. Freitas, *Sex and the Soul*, 115; emphasis in original.
90. Freitas, *Sex and the Soul*, 115.

and in control . . . sexualised images have featured in advertising since mass media first emerged. What is different now, however, is the unprecedented rise in both the volume and the extent to which these images are impinging on everyday life.[91]

Indeed, with the ubiquity of mobile phones, on-demand television and other sophisticated technology in today's society, along with easily accessible pornography in a variety of sites online, one need not even venture out of one's home to be inundated with vivid sexualized images in numerous forms. This surely must have a significant effect over time, particularly on impressionable young (or even, older) minds, and likely on their mindset and attitudes towards dating. The incentive to invest emotionally in any particular dating relationship is very likely reduced by the widespread availability of alternative means and avenues of pleasure and stimulation. The motivation to spend time and energy nurturing and cultivating depth in any one intimate relationship is likely decreased by the easy accessibility of such other quick sources of satisfaction in environments where interactions are viewed as generally "low risk" (in terms of posing little risk of emotional or physical harm).

Of the role of media and popular culture overall in presenting and encouraging particular conceptions of sexuality and gender, Hall laments the artificiality and shallowness of these portrayals in general and the markedly unhealthy effects on individual (especially female) behavior:

> Popular media and culture tend to promote a narrowly heteronormative vision. A good deal of attention continues to be given to simplistic and populist theories of evolutionary psychology. . . . While there may be a greater degree of sexual openness within UK society, much of this is presented within fairly rigid parameters of the acceptable and of what constitutes "sexy." This particularly affects women: surveys report that, constantly faced with heavily manipulated images presenting an unrealistic and extremely narrowly defined model of female attractiveness, they are deeply dissatisfied with their bodies even if not seeking surgical remedies, with eating disorders on the rise quite apart from widespread routine dieting.[92]

It is not unreasonable to conclude that such portrayals in popular media and culture significantly influence perspectives towards dating—particularly among the impressionable young but also possibly even among older

91. Papadopoulos, *Whose Life Is It*, 107–8.
92. Hall, *Sex, Gender, and Social Change*, 184.

CHAPTER 3: CONTEMPORARY ANGLO-AMERICAN CONTEXTS 107

age-groups—including their expectations of what constitutes attractiveness in a partner, and their resulting dating choices and behavior. If what is considered attractive or "cool" is a particular narrow brand of "sexiness," then that will tend to skew the popularity of dating partners in that limited direction, starving the many individuals involved of the richness, character and diversity of different definitions and expressions of attractiveness. Those who are particularly impressionable and anxious to appear in the "in-crowd" may be under particular pressure to conform to such narrow standards of attractiveness and thereby failing to apply wider, more realistic and substantial criteria in their choice of partners.

3.5 Technology, the Internet, and Online Dating

3.5.1 The Advent of the Internet

Fast-improving technology and the internet have led to the phenomenon, unprecedented in previous generations, of the ubiquity of social media, online dating and dating apps, with their accompanying advantages, risks, opportunities, and pitfalls. Among other things, it has fueled the development of several key features relevant to contemporary dating culture, including:

1. The widespread use of social media, including Facebook, Instagram, X (formerly Twitter), and so on
2. Online dating and various dating apps, made even more accessible by the rapid development of smartphone technology
3. Entrenched celebrity culture, particularly fueled by online platforms
4. A world saturated with images, many of them sexualized[93]
5. The easy availability and accessibility of "high-quality" pornography

The choices are wider than ever before. One may virtually "date" various prospects online in the comfort of one's own home, or one may choose to venture out and meet any particularly promising candidates offline after any preferred length of time spent considering each prospect virtually. The continued proliferation of dating sites and apps to

---

93. As, for example, Linda Papadopoulos has observed (*Whose Life Is It*, 108).

suit virtually every palate over the past couple of decades or so appears to have enabled these processes to take place ever more seamlessly. There are now dating apps to suit almost every style, preference, age, orientation, and taste. The wide variety of clickable options available these days ranges well beyond Tinder and Match to Hinge, Bumble, OKCupid, eHarmony, and more.[94]

There can be little doubt that the arrival of the internet along with the widespread availability of mobile phone technology have significantly increased at least the perception of choice and the easy availability of potential romantic contacts, as well as the ease of communicating with any prospects. Whether it is through email, the use of online dating sites or apps, or through social media, the opportunities and alternatives abound for meeting and dating, even across substantial geographical distances, as never before. The questions, however, arise: Does this augur well for the flourishing of interpersonal relationships? Does too much choice equate to little motivation to commit and settle down, thereby afflicting relationships in society with an unhealthy instability? Or do the internet and other technological advancements enable better decision-making, based on significantly more informed choice and the removal of the perception of scarcity which may in the past have imposed artificial pressures on individuals to commit to a particular relationship?

Illustrating concerns implied in the third question, Dan Slater observes: "People exhibit stronger positive illusions about a partner when they believe that access to alternative partners is scarce."[95] He also describes the typical condition, probably all too familiar for those who have been through it, of "relegating yourself to your current situation on the assumption or belief that no escape route exists, that you have no control," that is, "what the behavioral scientists call "learned helplessness" and what everyone else calls "settling.""[96]

Nancy Sales argues that the rise of the internet and dating apps have fueled the proliferation of casual sexual encounters (rather than the formation of long-term committed relationships), often benefitting men more than women.[97] There are alternative views, including those arguing that women are not necessarily disadvantaged in the Tinder-verse.[98]

94. For an overview, see, for example, Stodart et al., "Best Dating Sites."
95. Slater, *Million First Dates*, 119.
96. Slater, *Million First Dates*, 113.
97. Sales, "Tinder and the Dawn."
98. See, for example, Russell and Kissick, "Is Tinder Really Creating."

Further, social media and other online pressures have rapidly evolved. This includes the pervasive pressure to appear perfect or "happy." As Donna Freitas observes, based on interviews with students in college campuses across America:

> Students discuss the notion of the "real me" versus the "online me" and the dissonance they feel between these, the pressure to document publicly a certain kind of college experience, their fears about making themselves vulnerable on social media, and their worries about how to maintain real, meaningful relationships when a seemingly artificial online world dominates their social lives.[99]

Eli Finkel observes of the impact of the proliferation of choice, fueled by the internet, on committed relationships:

> You can say three things. . . . First, the best marriages are probably unaffected. Happy couples won't be hanging out on dating sites. Second, people who are in marriages that are either bad or average might be at increased risk of divorce because of increased access to new partners. Third, it's unknown whether that's good or bad for society. On one hand, it's good if fewer people feel like they're stuck in relationships. On the other, evidence is pretty solid that having a stable romantic partner means all kinds of health and wellness benefits.[100]

On the overall effects of the internet on dating, behavioral scientist Paul Dolan summarizes it well:

> Dating has become like shopping. We are now presented with people much like new shoes on our screens; we shop for the most attractive and add them to our dating basket. But with so much choice, filling up our baskets is not enough. New faces pop up all the time, with better hair, firmer abs and sexier hobbies. . . . The people on our screens are commodified: easily disposed of when a better, or simply newer, item comes in store. And we never stop shopping.[101]

There is a need, therefore, for the perception of the abundance of choice to be moderated. Dolan refers to Barry Schwartz's concept of "the paradox of choice" in his 2004 book, *The Paradox of Choice: Why More Is Less*,

---

99. Freitas, *Happiness Effect*, 10.
100. As quoted in Slater, *Million First Dates*, 119.
101. Dolan, *Happy Ever After*, 62.

to illustrate how work by psychologists has also highlighted "the psychological costs incurred when we are presented with too many choices."[102] At the same time, Dolan observes the positive aspects of modern technology for the landscape of dating, noting:

> Dating apps allow people to finetune their preferences in ways that were previously unachievable. Users can filter prospective dates by age, profession and desire to have babies, for example.[103]

He refers to studies that indicate that sometimes relationships that begin online have more successful outcomes than those that begin with in-person meetings.[104] This may be the case, while one must also note the inherent conflict between the commercial profit-oriented goals of dating apps and dating websites (often based on continued or repeat usage of their services) and any personal goals of users to find long-term love, the ease with which online users may be dishonest on their profiles, and the possible discrepancies between online matching and real-life compatibility. There also appears to be some significant pushback against the proliferation of dating apps in recent years, in various creative moves towards encouraging the forging of more meaningful in-person connections and fewer superficial "swipes" that seem to go nowhere.[105]

In the twenty-first century we live in a technologically-driven world. This is all the more apparent with the COVID-19 pandemic having further fueled an accelerating turn to technological tools to assist or enhance human interactions. Whether Gen Z, millennial, Gen X, boomer, or otherwise, it appears likely there will be an app (or other technologically-enabled tool or interaction) somewhere for you. This ongoing turn to technology may not necessarily be an adverse development, provided that care is taken to ensure that technology does not replace real-world interactions, and that there are safeguards against reductionistic and dehumanizing currents (discussed further in ch. 6).

---

102. Dolan, *Happy Ever After*, 62.

103. Dolan, *Happy Ever After*, 63.

104. For example, Cacioppo et al., "Marital Satisfaction and Break-Ups" (online dating associated with "slightly" lower chances of divorce and "slightly higher" marital satisfaction). See also Dolan, *Happy Ever After*, 63.

105. See, for example, Radin, "With Little Luck on Dating Apps."

3.5.2 Further Findings

A study involving Dutch eighteen- to thirty-year-old emerging adults to investigate motivations for using the popular smartphone dating app Tinder found that there were six primary motivations to use Tinder, that is, "love," "casual sex," "ease of communication," "self-worth validation," "thrill of excitement," and "trendiness," and that the frequency and distribution of these motivations varied according to age and gender. Interestingly and contrary to some popular perceptions of Tinder as a "hookup app," the study found that "love" was a stronger motivating factor than "casual sex" for Tinder use. Perhaps unsurprisingly, the "casual sex" motivation appeared with more frequency for men, along with the motivations of "ease of communication" and "thrill of excitement." The researchers concluded that "Tinder should not be seen as merely a fun, hookup app without any strings attached, but as a new way for emerging adults to initiate committed romantic relationships."[106]

A fairly sizeable study involving 678 participants, including college students as well as members of the general population, looked at the role of biological and personality traits in the use of online dating sites (ODSs). Although involving both heterosexual and homosexual participants, the study still provides relevant findings on the possible role of personality traits in contemporary heterosexual dating in the context of online dating websites. The personality model utilized in the study was the Big Five/OCEAN or five-factor model, encompassing the following five dimensions: extraversion, neuroticism, openness to experience, agreeableness and conscientiousness. It was found that both sex and sexual orientation bore a relation to personality traits and gratifications that participants sought from online dating sites. In particular, "women and homosexuals were found to be more neurotic, women were more agreeable, and homosexuals were more open to experiences" and "women were less likely to use ODSs to find sexual partners, but more likely to use ODSs to be social."[107]

A study reported in 2017 of 502 single adults (aged between eighteen to twenty-nine years old) was presented as the "first to investigate associations between the Big Five personality traits and Tinder use and motives."[108] It considered Tinder use in relation to the five-factor model of

---

106. Sumter et al., "Love Me Tinder," 67.
107. Clemens et al., "Influence of Biological," 120.
108. Timmermans and De Caluwé, "To Tinder or Not," 76.

personality (comprising openness to new experiences, conscientiousness, extraversion, agreeableness, and neuroticism).

For clarity, on these traits, I refer to the following definitions from John, Naumann, and Soto:

> Briefly, Extraversion implies an *energetic approach* toward the social and material world and includes traits such as sociability, activity, assertiveness, and positive emotionality. Agreeableness contrasts a *prosocial and communal orientation* toward others with antagonism and includes traits such as altruism, tender-mindedness, trust, and modesty. Conscientiousness describes *socially prescribed impulse control* that facilitates task-and-goal-directed behavior, such as thinking before acting, delaying gratification, following norms and rules, and planning, organizing, and prioritizing tasks. Neuroticism contrasts emotional stability and even-temperedness with *negative emotionality*, such as feeling anxious, nervous, sad, and tense. Finally, Openness to Experience (vs. closed-mindedness) describes the breadth, depth, originality, and complexity of an individual's *mental and experiential life.*[109]

The study found that users of Tinder tend to be associated with higher levels of openness and extraversion, and lower levels of conscientiousness, than nonusers (with no significant differences found in Tinder use for varying levels of agreeableness or neuroticism).[110] This may lead to a conclusion that individuals who are more extraverted and open to new experiences, while being less conscientious (in terms of levels of self-discipline and goal oriented–ness, in the five-factor model sense),[111] may be more predisposed to using mobile dating applications such as Tinder than those with other combinations of personality traits. Of course, other factors will influence decisions, but this study involving a significant number of respondents does point to some clear links between these specific personality traits and individual choices concerning Tinder use.

The study notes particular characteristics of the Tinder mobile application, including "the application's focus on physical attractiveness and location-based matching,"[112] offering "immediacy and proximity . . .

---

109. Oliver P. John et al., "Paradigm Shift," in John et al., *Handbook of Personality*, 138; emphasis in original.
110. Timmermans and De Caluwé, "To Tinder or Not," 74, 76.
111. Van Thiel, "Big Five Personality Traits."
112. Timmermans and De Caluwé, "To Tinder or Not," 75.

CHAPTER 3: CONTEMPORARY ANGLO-AMERICAN CONTEXTS 113

predominantly targeted at heterosexual singles."[113] Based on the study, these characteristics appear to particularly appeal to individuals with higher levels of openness and extraversion, along with lower levels of conscientiousness.

This study also considered associations between five-factor model personality traits and motives for Tinder use, with reference to a list of thirteen motives for Tinder use (social approval, pastime/entertainment, traveling, sexual experience, using Tinder to get over an ex-partner, belongingness, relationship seeking, flirting/social skills, sexual orientation, socializing, peer pressure, distraction, and curiosity).[114] The study found positive associations between the trait of openness and the "traveling" motive, and between the trait of neuroticism and the motives of "social approval" and using Tinder to get over an ex. It also found the trait of conscientiousness positively associated with "relationship seeking" and negatively with "pastime/entertainment" and "distraction." It further found the trait of agreeableness negatively associated with using Tinder for "sexual experience"/risky sexual behavior, and the trait of extraversion negatively associated with using Tinder for "relationship seeking" and "flirting/social skills" and positively associated with the "pastime/entertainment" motive.[115]

Further, the study found "none of the personality traits significantly predicted Socializing, which may imply that people are generally using the application to meet new people and to broaden their social network, regardless of their scores of the Big Five personality traits."[116] It also found "belongingness" to be the least common motive endorsed by participants for using Tinder, while "curiosity" was the second most common motive.[117]

A cross-sectional study involving 666 students recruited from four university campuses in Hong Kong who "completed a structured questionnaire asking about the use of dating apps, sexual history and sociodemographic information" investigated the relation between the use of smartphone dating applications and incidences of casual sex. The results found included that:

113. Timmermans and De Caluwé, "To Tinder or Not," 74.
114. Timmermans and De Caluwé, "To Tinder or Not," 75.
115. Timmermans and De Caluwé, "To Tinder or Not," 76–77.
116. Timmermans and De Caluwé, "To Tinder or Not," 77.
117. Timmermans and De Caluwé, "To Tinder or Not," 77.

1. "Users of dating apps were more likely to have had unprotected sex with a casual sex partner the last time they engaged in sexual intercourse."
2. "Using dating apps for more than 12 months was associated with having a casual sex partner in the last sexual intercourse, as well as having unprotected sex with that casual partner."[118]

A key finding from this study was "a robust association between using dating apps and having unprotected sex with a casual sex partner, implying that using dating apps is an emerging sexual risk factor." The study therefore recommended "that interventions promoting the safe use of dating apps should be implemented."[119]

Although this study was conducted in Hong Kong, I suggest that it sufficiently reflects conditions often found in contemporary Western university contexts (ease of interaction among students, accessibility, widespread use of up-to-date technology including smartphones, and so on) for the findings to be relevant in Western contemporary dating contexts too.

3.6 More Prevalent Economic Insecurity

It is pertinent to observe here that there are heightened economic concerns in Anglo-American societies particularly after the global economic crisis of 2008, and it is likely these are contributing to the phenomenon of young adults preferring to settle down later than the generation before them. Both American and British societies were significantly affected by the economic crisis of 2008, but it may be noted that economic insecurity was and is likely more severely felt in America than in Britain, due to the decline of key financial and social safety nets in America since the 1970s. Marianne Cooper highlights the phenomenon that American society has seen significant changes in risk and security in recent decades alongside a deepening divide between rich and poor.[120]

I suggest it is highly likely that (alongside other developments discussed in this chapter) these significant changes in risk and security in American society have affected dating and courtship behavior and

---

118. Choi et al., "Association Between Smartphone," 38.
119. Choi et al., "Association Between Smartphone," 38.
120. Cooper, *Cut Adrift*, preface.

perceptions towards marriage. In particular, propelled by such changes, Americans will most likely be less inclined to marry at a young age, but may instead wish to focus on achieving a measure of financial security before deciding, if they do at all, to "settle down." This may be reflected in the data, mentioned earlier, indicating the increasing age of first marriage for both men and women in America in recent decades.

British society has also been affected by the decline in job security and rising costs of living over the past decades, but I suggest that the continuing presence of the National Health Service—notwithstanding perceptions at times of declining standards of care amid increasing demands—is a possible factor in providing a measure of reassurance and security for both rich and poor. Despite long waiting times and varying standards of service, British residents have the assurance that they will not be left destitute or heavily in debt in the event of an unexpected health crisis. While this may not necessarily lead to higher rates of marriage or marriage at younger ages among British than among Americans (as other factors, including cultural changes and other developments discussed earlier will also significantly influence such behavior), it may well be that the relatively higher levels of financial security in Britain in terms of healthcare provision enable the earlier formation of stable couple relationships (including cohabitation) and longer-lived couple relationships/cohabitations. The availability of universal healthcare which is free at the point of use also helps ease divisions between rich and poor, making it possible for those who are less well off to achieve a level of stability and longevity in their intimate relationships.

In some contrast, American society may be less egalitarian than British society in terms of relative accessibility to the possibility of fulfilling and flourishing intimate relationships for all, due to divisions discussed earlier. Describing the stark socioeconomic inequality in America (which he also observes has increased significantly in recent decades), Finkel points out:

> Lower-class Americans are less likely to marry in the first place. And marriages that remain intact tend to be less fulfilling among the lower class than the middle or upper class. Furthermore, the link between low social class and poor marital outcomes has been getting stronger in recent decades.[121]

---

121. Finkel, *All-or-Nothing Marriage*, 155.

He discusses the following two hypotheses—which he informs are supported by empirical findings—for why, as he describes it, marriage "is in crisis among the lower class":[122]

i. "The precariousness of life for poorer Americans brings a level of unpredictability and stress that interferes with marital interactions."[123]
ii. "Poorer Americans have insufficient time and psychological bandwidth for cultivating their relationship."[124]

Jennifer Silva describes the contrast between today's perceptions concerning love, romance, relationships and marriage and those around fifty years or so ago, prior to the effects of the sexual revolution, and the resulting conflicting scripts or visions of love and romance that dating or married couples may have today—one perhaps inherited from earlier generations, based on "traditional" ideals of love and marriage centered around the nuclear family and traditional gender roles (with men as providers or breadwinners, and women as bearers of children and homemakers) and one based on visions of relationship as "therapeutic" or ideas of the "pure relationship" (described, for example, by Giddens, as discussed earlier) centered around emotional satisfaction and self-actualization.[125] Alongside the "emancipatory features of modern intimacy" emphasized by Giddens, she reminds that, in reality, achieving fulfilment in this "new kind of relationship" may necessitate "a particular set of emotional, linguistic, and material resources that are more accessible to the professional middle classes than to the working class."[126]

Silva points out that economic inequality, alongside such cultural expectations (which individuals may have internalized), results in working-class individuals being particularly disadvantaged when it comes to matters of love, intimacy and commitment. Lasting commitment and happy long-term marriages become practically unattainable for many of these individuals, due to the constant sense of deep economic insecurity. She summarizes the situation well:

> Feeling overburdened by the task of taking care of themselves in a precarious labor market and unable to meaningfully plan

---

122. Finkel, *All-or-Nothing Marriage*, 157.
123. Finkel, *All-or-Nothing Marriage*, 160.
124. Finkel, *All-or-Nothing Marriage*, 161.
125. Silva, *Coming Up Short*, 53–57.
126. Silva, *Coming Up Short*, 27.

for the future, for them commitment becomes yet another risk. Ultimately, young adults base their notions of successful intimate relationships on criteria that are structurally unavailable, leaving them resigned to being alone or perpetually seeking the one person who could magically meet their needs. Marriage, at least so far, is in these cases less of what Cherlin calls a "go-round"—an endless cycle of marriage, divorce, remarriage—and more of a nonstarter.[127]

Silva asserts that middle-class men and women have the "[financial], linguistic, material, and cultural resources" to "negotiate flexible forms of work and family arrangements" and thereby achieve emotional satisfaction in their intimate relationships, which working-class men and women lack.[128] This results in a stark inequality (between working-class and middle-class individuals) not merely in terms of financial resources, but in the means and chances of achieving success and fulfilment in their intimate relationships. Silva describes this bluntly as an "unequal access to intimacy [which is] often overlooked and will continue to have profound consequences for working-class men and women" and she highlights "the impossibility of traditional pathways of adulthood" for these men and women and their need to forge a different road ahead for themselves.[129]

Further on the British context, Gabb and Fink observe, based on data from their empirical study, that a recurring theme among couples in the twenty-first century includes that of:

> the difficulties of achieving an acceptable work-life balance and, moreover, the home is experienced as a space where feelings and experiences of unfairness coalesce and requests for support are left unheard.[130]

Elaborating on this, they note ongoing issues with gendered divisions of labor in the home:

> One of the most intensely experienced sites of anger and exasperation in the home is around the gendered inequalities that shape responsibilities for domestic chores and childcare, and

---

127. Silva, *Coming Up Short*, 78.
128. Silva, *Coming Up Short*, 78–79.
129. Silva, *Coming Up Short*, 79–80.
130. Gabb and Fink, *Couple Relationships*, 223.

particularly when women are also trying to manage the "double burden" of paid employment and the care of young children.[131]

Such tensions are particularly exacerbated when economic pressures and difficulties with employment are also ongoing. Gabb and Fink point out the substantial risk of communication breakdown in relationships resulting from a negative and tense home environment particularly when "extended or extensive proximity" are combined with "other stressors such as unemployment and a lack of financial resources," and contrast this with "couples in more secure situations in life," where "the home is experienced as a very positive aspect of the ways they are able to share hopes, desires, needs and anxieties with each other."[132]

At the time of writing, in the year 2024, it may perhaps also be argued that, worldwide (including in Anglo-American societies) there is more prevalent economic insecurity, not least among families and young adults, exacerbated by further economic uncertainty due to responses to the COVID-19 pandemic and war in Ukraine (and the Middle East). The pressures and effects on formation of intimate relationships discussed above are thus unlikely to recede soon.

3.7 Medical Advances Transforming Approaches Towards Sex

3.7.1 Key Medical Advances

Medical advances that have significantly lowered the traditional risks or costs of sexual interactions, and enabled the normalization of casual sexual interactions include particularly the widespread availability of reliable contraception and improved treatments for sexually transmitted infections (STIs). Mark Regnerus refers to three key elements which he argues have fueled a permissive sexual culture (which he terms "cheap sex") in contemporary American society: contraception, high-quality pornography, and online dating.[133] Regnerus defines "cheap sex" as "both an objective fact and a social fact, characterized by personal ease of sexual access and social perceptions of the same."[134] He continues:

---

131. Gabb and Fink, *Couple Relationships*, 223.
132. Gabb and Fink, *Couple Relationships*, 224.
133. Regnerus, *Cheap Sex*, 11.
134. Regnerus, *Cheap Sex*, 28.

CHAPTER 3: CONTEMPORARY ANGLO-AMERICAN CONTEXTS

> "Safe sex" facilitates cheap sex if the primary barrier to having sex with someone is concern about avoiding pregnancy. . . . Cheap sex has made some things more accessible—including but not limited to diverse sexual experiences—and some things more difficult, like sexual fidelity and getting and staying married.[135]
>
> Cheap sex becomes cognitively structured in the mind, affecting how men and women perceive subsequent encounters and even the purpose of sex. It becomes a mentality, not just an act.[136]

Undoubtedly there have been significant medical and technological advances since the 1960s, producing, among other developments, widespread reliable contraception and a variety of cures, remedies and treatments even for what in previous generations may have been regarded as dreaded or untreatable diseases. It is important to note also, however, that the overall context is not a straightforward rosy picture of medical advances resulting in untrammeled sexual freedom. Sexual health remains a key cause for concern, though not always at the forefront of individuals' considerations in the midst of a vibrant dating scene or when surrounded by superficially attractive prospects, as Hall reminds, sounding a note of caution on STIs in the British context.[137]

It is sobering to note that it may well be also that the overall perception of scientific and medical capabilities enabling the treatment and/or cure of a variety of STIs and illnesses has resulted at times in a complacent attitude towards sexual health, with widespread permissive sexual behavior resulting in the increased incidence of some of these infections in recent decades.

3.7.2 Further on Normalization of Practices of Casual Sex: Hookup Culture

A particular phenomenon in contemporary Western contexts, perhaps partly fueled by medical and technological advances enabling the normalization of casual approaches towards sexual interactions, and particularly by university campus culture (though the nature and features of such culture may vary significantly among different universities), and evident even beyond college campuses, is what has been termed

---

135. Regnerus, *Cheap Sex*, 29.
136. Regnerus, *Cheap Sex*, 30.
137. Hall, *Sex, Gender, and Social Change*, 176.

"hookup" culture. It is not possible to discuss exhaustively here "hookup culture," which has been the subject of numerous studies, books, and articles. In this section, I sketch an overview of this topic, aiming to highlight, within the limited space here, some of the key themes and features discussed by scholars in the field, particularly where these form a key part of the overall picture of heterosexual dating culture in contemporary Anglo-American society.

Jason King identifies four different types of campus hookup culture (stereotypical hookup culture, relationship hookup culture, anti-hookup culture, and coercive hookup culture)[138] and observes that "while those who do not hook up are not a majority, they are a sizable minority," although these "risk social marginalization."[139] In his description of "culture" in terms of "frames" (defined as "mental structures people use to understand their experiences") and "scripts" (defined as "mental structures people use to guide their actions"),[140] King observes that the frame and script of hookup culture is well known to students on campus, that "hooking up" is "a sexual act that does not imply commitment or attachment," and that the "hookup" script typically involves the following: "To hook up, one goes to a party, drinks, finds someone, and has a physical encounter (which can range from kissing to sex)."[141] Freitas points out that "three qualities that make up a hookup are its sexual content, its brevity, and its apparent lack of emotional involvement."[142]

Lisa Wade highlights the potentially harmful effects of pervasive hookup culture on American campuses, which she describes as "more than just a behavior; it's the climate."[143] She notes that while the actual behavior of hooking up may not be occurring as frequently as may be popularly perceived, the culture itself, "hookup culture" cannot be escaped, as it dominates American college campuses.

Wade points out in vivid terms the key issues confronting those who opt to take part in hookup culture:

---

138. J. King, *Faith with Benefits*, 5–12.
139. J. King, *Faith with Benefits*, 9.
140. J. King, *Faith with Benefits*, 12.
141. J. King, *Faith with Benefits*, 12.
142. Freitas, *End of Sex*, 24.
143. Wade, *American Hookup*, 19–20.

CHAPTER 3: CONTEMPORARY ANGLO-AMERICAN CONTEXTS

> [The] politics of its pleasure, punishing expectations of physical perfection, intimidating games of status, and possibility of becoming a victim or the agent of a sexual crime.[144]

She further sounds a cautionary note that hookup culture should not be perceived as being confined to college campuses. Based on her empirical research, she observes:

> It's everywhere. It has infiltrated our lives, obscuring our ability to envision better alternatives: sexualities that are more authentic, kinder, safer, more pleasurable, and less warped by prejudice, consumerism, status, and superficiality.[145]

Further along these lines, one may observe that the sexual revolution has not necessarily been liberating for women (though often perceived that way in terms of sexual freedom for women), and has tended to benefit men more, in terms of significantly less sexual responsibility due to the widespread availability of reliable contraception.

Armstrong, Hamilton, and England point out the spectrum of views and attitudes among writers towards hookup culture, observing the contrast in views, including between:

1. Writers opposing casual sex, such as Laura Stepp, author of 2007 book *Unhooked: How Young Women Pursue Sex, Delay Love, and Lose at Both*, whose view is that "hooking up ... places women at risk of 'low self-esteem, depression, alcoholism, and eating disorders.'"
2. "Pop culture feminists such as Jessica Valenti, author of *The Purity Myth: How America's Obsession with Virginity Is Hurting Young Women* (2010)" who "argue that the problem isn't casual sex, but a 'moral panic' over casual sex."
3. Writers like Ariel Levy, of *Female Chauvinist Pigs: Women and the Rise of Raunch Culture* (2005) whose concern "isn't necessarily moral, but rather that [young women involved in hookup culture] seem less focused on their own sexual pleasure and more worried about being seen as 'hot' by men."[146]

---

144. Wade, *American Hookup*, 23–24.
145. Wade, *American Hookup*, 24.
146. Armstrong et al., "Is Hooking Up Bad for Women?," 103.

Examining systematic studies of youth sexual practice which have been conducted by sociologists and psychologists in recent years, they observe in summary:

> The research shows that there is some truth to popular claims that hookups are bad for women. However, it also demonstrates that women's hookup experiences are quite varied and far from uniformly negative and that monogamous, long-term relationships are not an ideal alternative. Scholarship suggests that pop culture feminists have correctly zeroed in on sexual double standards as a key source of gender inequality in sexuality.[147]

They point out that "for most women, the costs of bad hookups tended to be less than costs of bad relationships."[148]

Among other observations, they remind that hookup culture should not be seen as a particularly new phenomenon peculiar to the current generation. They emphasize that it is the generation that came of age during the sexual revolution of the 1960s that experienced the most distinct changes in sexual behavior.[149] However, they also point out distinctive aspects of hookup culture in the current age, describing this as "a sort of limited liability hedonism" in that "contemporary hookup culture among adolescents and young adults may rework aspects of the Sexual Revolution to get some of its pleasures while reducing its physical and emotional risks," as "young people today ... are expected to delay the commitments of adulthood while they invest in careers."[150]

With similar observations on this, Jennifer Beste points out the competitive consumerist nature of contemporary hookup culture—and contrasts this with Metz's Christian worldview described in *Poverty of Spirit*.[151]

3.8 Conclusion

I have discussed and assessed in this chapter six key themes or features of contemporary Anglo-American contexts to be taken into account when constructing a Christian ethical framework for heterosexual dating.

147. Armstrong et al., "Is Hooking Up Bad for Women?," 104.
148. Armstrong et al., "Is Hooking Up Bad for Women?," 107.
149. Armstrong et al., "Is Hooking Up Bad for Women?," 104–5.
150. Armstrong et al., "Is Hooking Up Bad for Women?," 105.
151. Beste, *College Hookup Culture*, 127–43.

Although I have written much of this chapter in descriptive mode, I will discuss normative aspects in further depth in chapter 6.

I turn next, in the chapter that follows, to the field of psychology.

CHAPTER 4: COMPLEXITIES OF BEING HUMAN IN RELATIONSHIP

Psychological Aspects

4.1 Introduction

IN THE COURSE OF this chapter I will be discussing aspects of social psychology, evolutionary psychology, developmental and personality psychology, and anthropology which are relevant to answering my research questions. It will not be possible, within the limited space of this chapter, to consider exhaustively the numerous sources and vast amount of data and empirical research which are relevant. Hence I confine the discussion in this chapter to considering the work of a selection of key scholars whose work may be regarded as illustrative of psychological research in the extensive fields of couple relationships, personality, and the interface of psychology and theology.

Key scholars in these fields whose work I discuss have all published substantially in their respective fields, several with notable works, and are all authorities in their respective fields. Whilst I will also refer to the work of other scholars, it will not be possible to consider their work in detail, due to space constraint, and my discussion is therefore necessarily limited by these choices I have made. On romantic relationships, I have selected the work of Helen Fisher, Eli Finkel, David Buss, Elaine Hatfield, and Shelly Gable, alongside others, as illustrative of the variety of findings and perspectives in this field. On the psychology-theology interface, I will discuss work from Fraser Watts, Joanna Collicutt, and Jocelyn Bryan, and on personality and developmental psychology I have chosen to focus my discussion on the work of Dan McAdams, as I find their perspectives particularly persuasive in the context of this book.

4.1.1 The Psychology-Theology Interface

One cannot assume that theology always interacts seamlessly with psychology, of course. There are different models of interaction.[1] The findings of psychology may not necessarily map neatly onto the concerns of theology. Eric Johnson refers to the work of Alasdair MacIntyre to explain why the clash between the rival traditions of modern psychology and a historically grounded Christianity can seem so intractable, noting MacIntyre's argument that "the biggest obstacle to traditions engaging in mutual, beneficial interaction is the fact that each tradition's beliefs, standards and practices are the means by which an adherent evaluates another tradition, so the very means for determining rational superiority and weakness are themselves part of the debate."[2]

He observes that Christianity and the psychology that has emerged in late modernity are both "traditions interested in the nature of human beings and how to promote their well-being—two historically extended and socially embodied communities of inquiry and therapy." He notes:

> Christianity has its own substantial psychological and soul-care tradition, beginning in the Bible and continuing for the next two millennia, with many permutations over the generations, and consisting of many psychological and soul-care traditions (Catholic, Orthodox and Protestant) [while] the new psychology also constitutes a tradition, though of course it is much younger. However, its shorter history is more than compensated for by its vast output and the broad range of topics that it has addressed (and it too is made up of subtraditions ... psychoanalytic, behavioral, cognitive and so on).[3]

He points out that the rise of modern psychology has precipitated a crisis in the Christian community, primarily because "modern psychology has amassed a stunning set of empirical findings regarding human beings and developed many psychological theories of great complexity,

---

1. For helpful in-depth discussion of various approaches to the science-theology interface, see, for example, Messer, *Science in Theology*.
2. Johnson, *Psychology and Christianity*, 24.
3. Johnson, *Psychology and Christianity*, 24.

using novel empirical methods to discover aspects of human nature never before known."[4]

The response of Christians to this crisis has been varied. For example, among evangelicals, Johnson describes five different positions on the interaction between Christianity and modern psychology.[5] Of these, the "integration" view[6] is probably closest to the approach that I will take in this chapter. This view is often held by counselors and therapists, and is characteristically "more open to modern psychology than biblical counselling, but . . . generally more sympathetic to its critique than the levels-of-explanation approach," often advocating "interdisciplinary integration" between psychology and Christian theology, as they "believe both disciplines address, in different ways, the nature of human beings, how they develop, what has gone wrong with them and how they can overcome what has gone wrong."[7]

For completeness, I set out here the other four positions Johnson describes:

i. The "biblical counseling" view—advocates an approach to Christian counseling ostensibly based primarily on the Bible (with particular interpretations) as "sufficient for the spiritual needs of God's people" and resisting what is perceived as the "dominant Freudian and humanistic methods of counselling"[8]

ii. The "levels-of-explanation" view—"assumes a sharp distinction between the disciplines (or "levels") of psychology and theology" and holds that "all levels of reality [including the psychological and theological] are important" and that "each level of reality is accessible to study by the unique methods appropriate to it that have been

---

4. Johnson, *Psychology and Christianity*, 25.

5. Johnson, *Psychology and Christianity*, 37–38.

6. It should be noted that Johnson's typology of the relationship between psychology and Christianity does not map exactly onto Ian Barbour's well-known and influential fourfold typology of the science-religion interface. For example, Johnson's understanding of the "integrationist" approach does not necessarily equate to Barbour's "integration" model. When I refer to adopting an "integrationist" view in this chapter, this should be regarded as being most consistent with Barbour's "dialogue" model, as described in Barbour, *When Science Meets Religion*, 34–38. For example, Barbour observes that the "dialogue" model "portrays more constructive relationships between science and religion than does either the Conflict or the Independence view, but it does not offer the degree of conceptual unity claimed by advocates of Integration" (34).

7. Johnson, *Psychology and Christianity*, 34.

8. Johnson, *Psychology and Christianity*, 31.

developed by the corresponding discipline, and that the boundaries of each discipline . . . should not be blurred"[9]

iii. The "Christian psychology" view—generally involves Christians in psychology developing "their own theories, research and practice that flow from Christian beliefs about human beings—while continuing to participate actively in the broader fields," often resulting in approaches that are more strongly theologically grounded than the integration approach[10]

iv. The "transformational psychology" view—developed by Christian integrationists who sought to shift the focus to "ethical-relational concerns," arguing that "how Christians live out their Christianity in the field of psychology and counseling is at least as important as seeking to understand human beings Christianly," and linked to a resurgence in interest "in spiritual formation and spiritual direction"[11]

As mentioned, my approach in this chapter will generally be along the lines of an integrationist approach, in which I will draw on and discuss various aspects of psychological research which are relevant to answering my research questions, while at times advancing a critique (particularly from a theological or virtue-ethical viewpoint) of the views or perspectives of the psychological work discussed.

I turn now to considering briefly the work of three theologian-psychologists which may be seen as illustrative of contemporary work at the interface of psychology and theology. I also suggest that each of these theologian-psychologists, though perhaps in different ways and to varying degrees, may be seen as approaching the psychology-theology interface along integrationist lines, and this accounts partly for their selection here.

Fraser Watts

Theologian and clinical psychologist, Fraser Watts points out "four main forms of reductionism" which he sees in psychology:

i. In neuroscience: "The tendency to argue, as Francis Crick put it, that we are nothing but a 'bundle of neurons.'"

9. Johnson, *Psychology and Christianity*, 33.
10. Johnson, *Psychology and Christianity*, 35–37.
11. Johnson, *Psychology and Christianity*, 37–38.

ii. In evolutionary psychology: "The tendency to argue that we are just survival machines for our genes."
iii. In artificial intelligence: "There is a proposal that the mind is, in effect, just a computer program."
iv. "In some branches of social psychology, there is a proposal that human realities are just 'social constructs.'"[12]

Watts asserts the "critical contribution that theology can make . . . [is] to challenge reductionist interpretations of psychological research, though there is no direct challenge to detailed research work itself. Theology will want to urge much greater caution in the interpretation of research findings. . . It can aspire to clean up the reduction ideology that often distorts the way in which scientific research is presented [particularly in popular contexts]."[13]

He also presents ways in which a theological perspective may enrich a psychological approach on topics of mutual interest, such as guilt and forgiveness.[14] Concerning theological anthropology, Watts cautions against making claims that are made "just to fit in with other theological positions, and without theologians feeling any need to check empirically whether their claims are correct," also noting "there is too much theological generalization about human nature, and neglect of differences between people."[15]

He also asserts that both psychology and theological anthropology "need to recognize that human beings are physical, personal and social beings, and to find a way of understanding how those aspects intersect with one another," observing that "Christian theology currently tends to overemphasize relationality, and some areas of psychology overemphasize the biological aspects of human nature. Dialogue between them might help to correct each other's imbalances."[16]

He further observes:

> Both disciplines need to reconcile continuity of personality across different situations with change from one context to another. Theology tends to see unity of personality as normative,

12. Watts, "Psychology and Theology," 190.
13. Watts, "Psychology and Theology," 192.
14. Watts, "Psychology and Theology," 193–94.
15. Watts, "Psychology and Theology," 196.
16. Watts, "Psychology and theology," 196.

and diversity as breakdown of the norm. Psychology is more likely to start from the diversity of how people function in different situations, and to see integration as an achievement rather than a norm.[17]

These are important observations to bear in mind as one considers, in theological and psychological terms, what it means to be human, and, particularly for present purposes, what it means to understand and relate to the full person in the context of a dating relationship. This will be considered in detail in section 4.2.5.

In addition, Watts reminds that "psychology is both a biological and a social science," noting issues that arise from this partly due to biological psychology and social psychology "being different kinds of sciences, with different methodologies"—as biological psychology is a natural science, concerned with biological entities and processes, while social psychology relates instead to social aspects, such as social and cultural context and social processes.[18] He points out the conflict for supremacy sometimes occurring between these approaches, observing that "there is a recurrent tendency to prioritize biology, though that is sometimes countered by strong forms of social constructionism that want to prioritize the social."[19]

Watts's response to this conflict for supremacy is to suggest that "neither is prior in any general sense, and for all purposes," noting that different explanations—sometimes biological, sometimes social—may be required in different contexts, and that to comprehend complex phenomena (such as religious experiences), "multiple approaches that sit alongside one another" are necessary. He recommends "a systemic approach in which different explanatory discourses illuminate different aspects of whatever is under discussion."[20] Further, he points out a possible strength of this dual composition of psychology (being both biological and social), in that it may enable a richer understanding of human behavior, as "humans are both biological and social creatures."[21]

---

17. Watts, "Psychology and Theology," 196.
18. Watts, *Psychology, Religion, and Spirituality*, 172–73.
19. Watts, *Psychology, Religion, and Spirituality*, 173.
20. Watts, *Psychology, Religion, and Spirituality*, 172–73.
21. Watts, *Psychology, Religion, and Spirituality*, 173.

Joanna Collicutt

Theologian-psychologist Collicutt draws on the insights and findings of psychology at many points in her work, at times illustrating how such insights or findings can be compatible with Christian theology. For example, when discussing the positive psychology movement, she observes:

> Insights from positive psychology can inform the process of conforming to the character of Christ. This is the Spirit's work but, as Jesus reminds us in the words from Mark's Gospel at [Mark 12:29–30], it is an enterprise to which we must bring our *strength*.[22]

At the same time, she also points out places where the views of psychologists may not fit neatly with Christian perspectives. For example, she also notes that "some of the discourse of positive psychology jars with the traditional Christian habit of self-denigration," including, for example, as reminded in the exhortation to "deny ourselves and lose our lives (Matt. 16:24–25 and parallels)." She reconciles these possible tensions by reminding that such perspectives "need to be set alongside the fact that we have been created in the image of God (Gen. 1:26–27)."[23]

I will refer to further aspects of Collicutt's work later in this chapter.

Jocelyn Bryan

On what may constitute a human being's personality (while bearing in mind the complexity of this vast topic), Christian psychologist Bryan refers to a working definition from Lawrence Pervin and Oliver John, as follows: "Personality represents those characteristics of the person that account for consistent patterns of feeling, thinking and behaving."[24]

Bryan observes that key aspects of exploring personality include considering the:

i. What (describing observed qualities/features/characteristics)
ii. How (including exploring aspects of "nature"/genetic sources and nurture/environment/experiences)

---

22. Collicutt, *Psychology*, loc. 1247 of 6452; emphasis in original.
23. Collicutt, *Psychology*, loc. 1261 of 6452.
24. As quoted in Bryan, *Human Being*, 76.

iii. Why (including motivations, goals and values) of human personhood[25]

Applying this to the context of dating, I suggest that a good dating approach should involve the goal of getting to know the genuine person one is relating to—in all key aspects of human personhood, including the what, the how, and the why, including by asking constructive questions and engaging in diverse activities in different settings which may be helpful in this regard—rather than, perhaps, simply to "feel good" or "have a nice time" (which often characterizes various parts of contemporary dating). Honesty, as part of a Christian virtue-ethical approach, is also particularly important here, as opposed to the inclination—prevalent in some aspects of contemporary dating culture—to put forward an "attractive" false persona of oneself. I will discuss the complex matter of getting to know the "real" or "full" person further in section 4.2.5, but I offer the preceding thoughts as some preliminary comments on the matter while interacting with Bryan's work.

Bryan also observes regarding trait theory that:

i. "During the past 50 years the number of traits, and scales designed to measure them, has escalated and there is a bewildering array to choose from: often with little evidence of their validity and theoretical basis. . . . [The] focus [of the psychometric tradition] on traits and individual differences has led to sparse attention being given to the whole person and context in particular."

ii. "New approaches to personality have emerged in recent years which have broadened the theoretical base beyond trait theory and developed a more integrative approach."[26]

Further, pointing out three basic human needs, Bryan refers to Deci and Ryan's claim that "human beings have psychological needs to be competent [to manage our lives effectively], autonomous and related to others [in caring and mutually supportive ways]" and observes that "a considerable body of research confirms that satisfying these three psychological needs is essential for our well-being and psychological growth."[27]

Bryan reminds that "the psychology of motivation focuses on a meeting of essential needs and the energizing of desires" and that "there

25. Bryan, *Human Being*, 76–77.
26. Bryan, *Human Being*, 78.
27. Bryan, *Human Being*, 117.

are individual differences in both levels of motivation and kinds of motivation."[28] Commenting on the widely-known Maslow's hierarchy of needs—which groups human needs and desires into a hierarchy of five categories ("bodily needs for physical survival" such as for "food, shelter, sexual release," followed by the "need for protection and safety," then the "need for belonging and intimate relationships," and further "the need for esteem with achievement, competence, status and approval," and finally "the desire for the fulfilment of one's potential as a human being as self-actualization"), on the basis that humans only progress to higher level needs after lower level needs have been met—Bryan observes that "although it remains influential and has some validity, there are a number of problems with Maslow's approach,"[29] including:

i. "It over-simplifies the prioritization of needs. There are many counter examples of people pursuing higher needs when the lower ones are not met."[30]

ii. "The evidence from questionnaire studies does not support the hierarchy, but instead it seems that we have a hierarchy of motives and these differ in content and order from Maslow's hierarchy."[31]

iii. "We all make different choices regarding our motivations and priorities. It is these differences that contribute to the individual differences expressed in our personalities. Furthermore, our motivations and how we prioritize them is likely to change at different stages of our lives."[32]

Bryan, recalling that in McAdams's "three-level model" goals and values form the "second layer of personality over the first layer of dispositional traits," points out that "the two should not be thought of as separate layers," and notes that dispositional traits may be "correlated with . . . value dimensions."[33] She points out that "our motivations and goals become integrated into who we are and are related to our biological dispositions

---

28. Bryan, *Human Being*, 117.
29. Bryan, *Human Being*, 118.
30. Bryan, *Human Being*, 118.
31. Bryan, *Human Being*, 118–19.
32. Bryan, *Human Being*, 119.
33. Bryan, *Human Being*, 130.

[thus determining] our character, our habitus, and therefore how others experience and relate to us."[34]

Reminding of the human need for relatedness as "one of the three basic human needs along with agency and autonomy," she refers to Gen 2:18 (where God states, "It is not good that the man should be alone") as evidencing that "God acknowledges human relationships within the created order as a source of human flourishing and wellbeing."[35]

Bryan points out the primacy of relationality as a key aspect of human personhood:

> Human beings are created with a profound longing for relationship which is reflected in their human nature. A longing to love and be loved manifest in the need for intimacy [is] at the very core of what it means to be human.[36]

This forms a salient reminder that the matters discussed in this chapter need to be treated with great sensitivity and care.

4.1.2 Key Observations

Prior to detailed discussion, it may be helpful to highlight some key observations that I will be discussing based on psychological research, which have relevance to answering my research questions. In summary form, these observations are:

i. There are many different theories put forward by psychologists regarding the complexities of attraction and rejection in relationships, and how and why people fall in love with one person and not another. These include Finkel and Eastwick's theory based on "instrumentality," evolutionary theories, Le and Agnew's "interdependence theory," Sternberg's triangular theory of love, and Aron and Tomlinson's "self-expansion" theory of love.

ii. Various factors may influence one's choice of mate or the process of falling in love, across a variety of different situations. Among these, Helen Fisher has identified the following as being significant or commonly manifested: timing, physical attributes, attractive personality

---

34. Bryan, *Human Being*, 130.
35. Bryan, *Human Being*, 132–33.
36. Bryan, *Human Being*, 133.

traits, shared values, fulfilling needs and roles, and personal "love maps" formed through each individual's life experiences.[37]

iii. Scholars studying romantic relationships have identified different types of love. Most prominent among these are "passionate love" and "companionate love."[38]

iv. Of these, companionate love has been found in empirical research to be an important element in stable long-term marriages, including as observed by Shelly Gable and others.

v. Passionate love has been associated with a number of distinct physiological changes and behaviors, including as described in some detail by the anthropologist Helen Fisher.

vi. Because of its inherent physical and biological basis, casual sex may have bonding effects, even where these are unintended. It should be noted, however, also that individuals can vary widely in their levels of sociosexuality (defined in sec. 4.2.3). Further, the differences between men and women in their expressions of interest in casual sex are well established in empirical research particularly in Western contexts, including in a well-known (and well-replicated) study conducted by Elaine Hatfield and Russ Clark, although it remains unclear as to whether males and females actually differ in their personal responses towards experiences of casual sex.

vii. Romantic love also has its darker side, with romantic rejection and relationship breakdown often adversely affecting mental health, and with jealousy often identified in connection with romantic love, and significant numbers of incidents of abuse and violence being linked to intimate relationships.

viii. On personality traits, numerous studies by personality psychologists over the past several decades have resulted in a measure of convergence of views towards the grouping of traits into a few key clusters. Although there remain other theories which continue to be in use, one grouping of traits which is currently widely used in psychological research is that known as the "Big Five" or "OCEAN" (also mentioned earlier in chapter 3)—comprising "Openness

---

37. H. Fisher, *Why Him? Why Her?*, 143–58.

38. Shelly Gable, "Close Relationships," in Finkel and Baumeister, *Advanced Social Psychology*, 241. Definitions of both these terms are set out in sec. 4.2.2.

CHAPTER 4: COMPLEXITIES OF BEING HUMAN IN RELATIONSHIP   135

to Experience" (O), "Conscientiousness" (C), Extraversion" (E), "Agreeableness" (A) and "Neuroticism" (N).[39]

ix. Dan McAdams has developed a "three-level model" of personality that, as Jocelyn Bryan points out, unlike some other approaches, "focuses unashamedly on describing rather than explaining personality . . . supporting his assertion that too often psychology has moved towards explanation before carefully identifying the phenomena it is explaining."[40]

This three-level model includes consideration of each individual's (i) traits (particularly in relation to the "OCEAN" taxonomy), (ii) goals, motivations, and concerns, and (iii) notably also the narrative of his/her life as significant.

x. As to the question of whether individuals' traits change significantly over time, so that the norm may be that they are no longer the same as before (after, for example, a number of years), McAdams gives a suitably complex response:

Do people's traits mostly change or remain the same? According to years of research on the development of personality traits, the answer is *both*.[41]

Five Recommended Approaches

In this chapter I identify key findings (ten of which are summarized above) from psychological research relevant to answering my research questions. While acknowledging the potential helpfulness of an approach such as Hauerwas's law for married couples in a challenging season of their marriage who may need encouragement to persevere in their mutual commitment, I contend that for unmarried individuals or couples who are still dating, the advice needs to be significantly more nuanced. Rather than declaring, "You always marry the wrong person," and thereby almost encouraging an abrogating of responsibility to exercise due diligence in dating to make wise choices as far as reasonably possible, I recommend the five approaches that follow as possibly more helpful approaches, based on the psychological research discussed.

39. McAdams, *Art and Science*, 105–6.
40. Bryan, *Human Being*, 88.
41. McAdams, *Art and Science*, 104.

I suggest that these five approaches may also be seen as part of an outworking and application of my suggested fivefold ethic of temperance, courage, justice, prudence, and love and care (discussed in ch. 6) that takes into account the relevant psychological research. In this I am also applying an integrationist view (described in sec. 4.1.1 above regarding the psychology-theology interface). The five approaches that I recommend, based on the psychological research, are:

i. Be aware of the variety of dynamics that could be at work in the complex experiences of attraction and rejection in romantic relationships.

ii. Prioritize the value of companionate love for the long-term sustainability of intimate relationships.

iii. Be aware that casual sex may not actually be "casual."

iv. Be careful to minimize causing any unnecessary hurt or harm to the other, bearing in mind the potentially inflammatory nature and "dark side" of relationships when they go wrong.

v. Seek to understand and relate to the other person, and make decisions regarding the relationship (such as on compatibility), on the basis of seeking to discern the full person, in the multilayered aspects of his/her personality, rather than in superficial or one-dimensional ways—such as by focusing on physical attributes or surface traits.

For this I will be discussing in particular the work of Dan McAdams, particularly his three-level model of personality, and his consideration of developments in the life course. I suggest that McAdams's account of personality offers a fuller and more helpful account of what it means to be human, and what constitutes a person as far as personality is concerned, than other models such as Fisher's.

I will discuss the psychological research relating to these five recommended approaches in the sections that follow. The themes of approaches (i) and (v) are associated with particularly voluminous amounts of psychological research. Hence, even while focusing on only a few scholars' work, my discussion of the issues in these sections will be significantly lengthier than in the other three sections.

4.2 Discussing Psychological Research Relating to the Five Recommended Approaches

4.2.1 Complexities of Attraction and Rejection

The first aspect of the recommended approaches that I advocate in dating is to be as aware as possible of the complexities of attraction and rejection, which I now discuss in detail.

Why do we fall in love with one person, but not another? What causes the strong feelings of attraction one may feel towards one "special person," but not another? We do not all fall for the same person (although, of course, there are love triangles, and even more complex scenarios), but often, subjects of attraction differ from person to person.

4.2.1.1 Discussing Research from Eli Finkel

Eli Finkel and Roy Baumeister point out that there has been a resurgence of psychological research on interpersonal attraction in relationships in the twenty-first century, recovering from an earlier decline of interest in the field around the last two decades of the twentieth century (which was at the time partly in reaction to widespread concern about marital breakdown and societal instability caused by the sexual revolution of the 1970s, prompting increased research efforts in the field of "close relationships"—seeking, for example, to identify what contributes to stability and satisfaction in long-term relationships—rather than in the field of interpersonal attraction). This revival of research work in the general field of interpersonal attraction in relationships—along with a continued blossoming of work in the related, though relatively more recent field of attraction research based on evolutionary psychology (developing mainly from David Buss's work since 1989)—has occurred mainly due to "the advent of technological and methodological developments in dating practices and social networking in the real world, including online dating, speed-dating, and social networking."[42]

Among other scholars, Finkel also points out the helpfulness of speed-dating as a method in social-psychological studies of attraction, both in terms of "generalizability" and "strong experimental control":

---

42. Finkel and Baumeister, *Advanced Social Psychology*, 202.

> In speed-dating studies, participants volunteer for an actual speed-dating event in which they meet around a dozen preferred-sex partners for interactions of, say, four minutes in duration. The value of speed dating methods has come into sharper focus as concerns about replicability within social psychology have grown, because speed-dating events provide an efficient means of collecting high-impact data characterized by strong statistical power. . . . Such data enable researchers to answer questions that are unanswerable with most methods.[43]

Questions that these methods may helpfully address include, for example, the nature and extent of qualities that result in greater (or lesser) attraction from potential partners, or the particular roots of an experience of attraction in the context of other potential attractions.[44]

In 2015, Finkel and a fellow scholar P. W. Eastwick put forward the argument that at the heart of interpersonal attraction is what they term "instrumentality," that is:

> People become attracted to others who help them achieve needs or goals that are currently high in motivational priority.[45]

This developed on empirical research on close relationships, particularly on findings by Fitzsimons and Shah that "people tend to draw closer to significant others who are instrumental for such goals."[46]

Hence, Finkel and Eastwick, along with others, connect the phenomenon of attraction with each person's particular goals or concerns which are held to be important to that person personally. Of course, this may also imply that feelings of attraction experienced even by one person may vary from situation to situation, from context to context, depending on what her or his highly-prioritized personal goals or concerns are at that time.

Finkel and Eastwick also point out:

> In addition to functioning as the basis of attraction, instrumentality also serves as the (frequently implicit) foundation

---

43. Finkel and Baumeister, *Advanced Social Psychology*, 202.
44. Finkel and Baumeister, *Advanced Social Psychology*, 203.
45. E. J. Finkel and P. W. Eastwick, "Interpersonal Attraction," as quoted in Finkel and Baumeister, *Advanced Social Psychology*, 203.
46. Finkel and Baumeister, *Advanced Social Psychology*, 203. See also Fitzsimons and Shah, "How Goal Instrumentality Shapes."

for the major theoretical frameworks for understanding how attraction works.[47]

Further considering this theory of attraction based on instrumentality, one may note also the possibility that short-term attractions may arise based on particular conditions or circumstances which create a conducive environment for attraction, attractions which may not be sustainable in the long-term. An example may be where dating occurs in artificial "reality show" environments such as *Love Island* or *I'm A Celebrity, Get Me Out of Here*, television shows in which individuals who couple up during the duration of the show (based at the time on what they may well experience as "genuine" mutual attraction) may find that their relationships are not sustainable in the face of the challenges of living in the real world, after the show is concluded.

Being aware of the possibility of such attractions occurring on the basis of instrumentality (feeling drawn to those who are viewed as being helpful for achieving personal goals which one considers particularly important at the time) may help individuals to consciously take a more long-term perspective regarding any particular relationship in which feelings of attraction are encountered—to consider the long-term sustainability of the relationship, rather than being overly focused on feelings of attraction which may be based on short-term conditions.

The jury is probably still out on whether artificial environments, for example, on dating shows such as *Love Island*, are conducive for discerning real compatibility between two people for a long-term relationship. I suggest that while one may, by chance, be able to find "true love" in such contexts, environments such as these—which tend to encourage or facilitate the premature escalation of emotional and physical intimacy (and all the more so with the added incentive to "couple up" being presented by the prospects of publicity or winning)—are not particularly helpful in enabling the discerning, in a balanced and well-considered manner, real compatibility in key aspects of each of the individuals' lives which may be important for sustaining the long-term flourishing of a relationship.

Further, it may be observed that, in the attraction research considered above, no distinction appears to be made between attraction that is based on "love" (I use this term here to mean being primarily other-centered, such as being focused on appreciating what one considers beautiful in the other) and "lust" (here I use the term to mean desire

47. Finkel and Baumeister, *Advanced Social Psychology*, 203.

that is primarily self-centered, or driven by self-interest). I recognize the challenges involved (and possibly practical impossibility) of designing scientific experiments that would be able to draw out such distinctions. Of course, it is possible also (and this may occur quite frequently) that the emotions or attraction experienced by the persons involved may be comprised of a mixture of the two, both "lust" and "love." Be that as it may, from a theological and Christian virtue-ethical standpoint, I suggest that it is important (even with practical difficulties and imperfect outcomes) to distinguish between the two, and that attraction based on "love," rather than "lust," is most helpful for the long-term flourishing and well-being of the persons involved.

4.2.1.2 Discussing Helen Fisher's Work

Helen Fisher, the well-known anthropologist and expert on the scientific aspects of romantic love, identifies the following as factors that she considers significant in the process of falling in love/choosing one's mate:

i. Timing. Fisher argues that some events/transitions in life may make us more susceptible to falling in love than others.[48]

ii. Physical attributes—such as good looks, symmetry in facial features, body shape, and so on, though different temperament types may tend to have different preferences in the various aspects.[49] Fisher refers to studies that appear to indicate some preferences that manifest across different cultures/people groups in different parts of the world, such as a preference among men for a 70 percent waist-to-hip ratio in women, which she attributes to evolutionary motivations.[50]

iii. Fisher also points to certain personality traits she asserts are characteristics widely regarded as attractive, which "most people seek in a mate," indicating a sense of universal preference for certain qualities in a life partner. These include being "confident, smart, stable, friendly, generous, self-effacing, sensitive, financially secure, healthy and popular."[51]

---

48. H. Fisher, *Why Him? Why Her?*, 143.
49. H. Fisher, *Why Him? Why Her?*, 147–50.
50. H. Fisher, *Why Him? Why Her?*, 148.
51. H. Fisher, *Why Him? Why Her?*, 147.

iv. Shared values.[52] Fisher observes:

> Men and women are attracted to individuals who share their standards, ethics, morals and ideals... When it comes to *values*, similarity does attract.[53]

v. Needs and roles. Fisher refers to this as "exchanging needs" and "providing roles."[54] She refers, for example, to "social exchange theory" which "holds that men and women are attracted to those who can provide them with the resources they seek in exchange for the assets they can provide," and notes how this will vary from individual to individual, that "the exchange may be of any kind but it must be 'fair.'"[55]

vi. Love maps—Fisher observes that we all have unique love maps, which develop over time, formed by all the "forces and events" of our childhood and various past experiences which "converge to create a unique constellation of interests, values, beliefs and behavioral idiosyncrasies you carry in your head," influencing and guiding our dating behavior and choices.[56]

Overall, when approaching or considering a romantic relationship with a prospective partner, it will be helpful to be aware of the possibility of at least some of the above factors being in play in influencing one's choice of partner. Being aware of the possibility of such processes being at work may also enable one to approach a relationship with more well-informed judgment concerning the long-term suitability of the pairing (considering, for example, whether certain factors may be transient or not particularly reliable for determining long-term compatibility, while other factors may be given more weight).

Fisher asserts that "neuroscientists believe that the basic human emotions and motivations arise from distinct systems of neural activity, networks that derive from mammalian precursors." She notes that "psychological studies indicate that romantic love is associated with a discrete constellation of emotions, motivations, and behaviors" and describes the following as characteristics often associated with romantic love:

52. H. Fisher, *Why Him? Why Her?*, 152–54.
53. H. Fisher, *Why Him? Why Her?*, 153.
54. H. Fisher, *Why Him? Why Her?*, 154–56.
55. H. Fisher, *Why Him? Why Her?*, 154–55.
56. H. Fisher, *Why Him? Why Her?*, 157–58.

i. "Romantic love begins as an individual comes to regard another as special, even unique. The lover then intensely focuses his or her attention on this preferred individual, aggrandizing the beloved's better traits and overlooking or minimizing his or her flaws."

ii. "Lovers experience extreme energy, hyperactivity, sleeplessness, impulsivity, euphoria, and mood swings. They are goal-oriented and strongly motivated to win the beloved."[57]

Fisher considers romantic love to be "one of three discrete, interrelated emotion/motivated systems that all birds and mammals have evolved to direct courtship, mating, reproduction, and parenting," these three comprising:

i. The sex drive (associated with "lust")

ii. Romantic love/attraction

iii. Attachment[58]

She observes various brain chemicals and parts of the brain involved in manifestations of these:

i. The sex drive is "characterized by the craving for sexual gratification [and may be] directed toward many partners," and in humans is associated with the androgens, particularly testosterone"[59] and "specific networks of brain activation . . . [which] vary . . . among them [being] the hypothalamus and the amygdala."[60]

---

57. H. Fisher, "Drive to Love," 88.

58. H. Fisher, "Drive to Love," 89. This discussion is based on Fisher's chapter in the first edition of *New Psychology of Love*. There does not appear to be a chapter along similar lines in the second edition of *New Psychology of Love*. However, it may also be noted that in a Feb. 2019 interview, Fisher reiterates her description of key brain chemicals influential in what she asserts are "three distinctive brain systems" evolved in human beings concerning romantic relationships—comprising the sex drive, romantic love, and deep attachment. See Brain World, "Sex, Love, and Attachment." In the interview, and based on her empirical research and the personality model she has developed, she also observes that "explorers" ("people very expressive of the dopamine system") tend to be attracted to each other; and "builders" (those expressive of serotonin, tending to be "more traditional, conventional, calm") also tend to be attracted to each other; but that "directors" (those high in testosterone and who are typically decisive and logical) tend to be attracted to their opposite, "negotiators" (those high in estrogen, who tend to be "holistic thinkers").

59. H. Fisher, "Drive to Love," 89.

60. H. Fisher, "Drive to Love," 89–90.

CHAPTER 4: COMPLEXITIES OF BEING HUMAN IN RELATIONSHIP 143

> ii. Attraction, "the mammalian/avian counterpart to human romantic love," is "characterized by increased energy, focused attention on a specific mate . . . possessive mate-guarding, and motivation to win a preferred mating partner," is "primarily associated with elevated activity of dopamine in the reward pathways of the brain" and "most likely . . . also associated with elevated activity of central norepinephrine and suppressed activity of central serotonin, as well as other brain systems."[61]
>
> iii. Attachment is "characterized in birds and mammals by mutual territory defense and/or nest-building, mutual feeding and grooming, maintenance of close proximity, separation anxiety, shared parental chores, and affiliative behaviors" and "in humans . . . is known as companionate love" and is also associated with "feelings of calm, security, social comfort, and emotional union with a long-term mate," with "animal studies [suggesting] this brain system is associated primarily with oxytocin and vasopressin in the nucleus accumbens and ventral pallidum, respectively."[62]

For her account of the phenomenon of humans falling or being in love, Fisher focuses her discussion on the neurobiology/hormones/chemicals in the brain during these processes. In particular, she highlights elevated levels of dopamine and norepinephrine, along with low levels of serotonin, as key influences on the behavior of men and women in love.[63] She even draws parallels between the behavior of those newly in love with those laboring under obsessive-compulsive disorder (!).[64] While there may well appear to be some similarities in some aspects of such behavior, including as observed by Fisher, and while recognizing also that Fisher herself may not be implying that this is what romantic relationships basically boil down to, I suggest from a theological perspective that it is important to take particular care to avoid a reductionistic approach, particularly to the complex phenomenon of human relationships. Yes, falling in love does involve, on a biological level, various aspects of brain activity and the functioning of various hormones/brain chemicals (and these must be taken seriously into account when assessing what is taking place when a human being professes to be in love), but falling and being

61. H. Fisher, "Drive to Love," 90.
62. H. Fisher, "Drive to Love," 90.
63. H. Fisher, "Drive to Love," 91–92.
64. H. Fisher, "Drive to Love," 92.

in love is not simply about hormones. There are often a myriad of other factors involved. Falling in love, and being in love, cannot and should not be reduced to the mere working of some chemicals. At the same time, it is helpful to be aware of the neurological processes that may be involved when one is experiencing what may feel like overwhelming emotions while encountering romantic love, and to understand that these may arise from various triggering factors. All states of mind are associated with neurochemical brain states. Any mental event is also a physical event, and the various experiences one goes through in dating will each have their neurological correlate.

Concerning anthropological aspects,[65] Fisher has observed trends of female preferences for indicators of status, power or wealth in male suitors and male preferences for beautiful and shapely females as partners,[66] which appear based on evolutionary motivations—that is, the tendency among many women to prefer to select males of perceived high status/power/earning potential (whom adherents to evolutionary principles would likely identify as being perceived as most suitable mates to procreate with, considering biological features such as the female reproductive cycle, limited number of eggs, and so on), and the tendency among many men to select physically attractive females with specific physically appealing assets (whom adherents to evolutionary principles would likely identify as displaying traits of being able to produce and nurture thriving offspring).

Fisher's views may be compared to (or contrasted with) the writings of other dating and relationship experts popular in the field who may rely more on extensive experience in counseling singles and couples on the complex matter of romantic relationships. For example, Paul Dobransky—a popular writer, psychiatrist, and dating and relationship specialist—advances his view, based on extensive relationship counseling experience, that long-term sustainable love and pair-bonding consists of three aspects:

i. Sexual attraction

ii. Friendship and romantic bonding

iii. Commitment and intellectual intimacy[67]

---

65. For further on Fisher's anthropological perspective, see H. Fisher, *Anatomy of Love*.

66. H. Fisher, *Why Him? Why Her?*, 148–49.

67. Dobransky and Stamford, *Secret Psychology*, loc. 143 of 4370.

Dobransky's hypothesis is that a successful relationship has to be based on three essential elements, which he suggests are connected to three major parts of the brain—the "reptilian" brain focused on instincts such as the drive for food or sex, the "mammalian" brain focused on emotional attraction and the "higher" brain focused on ideas, values and other aspects of intellectual attraction—with parallels to sexual, emotional, and intellectual intimacy.[68] Dobransky's view is that relationships that are formed of only one or two of the above elements, but not all three, are on shaky foundations.

In some contrast, Fisher's basic premise appears to be what she asserts is our biological inheritance which she in various places advocates a return to. Among other things, she makes various observations from/draws various similarities with the animal kingdom, including from the behavior of primates, and from hunter-gatherer cultures, noting differences from practices in human farming culture. She also cites recent data from various empirical studies in contemporary contexts, including studies she has been involved in/conducted through the years.

4.2.1.3 Further Theories of Love

Ogolsky, Lloyd, and Cate offer an overview of "theories and models of romantic partnering," describing compatibility theories (based, for example, on complementarity of traits or similarity of values or attributes), stage models, social exchange theories (proposing "that the partnering process is driven by people's desire to maximize their rewards and minimize their costs"), adult attachment theory, uncertainty reduction theory, dialectic perspectives (emphasizing "the inherent tensions that . . . romantic relationships embody"), gender and feminist perspectives, evolutionary theory, and social ecological models (focusing on partners' interactions being influenced by "individual," "relational," and "macroenvironmental" contexts).[69]

Ayala Pines highlights the importance of childhood experiences, particularly the influence of the dynamics of one's relationships with one's parents and an "internal romantic image" on one's romantic choices and relationships.[70]

---

68. Dobransky and Stamford, *Secret Psychology*, loc. 183 of 4370.
69. Ogolsky et al., *Developmental Course*, ch. 3.
70. Pines, *Falling in Love*, 137–40.

Sternberg's triangular theory of love has been widely cited, and echoes of it may perhaps be seen in other psychologists' views. His triangular theory of love comprises: intimacy (related to emotional aspects), passion (related to motivational aspects), and commitment (related to cognitive aspects). He identifies eight types of love based on these elements:

i. Non-love (relationships lacking all three elements)
ii. Liking (based on intimacy, but without passion or long-term commitment)
iii. Infatuated love (love primarily based on passion)
iv. Empty love (committed love, without intimacy nor passion)
v. Romantic love (combining intimacy and passion, but without long-term commitment)
vi. Companionate love (love with intimacy and commitment, but lacking passion)
vii. Fatuous love (love based on passion and commitment, usually of the whirlwind variety, but without the stabilizing effect of intimacy developed over time)
viii. Consummate love (what Sternberg considers "complete love," comprising all three elements: intimacy, passion, commitment, noting that this can sometimes be challenging to maintain consistently).[71]

The "self-expansion theory of love," developed in the 1980s, appears well supported by research. It sees love as "the desire to expand the self by including a desirable other in the self,"[72] with two principles:

i. The "motivational principle" (in relation to the "drive for efficacy or competence")
ii. The "inclusion-of-other-in-the-self principle" ("through close relationships")[73]

Aron and Tomlinson relate their self-expansion theory of love to other theories on love, including:

---

71. Sternberg, "Triangular Theory of Love."
72. Aron and Tomlinson, "Love as Expansion," 2.
73. Aron and Tomlinson, "Love as Expansion," 1–2.

i. Interdependence theory—commitment based on "combination of high satisfaction, low quality of alternatives, and high levels of investment in the relationship." The authors relate self-expansion theory to this in terms of providing "some clear predictors" of what may lead to each of these features.[74]

ii. Attachment theory

iii. Communal/exchange theory

iv. Evolutionary theories

v. "Love as a story"

vi. Sternberg's triangular theory of love[75]

Engaging with self-expansion theory from a theological ethical and integrationist/dialogical perspective, I suggest that caution should be exercised, particularly bearing in mind that while there should be space in a virtue-ethical approach for emphasis on advancing human well-being and flourishing, it cannot be all about prioritizing self-fulfilment.

Based on the above discussion, I suggest it is helpful to be aware of how strong a motivating and driving factor "self-expansion" can be in experiences of attraction and falling in love (sometimes without any conscious intent by the individuals involved). I contend that applying an ethic of prudence in romantic relationships should include careful choice of one's romantic partner, including with awareness of the strong propensity individuals may feel towards "self-expansion" in the course of their lives. This may involve, for example, resolving to think beyond short-term needs and desires, and endeavoring to think in terms of long-term considerations as far as possible (including in terms of the likelihood of being able to sustain fidelity in the relationship, bearing in mind one's self-expansion needs).

Further, based on my assumption that lifelong monogamy is normatively a good to be upheld, I suggest that there will have to be limits to the extent in which the self-expansion model can be followed. While it will assist the flourishing of a romantic relationship and marriage if the individuals involved pay close attention to the self-expansion needs of the other (and indeed, awareness of and attention to this may well help sustain good marriages for the long-term), at the same time, particularly

---

74. Aron and Tomlinson, "Love as Expansion," 17.
75. Aron and Tomlinson, "Love as Expansion," 17–18.

within marriage—when a commitment to love and cherish the other "for better, for worse" has been made, self-expansion cannot be the decisive factor for the longevity of the relationship. For example, if one or both individuals at some stage in the marriage happen to feel attracted or drawn to others outside the marital relationship—including due to the motivation for self-expansion—at such times, virtues such as justice, love and care, and fidelity will need to be activated that take priority over any feelings of attraction to anyone other than one's spouse.

However, I also suggest that the response to such feelings of attraction to those other than one's romantic partner should differ depending on whether one is already married (having made a clear informed choice and commitment to be with one's partner through thick and thin) or whether one is still at a stage of dating or courtship (where one is still getting to know oneself or others, and still in the process of deciding whether making a commitment to this particular romantic partner for the long-term would be wise). Where one is still at the stage of dating or courtship, I suggest that some close attention should be paid to experiencing feelings of attraction for someone other than one's current romantic partner—particularly if those feelings are strong and sustained, based, for example, on a substantial need for self-expansion, and so on. While frivolous or transient feelings of attraction to others may well be disregarded, particularly when compared to the more substantial aspects of one's relationship with a current partner, if the experience of attraction to others has deeper and more sustained roots, an ethic of wisdom or prudence may well call for a suspension (or possibly eventual termination) of one's current dating relationship to evaluate the long-term viability of the romantic relationship. An ethic of courage may also be necessary, to call time on a dating relationship which may well have insufficiently deep roots, along with an ethic of love and care, and justice, to navigate the potential breakup of the current relationship in a manner that sensitively prioritizes the well-being of the persons involved.

Needless to say, a commitment to marry (and so to stay with one's partner "for better, for worse"), while an important step to realizing the good of marriage and lifelong monogamy, should not be entered into lightly—particularly when bearing in mind all the complexities of attraction, rejection, and "falling in love" that one may experience through different stages of life.

4.2.2 The Value of Companionate Love and Long-Term Compatibility

Long-term compatibility may result from various factors. Companionate love is one of these, and appears to be a key determinant of marital longevity.

Social psychologist Shelly Gable points out that in the study of romantic relationships, love is viewed by scholars not so much as an emotion, but rather more as a "subjective experience that involves particular motives and thoughts," and she observes that the two varieties of love that have been the subject of most focus are "passionate love" and "companionate love." She defines passionate love as "the intense excitement about, preoccupation with, and attraction to another person," and notes that "evolutionary theorists argue that feeling passionate love and intense desire facilitates relationship formation by focussing attention on the potential mate."[76]

In somewhat different tone, companionate love is "the deep sense of warmth, affection, and liking we feel for another person." Notably, Gable points out that this type of love is an important ingredient for the longevity of marriages, referring to research by Reis and Aron finding that "companionate love is associated with bonding and intimacy and is a defining feature of communal relationships." Citing a study by Huston, she continues:

> Companionate love is... the best predictor of long-term stability in marriages. In particular, Huston (2009) has been carefully following a set of newlywed couples, and after 13 years, he found that the best predictor of later divorce was low warmth and affection (i.e. low levels of companionate love) at the beginning of the marriage.[77]

Highlighting the importance of supportive companionship for the flourishing of intimate relationships, Gable observes that researchers have found that "high-quality relationships are characterized by partners who effectively offer one another support and are responsive to each other's needs"[78] and further that "the degree to which relationship partners sup-

---

76. Shelly Gable, "Close Relationships," in Finkel and Baumeister, *Advanced Social Psychology*, 241.

77. Shelly Gable, "Close Relationships," in Finkel and Baumeister, *Advanced Social Psychology*, 241.

78. Shelly Gable, "Close Relationships," in Finkel and Baumeister, *Advanced Social Psychology*, 242.

port personal growth, exploration, and goal pursuit also has an impact on individual well-being and overall relationship quality."[79]

Further, Alan Carr has observed that studies have shown a connection between the following demographic factors and marital satisfaction: "high level of education," "high socioeconomic status," "similarity of spouses interests, intelligence, and personality," "sexual compatibility" and "for women, later marriage."[80] In particular, highlighting the importance of similarity between partners, he has pointed out that "the research results show that similarity is associated with marital satisfaction, probably because of the greater ease with which similar people can empathise with each other and pursue shared interests."[81]

Research by Brian Ogolsky et al. on compatibility in dating couples identified four different couple types in terms of commitment processes: "(a) dramatic, (b) conflict ridden, (c) socially involved, (d) partner focused," and found that the "partner-focused couples" had the "highest levels of relationship satisfaction" and "strongest likelihood of advancing in stage of involvement."[82]

Further on psychological research on compatibility, Aristide Saggino et al. applied in an Italian context a compatibility quotient developed by Wilson and Cousins to measure partner compatibility and for which studies have found that relationship satisfaction is "positively correlated with the level of similarity between partners." Of the 184 Italian married heterosexual couples studied, they found that "couples with high compatibility scores have higher level of marital satisfaction" and that "Energy, Conscientiousness, Emotional Stability, Openness and Agreeableness were also related to couple compatibility."[83] In a study involving "long-wed older adults," researchers found "statistically significant associations" between marital satisfaction and four of the Big Five personality traits, when examining "the dynamics of personality within and between couples [including between-spouse similarities]."[84]

79. Shelly Gable, "Close Relationships," in Finkel and Baumeister, *Advanced Social Psychology*, 243.

80. Carr, *Positive Psychology*, 466–67.

81. Carr, *Positive Psychology*, 467.

82. Ogolsky et al., "Pathways of Commitment," 307.

83. Saggino et al., "Compatibility Quotient," 83. See also Wilson and Cousins, "Partner Similarity." Wilson and Cousins developed their measure of partner compatibility "based on similarity in physique, personality, intelligence, social background, attitudes, habits and leisure preferences" (161).

84. O'Rourke et al., "Personality Trait Levels," 351.

A 2012 study involving Fisher concerned neural aspects of long-term romantic love and recruited heterosexual couples, all with relatively high levels of household income.[85] The brains of ten women and seven men,[86] who had been happily married an average of 21.4 years (and who reported still experiencing intense romantic love for their partner), were scanned using functional magnetic resonance imaging (fMRI) while they were shown facial images of their partner.[87] Main findings included that there were significant similarities noted in the brain/neural activity (including neural activation in dopamine-rich regions of the brain associated with reward and motivation) of long-term married couples who are still in love with that of newly-in-love couples (found in previous studies on early-stage romantic love), but with a key difference: many more areas of the brain are involved for those long-term in love, including those connected with attachment and pair-bonding (involving significant levels of oxytocin and vasopressin, and other aspects), with correlations also with lowered stress for those long-term in love (likely associated with lower cortisol, and increase/regain of normal levels of serotonin) and increased calmness (rather than obsession)—a significant difference for those long-term in love from those in early love.[88] Overall, the study also affirmed that it is possible for romantic love to last, standing the test of time, but with elements that make such love sustainable over the long-term.

Further on marital longevity, it may be noted that Paul Dolan points out the importance of happiness in marriages to overall well-being. Citing a recent study on marital happiness and long-term health, he points out a key finding based on cross-sectional research that the positive health benefits of marriage only accrue to couples whose marriages are happy; if the marriages are not happy ones, then people would be healthier if they had never married.[89]

---

85. Household income itself will likely need to be a subject of future study to explore its effects and relation to romantic love, as the leaders of this study also observed (Acevedo et al., "Neural Correlates," 156).

86. Key limitations of the study include the small number of participants involved.

87. Acevedo et al., "Neural Correlates," 145–47.

88. Acevedo et al., "Neural Correlates," 156.

89. As cited in Dolan, *Happy Ever After*, 77.

4.2.3 Casual Sex May Not Actually Be "Casual"

My definition of "casual sex" in this chapter is in general terms, "sex without strings attached"—that is without commitment or emotional attachment. It may include hookups on campuses, "situationships," sex with strangers, or with acquaintances whom one has known for a very short length of time (such as less than a week), or with other acquaintances or possibly even friends (such as in "friends with benefits" arrangements) with whom one is not in a romantic relationship.

Helen Fisher famously discusses the science involved in physical intimacy, including by describing various chemical reactions that often take place in the course of intimate interactions, and the implications of this for dating. In a section discussing casual sex, she puts forward the view that intimate sexual relations are not a matter to be approached lightly, and goes on to sound a note of caution that one should "think before [stepping] into its deep waters."[90]

Fisher begins the discussion by noting the clear health benefits of sex, specifically, good sex "with the right person at the right time." The benefits she lists include the reduced risk of heart disease, improved fitness, pain relief, decrease in the occurrence of colds and flu, and improved bladder control.[91]

However, she goes on to argue strongly that "when you have sex with someone you hardly know, you can stimulate [powerful neural juices such as dopamine and norepinephrine], pushing you toward feelings of passionate romantic love."[92] In fact, she goes so far as to assert, in her expert view, that "casual sex is *rarely* casual."[93] In support of her argument, she describes the powerful chemical reactions involved when individuals are physically intimate (even when they are not emotionally committed to each other)—including that:

i. Dopamine (which she describes as "the brain chemical associated with feelings of intense romantic love") is released when genitals are stimulated.

ii. Norepinephrine (which she describes as "associated with energy, exhilaration and focused attention") is produced just after orgasm.

---

90. H. Fisher, *Why Him? Why Her?*, 220.
91. H. Fisher, *Why Him? Why Her?*, 219.
92. H. Fisher, *Why Him? Why Her?*, 219–20.
93. H. Fisher, *Why Him? Why Her?*, 219; emphasis in original.

CHAPTER 4: COMPLEXITIES OF BEING HUMAN IN RELATIONSHIP 153

> iii. Significant amounts of oxytocin and vasopressin (which she refers to as "the 'cuddle chemicals' associated with attachment") accompany orgasm, leading to feelings of bonding with one's sexual partner.[94]

She also refers to a study by anthropologist Justin Garcia, involving participants on an American college campus, which found that "50 per cent of women and 52 percent of men who initiated a 'one-night stand' were eager to jump-start a longer connection with this partner and one-third of these 'hook-ups' turned into romantic relationships," while "when this strategy failed to trigger a relationship, one of the partners regularly became depressed—suggesting that this individual had hoped for a longer, more meaningful connection."[95]

It may well be that the health benefits associated with sex that Fisher lists earlier are some of the benefits enjoyed (at least in part—along with its pleasurable, albeit sometimes temporary, aspects) by those who argue in favor of casual sex, that it is to be preferred to not having sex at all. However, based on Fisher's discussion of this issue as a weighty matter, rather than a subject to be approached lightly—as detailed above—I suggest that there is more to "casual sex" than is often assumed by its outwardly transitory nature (in terms of appearing to come with "no strings attached"), and that it will be of benefit to individuals involved in sexually intimate interactions to bear in mind the potentially potent bonding effects of sex, even casual sex.

It remains unclear how long the chemical effects of sexual interactions (including as described by Fisher) may last (whether they may be relatively short lived or may endure for significant lengths of time) and what the specific long-term implications may be. It may also be the case that the degree and severity of effects will vary from individual to individual, depending on different factors rendering some more susceptible than others to the effects of such chemicals. Be that as it may, I suggest that the above discussion may form the basis for sounding a cautionary note concerning indiscriminate sexual interactions, such as those experienced as part of "hookup culture." Illustrating this with an analogy to the adhesive properties of glue (and particularly with reference to the chemical reactions discussed above), I suggest that sexual interactions have "glue-like" tendencies. Just as one ought to be cautious of applying glue carelessly (such as between surfaces that one does

---

94. H. Fisher, *Why Him? Why Her?*, 219–20.
95. H. Fisher, *Why Him? Why Her?*, 220.

not intend to be joined together permanently), so as to be spared the complications of later trying to peel apart two surfaces that have been unintentionally glued together, one should also exercise caution not to delve into physically or sexually intimate interactions which may result in indiscriminate and unintended bonding effects.

Because of its inherent physical and biological basis (accompanied by the chemical reactions explained above, based on Fisher's observations), casual sex may have strongly addictive effects, even where these are unintended. Jason King in his study of campus hookup culture (discussed in ch. 3) observes that "hooking up can also become addictive, like drugs or alcohol, because the physical experience is powerful."[96] Here he quotes poignantly one of the students he interviewed, 'Anna,' as she shares candidly about her experiences of hooking up:

> You can stop, but it is like a drug. You feel bad about yourself the first time and the second time, but, later, you're like "this is great." The physical is not everything, but it means something. We are made to love, and the physical makes us feel loved. You can get out of it, but it takes time and patience and a strong desire not to be in it any more. . . . It is hard to stop, especially if your self-esteem is low. It is like drinking alcohol.[97]

Also based on extensive empirical research, Mark Regnerus and Jeremy Uecker observe that many American young women combine relatively "permissive sexual attitudes with a principled objection to relationshipless sex," as:

> They are not opposed to sex, and many of them are not virgins. But sex is largely unwanted apart from an emotional connection. Many have tried to have sex without emotion and found it impossible to sustain.[98]

It may be that there are differences between men and women where this is concerned, that is, in terms of the effects that casual sex may have on them biologically, neurologically, and emotionally. That cannot be explored in detail here. However, empirical studies have revealed that there are at least some male-female differences in perceptions towards casual sex. These I now discuss.

---

96. J. King, *Faith with Benefits*, 36.
97. J. King, *Faith with Benefits*, 35–36.
98. Regnerus and Uecker, *Premarital Sex in America*, 135.

CHAPTER 4: COMPLEXITIES OF BEING HUMAN IN RELATIONSHIP 155

The differences between men and women in their reactions towards casual sex are well established in empirical research. A well-known study by Elaine Hatfield and Russ Clark in 1978 (which has sparked numerous responses, including various replications of the experiment) "designed to test the classic evolutionary theory that men are generally more receptive to sexual offers than women" resulted in the stark finding that "seventy-five percent of men accepted [an] offer of stranger sex while none of the women did."[99] Even with societal developments in recent decades and what some may identify as a further liberalization in female attitudes towards casual sexual encounters, including on college campuses across America, male-female differences on this matter still remain. Hatfield, Rapson and Purvis observe in balance that:

> It is unclear to what extent men and women differ in their actual willingness to experiment with casual sex. However, it is one of the most replicated findings in social psychology that men are more likely than women to indicate a desire for short-term mating, that is, casual sex [referring to a further study by Hyde in 2005, "The Gender Similarities Hypothesis," in *American Psychologist* 60].[100]

Even where women may appear as willing as men to engage in casual sex, there may be a pragmatic reason behind their apparent eagerness, rather than a mere preference for recreational sex. As Hatfield, Rapson, and Purvis also point out, from an evolutionary perspective:

> Casual encounters can also be entered into with a vision for the future. Women may participate in casual sex in the hopes of attracting an appealing mate for the long term. Even in a one-night stand, they might search for professional men with ambition, status, good earning capacity ... men who are kind and considerate ... men who like children. These qualifications for casual sex would indicate potential hope for a more long-term relationship.[101]

They also note that a sexual double standard still remains, with a stigma affecting women rather than men.[102] As they quip aptly:

99. Hatfield et al., *What's Next in Love*, 122. See also Clark and Hatfield, "Gender Differences."
100. Hatfield et al., *What's Next in Love*, 129.
101. Hatfield et al., *What's Next in Love*, 132.
102. Conley et al., "Backlash from the Bedroom," as cited Hatfield et al., *What's Next in Love*, 141.

> A man sleeps with a lot of girls and he's a stud; a woman does the same thing and she's a slut.[103]

As to the effects of casual sex encounters, research has found that both young men and women may experience a wide range of emotions after a hookup—with some feeling positive, excited or stimulated, others feeling "nothing in particular," and still others feeling "embarrassed," "regretful," "nervous," "scared," or "confused."[104] Some researchers have also found more long-term negative effects:

> Men and women with a history of casual sex may possess lower self-esteem, feel more guilt, have less of a sense of well-being, and experience more psychological distress and depression than do their peers. They also risk more delinquent behaviors than do their peers.[105]

Whether or not it may be the case that such negative outcomes affect mainly those who may be more vulnerable in various ways, while others "survive" casual sex encounters relatively unscathed or even with overall positive outcomes, it should be borne in mind, nevertheless, that such negative effects are a reality for a significant number of individuals, and that "casual sex" may often not be as straightforward and "hassle free" as the word "casual" may imply.

It is not necessarily the case, of course, that casual sex is always detrimental to well-being. After all, casual sex may itself have many varieties, and an encounter of casual sex may, with the "right," considerate partner, even be described as "good" sex in terms of being enjoyable and pleasurable. Further, relationships that start with casual sex may sometimes lead to "something more." As mentioned above, as Fisher has also observed, based on empirical findings, individuals may embark on casual sex with the desire to progress eventually to a committed relationship, and may even harbor the wish that casual sexual relations will jump-start progression to commitment.

Psychologists have also identified sociosexuality, expressed in terms of a propensity towards casual sexual relations, as a characteristic that some individuals possess more than others. Individuals can in fact vary widely in their levels of sociosexuality—defined here as

---

103. Hatfield et al., *What's Next in Love*, 141.
104. Hatfield et al., *What's Next in Love*, 141.
105. Hatfield et al., *What's Next in Love*, 141.

"the predisposition to engage in uncommitted sex."[106] It may well be that individuals with relatively unrestricted sociosexuality are able to enjoy casual sex more freely and with less worries about effects on their emotional or mental well-being. There may also be other factors in play which make it unworkable to identify any direct link between incidences of casual sex and detrimental effects on mental health.

In terms of the effect that sociosexuality may have on marital outcomes, there is some empirical evidence that a lifestyle of casual sex or unrestricted sociosexuality may be associated with less successful outcomes where an eventual marriage is concerned. In recent research in America involving two independent longitudinal studies of over two hundred newlywed couples, it was found that "relatively unrestricted sociosexuality was associated with an increased probability of relationship dissolution through declines in marital satisfaction over time," while there was "preliminary evidence suggesting that frequent sex, high sexual satisfaction, and low stress weaken this association."[107] It may be therefore that strong inclinations towards casual sexual behavior result in increased pressures on a subsequent marital relationship, which may be somewhat alleviated by increased attention to ensuring high levels of sexual activity and sexual satisfaction within the marriage, accompanied by conditions of low stress.

4.2.4 The Potential for Harm in Relationships

On the often traumatic nature of romantic breakups, and the immensely sobering potential for significant harm, as the "other side of the coin of romantic love," when the loss of love is experienced, evolutionary psychologist David Buss observes:

> Losing love... remains traumatic, both for [the rejector] and for [the rejectee]. Just as evolution has installed serotonin reward mechanisms that flood our brains with pleasure when we mate successfully, so it has also equipped us with brain circuits that deliver searing psychological pain when we experience mating failure. The many failures of love can bring catastrophic costs, creating adaptive problems of great moment.[108]

---

106. This definition is from Rodrigues and Lopes, "Sociosexuality," 775, who take their definition from Simpson and Gangestad.
107. French et al., "Implications of Sociosexuality," 1460.
108. Buss, "Evolution of Love," 54.

Citing historical data, Buss notes that:

> In the United States, between 1976 and 1984, 4507 women were murdered annually, on average. . . . The majority were killed by men who loved them deeply. One study of women murder victims in Dayton, Ohio, reveals proportions similar to those of most studies: 19 percent were murdered by their husbands, 8 percent by a current boyfriend, 17 percent by an estranged husband, and 8 percent by a prior sex partner. These figures total an astonishing 52 percent of the women killed in Dayton. . . . Dayton is not unique. A massive study of homicides committed within the United States between 1976 and 1998 revealed that more than a third of the women were killed by an intimate partner [compared to 4 percent of the men being killed by a wife or lover]."[109]

In addition, Garcia-Moreno et al. have shown, among others, that there are established associations between romantic relationships and domestic violence.[110]

There are other significant aspects to be considered of the dark side of romantic love. These include the potentially traumatic effects of breakups/relationship breakdown and associated mental health issues. Experiences of rejection and/or the breakdown of romantic relationships have been shown to be significant causes of depression and self-harm/suicide attempts. For example, Monroe et al. found that romantic breakups are a key risk factor for adolescents first developing a major depressive disorder.[111] Canetto and Lester found that unrequited love may cause suicidal behavior.[112] Leary, Koch, and Hechenbleiker have shown that strong negative emotions, including sadness, anxiety, and shame, are elicited by interpersonal rejection, connected to "low perceived relational evaluation" or "relational devaluation."[113]

Further on the darker aspects of romantic love, Buss observes "the possibility that jealousy might be inexorably linked with long-term love."[114] He describes empirical data from a study of "651 university students who were actively dating, [noting that] more than 33 percent

---

109. Buss, "Evolution of Love," 54–55.
110. Garcia-Moreno et al., "Prevalence of Intimate Partner Violence."
111. Monroe et al., "Life Events and Depression."
112. Canetto and Lester, "Love and Achievement Motives."
113. Leary et al., "Emotional Responses," ch. 6, loc. 2368 of 4840.
114. Buss, "Evolution of Love", 51.

CHAPTER 4: COMPLEXITIES OF BEING HUMAN IN RELATIONSHIP   159

reported that jealousy posed a significant problem in their current relationship (Riggs, 1993). The problems ranged from the loss of self-esteem to verbal abuse, from rage-ridden arguments, to the terror of being stalked."[115] He concludes:

> Jealousy, paradoxically, flows from deep and abiding love, but can shatter the most harmonious relationships.... Jealousy is one of the most commonly found correlates of being in love.... It evolved to protect love not merely from the threat of loss, but also and more profoundly, from the threat of loss to a rival.[116]

The above, including the oft-occurring incidence of jealousy, appear to be part of the natural outworkings of romantic love, due to the deep, often intense, nature of sexual and emotional intimacy.

The rise of the internet has resulted in further varieties of ways in which jealousy, control or abuse in relationships may be expressed, even alongside its more beneficial aspects, as the authors of a 2016 study of adolescent romantic relationships on social networking sites have also observed.[117] Key findings from this study include the following:

   i. Social networking sites appear to be particularly helpful in facilitating the initiation of romantic relationships among adolescents, as "respondents found it easier to initiate conversations with their crushes and romantic partners as compared to starting a face-to-face conversation." This is perhaps in part due to the possibilities of alleviating the risk of rejection (or embarrassment) afforded by the range of methods of communication of interest provided by social networking sites.

   ii. The authors also point out that "next to signalling romantic interest by liking one's status updates and pictures, social networking sites were used by adolescents for the purpose of relational information seeking. In line with previous qualitative findings among adults, pictures were regarded as an important source of information to evaluate their crushes and potential romantic partners."

   iii. Feelings of jealousy are a common occurrence on social networking sites. Among other things, "respondents indicated that feelings of jealousy were elicited when others would comment on their

---

115. Buss, "Evolution of Love", 51.
116. Buss, "Evolution of Love," 51.
117. Van Ouytsel et al., "Social Networking Sites," 76.

romantic partners' status updates or photos or when their boyfriend or girlfriend appeared with someone else in a picture," and "one often mentioned way of coping with jealousy and relational insecurity was asking the romantic partner's password." Further, "next to controlling one's partner logging in to their private accounts, respondents also mentioned controlling the Friends Lists of their romantic partners and the checking whether they had read and would respond to their messages."[118]

Discussing this, the authors point out key concerns, including:

i. "Given the fact that romantic break-ups are common during adolescence, the exchange of passwords among romantic partners might be particularly risky as information from private accounts could get published online by a revengeful ex-romantic partner. Moreover, sharing passwords with friends has been linked with cyberbullying victimization [citing research]."

ii. "The fact that social networking site use within the context of a romantic relationship is found to elicit jealousy is troubling given the fact that research found that feelings of jealousy were often a precursor of dating violence perpetration and abusive behaviors in an offline context [referring to research]."[119]

From a virtue-ethical perspective (particularly applying the fivefold ethic advanced in ch. 6), given how easily feelings of jealousy arise in the context of close romantic relationships, I advocate a cautious approach that protects the well-being of individuals involved in dating, online or offline, including being careful not to be involved prematurely in physical or emotional intimacy, nor to publicize the relationship—online or offline—until both individuals are mature enough for genuine commitment and real compatibility has been ascertained over time. In an ideal world, breakups would be handled in a sensible and amicable/cordial manner. But in the reality of an imperfect world, what often occurs in a breakup is that either one or both parties—particularly due to strong emotions involved—may be prone to resorting to actions which may cause harm to the other. Hence I argue that where romantic relationships are concerned, and considering the immense potential for harm when a relationship goes sour, due to the strength of feelings involved, it is wise

---

118. Van Ouytsel et al., "Social Networking Sites," 83.
119. Van Ouytsel et al., "Social Networking Sites," 83.

CHAPTER 4: COMPLEXITIES OF BEING HUMAN IN RELATIONSHIP 161

to err on the side of caution in approaches to dating. Elaborated on in chapter 7, I also advocate a virtue-based approach to breakups when they occur—including involving wisdom, care, and sensitivity.

4.2.5 Seek to Understand and Relate to the Full Person

I now discuss psychological research relating to the final, fifth, aspect of the recommended approaches that I advocate in this chapter. This fifth aspect promotes an approach that relates to the whole person in the course of dating, rather than being skewed in terms of focusing on only a few or superficial aspects of the individual such as physical appearance, wealth, status or surface traits. On this aspect, I will be referring in part to the work of Helen Fisher, but will focus in particular on discussing the work of Dan McAdams. In the course of this section, I will also discuss some relevant observations from theologian-psychologists Joanna Collicutt, Jocelyn Bryan, and Fraser Watts on the subject of human personality.

On the topic of compatibility and temperaments, Helen Fisher puts forward her own theory of temperament, based on "Explorer," "Builder," "Director," and "Negotiator" types, with the view that most individuals have a primary temperament and a secondary temperament. She links each temperament to the substantial influence of a particular hormone— "Explorers" (whom she associates with intense energy, creativity and impulsivity) she links to dopamine, and "Builders" (whom she associates with precision, stability, orderliness and details) she links to serotonin. "Directors" (whom she describes as autonomous and competitive with strong systematizing and spatial skills) she links to testosterone, while "Negotiators" (whom she describes as having high levels of intuition, imagination and ability to make connections) she links to estrogen.[120]

Fisher discusses the role of temperament in mate selection and observes some general trends of attraction and levels of marital happiness/harmony for various combinations/pairings of temperament types. While finding that some pairings appear to have higher levels of couple harmony and happiness/satisfaction in the relationship, Fisher's view, overall, is that any combination of temperaments can work in a relationship, although each will have its unique set of strengths and challenges to work through.[121] It may well be that while some types of attractions

---

120. H. Fisher, *Why Him? Why Her?*, 42–123.
121. H. Fisher, *Why Him? Why Her?*, 162. Fisher asserts: "All can work, but each will

between certain combinations of personality types are more likely to occur (as it appears Fisher has observed), it remains the case that any combination of temperament may find its way to a successful relationship, provided that other important aspects of the relationship (some of which are discussed in this chapter) are attended to.

I turn now to discussing aspects of the work of personality and development psychologist Dan McAdams. This discussion is not meant to be an exhaustive discussion of personality. The field of psychological research into personality is vast, and it will not be possible to attempt a comprehensive coverage of the area within the limited space of this chapter. I will confine my discussion to considering aspects of the work of McAdams, particularly his three-level model of personality, and other aspects particularly relevant to my book, especially as set out in his 2015 book, *The Art and Science of Personality Development*. Though of course there are many other authorities in the field of developmental and/or personality psychology, due to space constraint I limit my discussion here to considering McAdams's work. I have chosen his work for its particular relevance to my book, and for the persuasiveness and strength of his theory for applicability in answering my research questions. I will also refer at times to relevant observations from theologian-psychologists Joanna Collicutt, Jocelyn Bryan, and Fraser Watts on the topic of human personality.

The strength of McAdams's work has been recognized by other scholars, for example, by Jocelyn Bryan who describes, and refers to as particularly helpful, McAdams's complex "three-level model" for personality psychology,[122] noting that it encompasses:

i. Aspects of the Big Five theory on traits (often referred to with the acronym "OCEAN" describing five key aspects of personality traits in terms of: openness to experience, conscientiousness, extraversion, agreeableness, neuroticism)[123]

ii. Goals and motivations[124]

iii. The significance of narrative/story in an individual's life[125]

---

have its ups and downs."

122. Bryan, *Human Being*, 88–95.
123. Bryan, *Human Being*, 89–91.
124. Bryan, *Human Being*, 91–92.
125. Bryan, *Human Being*, 93–95.

CHAPTER 4: COMPLEXITIES OF BEING HUMAN IN RELATIONSHIP 163

From a Christian theological point of view, Bryan observes:

> The notable omission of both the relational and spiritual aspects of personality is a deficiency in all of [the psychological models presented earlier in Bryan's chapter]. However, it is possible to find within McAdams's 3 level model scope for a more authentic representation and understanding of what it is to be human.[126]

She earlier notes that McAdams's inclusion of narrative in his three-level model of personality "has a compelling reality which accounts for features in our personalities beyond those identified in the cognitively bound social cognitive theory [which Bryan also discusses]."[127]

In my book, I advocate use of McAdams's three-level model of personality as a helpful way for individuals to approach the process of "getting to know the other person," and getting to know ourselves, better in the course of the practice of dating or courtship in contemporary Anglo-American contexts (although, of course, persons are necessarily complex by nature, and often in a process of development or change, hence it will not be practicable to speak of ever getting to know a person exhaustively). McAdams's three-level model of personality may also be viewed as a helpful "toolkit" for pastors and counselors when counseling couples or individuals. I suggest that it offers a fuller model of personality than many other models in the field, as (alongside the "level" of temperament traits), it also includes the concept of the agent with a history, and with goals and aspirations.

McAdams describes different key life stages in human development, asserting:

> The actor, agent, and author are the supreme psychological trinity for personality development over the human life course.[128]

He argues that "personality follows [these] three lines of development over the life course, each of which corresponds to a layer of psychological individuality."[129] He asserts:

> In personality development, stories layer over goals and values, which layer over traits.... The three lines/layers of personality

---

126. Bryan, *Human Being*, 89.
127. Bryan, *Human Being*, 88.
128. McAdams, *Art and Science*, 310.
129. McAdams, *Art and Science*, 308.

development each correspond to a particular perspective on the human self.[130]

McAdams observes that the perspective of the self as social actor (corresponding with level 1 of his personality model), based on dispositional traits, is the earliest to emerge in human development, as it develops even from birth, with each individual "[expressing] emotion and [displaying] characteristic behaviors, all of which is keenly observed (and evaluated) by our fellow actors on stage, who double as our audiences as well."[131] He notes that each actor's dispositional traits are basically about his/her "unique style of performance" and "reputation [within social groups]" that he/she develops, adding that:

> As observers, we sort actors out (ourselves included) in terms of the broad and basic dispositional traits that personality psychologists have enumerated over the past half century, now commonly catalogued in the Big Five.[132]

McAdams describes the perspective of the self as agent in connection with level 2 of his model of personality (focused on goals, motivations, and concerns), and he notes that this develops in significant terms a few years after birth, as "human beings express rudimentary agency even in the first days of life."[133]

He describes the self as it is expressed as "autobiographical author" in connection with level 3 of his model of personality, relating to "narrative identity,"[134] noting that this stage of personality expression in terms of "stories" is the last of the three to be reached in human development. It is apparent as a significant part of personality in the years of emerging adulthood, and usually begins in adolescence when "many human beings learn how to think of their lives as ongoing narratives, complete with settings, scenes, characters, plots, and themes."[135]

As mentioned earlier, McAdams observes the complex phenomenon that people's traits *both* change and remain the same over time.[136]

---

130. McAdams, *Art and Science*, 309.
131. McAdams, *Art and Science*, 309.
132. McAdams, *Art and Science*, 309.
133. McAdams, *Art and Science*, 309–10.
134. McAdams, *Art and Science*, 310. There are critics of the primacy of narrative, including, notably, Galen Strawson.
135. McAdams, *Art and Science*, 310.
136. McAdams, *Art and Science*, 104.

CHAPTER 4: COMPLEXITIES OF BEING HUMAN IN RELATIONSHIP   165

Further, Joanna Collicutt distinguishes between temperament and character, making the observation that temperament has a biological basis, and is often hereditary, although it can be managed, whereas character (for example, character strengths such as courage or temperance) may be developed over time.[137] She also points out empirical research showing the strong influence of particular situations on how people behave, that individual behavior may sometimes be more controlled by the situations encountered than by personality traits, and that "it is in the interaction between situation and temperament that the stuff of personality is formed."[138]

Fraser Watts also makes a similar observation, asserting that "there is a great deal of situational specificity in how people behave" and "it is widely recognized, as society gets more complicated and people have a wider range of social interactions, that the tendency for people to behave differently in different situations gets more acute and can lead to a loss of a core sense of self-identity that can be a source of distress."[139] The question of the stability and consistency of manifestation of personal traits across time and contexts therefore gives rise to a complex and multi-textured answer.

Watts further observes that "psychology is more comfortable than religion (or at least Christianity) with a plural self," particularly as "Christian assumptions about the unity of personality probably arise from the concept of the soul, which can be seen as the core of personality."[140] In some contrast:

> Psychology tends to start, more pragmatically, from the reality that people experience a degree of fragmentation . . . whatever sense of the unity of self is experienced seems a hard-won achievement, resulting from overcoming the natural fragmentation that arises from living in a wide range of different contexts.[141]

He observes that "it seems to be a human instinct to work at constructing a sense of self that, if not singular, can integrate disparate elements."[142]

137. Collicutt, *Psychology*, ch. 4.
138. Collicutt, *Psychology*, loc. 1120 of 6452.
139. Watts, *Psychology, Religion, and Spirituality*, 180.
140. Watts, *Psychology, Religion, and Spirituality*, 180.
141. Watts, *Psychology, Religion, and Spirituality*, 180.
142. Watts, *Psychology, Religion, and Spirituality*, 180.

He strongly urges the avoidance of extreme positions on this matter, and advocates instead a "middle way . . . not with a unitary sense of self, but with an integrative view of self that acknowledges diversity but also envisages some degree of integration," even if that process of ongoing attempted integration is incomplete.[143] Further, he points out a "growing psychology of narrative processes" and "much recent interest in narrative theology" which may relate to this.[144] There are parallels here with level 3 of McAdams's personality model, in which we see the maturing "author" attempting to knit together the diverse aspects of his/her life through the means of stories/narrative.

From a theologian's perspective, Watts also offers an important reminder that sound theology ought to hold together both the good and wicked aspects of human nature—notably, with the doctrine of the *imago Dei* reflecting the goodness and immense potential for good in humanity, and the doctrine of the fall reflecting the brokenness of humanity.[145]

I suggest it will be helpful to bear the above observations in mind when one is approaching the complex process of "getting to know" another person in the course of a dating relationship. Having realistic expectations about what a "real person" (as opposed to an "ideal" or imagined person) is like, complete with imperfections, and perceived as a "work-in-progress" rather than a "finished work of art," may help each individual to thrive in the relationship, accepting and being accepted for each other's flaws and all, and supporting each other in reasonable personal growth within realistic time frames.

Applying Level 1 of McAdams's Model

Applying level 1 of McAdams's three-level model to answering my research questions, I suggest that being aware to a reasonable extent of trait theories, particularly that psychologists have observed definite differences between individuals in personality traits—though the description and explanations for these differences do vary—can assist the process of dating/courtship and can also be helpful for building healthy relationships. Understanding that there are differences in traits and that these may have a significant influence on behavior and preferences, including

---

143. Watts, *Psychology, Religion, and Spirituality*, 181.
144. Watts, *Psychology, Religion, and Spirituality*, 181.
145. Watts, *Psychology, Religion, and Spirituality*, 168–69.

in dating or courtship practice and also in various choices about lifestyle, recreation, domestic and working life, and so on, enables better-informed decisions about a potential life partner, and may also provide helpful tools for constructively addressing situations of conflict in a relationship. While acknowledging that there are different theories of personality, and there is likely no settled explanation of personality differences—and, at any rate, there is insufficient space within the limits of this book to discuss these alternative perspectives and theories—I suggest, based on the preceding explanation, that even proceeding with some understanding of a trait theory such as the five-factor model is likely to assist the process of dating/courtship practice in ways that contribute to the flourishing and well-being of the individuals involved.

Is it possible that any combination of temperaments or traits can "work" between a couple? Helen Fisher appears to suggest this, as mentioned above.[146] As I have only explored the views of one author (Fisher) here, and have not reviewed empirical studies regarding this, I am not able to offer a definitive conclusion on the matter. On only a tentative basis, therefore, I suggest that it may be possible that any combination of temperaments or traits can "work" between a couple, that is, can result in a happy flourishing marriage, provided that there is a good understanding and acceptance between the couple of their individual differences, and similarities, in traits, and the strengths and weaknesses of their particular combination of traits. Perhaps there are particular combinations of traits that may occur more frequently than others (for example, giving rise to "opposites attract" theories, "sibling order" theories, and so on), for psychological reasons that are beyond the scope of this book to explore. Even so, I offer the tentative suggestion that there is no "magic" combination of traits that is most compatible between a couple, and that possibly any combination of traits may result in a happy flourishing relationship—depending on all the other complex variables in each particular relationship, and provided that there is good understanding and acceptance of the strengths and weaknesses of their particular pairing of traits.

In addition, I suggest that individual traits (such as described in the five-factor model) should not be confused with goals, motivations, and concerns (level 2 of McAdams's three-level model of personality), and that this aspect of personality (level 2, goals, motivations, and concerns)

---

146. H. Fisher, *Why Him? Why Her?*, 162.

is a more important factor for compatibility between a couple, for the long-term flourishing of their relationship.

Distinguishing Between Temperament and Character

As mentioned earlier, Collicutt draws a distinction between temperament traits, such as those described in the "Big Five" taxonomy (which she considers are "given" traits which are not easily changed though they may be managed), and character strengths, such as bravery, which she asserts "can be nurtured and developed."[147] She also notes that the turn by psychologists to studying character strengths is a recent phenomenon, which has developed with the growth of the positive psychology movement.

Applying Collicutt's analysis, that temperament and character ought to be distinguished, I suggest that this is a helpful distinction to make in the context of dating. For example, a person may have the temperament trait of high agreeableness (in terms of being generally inclined to go along with others' decisions or opinions and not liking to offend people), but may still be selfish, rather than genuinely kind. Agreeableness should not be equated with selflessness. On the surface, it may be possible to confuse the two (such as assuming the person with high agreeableness is selfless and kind, and concluding that the person with low agreeableness is unkind and self-centered). It may require more diligence in the process of getting acquainted for one to realize that the person with low agreeableness (who may not naturally be inclined to go along with others' opinions) may not actually be unkind. If such a person has also happened to have developed the character trait of kindness and selflessness, she/he may well be a person with low agreeableness (who is not afraid to disagree with others, or to go against the grain of peer pressure or majority opinion) who at the same time is kind, caring and considerate of others.

Further, I suggest that in the context of dating and relationships, character traits may well be more important than temperament traits (applying Collicutt's distinction again between temperament and character), although of course it will still be important for a flourishing relationship for each to understand the other's temperament traits, inclinations, strengths and weaknesses, and so on. For example, a relationship will be more likely to thrive if the persons involved are kind, caring, considerate,

---

147. Collicutt, *Psychology*, loc. 1172 of 6452.

and unselfish in character—even if one or the other is less agreeable in temperament or more inclined to disagree with others.

As a further example, the persons in a relationship are also more likely to flourish and their well-being protected if both individuals have the character trait of honesty, rather than being dishonest, deceptive or manipulative—whatever their temperaments might be. Here, again, I suggest that character is the more important aspect of personality to focus on.

Variations Over the Life Course: Applying Levels 1, 2 and 3

On personality changes during an individual's life course, McAdams points out that for level 1 (dispositional traits) studies have consistently found (though there are of course many variations among individuals) that as humans mature from their teenage years to young adulthood and through to the midlife years (thirties, forties, fifties, and sixties), they generally display increases in C and A and decreases in N—that is, through the years, they generally become more noticeably conscientious, agreeable and more emotionally stable.[148] Further, research shows that "changes in social roles [such as getting married, or transitioning from high school to vocational work] accompany, and often seem to cause, changes in dispositional traits."[149]

For teens and preteens, McAdams points out the difficulty of pinpointing particular age markers for adolescence, noting:

> In that it seems to begin earlier and end later than once expected, and in that its beginning looks nothing like its ending, adolescence is not what it used to be, if it ever was.[150]

In terms of seeming to start earlier, he points to "hormonal and psychological shifts heralding a transition to come" which can appear "years before the advent of puberty's most obvious signs—as early as age 8 or 9." In terms of seeming to continue for significantly longer than in earlier generations and to conclude later, he points to "surveys of North Americans and Europeans [showing] that an increasing number of individuals in their mid-20s and even older still do not consider themselves

---

148. McAdams, *Art and Science*, 131.
149. McAdams, *Art and Science*, 132.
150. McAdams, *Art and Science*, 313.

to be adults," particularly due to significant numbers not yet having attained the "roles traditionally associated with adulthood status—stable jobs, marriage, and parenthood."[151]

He thus finds it helpful to distinguish two separate "milestones in personality development" which he identifies as: (i) the preteen years, "marking the end of childhood itself (roughly ages 8–12 years)," and (ii) "marking emerging adulthood (the late teens through the 20s)."[152]

He describes the preteen years, heralding the start of adolescence, as a time characterized by "a rich and complex portrait of psychological individuality," as:

> Personality has now thickened to accommodate a second layer—goals and values layer over dispositional traits to structure psychological individuality. Factor-analytic studies of personality ratings suggest that it is around this time that a clear five-factor structure begins to appear for dispositional traits.[153]

He also points out key issues concerned with self-esteem during this period, as self-esteem appears to decline significantly among many children after about the age of eight.[154] He connects the significance of self-esteem as a key part of personality, revealed particularly during this time, to "at least two important developments":

1. "Rising expectations from parents and teachers regarding the child's achievements"
2. "The child's newfound tendency, rooted in cognitive development and the emerging sense of the self as motivated agent, to compare himself or herself to others in systematic ways"[155]

He further notes that it is during this developmental period that "researchers typically note the first clear signs of depression (especially in girls) and increases in antisocial behavior (especially in boys)" and that "scores on openness to experience also begin to rise in [these] preteen years."[156] Also, "as motivated agents," they start at this age to be able to direct their energies towards achievement of the particular goals

---

151. McAdams, *Art and Science*, 313.
152. McAdams, *Art and Science*, 313.
153. McAdams, *Art and Science*, 313.
154. McAdams, *Art and Science*, 314.
155. McAdams, *Art and Science*, 314.
156. McAdams, *Art and Science*, 314.

CHAPTER 4: COMPLEXITIES OF BEING HUMAN IN RELATIONSHIP   171

"on which their self-esteem depends, be they in the realm of sports, friendship, school, or values"—and away from goals which appear unsatisfying, "for which their own skills and traits, or their general life circumstances, may be poorly suited."[157]

McAdams also notes the propensity towards fantasizing among many young adolescents, particularly in imagining the story of their lives in terms of success, "accomplishment . . . or notoriety," which he argues (bearing in mind level 3 of his model of personality) "may be seen as a rough first draft of narrative identity."[158]

It may be observed that risk-taking (along with thrill-seeking) behavior appears to peak in the adolescent/teenage years, for reasons that may be related to stages of brain development and emotional contexts. Advocating a nuanced response to this, Sarah-Jayne Blakemore reminds that "there's no average teenager,"[159] while recommending that adult interventions focus on "the values that are important to young people . . . [including] feeling like a socially conscious, autonomous person."[160]

Of the young adult years, McAdams points to a consensus among "many social scientists . . . that the period running from about age 17 through the middle to late 20s constitutes an integral developmental epoch in and of itself, called emerging adulthood."[161] This may be particularly distinctive of "modern postindustrial societies," such as contemporary Anglo-American society, in which "schooling and the preparation for adult work extend well into the 20s and even beyond" and many young people delay marriage and parenthood until at least their late twenties.[162]

Notably, McAdams points out that "class and education" strongly influence how young people move through this developmental period, as working-class men and women who are less well educated may struggle to maintain fruitful employment, and thus lack the accompanying economic security, even while some may well decide to marry and start families during this time—in contrast to their more well-educated, middle-class peers who may likely spend years in training

---

157. McAdams, *Art and Science*, 314.
158. McAdams, *Art and Science*, 314.
159. Blakemore, *Inventing Ourselves*, 139; see also 134–38, 145–49.
160. Blakemore, *Inventing Ourselves*, 157.
161. McAdams, *Art and Science*, 315.
162. McAdams, *Art and Science*, 315.

and education before they decide to "settle down and assume the full responsibilities of adulthood."[163]

He observes that during the emerging adult years one may perceive a gradual positive increase in "traits associated with conscientiousness and agreeableness," and at the same time "a decline in neuroticism"—for, as emerging adults grow into their roles as stakeholding members of society, "their traits may shift upward in the direction of greater warmth and care for others, higher levels of social responsibility, and greater dedication to being productive, hardworking, and reliable."[164] At the same time, he notes the significance of other variables which affect outcomes in the life course, pointing out that "individual differences in traits combine with many other factors, including gender and class, to shape life trajectories during this time."[165]

McAdams points to the emerging adult years as a key developmental period when the various multiple facets of the complex personality and life of each individual gradually undergo the process of coalescing into a coherent meaningful whole. He also notes the importance of this task for preparing the individual for a fruitful future in an uncertain world.[166]

Of developmental changes in goals through adulthood, McAdams observes:

> Research has revealed developmental trends in the content and structure of personal goals, as well as changes in the ways people think about, draw upon, pursue, and relinquish goals as they get older. For young adults in modern societies, goals related to education, intimacy, friendships, and careers are likely to be especially salient. Middle-aged adults tend to focus their goals on the future of their children, securing what they have already established, and property-related concerns. Older adults show more goals related to health, retirement, leisure, and understanding current events in the world.[167]

Further, he points out that: (i) young adults tend to be concerned with "establishing an identity" and "exploring [a] range of life goals (and values) and committing to [a] subset that aims to provide life with meaning

---

163. McAdams, *Art and Science*, 315.
164. McAdams, *Art and Science*, 315.
165. McAdams, *Art and Science*, 315.
166. McAdams, *Art and Science*, 316.
167. McAdams, *Art and Science*, 194.

CHAPTER 4: COMPLEXITIES OF BEING HUMAN IN RELATIONSHIP   173

and purpose," focusing more on "promotion" than "prevention";[168] and (ii) concerning midlife, that "although very few people experience a full-blown 'midlife crisis,' studies suggest that many people in their 40s and 50s engage in what lifespan psychologist Abigail Stewart calls midlife reviews and midcourse corrections"[169] with goals tending to relate to "raising children, running a household, civic engagement" and "passing on cultural traditions"; while (iii) in later adulthood, people tend to focus more on "prevention" than "promotion" and a "winnowing of goals down to most important and meaningful concerns, often related to family," with "relatedness goals" being "greater than competence goals."[170]

As there appears to be a clear contrast between the life trajectories of "haves" and "have-nots" among emerging adults, so McAdams points out that there is also a contrast among adults in their forties and fifties—between the life stories of "the most active and generative adults" for whom midlife may be the "prime of life, even as role demands and conflicting goals threaten to overwhelm them," as "personal agency may be distributed across a broad spectrum of goals and responsibilities . . . the roles of parent, grandparent, child of aging parents . . . provider. . . colleague, neighbor, lifelong friend, citizen, leader, and so on" and that of others for whom the midlife years may be a time of "tremendous disappointment, mounting frustrations, and [stagnation]."[171]

He notes that "two decades of research on life stories shows that American adults in their forties and fifties demonstrate dramatic individual differences in narrative identity," as "those reporting low levels of generativity, high levels of depression, and depleted psychological resources construct life stories that fail to affirm progress and growth,"[172] whereas:

> Those who score high on measures on generativity and overall mental health construct redemptive self-narratives wherein protagonists repeatedly overcome obstacles and transform suffering into personal enhancement and prosocial engagement.[173]

Further, McAdams points out that overall there is a plateauing effect in midlife, that based on various research findings on

168. McAdams, *Art and Science*, 195.
169. McAdams, *Art and Science*, 193.
170. McAdams, *Art and Science*, 195.
171. McAdams, *Art and Science*, 316.
172. McAdams, *Art and Science*, 316.
173. McAdams, *Art and Science*, 317.

personality development—even where a "crescendo" is experienced during the midlife years of increased "rank-order stability in dispositional traits" with the traits of conscientiousness and agreeableness reaching a peak, and neuroticism reaching minimal levels—this "crescendo of midlife eventually subsides" and "the complexity of thought, feeling, and desire—as expressed at all three levels of human personality—seems to peak out in the midlife years."[174]

On the brighter side of things, it is also observed that during these years, midlife adults tend to "show a greater and greater positivity bias as they age," as they "savor positive experiences and memories and tend to downplay the negative."[175] Perhaps as part of a process of adjustment and acceptance of where they are in life, there is a noticeable process of consolidation that often takes place—for "as they begin to experience the physical and (in some cases) cognitive declines that accompany late midlife, adults may select goals and strategies for accomplishing them that optimize their best skills and compensate for their weaknesses."[176] McAdams thus concludes:

> Eventually, midlife adults may shift their perspective on life from one that emphasizes the expansion of the self and the bold exploration of the environment to one that emphasizes contraction, protection, and securing the gains they have already achieved. The shift is not likely to be sudden, may occur in some domains before others, and is sure to play out in different ways for different people. But however and whenever it happens, the shift marks a tipping out from a life narrative of ascent to one of maintenance and eventual decline.[177]

Of old age, McAdams points out in sombre tones that "the gain-loss ratio in life tilts toward the loss side as adults move into their later years."[178] Regarding motivations and goals, he observes soberly: "Fending off illness and dealing with loss may become the major goals of life."[179]

Concerning narrative identity, he points out that while "elderly adults may draw increasingly on reminiscences as they review the life they have lived," at the same time memory loss may well become a reality

---

174. McAdams, *Art and Science*, 316–17.
175. McAdams, *Art and Science*, 317.
176. McAdams, *Art and Science*, 317.
177. McAdams, *Art and Science*, 317.
178. McAdams, *Art and Science*, 318.
179. McAdams, *Art and Science*, 318.

CHAPTER 4: COMPLEXITIES OF BEING HUMAN IN RELATIONSHIP

for many, resulting in narrative identity becoming "fuzzy and vague in the later years."[180] Awareness of the reality of the end of life may also occupy the minds of the elderly, as "among the very old, the prospect of dying can never be too far away from consciousness, assuming the mind is still capable of conscious, rational thought."[181]

Yet, McAdams also sounds a positive note:

> Nonetheless, the last years of life are not invariably bleak. Many people retain significant psychological force until the very end.[182]

Drawing upon the story and writing of journalist Roger Angell, he emphasizes "the human need for connection," even in one's twilight years, referring to "our unceasing need for deep attachment and intimate love" even till the end of life itself.[183]

In view of all this, McAdams exhorts readers to "bind ourselves to other people in the social groups that give our lives meaning. . . . Artfully render our lives into life-affirming narratives of interpersonal communion."[184]

Applying the above observations on life stages to dating at different stages of life, it is helpful to bear in mind how goals, motivations, and concerns (alongside narratives) may tend to vary and change across age groups and different life stages. Boys and girls first starting to form paired relationships in their early experiences of schooling, in primary school, may be in the process of discovering the aspects of their lives that they will want to prioritize for building their personal sense of self-esteem. Teenagers forming couples in their adolescent years may be particularly open to risk-taking and thrill-seeking activities, particularly in their peer groups, while also discovering more about themselves and the importance of supportive friendships. College students may have to navigate the particular challenges of "hookup culture" in colleges and universities.

While some may marry early or settle early into long-term committed partnerships, many emerging adults in their twenties and perhaps even through to their early thirties, even as they continue to date and experience the thrills and challenges of romantic relationships, may also

---

180. McAdams, *Art and Science*, 318.
181. McAdams, *Art and Science*, 319.
182. McAdams, *Art and Science*, 319.
183. McAdams, *Art and Science*, 319. See Angell, "This Old Man."
184. McAdams, *Art and Science*, 320.

be especially driven by concerns about establishing their careers and achieving financial stability, before they feel able to "settle down and start a family." Those in their most generative adult years—usually beginning sometime in their thirties through to their forties, and into their fifties and early sixties, even while gradually also being possibly increasingly preoccupied with midlife concerns, may not be particularly active on the dating scene (many of them having already entered into committed relationships in one form or another, such as cohabitation or marriage, by this stage), unless divorced, widowed or still single (having perhaps in their earlier years been occupied with establishing careers). Often, even for those who are formally "available" to date, the demands of busy careers, raising children, and sometimes also caring responsibilities for their parents in elder years, may add further complications to an already challenging, albeit potentially enjoyable, experience of dating. As older adults continue to age, they will naturally likely also have increasing concerns about health in one way or another, while the greater amounts of leisure time available to those in their retirement years may motivate an increased interest in dating activities. All of these factors become relevant in their experience of dating, forming part of a "realistic package" of who they are as they relate one to another.

In all of these stages, while it is important to bear in mind the significant potential variation in goals, motivations, and concerns across different life stages, I also suggest that the five recommended approaches that I have advocated in this chapter, along with the fivefold ethic (prudence, justice, courage, temperance, love and care) that I propose and develop in chapter 6 remain relevant and applicable for all age groups involved in dating or courtship, in its many varied forms, throughout the life course.

I also suggest that being equipped with a good understanding of McAdams's three-level model of personality—discussed above—and its relevance at various stages of the life course, is particularly helpful for the process of seeking to understand and relate to the full person in the course of a dating relationship, and is likely to assist in the discerning of compatibility and suitability of the relationship for long-term flourishing in committed monogamy. Where individuals find, after a well-balanced period of dating and discernment over time, that there is a good matching of traits, goals, motivations, and concerns and also good mutual understanding of their two individual life stories and experiences, they have a good foundation for strong companionship, including to better understand and support one another into the future

CHAPTER 4: COMPLEXITIES OF BEING HUMAN IN RELATIONSHIP 177

in a long-term relationship or marriage through different stages of life. Should they then decide to take the next step in their relationship for a long-term commitment to lifelong monogamy (such as civil partnership or marriage), they will likely be well placed (with future nurturing) to realize the full potential of their relationship for the long term, including for meaningful companionship, mutual support, encouragement, and understanding, till the end of life.

4.3 Summary

I pointed out, in section 4.1.2, ten key observations based on psychological research in the fields of personality and romantic relationships, and elaborated on them in the course of this chapter. In answer to my research questions, I then suggested, based on the psychological research considered above, the following five recommended approaches:

i. Be aware of the variety of dynamics that could be at work in the complex experiences of attraction and rejection in romantic relationships.

ii. Prioritize the value of companionate love for the long-term sustainability of intimate relationships.

iii. Be aware that casual sex may not actually be "casual."

iv. Be careful to minimize causing any unnecessary hurt or harm to the other, bearing in mind the potentially inflammatory nature and "dark side" of relationships when they go wrong.

v. Seek to understand and relate to the other person, and make decisions regarding the relationship (such as on compatibility), on the basis of seeking to discern the full person, in the multilayered aspects of his/her personality.

With reference to the fivefold ethic that I will develop and advance in chapter 6, I suggest here that the above five recommended approaches may also be seen as part of an outworking and application of my suggested fivefold ethic of prudence (including practical wisdom), justice, courage, temperance, and love and care that takes into account the relevant psychological research.

Overall, I argue for better approaches to dating that build up, rather than tear down the human person. Bearing in mind the complex nature of personality, I advocate a more well-rounded approach to understanding the human person such as McAdams's three-level model of personality, which may be regarded as an extended theory of personality, for approaches that contribute to the flourishing and well-being of the human person, rather than causing harm or injustice to the person.

Romantic relationships have tremendous potential for good, as well as for harm. When they go well, much good can result and sometimes many persons (including, not least, the individuals involved in the relationship) may be built up and flourish in significant ways. However, when they do not go well, when they break down or continue in unhealthy patterns of relating (such as in situations of exploitation or abuse), great harm may result. I advocate deeply virtue-based approaches to dating and romantic relationships that can contribute to the good, well-being and flourishing of the persons involved, rather than cause harm or do not do justice to the whole person. I will elaborate on this in chapter 6.

First, I will turn to considering the lived experiences of ten long-term happily married couples in the next chapter.

CHAPTER 5: **SAINTS AMONG US (AN EMPIRICAL STUDY)**

Learning from the Lived Experiences of Ten Long-Term Happily Married Couples Embodying Virtues

5.1 Overview

5.1.1 Introduction

IN THIS CHAPTER, I seek to learn from the lived experiences of long-term happily married couples, to help shed further light on and point towards answers to my research questions.

It should be noted at the outset that my project was not centered primarily on my empirical study, and due to limitations of space, discussion of this study is confined to one relatively brief chapter of this book. Nevertheless, the empirical work completed and resulting findings do give supportive evidence and supportive data for the arguments that I seek to advance.

5.1.2 Methodology

My empirical study took place by means of semi-structured interviews of ten long-term happily married couples. As to how the couples were recruited, each of the couples was known to me personally, either as acquaintances—some quite distant—or as friends, and each of them had lived for a substantial length of time (at least several years) in or near the part of south Lincolnshire where I lived. Some of them were known to each other, others did not know the other couples at all. Each of the couples I had personally observed, and also understood from general knowledge in the community, as being happily married to each other. Upon that observation over a period of time, I approached each couple individually to ask if they would be happy to participate in this empirical research by means of a semi-structured interview. The sample interview questionnaire is attached at appendix A. A compilation of the interviewees' responses to questions relating to sections 5.2.2, 5.2.3, and 5.2.4 is included in appendix B.

It should be noted that all ten interviews took place prior to the COVID-19 pandemic. Each interview was held in person, face-to-face with each couple, in the privacy of either their family home or my home, according to their preference. All ten couples were resident in south Lincolnshire during the time of their interview and all were ordinary middle-class or working-class folk. None were celebrities nor multimillionaires. As it happened, although they were not selected for this reason, it was also the case that all ten couples were of the Christian faith, and most attended Church of England services.

At the time of their interview, each of the couples had been happily married for at least twenty-two years, many of them for a significantly longer period. Two of the couples comprised at least one partner who had been previously married and divorced, and hence was in their/her/his second marriage.

As to my criteria for being "happily married," I began each interview with the first key question: "Are you each happy with the marriage? If you could do so all over again, would you marry the same person?" Each of the interviewee participants answered clearly in the affirmative, yes to both these questions. If any of them had answered in the negative, the interview would have been stopped at that point, and I would not have proceeded with asking any further questions. As things stood, all ten of the couples I interviewed (all of whom I had some prior local knowledge, that they were in stable happy marriages, at least as far as was known in public) answered clearly in the affirmative, yes to both questions.

As mentioned in chapter 1, this is a high bar that I have set as part of key criteria for selecting couples to interview for my empirical study. This tougher standard was chosen in the hope that it would give rise to better quality answers for my interview questions (than if the couples were less than happy being with each other) for the purposes of my research questions. The initial diagnostic question of whether they would marry the same person again, if given the chance, was to help in the task of discerning in each case whether the couple were genuinely happily married to each other, a level further than being merely "content" (which would have applied to many more couples than the ones interviewed).

It may also be noted that it is possible some of the answers received may have been different if the interviewees were interviewed individually rather than as couples. However, I suggest that the overall findings would likely not have been materially different for purposes of my research questions—primarily as each couple remained married to the other, sharing bed and board, there would likely have been some sharing of their perspectives with each other even if interviewed separately.

Further, interviewing them as couples rather than individually allowed me to include some participant observation in the course of the interview, as I could see how they related to each other, and witness the dynamics of interaction between them as they answered each question—reacting or responding to each other's thoughts, and with some couples sometimes finishing each other's sentences, and addressing terms of endearment to each other.

This is a summary of the detailed process by which the transcripts were prepared and finalized:

i. Prior to starting the study I applied for and obtained ethical approval from the university to conduct the study. Prior to the start of each interview, the interviewees each signed a consent form (in the form approved by Durham University).

ii. Each interview lasted around one and a half to two and a half hours, and was recorded on audio tape.

iii. After each interview, I typed out the draft transcript based on the audio recording, and then forwarded each draft transcript to the respective interview couples for them to check, amend as necessary and approve when happy with the final version.

iv. There were some minor amendments from the initial drafts I sent, based on what the interview couples felt comfortable to stand as the final record and statement of their thoughts expressed at the interview.

v. The final transcripts (which I quote from) were each expressly approved by the respective couples as the official transcripts that they were each happy with, the official record and statement of their thoughts and conversation.

Reflexivity

As Davies reminds:

> Reflexivity, broadly defined, means a turning back on oneself, a process of self-reference. In the context of social research, reflexivity at its most immediately obvious level refers to the ways in which the products of research are affected by the personnel and process of doing research....
>
> In its most transparent guise, reflexivity expresses researchers' awareness of their necessary connection to the research situation and hence their effects upon it, what is sometimes called reactivity.[1]

Although reflexivity cannot entirely be avoided and its presence should certainly be noted in my research, the main precautions that I took to address reflexivity in my study include the standardization of interview questions—all participants were asked the exact same interview questions, as set out in appendix A—and my limiting my responses to the interviewees in the course of each interview, to help ensure, as far as practicable, that it would be primarily their voices that are heard in the findings.

5.1.3 Qualitative Research, Strengths and Limitations

This study was conducted through the lens of a qualitative scientific method, specifically involving the thematic analysis of in-depth interviews. As with others, this method has both strengths and limitations.

Key limitations of my methodology to be borne in mind are the small and unsystematically selected sample, the retrospective and cross-sectional design, the inability to prove causal relationships, and the influence of reflexivity (discussed above). Regarding the retrospective and cross-sectional (rather than longitudinal) design, participants were interviewed and asked questions about their past, rather than followed over time. While less costly to implement, this method also carries the

---

1. C. Davies, *Reflexive Ethnography*, 4, 7.

risk of lack of control over other factors and variables that may have influenced interviewees' responses.

In addition, Alan Bryman points out the possible lack of transparency in qualitative research regarding "what the researcher actually did and how he or she arrived at the study's conclusions."[2] I have endeavored to address some of such concerns by describing in some detail in section 5.1.2 the process of selecting participants, conducting research and gathering findings in my empirical study.

Bryman also reminds that three criticisms often raised about qualitative research are:

i. It is "impressionistic and subjective"—often relying on a researcher's "unsystematic views about what is significant and important" and on "personal relationships" often developed between the researcher and subjects.[3]

ii. It is "difficult to replicate," particularly due to its often unstructured nature and "reliance upon the qualitative researcher's ingenuity," since "the investigator . . . herself is the main instrument of data collection"[4] and "interpretation will be influenced by the subjective leanings of a researcher."[5]

iii. There are problems with generalizability of its findings, particularly "when participant observation is used or when qualitative interviews are conducted with a small number of individuals," as these participants cannot be considered representative of the general population.[6]

These are all aspects to be taken into account regarding my chosen methodology in this study and when considering its findings.

At the same time, the strength of my method is in creatively exploring the beliefs, ideas and themes of my subjects' self-understanding. I suggest that this method is particularly well suited for the purposes of my study, which primarily relate to identifying and drawing out key themes and recollections relevant to addressing my research questions.

---

2. Bryman, *Social Research Methods*, 399.
3. Bryman, *Social Research Methods*, 398.
4. Bryman, *Social Research Methods*, 398.
5. Bryman, *Social Research Methods*, 399.
6. Bryman, *Social Research Methods*, 399.

Swinton and Mowat point out that discussing distinctions between "idiographic knowledge" and "nomothetic knowledge" significantly "relates closely to the ongoing debate within the social sciences between qualitative and quantitative methods," noting that:

> Quantitative methods tend to assume the primacy of nomothetic knowledge while qualitative methods focus on idiographic knowledge.[7]

Further, they point out that these different approaches need not operate independently or exclusively of the other, as:

> These two research approaches are not bipolar opposites and, in fact, in practice need each other for the development of thorough understanding . . . of the way that the world is.[8]

They encourage an element of pushback against the tendency, in the world of social scientific research, to "[prioritize] nomothetic discourse . . . at the expense of the idiographic, with the latter often being downgraded to mere opinion or 'only descriptive.'"[9] They contend that both of these "modes of knowledge,"[10] the nomothetic (which is "knowledge gained through the use of the scientific method," based on the three criteria of falsifiability, replicability, and generalizability)[11] and the idiographic (which "presumes that meaningful knowledge can be discovered in unique, non-replicable experiences"),[12] are necessary and that in practice both are drawn on in the real world of lived human experience.[13]

I therefore suggest that the findings of my empirical study described in this chapter may form a contribution, albeit in a very small way, to further understanding the lived reality of couple relationships in contemporary Western contexts.

---

7. Swinton and Mowat, *Practical Theology*, 53.
8. Swinton and Mowat, *Practical Theology*, 53.
9. Swinton and Mowat, *Practical Theology*, 53.
10 Swinton and Mowat, *Practical Theology*, 52.
11 Swinton and Mowat, *Practical Theology*, 50.
12. Swinton and Mowat, *Practical Theology*, 52.
13. Swinton and Mowat, *Practical Theology*, 49–53.

5.2 Interview Findings

5.2.1 "How did you meet?" and "How long did you date/court for, before marriage?"

The couples met in several different ways, with no two experiences the same. The length of each period of courtship/dating before marriage also varied from couple to couple. What stood out was the variety of ways, and the different lengths of time, in which each of the two first became acquainted, went on to become a couple, and later married.

In the quotes and narratives below, names and place references have been anonymized to protect the privacy of the individuals referred to.

Timothy and Natalie met through village activities, courted for five years, and (at the time of the interview) have been married for twenty-eight years. Stephen and Hannah met at university, dated for four to five years, and have been married for forty years, now with two grown children and four grandchildren. George and Agnes met at a Royal Air Force dance, dated for eighteen months, and have been married for thirty-nine years. Clare and Walter worked together in a bank and had known each other for eighteen months before becoming a couple. They later moved in together before getting married after three to four years of dating/cohabitation and have been married for thirty-seven years. Nicholas and Wilma met through mutual friends, dated for three years, between two breakups, and have been married for fifty-three years.

Phyllis and Henry met at a coffee bar when they were both teenagers, dated for three years and married young. At the time of the interview they had been married for fifty-five years.[14] Rick and Cora lived in the same neighborhood and became friends over time. They got married nine months after becoming a couple and have been married for thirty-six years. Laura and Zachary met in the Air Force, dated other people, were friends for seven years, and became a couple at a time when Laura was recovering from breast cancer. They have been married for twenty-four years. Irene and Anthony said "our eyes met over a crowded bar" and were acquaintances for several years before becoming a couple and moving in together. They have been married for thirty-four years. Sandra and Edward met at college through a mutual friend, were friends for three years before becoming a couple, married soon after that, and have been married for thirty-three years.

---

14. Henry passed away in 2019.

5.2.2 "What were important criteria for you when you were dating? Why did you choose each other: (i) to date, and (ii) for marriage?"

There were several recurring themes in the interview responses on this question, including particularly shared significant interests (such as walking, countryside interests, work in the RAF), shared values on important matters (such as financial and spiritual matters), similar outlook on life, and good conversations. Physical attractiveness, intelligence, and a sense of humor were also familiar criteria. George said of Agnes: "It was her happy smile. She just smiled all night. It was very instant attraction." Some interviewees also referred to faithfulness/loyalty and character strengths in the other, particularly those perceived to be compensating for one's weaknesses.

The interviewees tended to describe these aspects as both their criteria for choosing each other to date and eventually to marry.

5.2.3 "What were your typical activities during dating/courtship?"

Typical activities varied quite widely from couple to couple, and included walks, meals, and going to the movies/pictures. Some exchanged letters, a couple went to the coffee bar a lot (during "coffee bar" era), some went to dances, some went to parties and other get-togethers. Some spoke on the phone regularly, some sent substantial time together attending activities of shared interests and hobbies, including Christian clubs and other ventures. Overall, it was apparent from the interview responses that each of the couples had spent significant time during their period of courtship/dating in conversation with each other, getting to know each other well in a variety of contexts, and discerning their mutual compatibility in the process.

5.2.4 "Any aspects of compatibility/fit that you think have worked for you, from experience of having been married now for these many years? Any changes from your criteria when you were dating?"

Key themes in response to this question included:

- Significant similar interests, likes and dislikes

- Similar significant values, including on financial, spiritual, and ethical matters
- Similar outlook on life/similar worldview
- Good conversations/interesting conversations/intelligent conversations
- Complementary character traits
- Loyalty and trust
- Mutual support
- Pulling in similar directions
- Resilience

Being interested in spending time together in similar activities, on similar pursuits—such as reading, gardening, walking, exploring, and so on—was highlighted as important for several respondents, while others also noted that they appreciated each allowing the other significant space for each to pursue their own interests. For some, supportive family/in-laws were important for their marriage, while for others, family/in-law support was lacking.

Sometimes the above criteria overlapped with, and sometimes these differed from their earlier criteria for choosing the other during dating/courtship.

Henry observed how much he grew to appreciate his wife's intelligence more through the years: "My mother was intelligent, more intelligent than my father. And that worked. I didn't realize it at the time, but over the years I realize that I was looking for somebody who was like my mother—intelligent. I was close to my mother."

5.2.5 Particularly Sensitive Questions

i. "Were you physically intimate with each other (e.g., kissing, cuddling) before marriage?"
ii. "Were you sexually intimate with each other before marriage?"
iii. "Did you live together before marriage?"

On these sensitive questions, while all ten couples answered a clear yes to question (i), there was a distinct variety in their answers to (ii) and (iii). While two couples (Hannah and Stephen, and Edward and Sandra) were of the strong conviction that sexual intercourse is best avoided prior to marriage, eight of the couples had been sexually intimate with each other before marriage, particularly after engagement, while four couples (Timothy and Natalie, Clare and Walter, Irene and Anthony, and Rick and Cora) had lived together before marriage.

Overall in numbers, of ten couples interviewed, the total of their answers is as follows:

i. Physically intimate before marriage (including kissing and cuddling): ten couples

ii. Sexually intimate before marriage: eight couples (but all indicated this was only after commitment was confirmed between them as a couple)

iii. Lived together before marriage: four couples

5.2.6 "What do you consider your significant similarities/ significant areas that you have in common? Which of those do you consider most important for helping you in your marriage/ relationship with each other?"

Again, sometimes echoing earlier themes, significant similarities which the couples said had helped their marriage included particularly:

- Similar significant interests
- Similar significant values, including on financial, spiritual, and ethical matters
- Good communication, including when disagreeing
- Friendship
- Loyalty and trust
- Family
- Involvement in community and church
- Shared history
- Fair division of labor
- Shared faith

- Forgiveness
- Adaptability, willingness to make adjustments for the other

George and Agnes mentioned they lived by a "code of honor," while Henry said: "It's learning. Learning not to be so selfish, and learning not to have a big battle about things."

5.2.7 "What do you see as your differences? Which differences do you find helpful and which do you find unhelpful in your relationship with each other?"

Various differences were also pointed out, most of which the couples observed were not detrimental to their marriage. In fact, a couple (Natalie and Timothy) even noted that some differences made life more interesting. Notably, these differences tended not to be in terms of life values/key concerns/direction in life.

Differences pointed out include:

- Differences in amount of sleep needed
- Some differences in interests, including levels of reading, types of books read, particular pursuits such as steam trains, clubs, and so on
- Some cultural differences, including growing up
- Personality differences
- Male/female differences
- Differences in "orientation" (for example, towards ideas or concepts versus towards people or relationships)
- Differences in tolerance towards alcohol

5.2.7 "What do you consider are your key influences in formation of your traits, values, goals/motivations/concerns, and so on, and your attitude towards dating/courtship and marriage?"

Parental influence—particularly in terms of the stability of many of their parents' marriages—featured as a key influence for several of the couples, along with values imparted more generally by extended family, the surrounding community, peer groups, friends, and religious faith.

Books were also a significant formative influence for participants who enjoyed reading.

Family upbringing featured significantly for most couples. Spiritual and faith influences, particularly church and Christian community, and sometimes Christian schooling and Christian activities, including as youths and/or at university, were also highlighted.

For older couples, the frugal values of the postwar years were an important influence. Further for older couples, the more conservative culture (particularly in terms of sexual values) of the postwar years was also a significant influence. One-night stands were quite unheard of. If a girl got pregnant, it was assumed she would be married soon after. Sexual activity was closely tied to commitment for most couples.

5.2.8 "Is there any general advice you would give to younger couples? Any aspects of premarital/dating/courtship behavior and contexts that you consider are helpful generally towards a healthy marriage?"

While a few were hesitant about offering advice, the primacy of enduring and deep friendship, alongside shared values and good communication, for their marital relationship, even in priority over other considerations such as sexual attractiveness, was a key theme brought up by several couples. Honesty, trust, and tolerance, along with give-and-take, were also key qualities that were pointed out as valuable for sustaining their relationships for the long term. Many emphasized the importance of friendship and trust, and pointed out that dating is an important time for establishing if the above elements are present in the relationship, and for checking for compatibility in values.

There was a significant variation in views among the couples as to whether premarital sexual relations would affect the quality of a marriage. As mentioned, a majority of the couples had been sexually intimate before marriage, particularly after engagement, while four of the ten couples had cohabited prior to marriage. However, there were also participants (including Stephen and Hannah) who voiced clear views that premarital sex is not advisable for a strong marriage. Hannah said: "I feel very strongly that the best advice is not to have sex before marriage. I feel it makes a very big difference to the quality of your marriage." This contrasted with Timothy and Natalie saying they felt that premarital cohabitation can be helpful for ascertaining compatibility and getting to know traits of the other person not discernible during usual dating activities.

Agnes advised: "Build a friendship. Know each other. Know the person."

Agnes also emphasized the importance of "good communication" and "tolerance," while Stephen said: "Keep communicating."

Natalie said: "Regard your partner as your best friend."

5.2.9 "Do you think there are aspects of the above advice that are less (or more) applicable in today's context, as distinct from when you were dating? What may be the reasons for this? Do you think there are significant differences between social expectations (particularly concerning premarital/dating behavior of couples) when you were dating and social expectations now?"

While observing societal changes and differences in social expectations from the time they were dating to now, opinions and views among the interviewees varied somewhat on this. Several noted that there are significantly lower standards, in terms of sexual permissiveness, nowadays. Some also pointed out that society is more forgiving nowadays, and also more affluent and materialistic nowadays.

George and Agnes said: "There's something timeless about values."

Phyllis and Henry observed: "It's so different nowadays. So many pressures on young people nowadays. . . . Also, because life was simpler then, expectations were different. And women weren't expected to work. Nowadays, people think they have to have this and that. . . . We wouldn't really know what to advise modern couples. Modern life is so different from when we were dating . . . modern life just seems so much more complicated."

5.2.10 "What personal qualities/virtues do you consider are important for a healthy marriage?"

Several similar themes came up in the responses to this question—some echoing those raised earlier—of the importance of strong friendship, trust, honesty, an attitude of tolerance, flexibility, and give-and-take, mutual respect, kindness, along with similar values particularly in matters of significance, such as finances and faith.

Friendship featured strongly for almost all the couples. They also mentioned:

- Loyalty
- Trust
- Similar sense of humor
- Financial compatibility, shared values concerning finances
- Significant shared interests
- Ability to adapt, resilience to adapt to life's challenges
- Forgiveness
- Communication
- Optimism, sense of humor
- Being easygoing, not being fussy about small things
- Give-and-take
- Respecting the other person
- Pulling together in the same direction
- Seeing each other's point of view

Agnes said: "[It's] being able to laugh at ourselves and also to laugh together. . . . It's not the material stuff that's important. It's what we have together." George and Agnes also emphasized the importance of "selflessness, rather than a "me-me-me" individualistic attitude."

5.2.11 "What other ingredients do you consider important for a happy healthy marriage? And any other general advice on dating/courtship/choice of life partner?"

In addition to the themes brought up earlier, including friendship, faith and honesty, practical considerations—including finances and budgeting and navigating parental wishes—were also highlighted as important for sustaining a healthy marriage in the long term.

Some advised not to expect perfection in a partner, while keeping in mind what is important.

Timothy and Natalie said marriage should be a "relationship of equals."

Phyllis observed: "There's got to be give-and-take. You can't be selfish."

5.3 Discussing Data in Response to Four Follow-Up Questions

After or in the final section of each interview, I asked each of the couples the following four follow-up questions:

> If you described your views and approach towards courtship/dating in terms of numbers:
>
> 1. On a scale of 1 to 10
>
>   (1 being most pragmatic/unromantic/functional in criteria—such as income, assets, skills—
>
>   10 being most romantic/non-pragmatic in criteria—such as romantic feelings, friendship—and
>
>   5 being a balance of both romantic and practical criteria),
>
>   your view/approach concerning criteria for choosing a life partner/marriage partner, <u>at the time you were dating/courting</u>, would be:
>
> 2. On a scale of 1 to 10 [as above, for question 1],
>
>   your view/approach concerning criteria for choosing a life partner/marriage partner <u>now</u> would be:
>
> 3. On a scale of 1 to 10
>
>   (1 being most absolute/nonpermissive—such as no sexual involvement before marriage—
>
>   10 being most permissive—such as "anything is fine, as long as both parties consent"—and
>
>   5 being mid-way/flexible in allowing there could be some sexual activity prior to marriage, but that should be directly connected to commitment/engagement),
>
>   your view/approach concerning practices in dating/courtship prior to marriage, <u>at the time you were dating/courting</u>, would be:
>
> 4. On a scale of 1 to 10 [as above, for question 3],
>
>   your view/approach concerning practices in dating/courtship prior to marriage, <u>now</u>, would be:

The answers received from the interviewees to each of these questions are set out in this table:

A. Natalie and Timothy	Natalie	Timothy
Answer to question 1	6	7
Answer to question 2	5	5
Answer to question 3	5	5
Answer to question 4	5	5

B. Hannah and Stephen	Hannah	Stephen
Answer 1	5	5
Answer 2	6	5
Answer 3	3	3
Answer 4	3	3

C. Phyllis and Henry	Phyllis	Henry
Answer 1	5	5
Answer 2	5	5
Answer 3	5	5
Answer 4	5	5

D. George and Agnes	George	Agnes
Answer 1	7	6
Answer 2	7	6
Answer 3	5	5
Answer 4	5	5

E. Wilma and Nicholas	Wilma	Nicholas
Answer 1	7	6
Answer 2	6	7
Answer 3	4	5
Answer 4	5	4

F. Sandra and Edward	Sandra	Edward
Answer 1	8	8
Answer 2	6	5
Answer 3	3.5	4
Answer 4	5	5

G. Laura and Zachary	Laura	Zachary
Answer 1	5	6
Answer 2	5	6
Answer 3	4	4
Answer 4	4	4

H. Irene and Anthony	Irene	Anthony
Answer 1	6	6
Answer 2	7	7
Answer 3	5	5
Answer 4	7	6

I. Rick and Cora	Rick	Cora
Answer 1	8	8
Answer 2	8	8
Answer 3	5	5
Answer 4	5	5

J. Clare and Walter	Clare	Walter
Answer 1	8	5.5
Answer 2	5	8.5
Answer 3	7	7
Answer 4	3	3

Accompanying Comments from Clare and Walter for answers 1 and 2:

> <u>Clare</u>: When dating it was probably about an 8. It's now more of a 5. You come to appreciate that the pragmatic things are what makes a marriage last. Though the romantic things are important, but not as important as before.
>
> <u>Walter</u>: For me, it was a 5 or a 6 when dating, but now, a few points more actually, about an 8 or a 9!

Accompanying Comments from Clare and Walter for answers 3 and 4:

> <u>Clare</u>: When dating, it was probably around 7. Now, probably right down to about 3. As you get older and see the consequences of the "free and easy" attitude, and seeing the effect on society of that "free and easy" attitude. And it makes me feel a more rigid structure has its merits. But there again, it's about tolerance, and not being judgmental.
>
> <u>Walter</u>: I would echo that, and for the same reasons.

The data from the above answers is also related to my proposed typology discussed in chapter 2. As set out in chapter 2, the scatter graph below represents the data from answers to questions 1 and 3 (views at the time of dating/courtship):

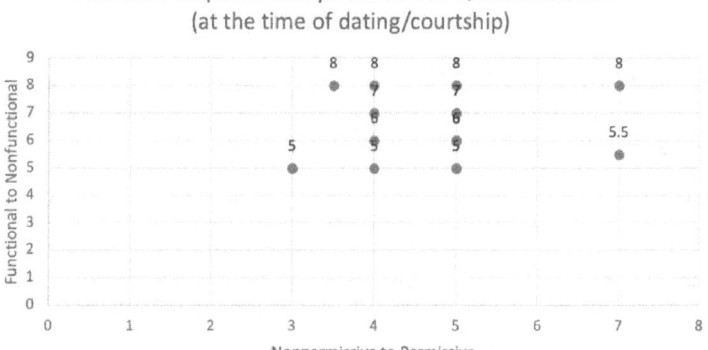

Data from Empirical Study: Answers to Questions 1 and 3 (at the time of dating/courtship)

The following graph represents data from answers to questions 2 and 4 (current views at the time of the interview):

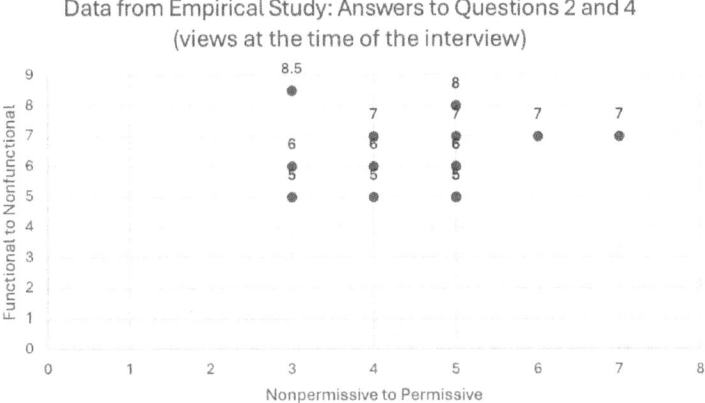

It is clear from both sets of data (as can be seen from the above graphs) that none of the answers were in the region of predominantly functional or predominantly nonpermissive approaches. At the same time, it is also clear that none were in the region of the highly permissive (9 or 10 on the X axis). Instead, as can be seen from these graphs, all the answers were in the region of either the center of the graph (moderate approaches), top center, or top right of the graph. Overall, this indicates that—based on the answers given—both in their views at the time of dating/courtship and at the time of the interview, type (3) approaches (and some type (2) views close to type (3)) were the prevailing type among each of the interviewees.

Space constraint does not allow for further exploration of the reasons for this phenomenon—including whether the answers given may have been different if the couples were interviewed as separate individuals rather than as a couple, and other possible factors and variables. This may form material for a future study.

5.4 Further Analysis of Findings

5.4.1 Key Themes Arising from Interview Responses

Key themes included:

(i) The importance of congruence of goals, motivations, concerns

Zachary said: "Software engineers would understand software engineers, but probably not get on so well with a clown, for example. They need to be compatible in their approach to life, and the things that are important to them. To really 'get' each other."

(ii) Resilience, fidelity, perseverance through thick and thin

Agnes said: "My grandma reminded me when I got married: "You're marrying the person. You're not marrying the person to turn him into what you want. It's accepting him for who he is, and marrying him for who he is."

(iii) Empathy, learning to see the other's point of view

Phyllis said: "As my mother said, 'You've made your bed. Now you must lie in it. If it's lumpy, thump it until it's soft' . . . Not meaning thump each other, but learning to see each other's point of view."

(iv) Devotion

Among some couples there was also a theme of devotion, being devoted to each other in loyal companionship.
    Irene said: "[Anthony is] my whole world. And the thing is, I'm his whole world too. That's why we have such a happy marriage. Because that's the way we feel. We have a strong friendship with each other. And total trust with each other. We trust each other to behave in ways that try to help."

(v) Adversity

Several of the couples faced adversity or challenging circumstances during their years of dating, courtship, or early years of their marriage—though in varying forms, including separation by distance (George and Agnes, Nicholas and Wilma), parental opposition (Hannah and Stephen), cancer diagnosis (Laura and Zachary), financial constraints (Irene and Anthony). Admirably, for these couples it was in persevering through these challenges that they became all the more certain that they wanted to marry each other.

5.5 Summary of Findings and Conclusions

From the extensive thoughts and practical wisdom shared by each couple, one can conclude that in the opinion of each of the couples their decisions, activities, and behavior *both* before marriage (that is, while dating or courting) and after getting married (that is, during the long years and different seasons of their marital life) mattered for the longevity and flourishing of their marital relationship. However, it should be noted that findings from this study have not been compared to data from unhappy marriages. Overall, while findings from my study regarding the self-understanding and perceptions of the couples raise several interesting themes, it will not be possible to establish a definite causal relationship regarding these matters without conducting quantitative research.

That said, all the interviews were rich discussions, through which many insights emerged. Each of the ten couples felt happy about their choice of whom they had married, that they had good compatibility with their spouse (and would marry their spouse again, if given the chance), and also felt that in the course of the many years of their marriage they had to keep growing and keep being and becoming, all the more, the right partner for their spouse. Each of their marriages had a good solid foundation to start with, in large part due to the choices they made during their time of dating/courting, and yet after getting married, they also had to keep nurturing their marital relationship and building on that strong foundation, so that they continued to flourish together in marriage.

As mentioned above, there was a significant variation in opinions among the couples as to the advisability of premarital sexual relations for strong marriages, and a significant variation in their experience of premarital sex and cohabitation prior to marriage. Referring to my typology discussed in chapter 2, though the interviewees' approaches varied between nonpermissive and moderate (mainly type (2) and type (3)), all agreed that sexual intimacy should be correlated in some way with level of commitment—some allowed for sexual intimacy after engagement, while others held that sex should be reserved for marriage.

Further, while physical attraction was a significant factor for many of the couples particularly in their younger years during their time of dating or courtship and formed part of their decision to marry, views varied among the couples as to whether sexual attraction continued to remain a key feature of their relationship in the long course of their married lives. A clear variety was also evident in the ways in which each couple met and dated.

There was near unanimity among the couples, however, about the importance of strong friendship (often signalled by a congruence or compatibility in their goals, values, motivations, and concerns), trust, honesty, good communication, mutual respect, kindness, and give-and-take for the longevity and flourishing of their marital relationship through the years, along with the propensity to stay committed during times of adversity. For many couples, the presence of these qualities discerned during their time of dating or courtship (and from the recollections shared, some activities and experiences during dating or courtship better enabled the discernment of the presence or absence of such qualities) prior to marriage tended to provide a strong foundation for the continued presence and growth of these qualities in the course of each of their marital lives.

It is possible that these findings were affected by the fact that all the couples interviewed were of the Christian faith (and other couples, perhaps of other faiths or none, may prefer other qualities in their relationship)—and it is pertinent to note that several of the couples highlighted the importance of their shared faith for their marital relationship. Yet, it is also possible that the above qualities identified by the couples as important for their marital relationship—strong friendship, trust, honesty, good communication, mutual respect, and so on—are universal qualities that may be valued by a range of couples (whether of the Christian faith or not) as being important for the longevity and flourishing of their marriages.

From the interview responses discussed, it may be possible to suggest that the most resilient marriages are built on dating practices and decisions that were based on a combination of the exercise of reason, emotion and physical attraction. All three elements appear to feature regularly in the couples' description of their practices and decisions during their time of dating or courtship.

For example, Zachary said: "I look at the whole package. If you weren't physically attractive to me, you wouldn't have been on my radar in the first place. We had good fun together. We enjoyed doing similar things."

Henry said: "I thought she was very intelligent. I loved her. I loved everything about her, and I still do. I thought she was beautiful, and very intelligent. You feel comfortable with the person. Or you also feel uncomfortable because you're afraid you'll lose her. I knew definitely that this is someone I wanted in my life."

Of exercising reason, George said: "We are both outward looking, we both have the same worldview. . . . There are other people, no matter how nice and beautiful, because they don't have the same outlook, it would have been a strain, and I couldn't get on with them. For Agnes it's the same."

Features of abiding emotion may be perceived in several of the couples' descriptions of loyalty, friendship and/or trust as a key aspect of their relationship. For example, Hannah said: "Loyalty and trust are important. Over the years, Stephen has always been very loyal, and I have always been able to trust him."

Physical attraction is also reflected in comments such as "I liked the look of him" (Wilma). It should be noted that this does not mean that either of the partners have to be particularly sexually attractive by conventional standards. As Nicholas observed memorably: "Physical attractiveness was relevant too, but that wasn't the primary consideration. I don't think either of us regard the other as 'God's gift to the [other sex]' or 'Mr. and Mrs. Universe.'"

I suggest this element implies that there continues to be ongoing physical intimacy between the couple, and that (along with intimacy on an emotional and intellectual level) there is a physical bond between the couple discernible through time, and clearly they are not physically repulsed by each other. Physical attraction between the partners (along with emotional and intellectual attraction) will thus mainly be a subjective phenomenon, based on factors unique to each couple. Hence it should not be surprising that at times there are strong resilient marriages in which the wife may be significantly older than her husband in years and may not appear as sexually attractive as younger counterparts. One may see this, for example (at the time of writing), even in high-profile couples such as Emmanuel and Brigitte Macron—defying stereotypical societal expectations that a "younger woman" necessarily makes a better wife.

Further, in the interviewees' responses, these eight key elements kept recurring, and I suggest that these are eight elements that are important to discern during dating/courtship, to help form a good foundation for marriage:

i. Strong friendship (particularly in terms of congruence of life goals, motivations, and concerns—including long term, not just short term)

ii. Honesty

iii. Trust

iv. Good communication

v. Mutual respect

vi. Kindness

vii. Give-and-take

viii. Propensity to persevere through difficult times

It may be observed that many of these qualities grew, and each couple's relationship was strengthened, often in the midst of the quotidian. Overall, responses from the interviewees in my empirical study showed the happiest relationships being characterized by mutual support and companionship. A parallel may be drawn here to findings from psychological research, discussed in chapter 4, showing the importance of companionate love for the longevity of romantic relationships. Extrapolating from this, I suggest that dating approaches that assist couples in discerning a strong foundation for long-term mutual support and companionship (rather than, say, approaches and practices which are focused on short-term pleasure-seeking) are significantly more likely to help promote happy, flourishing, lifelong monogamy.

Further, based on the interview responses described, themes along the lines of my proposed fivefold ethic (discussed in ch. 6) may also be discerned: themes of courage, justice, temperance, prudence, and love and care.

Recollections of "Dating" for These Ten Long-Term Happily Married Couples

What did "dating" mean for each of these ten couples who went on to stay happily married for more than twenty years (several for considerably more years)? What were the processes and activities they were involved in during their time of dating or courting? I have summarized the couples' responses in section 5.2.3.

It may be noted that for most of the couples, their dating activities and time spent together while dating were not focused nor centered on sex. Instead, they spent their time engaged in a variety of nonsexual pursuits together, in the process discovering whether they actually enjoyed spending "non-sexy" time with each other, getting to know the other person and eventually discerning if this person is who they could honestly make a lifelong commitment to. I suggest that these are good examples that contemporary couples may find helpful to follow. As many may have observed, sexual attraction in a relationship is unlikely to last forever, and often may continue only for a limited duration of time. If a couple are to be able to maintain a committed relationship for the long-haul, happily rather than grudgingly, more substantial "glue" is required for their relationship than sexual bonding alone, important though that may be. To discern whether the elements of this more substantial "glue" are present between the couple, a careful process of discernment is required in the course of dating.

What are the elements of this more substantial "glue"? As mentioned, based on data from the ten interviews in my empirical study, I contend that these elements revolve around a central theme of mutual support and companionship. Obviously, not everyone can get along swimmingly with everyone. We all vary, from one to another, in our personalities, interests, pursuits, life stories, goals, motivations, and concerns.[15] I suggest a good or "better" approach in dating will involve processes and activities that help each couple to discover and discern whether they each—with their unique personalities, values, life stories, interests and concerns—are substantially able to provide, experience and enjoy strong companionship and mutual support with each other.

If strong elements of mutual support and companionship are not clearly evident during a substantial time of dating or courtship, I suggest it would be unwise to expect or hope that such elements would somehow appear during marriage. If a couple are experiencing over a sustained length of time, well-grounded mutual support and companionship in a variety of ways (rather than, say, based only on superficial similarities and limited aspects of common ground), that continues to grow over time, I argue that this forms part of a good foundation for the couple to embark on a marital commitment if they so decide—while bearing in mind, certainly, that they will have to continue nurturing their relationship to continue growing along a generally upward trajectory of increasingly strong companionship and mutual support through the years.

---

15. Here again I refer to McAdams's three-level model of personality discussed in ch. 4, as a helpful tool for getting to understand ourselves and one another.

CHAPTER 6: LIVING MORE HUMAN(E)LY?

Towards Better Approaches

6.1. Introduction: Pushing Back Against Neoliberal Currents

IN CHAPTER 3 I identified and assessed the following six significant themes or features of contemporary Anglo-American contexts relevant to dating/couple relationships:

i. A continuing shift towards the form of "pure relationship" (referring to Giddens's definition of the term), partly as a trajectory of development from the sexual revolution

ii. Culture wars: Including on matters concerning sexuality, with often polarized positions between conservatives and progressives/liberals

iii. Economic insecurity: Heightened economic concerns, especially after the global economic crisis of 2008 but with roots and developments occurring decades before 2008, characterized by the decline of financial and social safety nets

iv. Medical advances significantly lowering the traditional risks or costs of sexual interactions and enabling the normalization of casual sexual interactions: particularly the widespread availability of reliable contraception and improved treatments for sexually transmitted infections

v. Increased sexualization of everyday culture: Including with the ubiquity of sexualized images in the vast majority of people's everyday experiences, and widespread availability of high-quality pornography, fueled by technology, including the internet and other media

vi. Fast-improving technology and the internet: Leading to the phenomenon, unprecedented in previous generations, of the ubiquity of social media, online dating and dating apps, with their accompanying advantages, risks, opportunities and pitfalls

Here I will suggest that both "purity culture" (associated, for example, with "promise rings," "purity balls," and programs such as "Silver Ring Thing" and so on) and "hookup culture" (including as described in ch. 3) are both at least partly manifestations (though expressed in markedly different ways) of a neoliberal worldview, which I suggest is antithetical to an authentically Christian worldview. It appears that an established "market" for sex exists and is a driving force for human sexual relationships in contemporary Anglo-American contexts, both among Christians and non-Christians, though manifested in varied ways (for example, in the "culture wars" between adherents of "hookup culture" and "purity culture").

Hence, pushing back to some extent against reductionistic and dehumanizing tendencies prevalent in contemporary contexts that approach human intimate relationships primarily in terms of "market," "exchange," and satisfaction of mostly temporal desires, I will advocate in this chapter a virtue-ethical (rather than purely deontological or utilitarian) approach to sexual ethics—and particularly for dating in contemporary contexts—that is neither in the direction of "purity culture" nor "hookup culture," nor following any (other) neoliberal currents, but which is grounded in full-fledged Christian theology and a vision of true humanity. I will propose a fivefold ethic for application to contemporary dating, composed of the four classical virtues (prudence, justice, courage/fortitude, and temperance) and an overarching recalibrating virtue of love and care. In the course of this chapter, I will seek to build this fivefold ethic as a Christian (possibly "Protestant") virtue-ethical approach applicable for contemporary sexual ethics.

I will then (in the next, concluding, chapter) draw together the findings of the preceding chapters along with my proposed fivefold ethic to suggest some "better approaches" overall to heterosexual dating in contemporary Anglo-American contexts, particularly in answer to my research questions:

i. Assuming a Christian version of happy, flourishing, lifelong, monogamous marriage (set out in ch. 1) is a good, are there any approaches to heterosexual dating in contemporary Anglo-American contexts that help realize or promote this good?

ii. And if so, what do they consist of?

As mentioned, I suggest that both "purity culture" and "hookup culture" are both at least partly manifestations (though expressed in markedly different ways) of a neoliberal worldview (defined here particularly in terms of a consumerist market-driven focus),[1] which I suggest is antithetical to an authentically Christian worldview. As Rodney Clapp surmises:

> Neoliberalism does not see the market as a facet of society, as embedded within and subordinated to the moral and spiritual aims of a people. Rather, for neoliberalism, the market encompasses and defines the entirety of society.[2]

Neoliberalism is a pervasive force around us that enthrones the market and the "fittest" according to rules of competition dictated by the prevailing powers.[3] Kevin Hargaden rightly cautions that "neoliberalism represents a theological problem for Christians because those who live under its reign are encouraged to share a vision for our common life that is unavoidably idolatrous" and observes that "as neoliberal subjects, we are trained in a rationality that seeks to apply the methods of economics to all aspects of life. . . . We are all neoliberal subjects; there is no alternative. Society increasingly serves the market."[4]

---

1. For example: "[Neoliberalism] can be associated with the slogan 'less state, more market.' . . . In the neoliberal perspective, individual liberty is conceived in economic terms, and the 'market'—the mechanism of price—is to play a central role in all aspects of social regulation" (Martikainen and Gauthier, *Religion in the Neoliberal Age*, 13). "It can be argued that the social acceptance of neoliberalism depends on a wider shift within Western societies, one which has to do with the rise of *consumerism* as a dominant cultural ethos. . . . In brief, mass consumption gave way to consumerism after the 1950s and has resulted in a profoundly morphed household, social and cultural reality, one in which the abundance and the circulation of objects and the continuous appeal to desire is central" (15).

2. Clapp, *Naming Neoliberalism*, ch. 2, loc. 662 of 4237.

3. This calls to mind Cavanaugh's prescient warning, in Augustinian vein, that "in the absence of a substantive account of the good, all that remains is sheer arbitrary power, one will against another. This is what Augustine calls the *libido dominandi*, the lust for power with which Pharaoh was possessed" (Cavanaugh, *Being Consumed*, 23).

4. Hargaden, *Theological Ethics*, 3–4.

I suggest that neoliberal instincts have seeped into and are evident in both "Christian" and secular approaches to dating in contemporary contexts. Such neoliberal currents may be discerned, for example, in the issues raised in books such as *Making Chastity Sexy*, where Christine Gardner observes, among other matters, a clever marketing strategy within the chastity movement in encouraging abstinence by promoting desire for ("say yes to") great sex within marriage.[5] This may also be observed in the "ring by spring" mentality (described in ch. 3) associated with "purity culture," and in the dehumanizing currents associated with hookup culture, discussed by authors such as Kari-Shane Zimmerman, Jason King, and Jennifer Beste.[6]

In perhaps a slightly different but related vein, Mark Regnerus (also discussed in ch. 3) observes—as what appears an objective reality—the existence of a "market" for sex in terms of a "social transaction," noting that there is in contemporary society "a basic exchange that typically constitutes the social setting in which sexual relationships begin, end, or continue—even one-night stands."[7] Advancing his claim that "cheap sex" has proliferated in contemporary American society,[8] he asserts:

> Cheap sex is both an objective fact and a social fact, characterized by personal ease of sexual access and social perceptions of the same. Sex is cheap if women expect little in return for it and if men do not have to supply much time, attention, resources, recognition, or fidelity in order to experience it. . . . My central claim . . . is that cheap sex is plentiful—it's flooding the market in sex and relationships—and that this has had profound influence on how American men and women relate to each other, which in turn has spilled over into other domains.[9]

Of the causes of this (also mentioned in ch. 3 above), Regnerus observes:

---

5. "For evangelicals, sex can legitimately take place only within the context of the marriage relationship, so marriage becomes not only the goal but also the implied reward for the abstinence commitment" (Gardner, *Making Chastity Sexy*, 47). "Great sex in marriage is promised to those who wait. Sex is no longer a taboo to be avoided but the prize to be earned" (50).

6. See, for example, Zimmerman, "Hooking Up"; J. King, *Faith with Benefits*; Beste, *College Hookup Culture*; Beste, "Hookups, Happiness."

7. Regnerus, *Cheap Sex*, 22.

8. And also noting Giddens's observation along these lines that "men mostly welcome the fact that women have become more sexually available" (*Transformation of Intimacy*, 11). See also Regnerus, *Cheap Sex*, 28.

9. Regnerus, *Cheap Sex*, 28–29.

> Cheaper sex has been facilitated by three distinctive technological achievements: (1) the wide uptake of the Pill as well as a mentality stemming from it that sex is "naturally" infertile, (2) mass-produced high-quality pornography, and (3) the advent and evolution of online dating/meeting services. All three are price "suppressors" that have significantly altered mating market dynamics, often in ways invisible to the individuals in the market.[10]

To reiterate, it thus appears an established phenomenon that a "market" for sex exists and is the driving force for human sexual relationships in contemporary Anglo-American contexts, both among Christians and non-Christians, though manifested in varied ways (for example, in the "culture wars" between adherents of "hookup culture" and "purity culture"). Indeed, in numerous ways, in the practices of dating in contemporary contexts (including, not least, dating apps, and more) the commodification and instrumentalization of human relationships and human persons—to the detriment, rather than the flourishing, of those human relationships and human persons—may be observed.

With this backdrop, and pushing back against such currents prevalent in contemporary Anglo-American contexts that approach human intimate relationships primarily in terms of "market," "exchange," and satisfaction of mostly temporal desires, I seek in this chapter—while thinking theologically about dating—to set out a virtue-ethical approach[11] to sexual ethics that is grounded in full-fledged Christian theology and a vision of true humanity. This will also entail some discussion (albeit not at length) of Christian theological anthropology and the doctrine of the *imago Dei*.

---

10. Regnerus, *Cheap Sex*, 11. Regnerus also argues here that these three "price suppressors," enabling the rise of "cheap sex," have resulted in "a massive slow-down in the development of committed relationships, especially marriage," along with other detrimental effects, including on the fertility of women and men's "economic and relational productivity."

11. My use of the term "virtue" throughout this book is in relation to the field of virtue ethics and should not be confused with an old-fashioned or Victorian understanding of the word primarily associated with "sexual purity."

6.2 On Christian Virtue Ethics

6.2.1 Christian Virtue Ethics Applied to Sexual Ethics

Regarding following a virtue-ethical approach to sexual ethics, it may be observed that a virtues-centered approach has also been adopted by other Christian ethicists, particularly Catholic theologians. For example, renowned theologian James Keenan proposed four cardinal virtues for application in relation to sexual ethics: justice, fidelity, self-care, and prudence.[12] In the context of Catholic culture, he advanced these virtues as "thickened" by the virtue of mercy.[13] With these proposed virtues, he also expanded on the traditional Catholic virtue applicable to sexual ethics, chastity.[14] In a recent chapter, Megan McCabe applied Keenan's proposed fourfold system of virtues as a "foundational ethic" to address the perplexing risk of sexual violence, stalking and abuse in the contexts of romantic relationships.[15]

As mentioned in chapter 1, Margaret Farley (though in an approach that some traditionalists may regard as unconventional) proposed seven norms for a just sexual ethic: do no unjust harm, free consent, mutuality, equality, commitment, fruitfulness, and social justice.[16] She derives these norms from "the concrete reality of persons" and builds these on "respect for their autonomy and relationality," thus "[respecting] persons as ends in themselves."[17] There is much to commend of Farley's proposals and I interpret her approach as bearing virtue-ethical strands, with norms built on two primary virtues, justice and love (or, more specifically, love/loving that is just). Further, Lawler and Salzman

---

12. Keenan, "Virtue Ethics." Keenan also argues that the classical fourfold system of cardinal virtues (justice, courage, temperance, and prudence) is inadequate for contemporary purposes (188–89). On the basis of human identity "being relational in three ways: generally, specifically and uniquely," Keenan advocates a cardinal virtue for each of these aspects: "justice" for being relational beings "generally," "fidelity" for being relational beings "specifically," and "self-care" for our being relational beings "uniquely" (189–90). While proposing this new fourfold system of virtues, he holds that the fourth virtue "prudence" in his proposed system continues to bear "the task of integrating the three [other] virtues into our relationships," similar to its role under the classical system (191). He also argues that "the older two virtues," fortitude (or courage) and temperance, "remain auxiliary and exist to support the realization of the other four" (190).

13. Keenan, "Virtue Ethics," 192–93.

14. Keenan, "Virtue Ethics," 181–82.

15. McCabe, "Relationships Instead of Hooking Up?"

16. Farley, *Just Love*, 216–32.

17. Farley, *Just Love*, 231.

have argued for three specific virtues—justice, love, and chastity—to be operative between humans particularly in the context of sexual relationships.[18]

While there may be resonances between my approach here and these eminent theologians' approaches (and generally with some Thomistic versions of virtue ethics),[19] there are also key differences (which should be apparent as I proceed to elaborate on my approach in the course of this chapter), particularly that the virtue-ethical approach that I propose here is advanced in more of a "Protestant"[20] vein—connected to a multifaceted integrated version of the *imago Dei* and Pauline theology, and developing on views expressed by N. T. Wright in a 2008 essay.[21] From this, I have derived a fivefold ethic, composed of a "recalibrated" version (borrowing Wright's/Pinches's terminology[22] here—that is, following a Christian mode of being human) of the four cardinal virtues of prudence, justice, courage, temperance, and a fifth overarching virtue of love and care, following the description of 1 Cor 13.

In sum, the version I propose is a Christocentric version of virtue ethics, centered on the concept of being and becoming more "truly human,"[23] that develops on the version outlined by Wright and is connected to my proposed multifaceted integrated model of interpretation

---

18. Lawler and Salzman, "People Beginning Sexual Experience," 557–65.

19. Especially in their emphasis on virtue ethics (rather than Kantian/deontological or utilitarian approaches) as a primary method to engage with contemporary sexual ethics.

20. To clarify, I use the term "Protestant" in this book in a broad sense of the term (that is, Christian but not identifiably Catholic nor Orthodox, and which can trace its roots to the Reformation emphases on the authority of Scripture, and salvation by divine grace alone and through Christ alone) which is not necessarily tied to Calvinist nor Lutheran tenets, which may at times include aspects of Anglican thought and which may perhaps have more affinity with Arminian expressions of the term.

21. N. T. Wright, "Faith, Virtue, Justification."

22. N. T. Wright, "Faith, Virtue, Justification," s.vv. "II: Virtues, Pagan and Christian." In relation to the term "recalibrate," Wright also refers to Charles Pinches's use of the term in his discussion of the Thomistic understanding of virtue, where he describes the cardinal virtues being "profoundly changed," "recalibrated" and "reordered" by the theological virtues (faith, hope, and love). See Pinches, "Virtue," 742.

23. The field is vast. For a helpful exposition of the concept of "humanity" and what being human might mean, see Bretherton, *Christ and the Common Life*, ch. 10, "Humanity." Bretherton also appears to affirm that an ethic of love and care is essential for genuine humanity: "Love of God and love of neighbor (which includes nonhuman creation) are the ground and fulfilment of what it means to be human" (ch. 10, s.vv. "Natality, Mortality, and the Teleological Nature of Being Human").

of the *imago Dei* (to be advanced in the next section). With its Christocentric focus and emphasis on consistency with Pauline theology (along with the overall trajectory of Judeo-Christian Scripture), I will offer this as a version of "Protestant" (or simply "Christian") virtue ethics for practical application in the field of contemporary sexual ethics.

6.2.2 A Brief Introduction to Virtue Ethics

I advocate a virtue-ethical approach, as an alternative to the dominant ethical approaches of deontology (often in the form of Kantian duty-based ethics) and utilitarianism (outcome-oriented ethics typically focused on maximizing pleasure and minimizing pain, based on calculations of "the greatest good for the greatest number"). I defend the importance and helpfulness of the cardinal virtues (prudence, courage, justice and temperance) from a Protestant Christian perspective and, to some extent, seek to harmonize the relevance of these virtues with Pauline theology—following N. T. Wright's approach of "recalibrating" the cardinal virtues in light of the highest Christian virtue, love, and also drawing on an integrated reading of the concept of the *imago Dei*.

Delineation of the four well-known cardinal virtues (of prudence, courage, temperance, and justice) may be observed in classical Greek writings at least as far back as Plato's *Republic*.[24] Aristotle, though with what appears to be a somewhat pluralistic approach to the virtues, discussed the acquisition of virtue through habituation, the development of a "second nature" through "the repetition of similar activities,"[25] and enumerated various attributes of excellence which may be considered relevant across different cultures and applicable in a variety of social situations. He also advanced the concept of "the mean," for understanding virtue in terms of being constituted of neither excess nor deficiency in a quality.[26] Among the scholastics, Thomas Aquinas stands out for his drawing on and recasting of Aristotelian thought on the virtues and detailed exposition of a distinctly Christian version of virtue ethics within

---

24. Plato, *Republic*, bk. 4.
25. Aristotle, *Nicomachean Ethics* 2.1.11104–2.2.1104a.
26. Aristotle, *Nicomachean Ethics* 2.2.1104a–2.9.1109b. For example, at 2.9.1109a he observes, "That is why it is also hard work to be excellent. For in each case it is hard work to find the intermediate . . . doing it to the right person, in the right amount, at the right time, for the right end, and in the right way is no longer easy, nor can everyone do it. Hence doing these things well is rare, praiseworthy, and fine."

a natural law framework, while also affirming the fourfold formulation of cardinal virtues.[27]

While ethical positions were generally focused on other perspectives (such as deontological or utilitarian approaches) in the eighteenth, nineteenth, and early twentieth centuries, particularly notable for the revival in the latter half of the twentieth century of scholarly interest in virtue ethics, along with Elizabeth Anscombe's groundbreaking 1958 article "Modern Moral Philosophy," is Alasdair MacIntyre's *After Virtue*, including with his emphasis on narrative, communities, and practices for the formation and sustenance of virtues.

Highlighting the intractable problems—particularly for resolving disagreements over moral dilemmas (MacIntyre refers to these in terms of "interminable" debates)[28]—associated with modernity and the Enlightenment project, he goes on to conclude that there are only two options left to choose: Nietzsche or Aristotle.[29] He advocates a return to the ways of Aristotle in which individuals are formed in virtue within their own communities, practices, narratives, and tradition.

Having put forward a key distinction between "external goods" and "internal goods," particularly through his memorable "chess analogy"[30] and other examples,[31] MacIntyre suggests the following preliminary definition for "virtue":

---

27. See, for example, Aquinas, *Summa Theologica* 2.2.61.
28. MacIntyre, *After Virtue*, 6.
29. MacIntyre, *After Virtue*, 118.
30. He gives the example of a child who is first drawn into playing chess through the inducement of candy, but whom one hopes will, through time and the experience of the integral thrills of chess playing, grow to love to play chess for itself and apart from any extraneous inducement. Following up on this example, he identifies "external goods" of chess playing as those for which there are "alternative ways for achieving such goods," for example, for the child in the illustration candy, and for adults "such goods as prestige, status and money." In contrast to this, he points out that "internal goods" for the practice of chess playing are those "which cannot be had in any way but by playing chess or some other game of that specific kind," and thus "those who lack the relevant experience are incompetent thereby as judges of internal goods" (MacIntyre, *After Virtue*, 187–88).
31. He also points out, through examples such as the practice of painting and cricket, that "external goods are therefore characteristically objects of competition in which there must be losers as well as winners," whereas "internal goods are indeed the outcome of competition to excel, but it is characteristic of them that their achievement is a good for the whole community who participate in the practice" (MacIntyre, *After Virtue*, 190–91).

> A virtue is an acquired human quality the possession and exercise of which tends to enable us to achieve those goods which are internal to practices and the lack of which effectively prevents us from achieving any such goods.[32]

Along these lines, he points out key virtues such as "justice, courage and honesty" as essential qualities for "any practice with internal goods and standards of excellence," if those goods internal to that particular practice are to be achieved (rather than merely external goods).[33]

Assuming that happy, flourishing, lifelong monogamy is an internal good in the field or practice of couple relationships, I suggest that virtues that help enable the realization of this good include in particular my proposed fivefold ethic, composed of prudence, justice, courage, temperance, and love and care.

It may perhaps be asked: "Why virtue ethics? What is so attractive about virtue ethics, compared to other approaches or moral theories?" (generally and particularly in the context of application to sexual ethics). In reply to such questions, I suggest that a virtue-ethical approach is more inclusive and flexible than a deontological or consequentialist approach, and may extend to include aspects of those other approaches. For example, exercising prudence in a particular situation may include having due regard for outcomes and helpful rules—while a virtue-ethical approach tends to be more focused on character, the being, rather than merely the action or doing.

As Biermann states well, "Virtue ethics is best seen not as an alternative or third way but, rather, as a wider view of the ethical task, one that encompasses the concerns and contributions of both deontological and [teleological or] utilitarian ethics."[34] Further, as Biermann (following Gilbert Meilaender) also points out:

> In contrast to a subjective morality of individual autonomy, an ethics of virtue contends that there do exist objective standards for human being, the pursuit of which is encouraged and enhanced by the adoption of virtues. . . . There are standards grounded in the authority of absolutes, and there is an end or a telos that serves as a goal for human beings.[35]

---

32. MacIntyre, *After Virtue*, 191.
33. MacIntyre, *After Virtue*, 191.
34. Biermann, *Case for Character*, ch. 1, 20.
35. Biermann, *Case for Character*, ch. 1, 22–23.

In a helpful overview of the different strands of contemporary Christian virtue ethics, Jennifer Herdt identifies the main strands as comprised mainly of:

i. "Natural Law TVE [theological virtue ethics]"—essentially amounting to Thomistic virtue ethics, that is, contemporary Catholic virtue ethics which Herdt describes as centered "primarily on Thomas Aquinas, and through Aquinas on his philosophical and theological sources and interlocutors," with distinguishing features including "its implicit commitment to the authority of Thomas's thought," "its defense of an integrated account of virtue ethics and natural law," along with its "distinction between the acquired and infused virtues and between the good as grasped through natural human capacities and the good as grasped by faith."[36]

ii. "Particularistic TVE"—described by Herdt as "generally [rejecting] the notion of a set of universal virtues grounded in human nature and basic natural inclinations," being generally "suspicious of natural law discourse" (along somewhat Barthian lines) and tending to be "more Augustinian in character," advanced in a Protestant vein (with the virtues perceived in terms of "gradual, grace-enabled formation" and the "growth of the gift of faith, rather than an autonomous, natural human achievement"), particularly seeking to "correct liberal theology without returning to a traditionalist orthodoxy" and characterized by an understanding of virtue ethics as "intelligible only within a shared tradition and way of life," focusing "on the Church as the site for the formation of genuine virtue" (exemplified, for example, in the thinking of Stanley Hauerwas).[37]

iii. "Analytic TVT" (theological virtue theory)—which Herdt notes is being advanced by scholars such as Linda Zagzebski (well known for her work in virtue epistemology, and going on to develop a "divine motivation theory" focused on "God's motives [as] perfectly good" and thus "God [as] the foundation of all moral value," with human beings meant to "imitate in particular God incarnate, Jesus Christ"),[38] "whose disciplinary homes are in departments of philosophy rather than in departments of religion or theology" and "[embracing] the traditional tasks of

---

36. Herdt, "Varieties," 226.
37. Herdt, "Varieties," 227–28.
38. Herdt, "Varieties," 229.

virtue theory: to systematize, simplify, and justify ethical discourse and practice.[39]

Herdt also points out "intersections" between Christian virtue ethics and strands of "agapic ethics" centered on love, along with debates regarding Fletcher's "situation ethics."[40]

On Thomistic virtue ethics, three key thinkers warrant further focus in this context. Within space constraints, I consider their views briefly here. First, Josef Pieper, in his approach to the virtues, sees himself in essence as endeavoring to "revive a classical heritage"[41] in which the cardinal virtues (of prudence, justice, courage, temperance), discernible at least as far back as in the works of Plato, and further in Aristotle, the Romans, Judaism and Christianity, are emphasized. Indeed, he describes the "doctrine of virtue" particularly in that fourfold framework as "one of the great discoveries in the history of man's self-understanding,"[42] and advances "that team of four, the basic virtues" as that which (following a classical phrase) "can enable man to attain the furthest potentialities of his nature."[43] In this task, Pieper finds it natural to draw on the work of Thomas Aquinas, whom Pieper considers to be a towering intellect in significantly advancing the Herculean task of reconciling reason with faith, "Aristotle" and "Bible,"[44] and through whom a voice of "the great tradition of human wisdom" can be heard.[45] Pieper's landmark work, *The Four Cardinal Virtues*,[46] thus contains many helpful reflections and practical insights as to how the classical

---

39. Herdt, "Varieties," 228.
40. Herdt, "Varieties," 230–31.
41. Pieper, *Four Cardinal Virtues*, Preface, xi.
42. Pieper, *Four Cardinal Virtues*, Preface, xi.
43. Pieper, *Four Cardinal Virtues*, Preface, xii.
44. Pieper, *Guide to Thomas Aquinas*, ch. 10.
45. Pieper, *Four Cardinal Virtues*, Preface, xiii.

46. In his interpretation of Thomas on virtue ethics, Pieper reminds of a hierarchy of the cardinal virtues, in the following order: prudence/wisdom, justice, fortitude/courage, temperance. According to Pieper (in his interpretation of Thomas) fortitude and temperance are necessarily subordinate to prudence and justice, that is, prudence and justice ought to be prior to fortitude and temperance—in order that evil might be kept in check. Thanks are due to Christopher Insole for reminding of this during lectures for the module God and the Good: Philosophy of Religion and Ethics, at Durham University.

tradition of the virtues, particularly in the fourfold formulation of the cardinal virtues, "[signifies] human rightness."[47]

Further, Jean Porter points out that: (i) Thomas always holds the virtues and natural law together in his moral theology,[48] and (ii) Thomas draws a clear distinction between the infused virtues and acquired virtues, particularly in the different ends that they are directed towards. In her account of Thomistic virtue ethics, while the theological virtues may only be infused (not acquired), the cardinal virtues may be infused by God or acquired (and thus directed towards different ends).[49] She observes that "Aquinas assigns to the theological virtues, and above all to charity, the unifying function toward which the cardinal virtues tend" and that "Aquinas holds that charity, rather than prudence, functions as the supreme organizing principle in the personality of the justified, by which not only all their actions but all their desires and impulses are directed toward God."[50] She also notes that Aquinas "insists that while, on the one hand, the cardinal virtues are finally inadequate without faith, hope, and charity, on the other hand, the theological virtues could not operate in an individual who lacked the proximate principles of human goodness, namely temperance, fortitude, justice, and prudence (I-II.65.3)."[51]

Finally, I consider briefly the views of Servais Pinckaers who is also authoritative in this field.[52] According to Pinckaers's exposition of Thomistic ethics, Thomas's system of moral theology was composed primarily of "virtues and gifts" and "dealt with sin only as the negation of virtue and saw legal precepts and obligations as aids to virtue."[53] He notes of this system as set out in the *Summa Theologica*:

47. Pieper, *Four Cardinal Virtues*, Preface, xi.
48. Porter, "Virtues and Vices," 272.
49. Porter, "Virtue Ethics," 93–94.
50. Porter, *Recovery of Virtue*, 169.
51. Porter, *Recovery of Virtue*, 171.
52. Among further scholars, Andrew Pinsent points out how distinct and different Aquinas's account of the virtues is from Aristotle's—even while Aquinas clearly has a detailed grasp of the *Nicomachean Ethics* and refers often to Aristotle (Pinsent, "Gifts and Fruits," 475–76). Alongside Aquinas's definition of "virtue," which is drawn from Lombard's *Sentences* rather than from the *Nicomachean Ethics*, and his distinct systems of "acquired virtues" and "infused virtues," it appears that Aquinas holds that only the infused virtues are "perfect" or "proper" virtues (475). In addition, alongside his vast detailed treatment of the virtues, Aquinas sets out an intricate network of gifts, beatitudes, and fruits of the Holy Spirit, which Pinsent (following Pinckaers) observes is connected in an "organic" way to the virtues in Aquinas's thought (476–77).
53. Pinckaers, *Sources of Christian Ethics*, 227.

> All his material was grouped around the major classical virtues provided by Christian tradition—faith, hope, and charity—and by those in the philosophical tradition—prudence, justice, temperance, and courage. To these, numerous other virtues were joined. All told, fifty-three virtues were discussed in individual questions or articles.[54]

Bearing in mind the key features of Thomistic virtue ethics highlighted by the above authorities, and adopting the language of Herdt's typology described earlier, it may be noted that my proposed fivefold ethic has more in common with the "natural law TVE" strand (Thomistic virtue ethics) than the "particularist TVE" strand. Hence, although I will offer my version of Christian virtue ethics as a possible version of "Protestant virtue ethics," it cannot be assumed that my version of virtue ethics shares any of the typical markers of the "particularist TVE" strand identified by Herdt. In the course of the next few sections of this chapter, I will show that my proposed version of Christian virtue ethics shares similarities with but also has key differences from the "natural law TVE" strand, typically understood to be Thomistic versions of virtue ethics—in particular that my proposed version is also built around the four classical cardinal virtues (prudence, justice, courage, and temperance), but these are underpinned and "recalibrated" (following Pinches's/Wright's use of the term) by the central, overarching virtue of love (particularly as described in 1 Cor 13), which I argue is also a (and indeed the primary) cardinal virtue.

Further (differing from both "natural law TVE" and "particularist TVE"), my version of Christian virtue ethics is grounded on an integrated reading of the *imago Dei* (explained in the next sections of this chapter) and Pauline theology, particularly on the question of what it means to be "truly human." In this more "Protestant" mode, I will therefore also be referring more to verses in Judeo-Christian Scripture, and aspects of Pauline theology, than to Thomas's *Summa Theologica* (while acknowledging the excellence of that great work and its enduring influence on subsequent thinkers). Further, as my version is centered around a universalizable concept of "true humanity," its focus will be on the cardinal virtues (in a fivefold formulation), and (differing from Thomistic versions) will not include discussion of separate theological or infused virtues (while I point out here that my version allows for the five proposed cardinal virtues to be acquired or infused).

---

54. Pinckaers, *Sources of Christian Ethics*, 227.

Briefly on how my version relates to Augustinian thought regarding the virtues, it is pertinent to note Saint Augustine's assertion in *City of God* that pagan virtue (that is, virtue without Christian faith) is not virtue after all[55]—giving rise to the concept of "splendid vices"—and his emphasis therefore on the theological virtues.[56] To clarify, I am not seeking here to overturn Augustine's understanding of true virtue as being ultimately centered in love for God and dependent on divine grace.[57] For present purposes and especially for application to sexual ethics, I only wish to point out that my proposed version of the cardinal virtues—particularly in terms of the fivefold ethic that will be elaborated on later in this chapter—differs from Augustine's version, including in his understanding of all the cardinal virtues as forms of love for God. While sharing Augustine's understanding of human agency as ultimately dependent on, and responsive to, divine grace, I wish to draw attention in my fivefold version of the cardinal virtues (building on Wright's thought) to the distinctive qualities of each of the classical cardinal virtues (prudence, justice, courage, temperance), that they each have their own unique character—and that stating that they are forms of love for God may mask the richness and complexity of each of these unique qualities as well as the horizontal dimension in the practice of these qualities[58]—even while I contend, agreeing with Wright, that they are "recalibrated" by the highest Christian virtue, love. I will explain this further when discussing my proposed fivefold ethic.

For my version of virtue ethics, differing from Augustine, I suggest that non-Christian virtue may still be genuine virtue to some degree—particularly as all (Christians and non-Christians) have still been made

---

55. See, for example, Augustine, *City of God* 19.25.

56. This appears consistent with, though perhaps also a further development from, Augustine's early views on the classical virtues, seeing them each and all as a form of love for God (Augustine, "On the Morals" 15.25).

57. In an excellent chapter explaining Augustinian thought on the virtues, Herdt highlights how human agency depends on divine grace for the formation of true virtue: "Augustine, then, argues that pagan philosophers and heroes are finally incapable of recognizing their own radical dependency on God in a way that opens them up to compassionate love of the world. In denigrating the humility of the Incarnation, they close themselves to the grace that would allow them to recognize the dependent character of their own agency and reach out to lift up the needs and cares of dependent others" ("Augustine on Grace and Worship," 116).

58. By "horizontal" I mean application in terms of relating to other creatures, human and nonhuman, contrasting with the "vertical," which is understood in terms of relating to God.

in the image of God, in the multifaceted sense that I will advance in the next sections. At the same time, I also suggest that Christians who have been deeply formed by Christian truth and are habitually responsive to the love and grace of God in Christ should be bearers of this image, including living this fivefold ethic, in its most discernible form, to closer to its fullest potential. In this, my thought is also along the lines of the Thomistic concept of "grace perfecting nature."

6.3 Developing a Multifaceted Integrated Model of Interpretation of the *Imago Dei* in Connection with Christian Virtue Ethics

6.3.1 Introduction

Given that there are many different versions of virtue ethics—even those identified as Christian strains of virtue ethics—it is necessary to consider the metaphysical and doctrinal underpinnings of the version of virtue ethics that I am advocating. To this end, I will turn to considering the key concept of the *imago Dei* in relation to the question of what constitutes true humanity and what it means to live in accordance to one's true, God-given nature.

It should be borne in mind that there remains no small amount of debate swirling around this concept.[59] At risk perhaps of some generalization, I approach this topic by means of a typology[60] (which has also been utilized by various contemporary scholars),[61] to assist in moving the discussion forward for this complex doctrine,[62] within the allowable space.

---

59. Cortez and Jensen describe the debates as "something of a test case for the relationship between biblical exegesis and systematic theology" (*T&T Clark Reader*, 73).

60. This may also be regarded as a form of heuristic device, somewhat akin, for example, to ideal types (discussed at the beginning of ch. 2).

61. For example, Shults, *Reforming Theological Anthropology*; Cortez, *Theological Anthropology*.

62. My thanks to Michael Burdett for excellent teaching, introducing me to the several diverse readings of the *imago Dei* discussed here.

Very briefly:

i. The term "structural" or "substantialist" model refers to classical models of interpretation of the *imago Dei* most closely associated with essentialism—typically based on capacities that are supposed to distinguish humans from nonhuman creatures, most prominently "reason" (or rationality) and "freedom."

ii. The term "functional" or "royal" model refers to views—often regarded as closest to the few biblical texts with this term—most widely held by scholars of the Hebrew Bible/Old Testament, interpreting Gen 1:26–27 in terms of vocation, role, or calling, particularly regarding humanity as God's (royal) representatives on earth, destined to rule over creation (but not necessarily by domination, and indeed more preferably through care and nurture).

iii. The term "relational" model refers to views based on relationality—humans relating to God, other humans, and other (nonhuman) creatures, and God relating to humans. It is often expressed in terms of (God's) divine address and human response. It may also find consonance with themes of relationality discernible within the doctrine of the Trinity, and themes of sociality and community.

iv. The term "dynamic," "Christocentric," and/or "eschatological" model refers to models centered on the person of Jesus Christ, and which pay special regard to New Testament discussions of the *imago*, particularly in terms of the *imago Christi*. These views tend to emphasize the dynamic (rather than static) nature of human beings, with the created potential for openness to others and to God, that may transcend the earthly self and which is focused ultimately on Jesus Christ, Christlikeness, and fellowship with God as the fulfilment of human destiny.

In this section, after considering four models of the *imago Dei*, I will contend that an integrated multifaceted model of the *imago Dei* (the dynamic or eschatological model, in combination with the relational model, and adapted aspects of the functional model, based on stewardship and a noble vocation to serve creation) is most helpful for application in contemporary contexts.[63]

---

63. Parts of this section, and the next sections, were included in my paper "*Imago Dei*." Thanks are due to those present at the Society for the Study of Christian Ethics' online conference who responded with helpful feedback.

Attempts to speak of "Protestant" versions of virtue ethics tend to provoke worries about "works righteousness" and the potential erosion of core tenets of Protestantism, such as *sola gratia* (by grace alone) and *sola fide* (by faith alone), though there have been various efforts by scholars through the years to reconcile the concepts of divine grace and human agency. In his 2008 essay N. T. Wright connects Christian virtue ethics with formation in Christian character, and develops a version of virtue ethics based on Pauline theology. As mentioned, the version of virtue ethics that I advocate in this chapter is based on an integrated version of the *imago Dei* (developed in this section), and builds particularly on Wright's approach in his 2008 essay. I contend that this Christocentric and eschatological approach to virtue ethics fits well with Protestant theology (and hence present it as a version of "Protestant virtue ethics"). I begin by discussing the concept of the *imago Dei*, to consider what being "truly human" in Judeo-Christian terms might mean,[64] particularly also as Wright's 2008 essay also refers to image bearing and a process of becoming more fully and truly human, particularly in Judeo-Christian terms.

6.3.2 Functional/"Royal" Model of Interpretation of the *Imago Dei*

Often revolving around the concept of "dominion" based on rule over creation, with humans acting as God's representatives on earth—and particularly arising from interpretations of the core passages of Gen 1:26-28 and Ps 8:5-8—this is one of the most recent models of the *imago Dei*, stemming from modern, particularly historical-critical, biblical scholarship.[65] It also takes account of significant findings about the practices of ancient Near East kings seen as reflecting the image of the

---

64. There are of course other significant topics in the vast field of theological anthropology that may be discussed besides the *imago Dei*, but these are beyond the scope of this book, and I argue here that particular consideration of the complex concept of the *imago Dei* (that human beings are created in the image of God) is an important place to start when speaking of "being human" in Judeo-Christian terms. I am also generally in agreement with Marc Cortez's argument that "the *imago Dei* stands at the center of any adequate theological anthropology," and his delineation of the following seven key affirmations—Christocentricity, relative uniqueness, mystery, relationality, responsibility, embodiment, brokenness—as "building blocks" for understanding the human person (*Theological Anthropology*, 37–40).

65. Shults, *Reforming Theological Anthropology*, loc. 2462 of 3467.

deity, and placing images of themselves in far-flung places to remind subjects of their dominion.

Although it prevails among Old Testament biblical scholars and is probably closest to the biblical texts on the image of God, a key objection to this model is that it carries the risk of abuse and application in patriarchal and/or oppressive ways. This is expressed notably in objections by feminist writers, and by those, such as Lynn White concerned about the environmental/ecological crisis.[66]

Yet, I contend it is helpful to bear in mind, as Van Huyssteen also notes, "Dominion is expressed in stewardship, nurture, and responsibility toward the things God loves."[67] This reminds of Jesus's exhortation, "For everyone to whom much is given, from him much will be required" (Luke 12:48 NKJV). Also affirming a functional interpretation of the *imago Dei*, Gordon Wenham asserts:

> The strongest case has been made for the view that the divine image makes man God's vice-regent on earth. Because man is God's representative, his life is sacred: every assault on man is an affront to the creator and merits the ultimate penalty (Gen 9:5–6) . . . this . . . describes the function or the consequences of the divine image; it does not pinpoint what the image is in itself.[68]

Hence it appears there is the concept of a noble vocation/calling implied in this model of the *imago Dei*, revolving around the idea of stewardship and humans' accountability to God for how we care for others, for fellow creatures, both human and nonhuman animals, and for all of creation. I therefore suggest that the functional model, if applied with this "stewardship" perspective, rather than abused (with an overemphasis on the idea of "dominion," too often associated with "domination"), should not be discarded and contributes an important angle to interpretations of the *imago Dei*.

6.3.3 Structural/Substantialist Model

Based around the idea of there being some quality/capacity inherent in human beings that makes the human unique and a bearer of the image of God, this view has probably the longest history reaching back to

---

66. Middleton, "Liberating Image?," 14. See also White, "Historical Roots."
67. Van Huyssteen, *Alone in the World?*, 121.
68. Wenham, *Genesis 1–15*, 31.

patristic times, and reaching its height in the Middle Ages, for example, in Aquinas's thinking. Notable is the significant influence of Greek philosophy (including from Aristotle and also Heraclitus, the Stoics, and others) on the early development of this model, particularly with the idea of rationality being the central defining characteristic of being human.[69] Boethius's definition (reflecting the influence of Augustine in his emphasis on the mind—constituted by memory, understanding, and will—as the image of God), asserted:

> [A person is] the individual substance of a rational creature.[70]

Of further concern, this emphasis on reason was also often connected with patriarchal inclinations, as it carried implications that males (viewed as being more endowed with reason than females) had stronger ties to the image of God than females who were viewed as being more bound by their embodied natures.[71]

Irenaeus's approach (while being focused on Jesus Christ as the image of God, and humans following in his likeness) distinguished between "image" (Latin: *imago*, Hebrew: *tselem*)—unaffected by the fall—and "likeness" (Latin: *similitudo*, Hebrew: *demut*)—affected by the fall. This was developed by Aquinas, who referred to the former as our essential nature ("rationality") and the latter as a supernatural gift, restored in Christ ("righteousness"). A move towards collapsing the "image-likeness" distinction—and contending that all of the human is marred by sin—tended to be significant for the Reformers,[72] who sought to "uphold total depravity" and emphasize justification by faith.[73] However, while there was some enthusiasm for "the early Reformer's insight that the image of God has to do with the real and whole human being"[74] (that is, that the real human is constituted of "both the dignity and the misery" of being human),[75] there seems to have been a lost opportunity here, as seventeenth-century Protestant Scholastics generally continued to be bound by medieval assumptions in this matter, and continued to adhere to structural approaches.

69. Grenz, *Social God*, 143–44.
70. Boethius, *Treatise Against Eutyches and Nestorius* 3.1.
71. Shults, *Reforming Theological Anthropology*, loc. 2381 of 3467.
72. Shults, *Reforming Theological Anthropology*, locs. 2355, 2406, 2413 of 3467.
73. Shults, *Reforming Theological Anthropology*, loc. 2457 of 3467.
74. Shults, *Reforming Theological Anthropology*, loc. 2432 of 3467.
75. Shults, *Reforming Theological Anthropology*, loc. 2423 of 3467.

Grenz points out two main capacities as distinguishing marks in humans of the divine image, according to this model: reason and will, seen by most early Christian theologians as "two [closely connected] aspects of the single rationality with which God endowed humans."[76] Qualities often emphasized for this model include rationality, spirituality, language, self-awareness, and culture.

Critique of this model comes especially from challenges from modern science—particularly evolutionary science—including discoveries which challenge concepts of the sanctity or uniqueness of human life. For example, animal studies show various nonhuman animals bearing certain similar capacities to humans, at least on a basic level, and at times even in surprisingly developed ways—including for rationality, self-awareness, and language. Space limitations do not allow for further discussion of this complex matter here.

As Middleton observes astutely, interpreters here have tended to ask "not an exegetical, but a speculative, question: in what way are humans like God and unlike animals?"[77] One of the matters of concern here is that following this model one may end up with quite arbitrary criteria of what characteristics pass the test and what do not—"test" characteristics which may be affected by whatever stream of thinking is currently in vogue in wider society, and also quite easily challenged by findings in modern science, including evolutionary science.[78]

6.3.4 Relational Model

An illustration of this model may be seen in Paul Ramsey's description of the image of God as "a relationship *within which* man sometimes stands, whenever like a mirror he obediently reflects God's will in his life and actions."[79] This model may be expressed in terms of the relationship of divine address and response between the Creator God and human creatures.

Possibly reaching its height during the nineteenth and twentieth centuries, this view is focused on the inherent sociality in human beings—that is, humans are created for community, to be relational, even

---

76. Grenz, *Social God*, 144.

77. Middleton, *Liberating Image*, 17.

78. Nevertheless, there are contemporary defenders of the substantialist model, and this model of interpretation of the *imago Dei* has not necessarily been superseded.

79. Ramsey, *Basic Christian Ethics*, 255; emphasis in original.

as God the Three-in-One is relational. This model is thus closely linked to the Trinitarian view of God, while also engaging with existentialist philosophy, addressing "current human existence rather than focusing on the first parents in paradise."[80]

While there are various prominent advocates of the model, including Brunner, Barth's particular influence towards its development may be noted, including as observed by Van Huyssteen:

> For Barth the image of God does not consist of anything humans are or do, but rather of the amazing ability or gift to be in a relationship with God.[81]

Notably also for Barth, humanity consists essentially of being male and female—on his account, Adam was fundamentally incomplete in his creation in the image of God until the creation of Eve, who became "I" to his "Thou."[82] Shedding further light on this, Lisa Stephenson observes that for Barth "humans display the *imago Dei* in a twofold sense: by being created as a 'Thou' whom God as an 'I' can confront, and by being created as male and female, existing in an I-Thou relationship to one another."[83]

This view is, however, not immune to criticism. One criticism, for example, in the context of Barth's version of it, is that it may not necessarily be clearly linked to and strongly grounded in the biblical texts on the *imago Dei*, although there have also been scholarly defences of the view, including arguments that a relational perspective may be considered integral to the Genesis texts.

6.3.5 Dynamic/Eschatological Model

With advocates such as Moltmann and Pannenberg (who emphasized the dynamic nature of human beings with the capacity for openness to others and to God, that transcends the self and which is focused ultimately on Jesus Christ, Christlikeness, and fellowship with God as the fulfilment of

---

80. Shults, *Reforming Theological Anthropology*, loc. 2488 of 3467.

81. Van Huyssteen, *Alone in the World?*, 136–37.

82. Barth, *Doctrine of Creation*, 308–9. For example, he states: "God's whole intercourse with man will now be strictly related to man conjoined as male and female and existing as I and Thou, and therefore to humanity" (308); "Masculinity and femininity themselves, in their differentiation and unity, constituted humanity" (309). It is also likely that in his reference to "I-Thou" relations, Barth relied at least to some extent on Martin Buber's thought (Buber, *I and Thou*).

83. Stephenson, "Directed, Ordered and Related," 439.

human destiny),[84] this model is both Christocentric and eschatological in focus. It is sometimes linked to the other models, particularly the relational. Developed partly "as a result of an increased exegetical focus on the message of Jesus Christ about the coming Kingdom of God,"[85] it views "the *imago Dei* as humankind's divinely given goal or destiny, which lies in the eschatological future and toward which humans are directed."[86]

In this interpretation, the concept of the image of God is rooted in Christ, the second Adam, as the fullness of God's image (Col 1:15–20 and 1 Cor 15:47–49). Christ is the "first-born" to whom believers "are to become like in form" (Rom 8:29).[87] Linked with the concept of sanctification, this model emphasizes that as humans become more Christlike, through the work of the Holy Spirit, they reflect God's image more (2 Cor 3:17–18). Pauline theology traces this hope for humankind—in a trajectory from fallen humanity, through the first Adam, to redeemed humanity in and through Christ, the second Adam. As Moltmann reminds:

> In the messianic light of the gospel, the human being's likeness to God appears as a historical process with an eschatological termination; it is not a static condition. *Being* human means *becoming* human in this process.[88]

Relationality may also be seen as an integral part of the dynamic/eschatological view.[89] As Moltmann also observes: "Likeness to God cannot be lived in isolation. It can only be lived in human community."[90]

Further, an important aspect of the dynamic/eschatological view of the *imago Dei* involves looking forward towards the resurrection—the

---

84. See, for example, Pannenberg, *Systematic Theology*, vol. 2, ch. 8, locs. 2724, 2799, 2811, 2862, 2875, 2899 of 8322.

85. Shults, *Reforming Theological Anthropology*, loc. 2512 of 3467.

86. Grenz, *Social God*, 177.

87. Moltmann, *God in Creation*, 218.

88. Moltmann, *God in Creation*, 227; emphasis in original.

89. A different but related expression of this view may perhaps be seen even in part in David Kelsey's magnum opus on theological anthropology, *Eccentric Existence*, that advances in Trinitarian and Christocentric perspective the centrality of God relating to all that is not God—including human beings—in terms of creation, eschatological consummation, and reconciliation. For Kelsey, human beings are "imagers of the image of God" in terms of being "finite living mysteries that image the triune living mystery" and this is centered on Jesus Christ, whom Kelsey describes as "the paradigmatic human creature" who "is paradigmatically the glory of God simply in his own creaturely humanity" (1009–10).

90. Moltmann, *God in Creation*, 222.

believers' hope of "bearing Christ's heavenly image in the resurrection," which the apostle Paul declares in 1 Cor 15:42–49.[91] Shults states this well:

> The essence of human creatureliness is disclosed by its end—being formed by the Spirit into the image of Jesus Christ. The *imago Dei* as the goal of personal and communal being, the telos of humanity, was revealed in the resurrection of the incarnate Word and the outpouring of the Spirit at Pentecost.[92]

This Christocentric emphasis may also be perceived in Daniel Migliore's assertions that the doctrine of the *imago Dei* must necessarily be centered on Christ (even as he affirms a relational interpretation of the doctrine):

> The image of God is not like an image permanently stamped on a coin; it is more like an image reflected in a mirror. That is, human beings are created for life in relationships that mirror or correspond to God's own life in relationship. In light of the history of Jesus Christ, Christian faith and theology are led to interpret the *imago Dei* as an *imago Christi* and an *imago trinitatis*.
>
> . . . For Christian faith, Jesus Christ is the fullest expression of what God intends humanity to be. This human being is the "image of God" (2 Cor 4:4, Col. 1:15) and our human destiny in him is to be conformed to the image of God. Hence the form of human life that we meet in Jesus Christ will surely be the decisive factor in any Christian statement of what it means to be genuinely human.[93]

6.3.6 An Integrated Multifaceted Model of the *imago Dei*

I suggest that an integrated multifaceted approach—combining dynamic/eschatological interpretations with the relational model and vocational/stewardship aspect of the functional model—is most compelling, as it is well grounded in the biblical texts relevant to the *imago Dei*, both in the Old and New Testaments, accords well with interdisciplinary studies and is robust in the face of contemporary challenges. Further, valuable parts of the classical/substantialist model (without the patriarchal or misogynistic implications of early versions of the model)—particularly

---

91. Grenz, *Social God*, 233.
92. Shults, *Reforming Theological Anthropology*, loc. 2573 of 3467.
93. Migliore, *Faith Seeking Understanding*, 145–46.

regarding the unique human potential to be in relationship with God—may be recovered and seen as integral to the relational or dynamic model, as these models encompass both the capacity and potential to be in relationship with God and others.

While proceeding with the dynamic/eschatological model as core, this approach also includes the vital aspect of the relational, as it reflects the Trinitarian nature of God, and the essential element of communion/fellowship at the heart of human existence, echoing also John 17:3. It further includes the important concept of vocation/calling and stewardship from the functional model, but avoids the overemphasis on "dominion" (which too often connotes "domination") and the substantial potential for abuse associated with this, as discussed above. The *imago Dei* should therefore, in accordance with the biblical material, be seen in terms of the human destiny to rule over (steward) the earth as God's representatives, but this should be grounded in love, following in the way of Christ.

This integrated model is consistent with the trajectory of the biblical story. With the fall, the original human vocation, which accorded with God's original purpose for humankind, had been distorted and corrupted into abusive forms of seeking and wielding power. There has however been restoration through Jesus's life, death and resurrection. Connected with this, the relational model bases human uniqueness on humanity's special relationship with God, while the dynamic model is most flexible, emphasizing the future, and transformation in Christ. This has practical application across a range of contemporary issues—including bioethics (particularly euthanasia, abortion, human enhancement), human rights, and sexual ethics, including where questions of human dignity and justice are concerned.

Aspects of this view may also be seen reflected in Middleton's argument based on the biblical texts that:

> Humanity created in God's image—and the church as the renewed *imago Dei*—is called and empowered to be God's multi-sided prism in the world, reflecting and refracting the Creator's brilliant light into a rainbow of cultural activity and socio-political patterns that scintillates with the glory of God's presence and manifests his reign of justice.[94]

---

94. Middleton, "Liberating Image?," 24–25.

CHAPTER 6: LIVING MORE HUMAN(E)LY? 229

It may be borne in mind that patristic[95] and medieval thinkers do have complex concepts of what constitutes human nature. However, it is also necessary to caution that views approximating the substantialist view should not be appropriated in such a way as to focus narrowly on features that distinguish humans from nonhuman animals and signal human likeness to God. It is necessary to point out that a substantialist view based on capacities has a reductionistic tendency that may not adequately reflect the full complexity of the concept of the *imago Dei*.[96] I endeavor to highlight more of this complexity by referring to other models of interpretation of the *imago Dei*, and ultimately by proposing a multifaceted integrated model of the *imago Dei* as a basis for discussion of what it means to be human in theological and ethical terms. David Clough also argues that the move away from substantialist interpretations of *the imago Dei* among theologians and the development of functional and relational models of this concept[97] indicates that "the long theological enterprise of seeking to identify a particular unique human characteristic with the divine image has been brought to an end."[98]

Overall, I contend for an integrated multifaceted model in which the *imago Dei* is understood in terms of the God-given potential in human creatures to be formed in Christlikeness and their vocation to be God's representatives in creation, which, particularly since the fall, is only fully realizable through the person and work of Jesus Christ. In this there are elements of both the "now" and the "not yet," of both the present and the future. With a functional/royal, Christological and eschatological focus, it is also deeply relational in emphasis. It encompasses humanity's destiny to "rule the earth," not in domineering, oppressive, manipulative nor exploitative ways, but, rather, in genuine self-giving love, stewardship, and humility, in the way of Christ.

Connecting this with Pieper's reference to the "furthest potentialities" of human nature, mentioned earlier,[99] I argue that this multifaceted and integrated interpretation of the *imago Dei* that I advance here is a

95. See, for example, Gabrielle Thomas's insightful study of Gregory Nazianzen's multifaceted concept of the *imago Dei* in Thomas, *Image of God*.

96. Also cautioning against narrow readings of the *imago Dei* and arguing for a performative interpretation—understanding the image of God in terms of a verb (imaging God) rather than a noun (in terms of a static focus on capacities)—see MacFadyen, "Redeeming the Image."

97. Described, for example, by Wenham, *Genesis 1–15*.

98. Clough, *On Animals*, 66.

99. Pieper, *Four Cardinal Virtues*, Preface, xii.

substantial expression of what these human potentialities consist of. What is humanity, what kind of creature is the human, and what is humanity called to be? I answer that humanity is made in the image of God—in the full-fledged functional/royal, relational, and dynamic and eschatological meanings of the phrase set out above: (i) that humanity is created royal, and hence called to lead or rule in creation (as the "children of God" [Rom 8:19–21 NIV]) not in domineering or dominating spirit, but in humility and love in the way of Christ; (ii) that the human being is at heart a relational creature and made for flourishing in relationship with God and others; and (iii) ultimately that the human being is called to be conformed to Christ (Rom 8:29) in all that Christlikeness means. In all of this—human vocation, purpose/telos, calling, and destiny—I agree with Pieper that the four cardinal virtues have a vital role, enabling the human being to "attain the furthest potentialities of his nature."[100] Elaborating on the word "potentialities," I understand this in terms of the multifaceted and integrated version of the *imago Dei* I have advanced and described above. Further, I add to Pieper's insights by contending, developing on N. T. Wright's argument in his 2008 essay, that to fully enable the human being to attain these "furthest potentialities of [her/his] nature," the four classical cardinal virtues need to be recalibrated by the highest Christian virtue, love, and that love should in fact be understood as a fifth and overarching cardinal virtue, in the spirit of 1 Cor 13.

I will elaborate on this in the next sections of this chapter. Further, it is my contention that the more mature and developed we human creatures are in growth in these five cardinal virtues, the closer we will be in living towards our full potential as bearers of the image of God.[101]

6.4 On the Cardinal Virtues, Judeo-Christian Scripture, and Christian Virtue Ethics

6.4.1 Virtue Ethics and Pauline Theology

There are various forms of virtue ethics, some not related to Christianity. A virtue-ethical approach typically involves considerations of virtue (*arête*), practical wisdom (*phronesis*), and, often, happiness/flourishing

---

100. Pieper, *Four Cardinal Virtues*, Preface, xii.

101. Realistically, this will take a lifetime and more, even for the most well-endowed humans, and I also accept that this process can only be fully completed through divine grace.

CHAPTER 6: LIVING MORE HUMAN(E)LY?

(*eudaimonia*).[102] Porter defines "virtue" as a "praiseworthy, admirable or desirable" trait, formed over time as a relatively stable quality, character, or disposition[103]—habituated, rather than easily changeable. She observes that Christian virtue ethics need not be restricted to Aristotelian/Thomistic versions or Hauerwas's communitarian approach, but may be discerned in a variety of different approaches.[104]

Despite tensions between concepts of divine grace and human agency and free will in discussions that attempt to reconcile Protestant thought with virtue ethics, it should not be assumed that Protestant theology is inherently opposed to a virtue-ethical perspective. Several scholars in recent years have published work relating Protestant theology to virtue ethics.[105] Indeed, Pieter Vos argues in his recent book that "Protestantism has never abandoned virtue ethics at all."[106]

As mentioned, I seek to advance in this chapter a version of "Protestant" virtue ethics based on my reading of the doctrine of the *imago Dei* (the integrated version advanced in the previous section), focused on a vision of what "being truly human" means in Judeo-Christian terms. My proposed version of virtue ethics also draws partly from the thought of the New Testament scholar, N. T. Wright, an expert on Pauline theology. In summary, Wright sets out his Christian approach to virtue ethics in eschatological terms as follows:

> The Christian teaching and practice of virtue, then, can be understood in terms of the life that is lived within the story whose goal, whose *telos*, is that complete, redeemed, renewed, and perfected human life, within God's new and redeemed heaven and earth and among God's restored people.[107]

Wright distinguishes his version of virtue ethics from Aristotle's including by noting that Aristotelian virtue is based on rationality, whereas Wright proposes a version of the classical virtues "recalibrated" by the

---

102. Hursthouse and Pettigrove, "Virtue Ethics."
103. Porter, "Virtue Ethics," 87.
104. Porter, "Virtue Ethics," 98.
105. Recent examples of Protestant approaches to virtue ethics include Biermann, *Case for Character*; Nolan, *Reformed Virtue After Barth*; Moberly, *Virtue of Bonhoeffer's Ethics*; Cochran, *Protestant Virtue and Stoic Ethics*. As mentioned above, Jennifer Herdt identifies different strands of contemporary Christian virtue ethics ("Varieties").
106. Vos, *Longing for the Good Life*, 14.
107. N. T. Wright, "Faith, Virtue, Justification," loc. 5214 of 10812.

highest Christian virtue, love. In this he also speaks in eschatological terms, emphasizing the life of love as part of the believer's telos:

> For the Christian, virtue is the practiced art of being the sort of person who is already anticipating, in the present, the life of the coming age. The point of 1 Corinthians 13 is that love is not our duty; it is our *destiny*.[108]

Thus, among other key themes, Wright discusses with significant regard the cardinal virtues from the classical tradition and "translates these into a Christian mode,"[109] particularly by bringing these into conversation with Pauline theology. Hence, in addition to the theological virtues of faith, hope, and love (notably of 1 Cor 13), he argues that the cardinal virtues of temperance, courage, justice, and prudence continue to be relevant "goals" on a Christian's journey and may be "redeemed," that is, regarded in terms of God's grace, rather than considered primarily in terms of "unaided human effort" (as in Pelagianism[110] or semi-Pelagianism).[111] As examples, he draws parallels between "temperance" and "self-control" (from Gal 5:23) and between "prudence" and "wisdom" in the Judeo-Christian tradition,[112] and describes "wisdom" as "recalibrating pagan prudence" in light of the highest Christian virtue, love.[113]

Building on Wright's thinking (and based on my integrated version of the *imago Dei* advanced earlier), I argue for a Christocentric and eschatological version of Christian virtue ethics—based on character formation in genuine Christlikeness as reflected in Judeo-Christian Scripture and becoming more truly human (fulfilling the spirit of the law, rather than merely the letter of it) in ways that Jesus made possible. This involves humanity living in view of its telos (an eschatological perspective, with a firm hope of resurrected life in the new heaven and new earth, through the finished work of Christ)—working in forming the virtues as particular "strengths" (as Wright describes it) to develop on our journey, in light of and in anticipation of our future—as redeemed humanity, eventually reaching the final goal of becoming "our full and

---

108. N. T. Wright, "Faith, Virtue, Justification," loc. 5214 of 10812; emphasis in original.

109. N. T. Wright, in email to author, July 16, 2016.

110. Which may be colloquially understood as "pulling oneself up by one's own bootstraps."

111. N. T. Wright, "Faith, Virtue, Justification," loc. 5176 of 10812.

112. N. T. Wright, "Faith, Virtue, Justification," locs. 5226, 5236 of 10812.

113. N. T. Wright, "Faith, Virtue, Justification," loc. 5224 of 10812.

true selves."[114] Discussing this process of formation and sharing some connections with traditional approaches to virtue ethics emphasizing narrative, communities, exemplars and practices, Wright also argues elsewhere that, in practical terms, such spiritual formation develops best in the "virtuous circle" that he proposes, emphasizing Scripture, stories, examples, community, and practices.[115]

Further on Protestant theology and formation in virtue, and the relation between divine grace and human agency, I propose to bring into the conversation observations from John Barclay, particularly from *Paul and the Gift*. Barclay reminds us that the gift of God's grace to us in Christ is not "cheap" and does not exclude the concept of a transformed life in response to that gift, as he observes:

> Already in [Rom] 5:12–21 there are indications that the Christ-gift is not morally vacuous, an unconditional gift that winks at human sin: it contains transformative power....
>
> Gifts convey power as gifts; attention to the ancient dynamics of gift would indicate that "cheap grace" (gifts expecting nothing in return) was not an option in ancient thought.[116]

Relevant to the present discussion regarding virtues and the place of the classical tradition, Barclay also reminds that the new Christian mode of thinking about the virtues is not entirely inconsistent with the prevailing tradition of that time, although there will be recalibration:

> The "transformation" Paul expects of believers in the "renewal of the mind" (12:2) will not clash at every point with the modes of behavior common in their surroundings: there will be some overlap in the recognition of what is "good" and "bad" (12:17;13:3) and no inevitable clash with the interests of the governing authorities (13:1–7). But the new orientation to the Lord (12:11) will involve a mindset whose assumptions, priorities, and dispositions are newly configured, in differentiation from "this age" (12:2).[117]

At the same time, Barclay draws out the newness of the life lived by the believer through the resurrection power of Christ, emphasizing that:

---

114. N. T. Wright, "Faith, Virtue, Justification," loc. 5137 of 10812.
115. Tom Wright, *Virtue Reborn*, 221–44.
116. Barclay, *Paul and the Gift*, 496, 499.
117. Barclay, *Paul and the Gift*, 509.

> Christian "obedience" thus responds to the prior, incongruous gift of God in Christ. . . . To live from faith is to "put on the Lord Christ Jesus" (13:14), whose presence in power motivates, enables, and shapes their patterns of behavior (15:1–3).[118]

Barclay also highlights the noncompetitive nature of the relationship between divine grace and human agency, "because the life of the believer is . . . [in a radical kind of eccentric dependence] derived from Christ,"[119] and, essentially, this enables each to grow in Christlike humanity:

> God's grace does not exclude, deny, or displace believing agents; they are not reduced to passivity or pure receptivity. Rather, it generates and grounds an active, willed conformity to the Christ-life, in which believers become, like Christ, truly human, as obedient agents (5:19).[120]

Further on the question of moral standards, it is important to note Barclay's clarification that "Paul certainly expects that the moral incongruity of the Christian life will be reduced over time," as Christian believers' being bound to righteousness in Christ "draws them toward holiness" and therefore "in that sense, what began as a morally incongruous gift will be completed as a morally congruous gift."[121]

Formation in Christian character/virtue as described above involves moral effort and habituation.[122] From a Protestant virtue-ethical perspective, such moral effort is not "unaided human effort"[123] but a response to God's love and grace (1 John 4:19) and enabled by the Holy Spirit. As Barclay observes, "Christian obedience is thus vital, but only ever in a responsive mode."[124]

6.4.2 Living the Life of Genuine Humanity: A Christian Virtue-Ethical Approach

On the matter of interpretation of passages of Scripture for formulating my approach, it is helpful to note that in *Proving Doctrine*, Kelsey lists the

---

118. Barclay, *Paul and the Gift*, 517.
119. Barclay, *Paul and the Gift*, 518.
120. Barclay, *Paul and the Gift*, 518.
121. Barclay, *Paul and the Gift*, 517.
122. Brad Kallenberg explains this well ("Virtue Ethics").
123. N. T. Wright, "Faith, Virtue, Justification," loc. 5147 of 10812.
124. Barclay, *Paul and the Gift*, 518.

following four diagnostic questions for analyzing different theologians' ways of approaching Scripture for authorizing their theological proposals:

i. What aspects of Scripture is (are) taken to be authoritative?

ii. What is it about this aspect of Scripture that makes it authoritative?

iii. What sort of logical force is ascribed to the Scripture to which appeal is made?

iv. How is the Scripture that is cited brought to bear on theological proposals so as to authorize them?[125]

Further, in considering how scholars authorize their theological proposals or conclusions, Kelsey suggests an approach following Stephen Toulmin's analysis, identifying, among other elements, "data" and "warrants," along with "backing" where necessary, to support a claim or conclusion.[126] This reminder from Kelsey of such questions in relation to hermeneutics is relevant for present purposes as I seek to establish a biblical basis for my proposed version of Christian virtue ethics (as distinct from traditional Thomistic versions) for application to sexual ethics. Due to space constraint, I will not be exploring Kelsey's approach beyond this. Without using the terminology mentioned nor venturing to discuss the merits or demerits of Kelsey's approach (which are outside the scope of this book), but considering the diagnostic questions posed above and as a partial answer to them, I propose in this chapter to draw on William Webb's redemptive-movement hermeneutic as a helpful lens through which to read texts of Scripture[127] to discern fruitful ways of interpreting the concept of the *imago Dei* and build a version of Protestant virtue ethics, particularly in terms of my proposed fivefold ethic, for application to sexual ethics.

A relevant question for this chapter is: "Based on Judeo-Christian Scripture, should virtue ethics (including the fivefold ethic advanced here) be a key focus for Christians?" To answer this question along the lines of the above diagnostic questions (and borrowing Webb's term of the "ultimate ethic" from his redemptive-movement hermeneutic), my claim is that Judeo-Christian Scripture should be read in light of the ultimate ethic to live in genuine humanity, particularly in terms of the

125. Kelsey, *Proving Doctrine*, 2–3.

126. Kelsey, *Proving Doctrine*, 125–38.

127. My thanks to Elizabeth Shively for first introducing me to David Kelsey's thought and William Webb's work.

image of God being restored in humans through the life, death, and resurrection of Jesus—and this may be seen particularly in the life of Christ, whom we are to follow and imitate, including as our ultimate moral exemplar (and King). In connection with this, I contend that a key aspect of living this life of genuine humanity is to reflect the character of God, as revealed in various parts of Scripture (some of which will be set out below) and in Jesus Christ. Cardinal qualities (from which other qualities may be understood as derived) of this character include justice, wisdom and truth, temperance, courage (all as described in various passages of Scripture), and love as described particularly in 1 Cor 13 and other relevant passages. My conclusion is thus that virtue ethics (including in terms of the fivefold ethic proposed in this chapter) should indeed be a key focus for Christians, and I argue that this is borne out in Judeo-Christian Scripture, interpreted as above.

Webb emphasizes a "redemptive-movement" hermeneutic that is consistent with Scripture[128] and allows for movement "beyond the concrete specificity of the biblical text,"[129] on the basis of movement toward an "ultimate ethic."[130] Webb contends that his redemptive-movement hermeneutic provides "crucial meaning" that is often lost when interpreters confine their readings to a static meaning within the text (that may perhaps be considered akin to a literalistic approach).[131] He argues for a more dynamic approach that involves applying "a trajectory or logical extension of the Bible's redemptive spirit that carries Christians to an ultimate ethic."[132] He asserts that a redemptive-movement hermeneutic is a subset (rather than a rejection) of the historical-grammatical method, and thus also reminds that historical or contextual aspects of the text should not be neglected in interpretation. Webb thus advocates redemptive movement *beyond* the outright provisions of the canon, towards an "ultimate ethic" consistent with the underlying spirit of the Christian story. This differs from a movement hermeneutic that is confined within the canon.

Without necessarily endorsing Webb's views on particular ethical issues (detailed discussion of which is not practicable here),[133] I seek to

128. Webb, "Redemptive-Movement Model," 217.
129. Webb, "Redemptive-Movement Model," 247.
130. Webb, "Redemptive-Movement Model," 217.
131. Webb, "Redemptive-Movement Model," 221.
132. Webb, "Redemptive-Movement Model," 217.
133. Webb sets out his views on slavery, women's roles, and homosexuality in detail in *Slaves, Women & Homosexuals*.

CHAPTER 6: LIVING MORE HUMAN(E)LY?

draw particular attention to the concept of the "ultimate ethic" advanced by Webb for interpretation of passages of Scripture relevant to ethics. In the present context, I suggest that this should be connected to the question of what it means to be truly human, and particularly to the core concept of the *imago Dei* discussed above. I therefore argue for reading and interpreting Scripture through a version of a redemptive-movement hermeneutic—based on the concept of an "ultimate ethic"—that is focused on what a life of genuine humanity or redeemed humanity involves—and I suggest that this can and should be allied to a virtue-ethical approach to reading Judeo-Christian Scripture, in the sense of the Christocentric version of virtue ethics that I seek to advance. I also contend that 1 Cor 13 is particularly central in this context.

While not going into the intricacies of debate concerning whether Judeo-Christian Scripture is virtue ethical in emphasis,[134] I seek to advance here a Christian version of virtue ethics which is true to Judeo-Christian Scripture as follows:

Based on the core concept of what it means to be "truly human,"[135] I expand on Webb's concept of the "ultimate ethic"[136] in his redemptive-movement hermeneutic for interpreting Scripture to argue that this "ultimate ethic" for reading Scripture (particularly for application on ethical issues) can and should be understood in terms of what it means to be truly human, to live a life of genuine or redeemed humanity. Further on this, I draw on the doctrine of the *imago Dei* to shed further light on what being "truly human" means, and in this I advance my proposed integrated version of the *imago Dei* (argued for earlier in this chapter) which is Christocentric and eschatological in emphasis, focusing on humanity's calling to reflect God's character in the many facets of living in creation, in anticipation of the fulfilment of God's promise to redeem creation,[137] and following the way of Christ, who is the image of the one true God (Col 1:15–17).

---

134. See, for example, John Barton's excellent overview of the topic ("Virtue in the Bible"). See also Briggs's helpful discussion of virtue ethics in relation to reading the Old Testament (*Virtuous Reader*, 17–44).

135. In terms of living the life of genuine humanity, which may be understood in terms of redeemed humanity, on the understanding that perfected humanity is only possible through the work of Christ and even then will be inchoate or unfinished on this side of eternity before the eschaton.

136. And may well go beyond what he has argued.

137. Based on passages of Scripture such as Rev 21:1.

I suggest that an authentically Christian and biblically-based version of virtue ethics may be understood in these terms and may also be regarded as related to natural law. From this understanding, I argue, building on N. T. Wright's insights, that the cardinal virtues of the classical tradition—prudence (or wisdom), justice, courage (or fortitude), and temperance (or self-control)—when "recalibrated" (borrowing Pinches's/Wright's term) by the central and overarching Christian virtue of love, form a fivefold ethic (with love as the overarching virtue, alongside the cardinal virtues of the classical tradition) which is consistent with Judeo-Christian Scripture. Further, I suggest, including based on the insights of Pauline scholar John Barclay (set out earlier) and Wright himself, that advancing virtue ethics in such terms does not contravene core Protestant doctrines, particularly justification by faith (rather than works) and reliance on God's saving grace. I therefore propose to advance this as a somewhat "Protestant" or simply "Christian" version of virtue ethics, distinct from the "particularistic TVE" and "natural law TVE" strains of virtue ethics identified by Herdt (described earlier).

6.4.3 On the Cardinal Virtues in Judeo-Christian Scripture

While there is mention in the deuterocanonical book Wisdom of Solomon of the classic fourfold formulation of the cardinal virtues (temperance, prudence, justice, and fortitude [Wis 8:7 KJV]), it may not appear immediately obvious that the ethical system in the context of the Hebrew Bible/Old Testament or the New Testament is built around the cardinal virtues. However, it is also worth noting that particularly in the Hebrew Scriptures themes revolving around the cardinal virtues of justice, prudence, courage, temperance (though they may not be referred to specifically in terms of "cardinal virtues") are quite apparent, and also often related to God's presence, character, and/or requirements or decrees. For example, consider the following verses: (i) on wisdom: "the fear of the Lord is the beginning of wisdom" (Prov 9:10), and indeed the whole rich corpus of wisdom literature in Jewish Scripture; (ii) on courage: memorably "be strong and courageous ... for the Lord your God will be with you wherever you go" (Prov 1:9); and (iii) on temperance/self-control: "Better a patient person than a warrior, one with self-control than one who takes a city" (Prov 16:32). Further, the priority of justice is emphasized in many

CHAPTER 6: LIVING MORE HUMAN(E)LY?

key passages of Scripture, including in verses such as Isa 58:1–10; 61:1–8; Amos 5:7–15, 22–24) and notably in Mic 6:8.

Finally, it should be undisputed that love (of God and neighbor) is (and should be) the central focus of Judeo-Christian Scripture, as Jesus states unequivocally in the Gospels, particularly in his setting out of the two Greatest Commandments: "Love the Lord your God with all your heart . . . soul and . . . mind. . . . And the second is like it: 'Love your neighbor as yourself.' All the Law and the Prophets hang on these two commandments" (Matt 22:37–40 NIV).

Along with the above, exhortations to virtuous character may be observed in many verses across the New Testament, including in 1 Cor 13; Gal 5:22–23; and several other passages. This is clear also from the verse "God gave us a spirit not of fear but of power and love and self-control" (2 Tim 1:7 ESV), reflecting the virtues of courage, love, and temperance.

Further from St. Paul, there is the resounding reminder "Finally, brothers, whatever is true, whatever is honorable, whatever is just, whatever is pure, whatever is lovely, whatever is commendable, if there is any excellence, if there is anything worthy of praise, think about these things" (Phil 4:8 ESV), which I suggest exemplifies a virtue-ethical approach, in its emphasis on focusing on all that is excellent, just, pure, lovely, and commendable.

Indeed, as Wright aptly observes:

> The ancient Jews thus assumed (and the early Christians carried on this assumption) that in all kinds of ways the vision of genuine humanity that they glimpsed in God, in Torah, and in Wisdom constituted the overarching goal that included within itself, even though it also transcended, the goal glimpsed by pagan philosophers.[138]

My proposed fivefold ethic may also be regarded as epitomized in Jesus, who, among much else that is crucial (including, not least, in soteriological aspects), is the ultimate Christian moral exemplar whom Christians are called to follow as Lord.[139] It is not possible within this limited space

---

138. N. T. Wright, "Faith, Virtue, Justification," loc. 5175 of 10812.

139. In my views here, there may be a degree of resonance with Glen Stassen's concept of incarnational discipleship and a "thicker Jesus." See Stassen, *Thicker Jesus*, for example, ch. 2, highlighting the three key themes of: (i) "God revealed in the incarnate Jesus of Galilee, thickly interpreted" (35); (ii) "the sovereignty of God or Lordship of Christ throughout all of life" (37); and (iii) "the Holy Spirit's evocation of continuous repentance," including in resisting "false ideologies" (39). See also the discussion of Stassen's views in Gushee and Williams, *Justice and the Way of Jesus*.

to adequately represent or describe the depth and richness of the life of Jesus, the incarnate Son of God in this regard. Be that as it may, in a brief sketch here, I suggest that one may observe, particularly recorded in the canonical Gospels, many examples of the cardinal virtues advanced in my proposed fivefold ethic, including: (i) his courage—most notably, for example, not shirking from heading to Jerusalem and a gruesome death at Calvary; (ii) his temperance—for example, when restraining Peter who sought to prevent his arrest at Gethsemane with violence, and in the many instances of temptation and trial, including his forty days in the desert before the start of his ministry, and in his trial before Pilate; (iii) his wisdom and prudence[140]—in his various encounters with friend and foe alike, along with his teaching and many parables, not least of all his exhortation to "be wise as serpents and innocent as doves" (Matt 10:16b NRSV);[141] (iv) his deep sense of justice—including in numerous instances of defending the poor, afflicted, outcasts, and overlooked in society; and (v) his love and care—in the numerous accounts of his healing the sick or disabled, and attending to those who were suffering physically or in mind or spirit,[142] and ultimately in self-giving love, even to death on a cross (Phil 2:1–8). Indeed, Jesus in his life of complete self-giving love exemplifies the apostle Paul's description of love in 1 Cor 13.

This virtue-ethical perspective should not be interpreted as implying that the understanding of important elements of Judeo-Christian Scripture in terms of law (or divine command) is displaced. Rather, I argue that Jesus Christ should be regarded as the ultimate fulfilment of the law (as understood in Judeo-Christian Scripture). As Jesus's statement recorded in Matt 5:17 reminds, he came "not to destroy the Law and the Prophets," but to fulfil them. We are also reminded in the Gospels of Jesus's call to follow him. Further, in Matt 22:40 he emphasizes that all the Law and the Prophets depend on the two Greatest Commands, to love God and neighbor, giving centrality to love as the overarching foundational ethic for all who follow him. Further, as St. Paul also reminds us, Jesus is in truth "the power of God and the wisdom of God" (1 Cor 1:24b NIV).

---

140. I use the term "prudence" in this book not in the narrow sense of akin to being "cautious" but in a fuller sense equating to wisdom.

141. Indeed, I contend that true wisdom or prudence is epitomized by Jesus's Sermon on the Mount, as recorded in the Gospels.

142. Most notably, as detailed in the four Gospels, Matthew, Mark, Luke, and John.

CHAPTER 6: LIVING MORE HUMAN(E)LY?

Along these lines, it may also be observed that there is a distinct call in Christian Scripture to imitate (and/or follow) Jesus Christ. For example, in addition to Jesus's call in the Gospels for his disciples (and all) to follow him, we have (from St. Paul again) the clear exhortation to "be imitators of me, as I am of Christ" (1 Cor 11:1 ESV).

Wright also reminds of the necessity, in following the way of Christ, for theology, and methods and means, to be "cross-shaped through and through."[143] I suggest this should also apply to approaches to dating—that authentically Christian dating approaches should be "cross shaped" in following Christ's way of love and care—and that this will include being against all manipulative, deceptive, abusive, and/or exploitative (and other reductionistic and/or dehumanizing) practices/approaches.

In all of this, I suggest it should also be borne in mind that there should be a pervasive countercultural quality to this version of Christian virtue ethics. As passages such as Phil 2:1–8 and Gal 5:13–15 remind, a genuinely Christlike spirit of love and care runs counter to the relentlessly competitive (and backbiting and other-devouring) drive of the surrounding culture. This also has particular relevance to sexual ethics, in that I contend that an authentically Christian approach to sexual ethics ought to run counter to prevailing self-focused, market-driven, and consumerist/neoliberal approaches.

6.4.4 Further on This Christian Virtue-Ethical Approach for Application in Contemporary Contexts

In my argument here, there is also some recourse to natural law reasoning, particularly in terms of contending for objective universal standards and criteria for what may be regarded as humane (as opposed to inhuman) behavior. This may be seen in terms of considerations of purpose and human potential, intended ends, and a normative concept of what it means to be "truly human" and to flourish as human creatures.

In this context, it is also pertinent to note Peterson and Seligman's findings of twenty-four character strengths which appear universally preferred across different cultures. Peterson and Seligman embarked on a "historical survey leading to the conclusion that six core virtues—wisdom,

---

143. N. T. Wright, *Challenge of Jesus*, 69.

courage, humanity, justice, temperance, and transcendence—recur across time and place."[144]

Based on that survey, a total of twenty-four qualities are advocated in Peterson and Seligman's book as character strengths on which consensus has been reached across different cultures as being universally worthy of cultivation. These qualities/strengths are:

i. Strengths of wisdom and knowledge: creativity, curiosity, open-mindedness, love of learning, and perspective (wisdom)

ii. Strengths of courage: bravery (valor), persistence (perseverance, industriousness), integrity (authenticity, honesty) and vitality

iii. Strengths of humanity: love, kindness, social intelligence (emotional intelligence, personal intelligence)

iv. Strengths of justice: citizenship (social responsibility, loyalty, teamwork), fairness, leadership

v. Strengths of temperance: forgiveness and mercy, humility and modesty, prudence, self-regulation (self-control)

vi. Strengths of transcendence: appreciation of beauty and excellence, gratitude, hope (optimism, future mindedness, future orientation), humor (playfulness), spirituality (religiousness, faith, purpose)[145]

Further, as also observed by some Christian ethicists, for example, Lawler and Salzman,[146] and following Wright's advancing of a "virtuous circle" for formation in virtues,[147] I suggest the following should be given particular focus as part of a virtue-ethical approach:

i. Good healthy communities

ii. Regular helpful practices

iii. Helpful moral exemplars

The above ideally should include provision of support (both through pastoral and other sources) and guidance in character formation (including

---

144. Peterson and Seligman, *Character Strengths and Virtues*, 53.

145. Peterson and Seligman, *Character Strengths and Virtues*, 28–30. My fivefold ethic proposed in this book does not map exactly onto Peterson and Seligman's classification, but there are substantial areas of overlap.

146. Lawler and Salzman, "People Beginning Sexual Experience," 562.

147. Tom Wright, *Virtue Reborn*, 221–44.

in virtues forming part of my proposed fivefold ethic advanced here), including in the context of dating and interpersonal relationships.[148]

6.5 A Fivefold Ethic

I have set out above the metaphysical, ontological, and doctrinal basis for my proposed fivefold ethic which I will advance here. In sum, I propose this fivefold ethic as a key part of living in genuine humanity, as bearers of the image of God (in the multifaceted integrated sense advanced earlier) and following N. T. Wright's approach of "recalibrating" the classical virtues in the light of the highest Christian virtue, love. The combination of five cardinal virtues that I propose here may also be regarded, in a natural law vein, as a variation on the six core virtues or strengths identified by Peterson and Seligman across different cultures mentioned earlier,[149] but with "prudence" understood here as synonymous with wisdom, rather than a quality of temperance, and with some differences in classification.

I therefore advocate the following fivefold ethic for Christian sexual ethics: An ethic of prudence, justice, courage, temperance, and love and care (as an overarching ethic), based on 1 Cor 13. I argue that these five virtues are cardinal in terms of being fundamental "hinge virtues" (from the Latin word *cardo*) in that other virtues derive from them. For example, honesty may be understood as flowing from justice and love, self-care from prudence, gratitude from justice, and humility and patience from love. Following the integrated version of the *imago Dei* that I have argued for, I contend that these five cardinal virtues also indicate key aspects of the character of God which humanity are called to reflect while living in creation, and particularly in our relationships with one another and the rest of creation. They express what constitutes genuine humanity, particularly in a relational context. I thus advance this as a fivefold ethic of cardinal virtues particularly for humans living in relationship with one another and our fellow creatures, including for intimate or sexual relationships.

---

148. I suggest that such a framework may have still been quite widely in place (though by no means perfect) in Anglo-American society before the sexual revolution of the 1960s—the presence and strength of communities—and that this also contributed to the strength and resilience of interpersonal relationships of that time—as can be seen, for example, in responses to the challenges of the Second World War.

149. Peterson and Seligman, *Character Strengths and Virtues*, 28–30.

As mentioned, this fivefold ethic is composed of the four cardinal virtues from the classical tradition, alongside and "recalibrated" (or modified wherever necessary) by the overarching virtue of love (understood in terms of 1 Cor 13). As an example of this "recalibration," wherever prudence or courage are exercised as virtues, these should not be exercised in a spirit of selfish ambition or pride (in order to be true virtue under this new system). While in the classical tradition, it may have been possible (or even encouraged) to display courage or wisdom alongside pride and self-advancing ambition, I suggest that with this recalibrated version, such display would not constitute the exercise of these virtues according to their true character, in the sense of living true to one's calling to genuine humanity (including to reflect the character of the living God, most exemplified in the person, Jesus Christ).

To summarize, in this fivefold ethic that I advocate:

i. Love is one of the five cardinal virtues, but it is also the overarching "recalibrating" virtue—based on 1 Cor 13 (particularly 1 Cor 13:1–3).

ii. Each of the other four cardinal virtues are virtues in their own right, with their own character—they are not collapsed into love. While love is the overarching virtue, they are not just forms of love.

A question may arise as to whether the other theological virtues, "faith" and "hope," should be included in this ethic. In answer, I would say that faith and hope are included to a significant extent, at least in the context of relationships, within an expansive understanding of love based on 1 Cor 13:7 ("[love] always trusts, always hopes, always perseveres" [NIV]).[150] In my fivefold ethic, I have not specified faith and hope as separate cardinal virtues, as I argue that the primary focus should be on love as the cardinal (as well as theological) and preeminent virtue which recalibrates the other cardinal virtues (and as said, I also contend that faith and hope are included within, and should flow from, love).[151]

---

150. N. T. Wright also makes this point: "Paul, indeed, gives both faith and hope as qualities of love: love bears all things, believes all things, hopes all things, endures all things (13:7)" ("Faith, Virtue, Justification," loc. 5234 of 10812).

151. In this I am also suggesting that, in addition to the "vertical" dimension that faith and hope are traditionally associated with (as theological virtues), that is, primarily in relationship with God, there is also a horizontal dimension to these virtues—that is, in relationship with our fellow creatures.

CHAPTER 6: LIVING MORE HUMAN(E)LY?

This is a key aspect in which my version of virtue ethics (building on Wright's version) differs from Thomistic versions, which generally maintain the two distinct categories of the theological virtues (faith, hope, and love) and the cardinal virtues of the classical tradition (prudence, temperance, courage or fortitude, and justice), although there is also much in common. Overall, in the version that I advance here there is a clearer emphasis on love as the central virtue (which, as I suggest above, encompasses faith and hope in a relational context), both as a cardinal and a theological virtue, recalibrating the other cardinal virtues.

As said, my argument that these five virtues are cardinal (or fundamental, core or "hinge" virtues) is connected to the central concept of being truly human (as opposed to "inhuman"), or living the life of genuine humanity (as opposed, for example, to dehumanizing behavior). This links back to my discussion of the *imago Dei*, as I also suggest that when humans (even non-Christians) exercise some form of these virtues—being courageous, just, temperate, prudent or kind, for example—even in an imperfect form, they are displaying the image of God in which they have been created, even though this image has been corrupted by the fall, and thus these virtues are not entirely false even when practiced by non-Christians in an imperfect or inchoate form.[152] Further, as also said earlier, this image is redeemed by and perfected by the work of Christ. Therefore I also suggest that the cultivation and growth of these cardinal virtues—recalibrated by the highest Christian virtue, love, responding to God's grace in a restored relationship with God through Christ, and enabled by the Holy Spirit—should be all the more evident in the life of the Christian.[153] A fine combination of these five cardinal virtues—courage, temperance, prudence, justice, and love and care—may be seen, for example, in the life of Dietrich Bonhoeffer who, in addition to ministry and published work packed with wisdom and great insight, courageously put his life on the line, and ultimately lost his life, in joining the resistance movement and the plot to assassinate Hitler for the greater good.[154]

---

152. This is a further aspect in which my version of virtue ethics differs from that of Augustine who, as mentioned above, holds that virtue without true Christian faith is false virtue—thus giving rise to the concept of "splendid vices."

153. Even though, for various reasons in our contemporary world, this may not be discernible in many cases. I contend that a greater focus on formation in Christian circles in these cardinal virtues, alongside theological virtues, may partly assist in addressing such problems, especially, in the context of the present chapter, where these concern sexual ethics.

154. There are various accounts of Bonhoeffer's life detailing this. See, for example, Metaxas, *Bonhoeffer*; Tietz, *Theologian of Resistance*.

In the context of heterosexual dating, this fivefold ethic may be applied in different ways. One may apply this when considering criteria for deciding who to date, and eventually who to marry. In this, it may be unwise to follow mere "evolutionary" instincts—whereby men may tend to be drawn to physically attractive and shapely women who appear to signal potential for bearing the fittest offspring, while women may tend to be drawn to men who hold greater status, wealth or power in society who thus appear to offer greater potential to provide for offspring and enable them to succeed in the race of life.[155] Basing one's choice of life partner on who is most physically attractive, or who holds the greatest position of wealth or prestige, may be a short-sighted approach that ignores more important considerations such as whether one's prospective life partner lives by an ethic of love and care, or whether she or he is habituated to an ethic of justice in her/his relationships.

Another way of applying this proposed fivefold ethic is to encourage formation in these five proposed core virtues which I suggest will help enable flourishing in relationships, including intimate/dating relationships, and better decisions regarding marriage. For example, exercising temperance and prudence will help one to make more well-considered choices as to who to date, how to date, who to marry, and so on. I elaborate on each of these five proposed core virtues for application to sexual ethics in the paragraphs that follow.

Reiterating how the classical cardinal virtues relate to love in my proposed fivefold ethic, the other four cardinal virtues should not be collapsed into the virtue of love. The cardinal virtues do each have their own distinct quality, and can be distinguished one from the other (courage is not the same as temperance, which is not the same as justice, which is not the same as prudence, which is not the same as love, and so on), while they are also intricately related one to another. At the same time, I suggest that each of the classical virtues, while having value in and of itself, is perfected by love, specifically agape love, in the spirit of 1 Cor 13.

Courage is glorious, prudence is wonderful, and so on, but each might also be tarnished by pride or selfishness, if not undergirded by love—love which is patient and kind, that does not envy nor boast, is not arrogant nor rude (1 Cor 13:4–5), and further still in the spirit of all of that great chapter.

---

155. See, for example, the discussion in Buss, "Sex Differences."

An Ethic of Prudence

Josef Pieper interprets Aquinas's thought as meaning that prudence is the preeminent virtue among the cardinal virtues, and the root of the other virtues:

> Prudence is the cause of the other virtues' being virtues at all. . . . Virtue is a "perfected ability" of man as a spiritual person; and justice, fortitude, and temperance, as "abilities" of the whole man, achieve their "perfection" only when they are founded upon prudence, that is to say upon the perfected ability to make right decisions.[156]

> Prudence "*informs*" the other virtues; it confers upon them the form of their inner essence. . . . Prudence works in all the virtues; and all virtue participates in prudence.[157]

> Everyone who sins is imprudent. Thus prudence is cause, root, mother, measure, precept, guide, and prototype of all ethical virtues; it acts in all of them, perfecting them to their true nature; all participate in it, and by virtue of this participation they are virtues.[158]

Further, while pointing out the "reciprocal dependence"[159] of the cardinal virtues, Pieper reminds us "how greatly prudence, upon which all virtue depends, is in its turn dependent at its very fundaments on the totality of the other virtues, and above all on the virtue of justice."[160]

In the context of romantic relationships, the exercise of prudence also includes the practice of foresight, deliberation and cultivating the habit of making wise choices, for example, choices not based on external appearances or superficial considerations nor motivated by peer pressure or what would impress one's friends or family—challenging though this may be particularly during certain seasons of life—but rather based on more substantial considerations, such as matching levels of spiritual, intellectual and emotional depth. The exercise of prudence in the context of dating relationships should also involve discernment and differentiating between a "good catch" and a "good fit." For example, a person

---

156. Pieper, *Four Cardinal Virtues*, 6.
157. Pieper, *Four Cardinal Virtues*, 7; emphasis in original.
158. Pieper, *Four Cardinal Virtues*, 8.
159. See also Aristotle, *Nicomachean Ethics* 4.13, for example, at 1144b: "We cannot be fully good without prudence, or prudent without virtue of character."
160. Pieper, *Four Cardinal Virtues*, 15.

may appear particularly appealing in terms of being a "good catch" (for example, with significant wealth and status in society, or other attractive assets, or even with a wealth of desirable characteristics) but may not necessarily be a "good fit" in terms of matching well with one's goals, motivations, and concerns. Exercising prudence should thus also involve being attentive to outcomes, including warning signs, though these are not always straightforward, particularly when a dating partner is deceitful—to the extent that outcomes are reasonably foreseeable in a particular situation encountered in the course of dating.[161]

An ethic of prudence should include an ethic of self-care, including the exercise of care to ensure that one is not drained—emotionally, physically, spiritually, or in terms of resources—in the course of being in a romantic relationship. It is particularly important to be attentive to this in such contexts, as the heady experiences of romance can often appear overwhelming or all consuming, to the detriment of other aspects of one's life.

An ethic of prudence is also particularly relevant for the everyday practice of dating when expressed in terms of the exercise of practical wisdom, for which echoes may be found in advice from relationship counselors and psychologists experienced in the field. For example, Young and Adams in their *Ten Commandments of Dating* set out what they consider are ten helpful practical rules of thumb based on years of experience in counseling singles and dating couples. While I am not necessarily in agreement with all the "rules" they advocate, I suggest that at least a few of these may be regarded as examples of the application and outworking of practical wisdom in the context of dating. These include the following "laws" that continue to be particularly helpful in contemporary contexts: (i) "Thou shalt get a life": cautioning against over-absorption in a romantic relationship, to the exclusion of other aspects of life; (ii) "Thou shalt use your brain": cautioning against being led by one's emotions and/or hormonal impulses; (iii) "Thou shalt be equally yoked": emphasizing the importance of compatibility in life purposes and goals, including in spiritual matters; and (iv) "Thou shalt set clear boundaries": reminding of the importance of maintaining good boundaries even in

---

161. This is where a virtue-ethical approach may encompass utilitarian/consequentialist/outcome-oriented approaches, although it should not be dictated entirely by outcomes nor unduly burdened by complicated calculations of possible outcomes, many of which are unpredictable.

matters of the heart and intimate relationships.¹⁶² Along similar lines as "thou shalt set clear boundaries," Cloud and Townsend, experienced psychologists/counselors strongly advocate "boundaries in dating" as part of their advice characterized by down-to-earth wisdom.¹⁶³

As perhaps an example of adapted wisdom, John Gray, relationship counselor and author of the controversial 1992 bestseller *Men Are from Mars, Women Are from Venus*, argues in a recent book for new and/or enhanced relationship skills to navigate what he considers significant societal changes in the past couple of decades, particularly with higher levels of stress due to "the increasing pace of work and life" for both men and women, while there are "millions more women in the workplace" and men are contributing more to household duties.¹⁶⁴

Further, developing on findings discussed in chapter 5, I suggest that an ethic of prudence applied to dating should include taking into account both romantic and practical considerations in one's choice of a life partner, along with an approach towards physical and sexual intimacy that is correlated to commitment.

An Ethic of Courage

Starting with the classical understanding of courage, applying here the Aristotelian concept of the mean in relation to virtue, it should be borne in mind that courage is the mean between cowardice and recklessness—that is, neither too much nor too little fear.¹⁶⁵

Courage is an important virtue that may be relevant to the practice of dating in various ways. This may include, for example, the courage

---

162. Young and Adams, *Ten Commandments of Dating*. They advocate the following "time-tested relationship laws": (1) "Thou shalt get a life," (2) "Thou shalt use your brain," (3) "Thou shalt be equally yoked," (4) "Thou shalt take it slow," (5) "Thou shalt set clear boundaries," (6) "Thou shalt save sex for later," (7) "Thou shalt not play house," (8) "Thou shalt fight fairly," (9) "Thou shalt not ignore warning signs," and (10) "Thou shalt choose wisely."

163. Cloud and Townsend, *Boundaries in Dating*.

164. Gray, *Beyond Mars and Venus*, loc. 123 of 5595. For example, at the same location, Gray asserts: "Both men and women require a new kind of emotional support that embraces greater authenticity, intimacy, and personal expression. Gone are the days when a woman was required to be submissive and dependent on men, and a man had to carry the burden of providing for his family alone."

165. See, for example, Aristotle, *Nicomachean Ethics* 2.2.1104a: "If, for instance, someone avoids and is afraid of everything, standing firm against nothing, he becomes cowardly; if he is afraid of nothing at all and goes to face everything, he becomes rash."

for an interested male[166] to approach the subject of his interests, risking the possibility of rejection or, even if the relationship progresses well, the challenges that accompany increasing intimacy and vulnerability in a personal relationship. Also important is the courage to end or walk away from a relationship which may be harmful (such as in cases of exploitation or abuse), even where there may be strong "pull" factors (such as sexual attraction, financial or emotional dependence, or even emotional blackmail) that make it difficult to leave such a relationship.

Further, this virtue includes the courage to face challenges and persevere through difficult times, fortitude—a particularly important quality for marriage, as every marriage, no matter how well matched, will face challenges/difficult times, though this will vary in nature and degree.

At the same time, an ethic of courage is important to enable or encourage one to choose or remain in a state of singleness and celibacy at least for a season of life, when there may be no suitable companion available at present—even in the face of societal or peer pressures to "hook up" or "couple up." This includes the courage to "dare to be different," even when one may be on the receiving end of disparaging treatment from those in society who may tend to view those who are "coupled up" as being somehow superior as a species. Cultivating and exercising this virtue is also helpful for enabling one to exercise the other virtues (such as prudence, temperance or justice) in the process of making wise choices concerning a possible future life partner, rather than compromising (or as is sometimes referred to in everyday parlance, "settling") by coupling up, say, with the nearest available agreeable person out of a fear of being alone.

Courage is also linked to honesty. This includes the courage to tell the truth about oneself, even if that truth may be less than flattering. In a romantic relationship, courage may include being brave enough to disclose details about oneself which may be less than impressive, and trusting that the other will not belittle nor exploit that information in any way. Courage should include being honest about aspects of one's life which may not be that impressive, rather than putting on a front or

---

166. This may also apply to an interested female, of course, as this is stated merely as an example. The intricacies of whether it should always be males who approach females for dating/courtship purposes, rather than the other way round, or either way, comprise a discussion which are beyond the scope of my chapter, hence it may be assumed for present purposes that I am neutral on this issue.

trying to gain the advantage in a relationship by means of deception or manipulation.

An Ethic of Temperance

I begin here with the classical understanding of this virtue, which refers primarily to making right choices particularly in relation to one's desires or appetites.[167] Following Wright's suggestion in his 2008 essay, I suggest that temperance is closely related to self-control (included in the fruit of the Spirit of Gal 5:22–23). An ethic of temperance or self-control may also be regarded as related to an ethic of chastity (though not necessarily celibacy or asceticism).

Further, applying findings discussed earlier in chapter 5, I also suggest that, as part of "better approaches" to dating proposed here, physical and sexual intimacy should be correlated to a person's level of commitment to the other in a romantic relationship—and preferably that sexual intimacy should be reserved for the period of engagement at the earliest. An ethic of temperance should thus also involve regulating one's desires, emotions and physical inclinations in accordance with this.

Further, in contemporary Anglo-American societies in which instant gratification is encouraged at every turn, fueled in dating culture by the proliferation of online dating and mobile dating apps, I contend it is all the more a priority to promote the cultivation of temperance as a virtue—so that for anyone on the dating scene delayed gratification becomes a real possibility and a practice, enabling better decision-making for the long term and enhancing overall well-being and flourishing for the individuals and couples involved.

This virtue is also particularly important to enable one not to be led, or misled, by experiences or feelings of sexual attraction in the important decisions concerning dating, courtship and selection of one's partner for life. It may be observed that in contemporary contexts decisions in such matters are too often dictated by experiences of desire and sexual attraction, at the expense of more weighty considerations such as a person's character, goals, motivations, and long-term concerns. Cultivating and exercising a habit of temperance will assist the individual in resisting such

---

167. See, for example, Plato, *Republic*, 75, where it is said, "Temperance, I replied, is the ordering or controlling of certain pleasures and desires; this is curiously enough implied in the saying of 'a man being his own master.'"

impulses and enable better decision-making in such matters. This is all the more critical as such decisions often have long-term ramifications.

This ethic of temperance or self-control may be exercised in connection with helpful practical advice in the context of dating on the importance of establishing and maintaining good boundaries in dating relationships—for example, as advised, notably, by Cloud and Townsend in *Boundaries in Dating*. The exercise of temperance is also especially important for control, regulation (and if necessary, reorientation) of one's appetites and desires in the context of life choices made concerning dating and singleness. If no suitable person (in terms of compatibility in important aspects) is available on the horizon, it may well be necessary for an individual to be prepared to be single and celibate at least for a period of time. As mentioned earlier, I suggest that being willing and able to be single and celibate, at least for a season of life, should be part of one's approach to dating (rather than making unwise compromises on compatibility out of fear of being alone or single). Temperance will be particularly necessary in such contexts.

An Ethic of Justice

As has been observed, "there are various ways of dividing up the domain of justice," but "the most famous distinction is probably Aristotle's"[168]—that is, between "corrective justice" and "distributive justice."[169] Bix notes that corrective justice "involves rectification between two parties, where one has taken from the other or harmed the other," while distributive justice "involves the appropriate distribution of goods among a group ("giving each person his or her due")" and this includes "most of the better known modern discussions of justice, which usually treats justice primarily as about the proper structuring of government and society."[170]

Pieper, on a Thomistic perspective of justice, points out "three basic forms of justice":

> Reciprocal, or mutually exchanged justice . . . which orders the relation of individual to individual partner; ministering justice . . . which brings order to the relations between the community as such and the individuals who are its members; legal

---

168. Bix, *Jurisprudence*, 172.
169. Aristotle, *Nicomachean Ethics* 5.3.1131a–5.4.1132h.
170. Bix, *Jurisprudence*, 172.

CHAPTER 6: LIVING MORE HUMAN(E)LY?

or general justice . . . which orders the members' relations to the social whole.[171]

Amid the diversity of views as to what justice may be composed of, Pieper points to one clear basic formulation:

> Nevertheless there is a notion of the utmost simplicity to which that bewildering variety can be reduced. . . . All just order in the world is based on this: that man give man what is his due.[172]

At the same time, however, as Pieper also notes, discerning and ascertaining what "giving one his due" actually amounts to in practice, and in various specific scenarios, can be a very complex matter.

I therefore define this in terms of "giving to the other what is due," while bearing in mind the complexity that may be involved in determining what this involves in different situations. In the context of dating, I suggest this virtue will also include being honest—ensuring that one's date or partner has the appropriate, relevant and accurate facts about you, rather than lying or putting on a front. The degree of disclosure of (sometimes quite private) details about oneself should of course be appropriate to the stage the relationship is at. One, quite sensibly, should not be passing on unnecessary personal information to an acquaintance on a first date, while of course one should also not lie. If, however, two people have been steadily dating for about two years or so, and are contemplating engagement or marriage, an ethic of justice should certainly involve disclosing to the other all key personal details, particularly any and all details which may have an effect on the decision whether or not to marry. This may perhaps be likened to the duty of "utmost good faith" (*uberrimae fidei*) in insurance contracts, in which an applicant has the duty to disclose all relevant facts that may affect an insurer's decision whether or not to insure.

Further, an ethic of justice should exclude manipulative or deceptive practices and all forms of exploitation or abuse in a relationship. Gender inequality and sexual double standards should be challenged and abolished.

It has been suggested that gratitude—the propensity to be thankful for how others have contributed to the good in our lives—forms a part

---

171. Pieper, *Four Cardinal Virtues*, 70–71.
172. Pieper, *Four Cardinal Virtues*, 44.

of the virtue of justice.[173] A virtue of justice may also be related to fidelity, and should encompass the ability and propensity to be faithful and trustworthy in relationships.

This ethic is also particularly applicable in situations of breakups. Doing justice, even when a breakup may be deemed necessary, involves also proceeding by means that render to the other all that is due, and treating him/her with respect. Hence, this should exclude breakup practices such as "ghosting," suddenly disappearing off the scene without a word of explanation, or breaking up with a mere "tweet" (unless there are good reasons for concluding that one's life would somehow be put at risk by means of a breakup mode where one is more present to the other)—while appropriate boundaries should be maintained.

I now turn to discussing a case study relevant to this matter from recent Christian history. Reading Stephen Plant's account, based on meticulous research, of the relationship between Karl Barth, Charlotte von Kirschbaum, and Nelly Barth,[174] it is difficult to escape the sense that Charlotte von Kirschbaum's experience in the long heartrending affair particularly lacked, and was particularly in need of, just dealing. One must recognize that the practical exercise of prudence in such a complex situation is particularly challenging, and yet it is difficult to escape the sense of desiring for Kirschbaum that she should have been better advised and supported in the matter, particularly in the early stages of her relationship with Karl Barth—who held the balance of power, experience, and influence in his favor. Perhaps, if Kirschbaum had been better advised and supported, the trajectory of her life may well have turned out quite differently. Clearly talented, intelligent, physically attractive, and amiable in personality, she may well have married a suitor other than Barth, and continued in a happy marriage in which her talents were allowed to flourish and her clear potential truly affirmed and developed.

An Ethic of Love and Care

From a Christian viewpoint, I argue that an ethic of love and care—based primarily on St. Paul's memorable exposition in 1 Cor 13—should be the central virtue in practically all matters of life, and particularly in the matter

---

173. See, for example, Robert Solomon, "Foreword," in Emmons and McCullough, *Psychology of Gratitude*, x.

174. Plant, "When Karl Met Lollo."

CHAPTER 6: LIVING MORE HUMAN(E)LY?

of interpersonal relationships. I use the term "love and care" here to identify this virtue in terms of love as described in 1 Cor 13 (and the central Christian command to love),[175] and to distinguish it from the myriad other forms or usages of the word "love" (such as references to romantic love, passion, affection, and so on).[176] It should thus be understood primarily in terms of agape love, that is, oriented toward the good of the other (although not necessarily entirely exclusive of self-love). In my proposed fivefold ethic, I contend that an ethic of love and care should be the overarching ethic that governs and "calibrates" (adapting Wright's/Pinches/ term) the exercise of the other virtues. This is based on 1 Cor 13:

In St. Paul's memorable words:

> If I speak in the tongues of men and of angels, but have not love, I am only a resounding gong or a clanging cymbal. If I have the gift of prophecy and can fathom all mysteries and all knowledge, and if I have a faith that can move mountains, but have not love, I am nothing. . . .
>
> Love is patient, love is kind . . . it is not self-seeking, it is not easily angered, it keeps no record of wrongs. . . . Love never fails. (1 Cor 13:1–8a NIV)

In his commentary on 1 Corinthians, Richard Hays reminds of the central aim of this passage:

> The purpose of chapter 13 is to portray love as the sine qua non of the Christian life and to insist that love must govern the exercise of all the gifts of the Spirit . . . the purpose of this chapter is straightforwardly ethical. By describing the qualities of love, Paul is seeking to promote the *character formation* of the members of the Corinthian community.[177]

Further, on the matter of spiritual gifts which Hays notes that Paul is addressing in particular, he observes love's "governing role" in this context:

---

175. For example, in Mark 12:31 and elsewhere.

176. It may be quite easily observed that there are many different possible meanings of "love." See, for example, Lewis, *Four Loves*. Josef Pieper argues that "the boundaries between eros and agape" (that is, between "self-love" and "unselfish love") are "fluid" and inseparable (*Faith, Hope, Love*, 209). In this he disagrees with views along lines "that creation and redemption have nothing to do with one another" (209)—notably such as Anders Nygren, *Agape and Eros*—which draw sharp distinctions between eros and agape, and, in conformity with Luther and Calvin, seek to overturn what they perceive as the Thomistic synthesis of natural and supernatural loves.

177. Hays, *First Corinthians*, 336–37.

> [Paul]'s point is not that love should supersede spiritual gifts but that it should govern their use in the church. . . . Love is not a higher and better gift; rather, it is a "way" (12:31b), a manner of life within which all the gifts are to find their proper place.[178]

As Craig Blomberg also reminds, "First Corinthians 13:1–3 makes the point that without love the gifts are worthless . . . without love the most exemplary use of a particular gift profits a believer nothing."[179]

I suggest that this overarching and "governing" (or calibrating) role of love in relation to the spiritual gifts should also apply in the relationship between love and the other virtues—prudence, courage, temperance, and justice—in my proposed fivefold ethic.

Faithfulness—"love always perseveres, love never fails" (1 Cor 13:7b–8a)—and fidelity (in the right context—particularly when the partners in the relationship have reached the stage when they are ready to make a firm commitment to each other) are also included within an ethic of love and care. However, this does not imply that breakups should never occur, particularly when prior to marriage the individuals have discovered weighty grounds of unsuitability for marriage, and particularly also when relationships are found to be abusive.

Further, this ethic should include the practice of truth and honesty, rather than deception or pretences (as "love does not delight in evil, but rejoices with the truth" [1 Cor 13:6 NIV]). This has particular practical application to dating in contemporary Anglo-American societies, running counter to prevailing tendencies towards maintaining attractive appearances (fueled also by a social media–driven culture, with the widespread usage of Facebook, Instagram, X/Twitter, and so on) which may be promoting personalities that are illusory rather than real.

This ethic thus encompasses truth/honesty, along with joy,[180] humility,[181] and other key qualities described in 1 Cor 13—thus going distinctly beyond Aristotelian concepts of virtue.

Importantly, this ethic excludes any form of abusive, manipulative or exploitative behavior in relationships. This should also exclude all violence and any coercive or controlling behavior, even though such forms of behavior may often be associated with intimate relationships.

---

178. Hays, *First Corinthians*, 338.
179. Blomberg, *1 Corinthians*, 345.
180. Particularly in relation to truth (1 Cor 13:6b).
181. Love "does not boast, it is not proud" (1 Cor 13:4b NIV).

Further, it should be emphasized that applying an ethic of love and care also involves relating to the other as a person, rather than a "thing" or an object. This should therefore exclude objectifying and instrumentalizing approaches. By "person," in the present context,[182] I mean a human being, made in the image of God—and here I refer again to my understanding of the *imago Dei* which I have advanced earlier in this chapter. Practically therefore, this ethic involves life-affirming practices and excludes any behavior or practices that are reductionistic or dehumanizing in effect—for example, in contemporary contexts, behaviors such as "negging"[183] and unwarranted "ghosting."[184] Practicing an ethic of love and care would involve prioritizing the good and flourishing of the other, rather than prioritizing the seeking of personal advantage for oneself.

Reiterating the Uti/Frui Distinction

Further discussing this virtue of love and care through a theological lens, I refer again to the Augustinian insight (discussed in ch. 1) regarding the use/enjoyment (or *uti/frui*) distinction in relation to love,[185] and apply this to contemporary dating/couple relationships. My contention here is that it is important to recognize and remember, in every relationship with our neighbor, even in the closest of couple relationships, that we each first and foremost belong to God—that the other (even our partner in life) belongs first and foremost to God—and we should not seek to impose our will upon him/her (the other/our neighbor), but we should instead always ask (and seek) that God's will be done in all our lives, in the life of the other/our neighbor/our partner, and in our life. In my view, this is part of what it means, in practice, to "love our neighbor in God," applied to the context of couple relationships.

---

182. I say this while recognizing that "person" may in other contexts refer to nonhuman creatures, particularly those bearing key characteristics, such as language, that may be considered by some thinkers in the field to be markers of personhood.

183. For a definition, see, for example, https://www.dictionary.com/browse/negging.

184. Helpful discussions include Gould, "What Is Ghosting?"; Vilhauer, "What to Do."

185. See again, for example, Van Nieuwenhove, *Introduction to Medieval Theology*, 25.

This seeking to impose one's will upon the other, in the context of dating/couple relationships, may be discerned in various forms (and by grace, can hopefully be resisted)—including in various forms of controlling, predatory, exploitative, manipulative, or deceptive behavior. This may be seen, evidently, in cases of domestic abuse (whether physical or emotional), so prevalent in contemporary society. Still, in addition to this, the permutations and combinations of such behavior in the context of today's digital age (including not least, with sophisticated technology, the internet, social media, and dating apps) are likely endless.

To reiterate, in resistance to such ways, practicing an ethic of love and care should instead involve continually seeking that God's will be realized or accomplished in both our neighbor's and our lives. In my view, this is part of what it means, in practice, to "love our neighbor in God," applied to the context of couple relationships. It should involve entrusting both lives, our life and our neighbor/partner's life, to God—and desiring that God's will should come to fullness in each life/both lives.

Intimate relationships, especially involving sexual relations, are primary contexts where abuse or manipulation in its various forms may easily occur—not least because of the dynamics of power and possession often involved in such relationships. An ethic of love and care involves putting the welfare and well-being of the other (the good of the beloved) ahead of one's own desires for control or security.

Overall, while I am seeking to advance a fivefold ethic that is universalizable, I also suggest that the practice and manifestation of this fivefold ethic is enhanced by active Christian faith. For example, an ethic of love and care towards others can be all the more enhanced, energized, and enabled by having an active and secure loving relationship with God. As mentioned, each of these five cardinal virtues may be infused by God or acquired.

6.6 Further on This Fivefold Ethic

6.6.1 Unity of the Virtues

In this proposed fivefold ethic, I suggest that, while love is the overarching recalibrating virtue, all five virtues ought to be cultivated to enable full expression of one's humanity.[186] Ideally, there should not be a deficiency

---

186. In terms of living the life of genuine humanity, which may be understood in terms of redeemed humanity, on the understanding that perfected humanity is only

in one or more of the virtues—as all five are cardinal or "hinge" virtues and contribute to the whole of the expression of one's true humanity. In this sense, there is unity in the virtues that constitute this fivefold ethic.

Should one return to an abusive marriage? Should another leave his/her spouse for someone who appears to be a "better fit"? Should a woman date a man who is decades younger than her, if it turns out that he genuinely cares for her? Should a man cohabit with a woman when he has no intention of marrying her?

For all these questions and others, there will be a myriad of unique circumstances and factors on which a decision might turn. Certainly, further questions will need to be asked in each case and further details elicited.

Yet at the same time, for all of these matters, I advocate key questions based on my proposed fivefold ethic to assist in finding a way forward through the moral dilemma considered—these questions, applying my proposed fivefold ethic to each proposed action, would be along the lines of:

- Would the proposed act or decision be wise?
- Would it be just?
- Would it be courageous?
- Would it be temperate?
- Would it be loving and kind?

I propose this fivefold ethic as an expression of what "being truly human" means in moral terms—as opposed to living in inhuman or dehumanizing ways. This is related to and yet not altogether the same as the fruit of the Holy Spirit described in Gal 5:22–23,[187] which is available only to believers (I consider this further in a brief excursus below). I suggest that through the enabling and empowering of the Spirit, believers are better placed and should be able to practice and live out this fivefold ethic all the more, in both vertical ways (towards God) and horizontal ways

---

possible through the work of Christ and even then will be inchoate or unfinished on this side of eternity before the eschaton.

187. I suggest that Gal 5:22–23 is not intended to be a systematic exposition on virtue ethics but is part of a description (with examples of qualities) of a Christian's life in the Spirit. Hence it should not be regarded as contradicting an emphasis on love as an overarching virtue or on love recalibrating the cardinal virtues in their classical formulation (both of which are central to my proposed fivefold ethic).

(towards our fellow creatures, including our fellow humans). I say *should*, because for various reasons (beyond the scope of this chapter to explore) this sometimes (or in some contexts, often) does not happen, and it may sometimes appear that Christians are "less virtuous" in various aspects than non-Christians—a regrettable matter, which I suggest is not in accordance with humanity's full potential and telos.

My proposed multifaceted model of interpretation of the *imago* Dei is focused on Jesus Christ as the true image of God whom we are to follow.[188] The *imago Dei* is relevant both to questions of how we treat and relate to our fellow creatures and how we treat and relate to ourselves. When relating to our fellow human creatures, we need to remember that each is a bearer of the image of God, and render all the regard, reverence, and dignity that entails. When asking how we should regard and treat ourselves, how we should live and what choices we should make, we also need to bear in mind that we are bearers of the image of God, and remember all the awe and respect that should also flow from this. Particularly for application to Christian sexual ethics, my proposed fivefold ethic (composed of prudence, justice, courage, temperance, and an overarching virtue of love and care) is a proposed outworking and practical expression of this, of living as bearers of the image of God and relating to our fellow creatures as bearers of the image of God.

6.6.2 A Brief Excursus on the Fruit of the Spirit

A question may arise as to how this ethic relates to the fruit of the Spirit mentioned in Gal 5:22–23. Overall, my proposed fivefold ethic is about virtue ethics and is consistent with Gal 5:22–23, but it does not fully overlap with the content of these verses. I suggest that Gal 5:22–23 is not meant to be an exposition on cardinal virtues for the Christian life, but offers an illustrative (rather than exhaustive) list of qualities that are descriptive of the Spirit-filled life. For example, I am concerned about the lack of mention of justice in the fruit of the Spirit, and courage/fortitude is only implied in "faithfulness," while wisdom/prudence (although very much in the wisdom literature of the Hebrew Bible/Old Testament) is not mentioned. Further, a strict ninefold formulation of the fruit of the Spirit does not clearly highlight love as a (or the) primary virtue, which I contend should be the overarching recalibrating virtue—following 1 Cor 13.

---

188. See, for example, 2 Cor 3:18; 4:4–6.

6.7 Conclusion

As a further original contribution to the fields of theological ethics and sexual ethics, I have advanced my integrated multifaceted model of the *imago Dei* to ground my proposed fivefold ethic. I have developed and advocated this fivefold ethic, connected to this integrated multifaceted interpretation of the *imago Dei*, as a key aspect of living in genuine humanity, building on Josef Pieper's reference to "[attaining] the furthest potentialities of [human] nature"[189] and drawing on observations from N. T. Wright's 2008 essay, "Faith, Virtue, Justification, and the Journey to Freedom."

There has been considerable scholarly work both in the fields of exploration of the doctrine of the *imago Dei* and of Christian virtue ethics, but there have as yet not been substantial connections developed between the two fields, although there have been engagements between aspects of the *imago Dei* tradition and aspects of virtue discourse.[190] I offer my proposed fivefold ethic, connected to my integrated multifaceted interpretation of the *imago Dei*, to advance the conversation on what it means to be truly human, particularly for application in the fraught field of sexual ethics. This also forms part of my contribution to assist in answering two key questions regarding human existence in this context: "Who are we?" and "How are we meant to live?"

I advocate this proposed fivefold ethic as a key way in which the image of God in humanity may be manifested. In other words, I contend that humanity's imaging of God is partly actualized in the practice of this fivefold ethic. I suggest that when we humans practice the virtues, including particularly this proposed fivefold ethic—composed of the four classical cardinal virtues, along with and recalibrated by an overarching virtue of love and care—we are living in accordance with our telos, as bearers of the image of God.

Overall, pushing back against reductionistic and dehumanizing (including neoliberal) currents in contemporary dating approaches, I advocate the Christian virtue-ethical approach set out above—centered on a vision of genuine or redeemed humanity (what it means to be "truly human") developed in relation to my proposed multifaceted and integrated version of the *imago Dei* that is Christocentric in focus—expressed in the

189. Pieper, *Four Cardinal Virtues*, Preface, xii.
190. For recent examples, see Ployd, "Inseparable Virtue"; Keenan, "Linking Human Dignity"; Keenan, *Moral Life*, ch. 7, "The Virtues."

form of my proposed fivefold ethic (composed of five cardinal virtues: prudence, courage, temperance, justice and an overarching, recalibrating ethic of love and care) for practical application in the field of contemporary sexual ethics. I therefore advocate this fivefold ethic as a key expression of living as bearers of the image of God in the multifaceted integrated sense I have argued for earlier, that is, as a vital part of living to the "furthest potentialities of [human] nature."[191]

---

191. Pieper, *Four Cardinal Virtues*, Preface, xii.

CHAPTER 7: LIVING MORE HUMAN(E)LY?

Further Application and Concluding Thoughts

7.1 Drawing Together Findings from the Preceding Chapters

THUS FAR, IN ANSWER to my research questions set out earlier, I have suggested that, to help realize the good of happy, flourishing, lifelong monogamy (as defined in ch. 1), in approaching heterosexual dating in contemporary Anglo-American contexts (as described and discussed in ch. 3—including in view of a continuing shift towards the form of "pure relationship," culture wars, economic insecurity, medical advances enabling the normalization of casual sexual interactions, the increased sexualization of everyday culture, along with the growth of the internet and fast-improving technology resulting in the ubiquity of social media, online dating, and dating apps), and bearing in mind the typology of different approaches, historically and cross-culturally, to dating, courtship, and marriage (that I developed and set out in ch. 2):

1. The fivefold ethic I have advanced in chapter 6 should be prioritized.[1] When asking what qualities are important in a life partner, I propose that the qualities forming the fivefold ethic should be prioritized: prudence, justice, courage/fortitude, temperance, love and care (rather than, say, superficially focusing on physical attributes or surface personality traits or abilities).

---

1. Here, I am moving tentatively beyond the predominantly descriptive mode of earlier chapters to normative proposals based on the preceding discussion.

Individuals dating should (ideally) take substantial lengths of time to discern whether their prospective romantic partner has these qualities in genuinely substantial measure. While recognizing that we are all works-in-progress—and everyone will need more work in one or more of these areas—I suggest that these are important qualities that enable the flourishing of relationships, not least of all intimate romantic relationships. In preparation for navigating the convoluted world of dating and romantic relationships in contemporary contexts, I advocate a focus on cultivating these qualities, through habituation and character formation.

Of course, nobody is perfect, and formation in virtue requires time and effort, a lifelong process which cannot be completed this side of the eschaton. I suggest that a threshold is required for each individual to assess whether the degree of courage/temperance/prudence/justice/love and care that they discern in the other is sufficient for them to proceed with a decision to commit to lifelong marriage, and that it is for each individual to decide (soberly and as carefully as possible), in each of their unique circumstances, what that threshold should be and where the line should be drawn.

2. Rather than "purity culture" or "hookup culture" (discussed in ch. 3), and following my findings in chapter 2 and chapter 5, I recommend approaches in heterosexual dating that are along the lines of type (3) (and versions of type (2) close to type (3)) of my typology, that is, (with reference to my graph representing my typology in ch. 2) approaches that include both a vertical axis and a horizontal axis, and involve: (i) on the vertical axis, both romantic and practical considerations when choosing a partner for life, and (ii) on the horizontal axis, a moderate approach on the nonpermissive to permissive scale regarding intimate relations prior to marriage, and particularly that these should be correlated to levels of commitment in the relationship.

On the popular lifestyle choice of cohabitation in contemporary Anglo-American contexts, I reiterate my arguments in chapter 2, following Lawler and Salzman, and Thatcher, in distinguishing between "non-nuptial cohabitation" (using Thatcher's terminology) and "pre-nuptial cohabitation."[2] I suggest that cohabitation without a clear

---

2. Thatcher: *Living Together and Christian Ethics*, ch. 2; *God, Sex, and Gender*.

intention towards long-term commitment is in the nature of type (4) of my typology, while cohabitation in preparation for or as part of a process of long-term commitment (culminating in the formal procedures of marriage) is in the nature of type (3) of my typology.

3. Further, learning from the field of psychology, I advocate applying the five "recommended approaches" that I proposed in chapter 4—based on psychological research into romantic relationships and aspects of personality. In summary again, these five approaches are:

   i. Be aware of the variety of dynamics that could be at work in the complex experiences of attraction and rejection in romantic relationships.

   ii. Prioritize the value of companionate love for the long-term sustainability of intimate relationships.

   iii. Be aware that casual sex may not actually be "casual."

   iv. Be careful to minimize causing any unnecessary hurt or harm to the other, bearing in mind the potentially inflammatory nature and "dark side" of relationships, particularly when they go wrong.

   v. Seek to understand and relate to the other person, and make decisions regarding the relationship (such as on compatibility), on the basis of seeking to discern the full person, in the multilayered aspects of his/her personality. In relation to this, as mentioned, I recommend McAdams's three-level model of personality, discussed in detail in chapter 4, as a helpful tool for assisting couples to get to know each other in various key aspects of their personality.

   As stated in chapter 4, I contend that applying the above five "recommended approaches" may also be perceived as part of a practical working out of prudence in terms of being attentive to our finitude, limitations and embodiment as human creatures.

4. In addition, learning from the lived experiences of couples who enjoy the fruits of happy flourishing long-term monogamy, I suggest that the following insights should also be borne in mind, as I have discussed in detail in chapter 5:

   To reiterate, applying the findings of my empirical study based on semi-structured interviews of ten long-term happily married couples in Lincolnshire, I suggest that the following eight key elements are important for discernment during the period of dating or courtship, to help form good foundations for lifelong marriage:

i. Strong friendship (particularly in terms of congruence of life goals, motivations, and concerns—including long-term, rather than just short-term concerns)

ii. Honesty

iii. Trust

iv. Good communication

v. Mutual respect

vi. Kindness

vii. Give-and-take

viii. A propensity to persevere through difficult times

In addition to these, I also suggest that themes along the lines of my proposed fivefold ethic can be discerned from the interviewees' responses in my empirical study—themes of courage, temperance, prudence, justice, and love and care.

Further, as I have contended in chapter 5, it may also be possible to suggest, based on the findings of my empirical study, that the most resilient marriages are built on dating practices and decisions that are based on a combination of the exercise of reason, emotion, and physical attraction.[3] All three elements can be discerned from my interviewees' descriptions of their practices and decisions during their period of dating or courtship.

Along with the above, there are many indicators from the interview responses in my empirical study that enduring mutual support and companionship through the years (and the discerning of good potential

---

3. As stated in ch. 5, it should be borne in mind that this does not mean that either of the partners is required to be particularly sexually attractive by conventional standards. By inclusion of this element I mean that there is ongoing physical intimacy between the couple, and that (along with intimacy on an emotional and intellectual level) there is a physical bond between the couple that can be discerned through time, and they are not physically repulsed by each other. As said, stereotypes (such as assumptions that a younger woman is necessarily a better wife based on physical attractiveness) should be avoided, and I suggest that physical attraction between the partners (along with emotional and intellectual attraction) will thus mainly be a subjective phenomenon, based on factors that are unique to each couple. In this sense, while it may appear there are common elements and familiar themes, no two couples are the same.

for this during the time of dating and courtship) are key foundational elements for the thriving and flourishing of the couple relationships in the long term. I also argue that applying these findings and insights from my empirical study, albeit a small and modest study, listening to the voices of those who have gone before, may also be regarded as a further practical working out of the virtue of prudence (or wisdom) for the practice of dating.

Together, the above findings and proposals form the building blocks for a Christian ethical framework for heterosexual dating in contemporary Anglo-American contexts.

Utilizing MacIntyre's language of "goods" and "virtues," as discussed earlier in chapter 6, I argue that happy, flourishing, lifelong monogamy is an internal good in the field or practice of couple relationships and, further, that virtues that help enable the realization of this good include in particular my proposed fivefold ethic, composed of prudence, justice, courage/fortitude, temperance, and love and care.

7.2 Further Applying This Christian Virtue-Ethical Approach to Contemporary Dating

This virtue-ethical approach that I advocate is against "throwaway culture" which appears so endemic in contemporary Western experience. Related to this, it also stands against "meaningless sex" and similar practices. Hence, it is also against the meaningless breakup of committed relationships for no substantial reason—recognizing in particular the injustices that such breakups often may cause. At the same time, it would caution against a careless attitude towards the formation of relationships, recognizing that once an intimate relationship has grown, no matter how ill advised such a relationship may be, the ending of such a relationship—even when the breakup would in the long term be conducive to the well-being of the individuals involved—often results in some level of harm, detriment or pain to those involved.

The Christian virtue-ethical approach that I advance here seeks to support the practice and development of key virtues which I suggest are important for the flourishing of human intimate relationships. Such virtues should include particularly my proposed fivefold ethic of justice, courage, temperance or self-control, prudence or wisdom, and love and care, including patience, kindness, faithfulness, and honesty that upholds truth (1 Cor 13), along with further qualities highlighted in various parts of Christian Scripture (such as the Beatitudes and Gal 5:22–23), including joy, peace, gentleness, goodness. This differs significantly from various approaches sometimes popular in the dating market which involve various seduction techniques, manipulation or deception. This approach also implies not necessarily following one's "biological" instincts, such as female preferences for indicators of status, power or wealth in male suitors and male preferences for beautiful and shapely females as partners, which appear based on evolutionary motivations (as discussed earlier).[4]

7.2.1 A Christian Virtue-Ethical Approach to Unrequited Love and Breakups

One key distinction between the dating relationship and marriage is the often, or sometimes, temporal nature of the relationship. Dating relationships may be terminated more frequently and easily than marriages and without any recourse to nor remedies from the law. It may well be that this is an acceptable situation given that parties who are in a dating relationship but do not feel ready for the serious commitment that marriage involves could be at a stage where either or both partners still have reasonable doubts about the long-term viability of their relationship. A dating relationship, rather than the more serious commitment of marriage, gives the persons involved time and space to explore their mutual compatibility and evaluate long-term possibilities.

My proposed fivefold ethic may also be applied in situations of:

i. Unrequited love
ii. Breakups.

This may include applying the five recommended approaches discussed in chapter 4 on psychological aspects, and particularly, being sensitive to the potentially inflammatory nature of romantic relationships and breakups.

Laura Smit also promotes a virtues-centered approach to romantic relationships, including by applying, among other qualities, the fruit of the Spirit of Gal 5:22–23 as virtues practiced in the context of romance.[5] Overall, she argues that unrequited love, where love is not returned—if

---

4. See again, for example, as mentioned, the discussion in Buss, "Sex Differences."
5. Smit, *Loves Me, Loves Me Not*, 130–34.

that love is real, rather than based on fantasy or the imagination—can be a good that draws one closer to God.[6] She illustrates well the application of an ethic of love and care to experiences of unrequited love or rejection. This contrasts with violent or harmful responses (for example, as described in ch. 4).

Further, I suggest the exercise of a virtue of prudence in the oftentimes challenging situations of unrequited love and breakups should involve a mentality that seeks to discern a "good fit," rather than one focused on getting a "good catch." A prospective romantic partner may appear very appealing in terms of possessing qualities that are often considered a "good catch" in contemporary contexts—such as a high status in society or well-paying job (particularly for men) and "perfect ten" physical attributes (particularly for women),[7] but may not actually be a "good fit" in terms of real-life compatibility. I have discussed matters of compatibility in chapter 4, and will discuss this further, later in this chapter.

In addition, when navigating the various and often complex sets of circumstances which breakups involve, the other virtues in the fivefold ethic that I propose may also be particularly necessary, in addition to prudence. For example, courage may be required to face up to the reality of an abusive relationship and to walk away even in the midst of opposition. Temperance may be particularly called for to control the sometimes deeply held emotions and desires that may cloud one's sense of judgement about the health of the relationship. Justice is necessary to ensure that even in the difficult circumstances of breakups, each is fairly attended to and is rendered his or her due. And overall, love and care are required, so that the potentially harmful effects of breakups and/or unrequited love may as far as possible be minimized, and so that the complex issues involved are handled with compassion and sensitivity, alongside wisdom.

7.2.2 Further Proposals for Better Approaches

There appears to be a prevailing expectation in contemporary Anglo-American society that sex should normally become a part of a dating relationship before too long, unless an exception is made with good reason. This may be discerned from much contemporary dating advice, including

---

6. Smit, *Loves Me, Loves Me Not*, 59–60, 247–50.

7. As discussed in ch. 4, such traits have been identified often as attractive to romantic prospects, from evolutionary perspectives.

The Rules, for example, in lines such as: "It's only fair that if you're dating a man for a month or two and don't plan to sleep with him for a while to let him know. Otherwise, you're being a tease..."[8]

From a theological perspective, I would argue (following the discussion in ch. 1) that sex is meant to seal an already well-fitting relationship[9] between two people who have reached a well-considered decision to be in covenantal commitment to each other, and to enable/support the couple in continuing to grow long term in ever deeper relational oneness. It is not meant to paper over deficiencies in a relationship nor to create the illusion of compatibility based on hormone-fueled emotions, nor to jump-start intimacy between two virtual strangers, nor as a recreational "toy" for "quick-fix" pleasure—though so often in contemporary culture this is how sex appears to have been used (misused).

Further, my concern about contemporary dating advice along lines such as "How to get the guy" or "How to get the girl" is that such advice does not encourage readers to live close to their full potential as human beings, particularly as bearers of the image of God (in the multifaceted and integrated sense I have argued for earlier), and particularly in terms of practicing and growing in the cardinal virtues of courage, temperance, prudence, justice, and love and care, which enable genuine human flourishing. As Jesus has observed: "What good is it for someone to gain the whole world, yet forfeit their soul?" (Mark 8:36 NIV).

From a Christian virtue-ethical perspective, I therefore suggest the following further "better approaches" to heterosexual dating in contemporary Anglo-American contexts:

i. Emphasis on encouraging the formation/growth of "more good men" and "more good women," along the lines of my proposed five-fold ethic

ii. Focus on relationships, approaches, and practices that build up, rather than tear down (or wound, exploit or harm) each person

Following on from the above, these particular twin issues need to be addressed when considering helpful approaches to dating:

---

8. Fein and Schneider, *Complete Book of Rules*, rule 20: "Don't Rush into Sex and Other Rules for Intimacy."

9. Meaning "well fitting" in core spiritual, cognitive/rational, and affective/emotional aspects.

i. The sexual drive and natural working and effect of hormones, which often becomes an impetus towards early sexual involvement/marriage (particularly among emerging adults, but also relevant in other life stages)

ii. Compatibility—including the sensible need to know a prospective mate well enough before entering into the weighty commitment of marriage (with its substantial emotional, practical and legal ramifications)

Contemporary secular dating culture appears to lean towards addressing the latter by being relatively lax concerning the former (permissive attitudes regarding sex before marriage). Conservative Christian/church attitudes have tended to lean in the opposite direction, that is, by emphasizing sexual purity before marriage, and possibly indirectly encouraging young people to rush into marriage (to address the former—sexual drive) without sufficient consideration of the latter (weighty issues of compatibility).[10] Such an approach is regrettable, often resulting in a "lottery" of marriages which may turn out well matched or ill suited. This leads in turn to perplexing dilemmas concerning the acceptability of divorce in contemporary Christian culture, and I contend here that significant numbers of couples may well be spared the complex and often challenging issues concerning divorce if dating culture can be sufficiently reformed to take adequate and serious consideration of both issues (i) and (ii) above.

Addressing (i) and (ii) above, I advocate reformed dating culture which encourages both:

i. Physical intimacy that is correlated to the level of commitment within the relationship

ii. Sufficient substantial[11] time and focus on getting to know the other person (in all key aspects of personality—referring again to

---

10. Referring to my proposed typology and graph representing the typology set out in ch. 2, I suggest that there has been an overemphasis in conservative Christian circles on matters relating to the horizontal axis (permissive as opposed to nonpermissive approaches to sexual relations prior to marriage) and insufficient focus on matters relating to the vertical axis (reasons for choice of one's marriage partner).

11. This acknowledges that what constitutes "sufficient" or "substantial" will vary according to different couples' and individuals' circumstances, but I suggest that the general principle of "sufficient and substantial" should be emphasized, while allowing for variation based on different contexts.

psychological aspects, including McAdams's three-level model of personality) when dating, to ascertain whether there is real compatibility.

7.3 Further Discussion of "You Always Marry the Wrong Person"

The Relevance of "Compatibility"

Does "the one" exist? How about soulmates? Perhaps (as some who may have been fortunate enough to have found love several times in their lifetime may attest), it is unrealistic to assert that there is only "one" person with whom a blissful marriage can be built. Yet, we probably all know of couples who have formed pair-bonds so strong that each regards the other as a "soulmate." Perhaps such bonds are forged mainly through "working at it" through the years, as some may insist. I certainly agree this is important. Yet, I suggest that some sort of "compatibility" will be at work in such relationships as well.

Further to discussion of this in chapters 1 and 4, my contention is also that prioritizing some level of "compatibility" as part of the criteria for choice of one's life partner is a further part of the practical outworking of the virtue of prudence (or practical wisdom) and does have backing from Judeo-Christian Scripture. For example, it may be observed that Judeo-Christian Scripture contains hints of the importance of compatibility in life's significant relationships, though not necessarily directly addressing romantic relationships. This may be discerned from verses such as "Can two walk together unless they are agreed?" (Amos 3:3 NKJV) and "Do not be unequally yoked together with unbelievers" (2 Cor 6:14a NKJV).

What might this "compatibility" consist of? What is more important, and less important? My advocating for more of a focus on discerning genuine compatibility (including in Christian dating) is further supported by reference to expert advice, such as from experienced divorce lawyer Baroness Shackleton, who recommended ten questions for couples to ask before marriage, including the following:

- "Are we a 'good fit'?
- "Do we have a strong basis of friendship?"
- "Do we want the same things?"

- "Are our expectations realistic?"
- "Do we generally see the best in each other?"
- "Do we both work at keeping our relationship vibrant?"
- "Do we feel we can discuss things and raise issues with each other?"
- "Are we both committed to working through hard times?"
- "Would we pull together to get through stressful times?"
- "Do we each have supportive people around us?"[12]

As a further example of applying practical wisdom, nationwide relationship counselors Relate highlight the importance of shared values for the longevity and thriving of relationships, stating:

> Usually, you tend to have more satisfying and longer lasting relationships with people that share your values. That's the deeply held stuff that really makes up the core of who you are and what you believe—your ideas about work, leisure, money, religion, family and so on. . . .
>
> Having the same interests or sharing a physical attraction can make a real difference too—but when it comes down to it, values tend to be what lasts the longest.[13]

On the importance of congruence of goals, motivations, and concerns, I suggest that this aspect may also be related to different indices for measurement of attractiveness which may vary considerably from person to person (and even for the same person through different seasons of life). For person A, physical looks and physique may be high on the list of "must-have" attributes in a potential partner, while for person B intellectual ability in certain fields may be particularly important, while for person C specific features of personality, habits, and interests may be preferred. It would be advisable during the period of dating or courtship to ensure there is honest communication between the two individuals as to what aspects or features each genuinely finds attractive, and whether these are short-term or longer-lived inclinations, and which are likely to be sustainable in the long term.

In relation to this, it is also helpful to note Pope Francis's reminder:

---

12. Freeman-Powell, "Could Love Island."
13. Relate, "How to Find Someone," paras. 5–6.

> Nothing is more volatile, precarious and unpredictable than desire. The decision to marry should never be encouraged unless the couple has discerned deeper reasons that will ensure a genuine and stable commitment.[14]

Part of the main focus of my project, as reflected in the preceding chapters, is to seek to discern—learning from history, sociology, psychology, people's lived experiences and Christian virtue ethics—what these "deeper reasons" should consist of, in order to help enable "a genuine and stable commitment," held to be a priority above.

This may be helpfully evaluated with the question from Stassen and Gushee referred to in chapter 1: "Whom can I trust to live my life with, to be faithful to and to be faithful to me?"[15] I suggest that such questions are better answered when one is equipped with a more well-rounded knowledge of oneself and the other, based, for example, on McAdams's three-level model of personality discussed in chapter 4, considering (i) traits; (ii) goals, motivations, and concerns; and (iii) one's personal story/journey/narrative.

At its core, I suggest that true compatibility should be about each person knowing the other well, and loving and accepting the other for all that he/she is (as the saying goes, "warts and all") and, as I have suggested in chapter 4, taking into good account the various aspects and levels of the other's personality, while enabling him/her to flourish and live to his/her full potential, and accepting that these may change/develop through the years. Ideally, dating should be a process in which true compatibility can be discerned, to form a foundation for a lifetime commitment to continue to grow and flourish together in a dynamic process of deepening compatibility.

7.4 Further Observations in Connection with a Discussion of Compatibility

7.4.1 On Friendship and Love

In Aristotle's *Nicomachean Ethics*, three types of friendship are described:

i. Friendship of pleasure

---

14. Francis, *Amoris Laetitia*, para. 209.
15. Stassen and Gushee, *Kingdom Ethics*, ch. 14, loc. 6099 of 12445.

ii. Friendship of utility

iii. Friendship of character/virtue/excellence/good people—Aristotle refers to this as "complete friendship," encompassing aspects of the first two types, but based in goodness/the character of the friends and hence more substantial, with most potential for enduring through different circumstances.[16]

Due to space constraint, I will not be discussing in detail the different scholarly interpretations of Aristotle's views regarding friendship. Very briefly, it may be noted that some interpret Aristotle to mean that only (iii) (friendship of character) is the perfect form of friendship, and the others are considered imperfect forms. There are also scholars who disagree with the above view—for example, by regarding friendship as part of a formative influence and experience which assists in moulding one's character in virtue/goodness.

Applying this discussion to dating, courtship and romantic relationships, and my fourfold typology discussed in chapter 2, I suggest that there appears to be a degree of parallel between friendships/relationships of utility and type (1) (functional approaches), while types (2), (3), and most of (4) (except the functional expressions of type (4))—based on companionate or romantic approaches—may correlate with the idea of friendships of pleasure, but critically some key expressions particularly of type (3) and some of type (2) may be examples of Aristotle's concept of friendship based on character/virtue/goodness.

Further, connecting this to my empirical study and findings regarding the key role of friendship as an ingredient of happy long-term marriages, I suggest that better approaches in dating should include an emphasis in discerning whether there exists between each couple genuine friendship as Aristotle describes it—friendship of character/virtue. This is likely a significantly more stable and enduring basis for long-term intimate relationships than friendships or relationships based merely on pleasure or utility.

As Pope Francis has also reminded regarding the primacy of good friendship for marriage:

> After the love that unites us to God, conjugal love is the "greatest form of friendship." It is a union possessing all the traits of a good friendship: concern for the good of the other, reciprocity,

16. Aristotle, *Nicomachean Ethics* 8.3.

intimacy, warmth, stability and the resemblance born of a shared life. Marriage joins to all this an indissoluble exclusivity expressed in the stable commitment to share and shape together the whole of life.[17]

This is further borne out by the questions for couples suggested by Baroness Shackleton mentioned earlier.

7.4.2 Further Observations from *An Uncommon Correspondence*

In *An Uncommon Correspondence*, documenting the deeply thoughtful correspondence between Ivy George and Margaret Masson, these two friends describe their very different experiences of romance and courtship in the respective cultures (East and West) they grew up in. In the course of the correspondence, Ivy describes her experiences of the culture of arranged marriages in her home country, India, and her reservations/frustration with the system. At the same time, George also poignantly points out the deficiencies and ultimate hollowness of an overly "romanticized" culture of love, dating and courtship in the West, which often leaves one yearning for more.[18] Later, after turning away suitor after suitor, Ivy agrees to marry a suitor called Abraham, of whom she initially writes after their first couple of meetings:

> Into our conversation I began to get the sense that this man was mature and decent enough not to misinterpret me to his family. I started to feel safe with him. We started to talk about other things quite freely—women's issues in India, liberation theology, questions of social justice and so on.[19]

Although Ivy is unable to give Abraham a definite answer at their initial meetings, quite unconventionally for their context (of the culture of "arranged marriages"), she and Abraham agree to continue a correspondence—by letter and telephone—giving them several months to consider their relationship. In the course of her developing relationship with Abraham, still conducted along the lines of safeguards provided by the "arranged marriages" culture, including with strict limitations

---

17. Francis, *Amoris Laetitia*, para. 123.
18. George and Masson, *Uncommon Correspondence*, 37–39.
19. George and Masson, *Uncommon Correspondence*, 122–23.

on physical intimacy prior to marriage, Ivy writes approvingly of such restrictions.[20] Eventually, she marries Abraham.

As many in successful arranged marriages have likely observed through the centuries, love can grow over time, when important aspects are in place. For some, though there may be no initial romantic "spark" on their first meeting, if fundamentals are sound, the relationship can still blossom into a strong, meaningful and intimate partnership. Ivy places priority on key qualities in Abraham's character (virtues), and values their compatibility spiritually, intellectually, and socially, while also highlighting the helpfulness of abstinence and exercising self-control in intimate relationships. These are practical considerations but can also form the basis of strong and sustainable romantic relationships.

7.4.3 Further Observations from Szreter and Fisher Contributing to Practical Wisdom

Concerning criteria in dating and courtship, Szreter and Fisher advocate resisting the tendency to think in terms of "either/or" considerations when it comes to marriage and romance. An approach that balances both practical and romantic considerations may be helpful, and they found this to be borne out in parts of their interviewees' responses. They assert:

> In talking of their decisions to get married interviewees constructed a balance between romance and realism, which robustly deprecated anything too sentimental or soppy, while still reserving a space for acknowledging the importance of love and intimacy, albeit within the practical context of the kind of hard-working partnership that would be necessary for a successful marriage.[21]

Reminding of the complex nature of factors in play and the range of experiences reflected in their respondents' testimonies, Szreter and Fisher observe evidence of both unhealthy ignorance and inhibitions, "on the one hand," and of healthy respect for the privacy of marital/sexual relations (connected with marital pleasure and intimacy), "on the other hand," undergirding many interviewees' responses.[22]

---

20. George and Masson, *Uncommon Correspondence*, 141.

21. Szreter and Fisher, *Sex Before the Sexual Revolution*, ch. 4, s.v. "Conclusion."

22. Szreter and Fisher, *Sex Before the Sexual Revolution*, ch. 10, s.vv. "Conclusion: Private Lives."

While recognizing the "various progressive critiques of sex [which have] emerged [throughout the early and mid-twentieth century] [denouncing] silence and secrecy surrounding sex as conducive to ignorance, inhibitions, incompetence, intolerance and sexually unsatisfying marriages" and the "radical and conservative voices alike" during this period which "increasingly saw sexual satisfaction as a cornerstone of marriage and urged couples, especially men, to educate themselves in improved sexual technique" which overall have "informed and stimulated various sexual debates and transformations throughout the twentieth century particularly since the 1960s when the (contested) idea of 'liberation' was heralded as a break from the 'repression' of the past [which was labelled 'Victorian' and characterized by] ... restricted, taboo sexuality],"[23] Szreter and Fisher's "oral history evidence explodes ... stereotypes."[24] They conclude that the widely held narrative, which presents a "'modern' eroticised version of marriage against a 'traditional' [pre-1960s] 'repressed' version, dominated by ignorance and an absence of communication between partners," is simplistic and "posits too crude a contrast between sexual pleasure versus sexual shyness, inhibition and reticence."[25]

Following Szreter and Fisher's conclusions, I contend for a balanced approach to the "sexual revolution" in contemporary Anglo-American contexts. Certainly, it is necessary to encourage individuals to be comfortable and confident in their self-understanding, personal identity, and sexuality (rather than endorsing repression, ignorance, and other unhelpful mindsets). At the same time, it is also necessary to remind of the value of privacy and respecting the genuine worth of the good gift of sex in healthy contexts that promote human flourishing, rather than simply opening the floodgates to encouraging promiscuous lifestyles that may not necessarily be conducive to human well-being.

7.5 Further Drawing Together the Findings of the Preceding Chapters

To reiterate, in this book I have sought to answer the following questions:

---

23. Szreter and Fisher, *Sex Before the Sexual Revolution*, ch. 10, s.vv. "Conclusion: Private Lives."
24. Szreter and Fisher, *Sex Before the Sexual Revolution*, ch. 10, s.vv. "Conclusion: Private Lives."
25. Szreter and Fisher, *Sex Before the Sexual Revolution*, ch. 10, s.vv. "Conclusion: Private Lives."

CHAPTER 7: LIVING MORE HUMAN(E)LY?   279

  i. Assuming a Christian version of happy, flourishing, lifelong, monogamous marriage is a good, are there any approaches to heterosexual dating in contemporary Anglo-American contexts that help realize or promote this good?
  ii. And if so, what do they consist of?

To answer these questions, I first set out (in ch. 1) my assumptions regarding the version of marriage that I regard as a good (happy, flourishing, lifelong monogamy). I then considered in some detail:

  i. Historical and cross-cultural aspects of dating and courtship culture, in which I developed a typology of dating and/or courtship practices (ch. 2)
  ii. Sociological aspects, in which I discussed six key features or themes that I consider particularly significant in relation to heterosexual dating approaches in contemporary Anglo-American contexts (ch. 3)
  iii. Psychological aspects, engaging with psychological research relevant to answering these questions, in which I developed and recommended five "recommended approaches" (ch. 4)
  iv. Empirical data and responses from my empirical study, consisting of semi-structured interviews of ten long-term happily married couples in Lincolnshire (ch. 5)
  v. Christian virtue ethics, in which I developed, discussed and advanced my proposed fivefold ethic for application to dating in contemporary Anglo-American contexts (ch. 6)

I advocate my proposed fivefold ethic as helpful for the formation of stable, flourishing and mutually supportive couple relationships[26] in twenty-first-century Anglo-American contexts and as being particularly conducive to the well-being and flourishing of individuals involved in heterosexual dating practices in these contexts. This approach also focuses on mutual

---

26. This leaves slightly open the issue of whether marriage (in legal terms) is the best form of couple relationship for human well-being and flourishing. Full discussion of this topic is beyond the scope of my book, although much of my book is advanced on the premise that, in general, a healthy marriage (or, now under UK law, a civil partnership) is still the form of couple relationship that is most conducive to human flourishing and well-being, in terms of mutual commitment, long-term stability, and the legal and public protection that is provided to married spouses (or, also, civil partners under UK law) in America and the United Kingdom, which is not generally available to unmarried cohabitees or to those in other forms of couple relationships.

support and companionship as a foundation for a good marriage that also enables the well-being and flourishing of the individuals involved and society around them. Although this ethic has been advanced in a "Protestant" mode, it is likely evident that in some ways it has more resonance with Anglo-Catholic approaches.

Applying an Aristotelian concept of the mean, eschewing both excess and deficiency, I also suggest that my proposed approach may be further understood by considering the typology of dating practice that I developed and described in chapter 2, and is also supported by findings from my empirical study discussed in chapter 5. In particular, this approach may be perceived as being akin to type (3) (or versions of type (2) which are close to type (3)) of the typology of dating practice developed in chapter 2. Data from my empirical study, interviewing ten long-term happily married couples in Lincolnshire, also show strong correlation with type (3) (or versions of type (2) close to type (3)) features, as I have discussed in chapter 5.

I suggest that the overall approach I have described above also has some features in common with dating/courtship culture in 1930s–50s Anglo-American contexts, prior to the sexual revolution of the 1960s and 1970s. While approaches to dating, courtship, and/or marriage during this period have often been criticized as ignorant, repressive, and/or unfulfilling,[27] I advocate a more nuanced view of the complex picture of intimate life in those times, supported by research such as that of Szreter and Fisher[28] and others (further described in ch. 2 on historical and cross-cultural aspects), while also bearing in mind that such approaches clearly need to be adapted to our twenty-first-century contexts. While such adaptation is certainly necessary, I suggest that even so, substantial elements remain that are relevant and helpful from dating and/or courtship practices and approaches during that period—or subsequent to that period but significantly influenced by that period, such as children applying approaches learnt from their parents—this may be observed, for example, from responses from the interviewees in my empirical study described in chapter 5, particularly regarding significant influences from their parents or community on their lives and practices. I recommend

27. See, for example, literature such as McEwan, *On Chesil Beach*; Giddens, "Global Revolution," in which Giddens concludes his argument against "the traditional family" by referring to the long sixty-year marriage of his great aunt, which he describes as "deeply unhappy . . . the whole of that time" (33).

28. See, as discussed above, Szreter and Fisher, *Sex Before the Sexual Revolution*.

CHAPTER 7: LIVING MORE HUMAN(E)LY?   281

recovery of some of those elements (which may be identified from findings in my empirical study, and also particularly where they may be understood in terms of the virtues I have discussed in ch. 6) for application in contemporary Anglo-American contexts in ways that may be of significant help in addressing contemporary problems.

Overall, therefore, I advocate a Christian virtue-ethical approach primarily in the form of the fivefold ethic that I have developed and discussed in chapter 6 (for application in contemporary Anglo-American contexts, discussed and described in ch. 3), an approach which in practical terms, applied to sexual ethics, may also be understood as being along the lines of type (3) (or versions of type (2) close to type (3)) of my proposed typology developed and described in chapter 2, and which may also be applied along psychological lines through the five "recommended approaches" that I developed and discussed in chapter 4.

The decision to make a lifelong commitment to one person is a very weighty decision, and (as some marriage services still include a reminder of) not a decision to be entered into lightly. Marriage, particularly maintaining lifelong monogamy in the contemporary world, is tough. Staying faithful and happily married to one person in contemporary Anglo-American contexts is a tremendous challenge, but I contend that it is a good worth fighting for (as set out in ch. 1), and I also contend (through chs. 2–6) that starting a marriage with a strong foundation (rather than assuming, say, that "you always marry the wrong person")—particularly in terms of practicing the "better approaches to dating and courtship" advocated in this book—contributes significantly to enabling the building and continued maintenance and flourishing of happy, lifelong, monogamous couple relationships.

Of course, practicing the virtues of prudence, justice, courage, temperance, and love and care should not simply stop at the altar or the registry office. Marriage (or civil partnership) should be a lifelong journey in which each couple continue to develop and grow together, deepening and nurturing their intimate relationship in a myriad of different ways, so that its potential for flourishing is realized all the more through the years. I contend in this book for a good foundation on which such flourishing intimate relationships can be built and enabled to last the years. Advocating a Christian virtue-ethical approach particularly in terms of my proposed fivefold ethic advanced here, I suggest that the more developed that individuals and couples are in the virtues discussed when they engage in dating in contemporary Anglo-American contexts, the better—the more conducive to well-being and flourishing—will be the experiences and outcomes of their dating practices, even through the uncertainties and vicissitudes of life, and the better and stronger will be their long-term committed relationships should they decide to commit long-term to a particular relationship, usually in marriage or a civil partnership.

From a Christian standpoint, but with a view to universal applicability, I suggest that even being well developed in the various "nontheological" classical cardinal virtues (traditionally identified as prudence, justice, courage, and temperance) will significantly improve the quality, experiences and outcomes of dating practices in contemporary Anglo-American contexts. I suggest that in addition, being developed in the virtues (traditionally described as "theological") of faith, hope, and love (in the spirit of 1 Cor 13)—which in accordance with traditional Christian teaching is available only to believers through infusion by the Holy Spirit—will provide an additional, richer, deeper and more fruitful dimension to those dating practices and relationships. As discussed, overall, I advocate a fivefold ethic—composed of five cardinal virtues: prudence, justice, courage/fortitude, temperance, and (an overarching, recalibrating virtue of) love and care—for universal applicability in couple relationships.

7.6 Limitations of This Study and Suggested Areas for Future Research

As this study is interdisciplinary, with an emphasis on breadth, covering several specialist fields, including by engaging historical, sociological, and psychological research relating to couple relationships, it has not been possible to consider comprehensively nor exhaustively the extensive material in each of these fields. While I have endeavored to present a fair selection of significant scholarly work in each of these fields relating to my research questions, there will inevitably be areas of research which I have not been able to venture into due to space and time constraints. Future research could focus on delving further into each of these fields (history, cross-cultural studies, sociology, psychology) in relation to couple relationships, with theological ethics and virtue ethics interacting with each of these, including by exploring further each of the themes I have highlighted in the preceding chapters.

In addition to this, due to limitations of time and space, the empirical study I conducted and reported on in chapter 5 is very modest with a small sample size of ten happily married couples (twenty participants). I am aware there are routinely much bigger studies conducted, involving hundreds, even thousands, of couples in the field of couple relationships. Thus, future research may also focus on conducting further studies—perhaps reusing or expanding on the questions that I asked my interviewees in this study. I will be interested to see if the findings are along different or similar lines to the findings and data I have presented in my typology-based graph in chapter 2 and discussed in chapter 5.

7.7 Concluding Thoughts

I refer again to the analogy of the house and foundation that I described in chapter 1, in relation to the topic of compatibility. To that analogy I now add a further analogy, an agrarian or gardening analogy. Consider that building a good marriage is somewhat like endeavoring to grow a healthy zucchini plant or apple tree. If the original plant or baby tree is planted in soil that is not conducive for growth of the tree or plant, it will not thrive and may eventually wither—even if good care is poured on it thereafter. If however the plant or baby tree is first planted in good soil—with healthy nutrients and in a good location with sufficient air, light, and so on (as good primary school science teachers would have reminded us)—subsequent care and nurture, such as regular watering of the plant and careful removal of weeds, will enable the growth of the plant without major hindrance. I suggest that "better approaches to dating" are like building a good foundation for a house or good soil for the growth of a tree. On a good foundation, an enduring house can be built and, with good maintenance, will last the years. In good soil, a plant or tree can flourish through the years, with nurture and care. My main research questions in this book (first set out in the Introduction) may be understood also in terms of asking: What does this "good foundation" consist of? What does this "good soil" consist of? In other words, what are these "better approaches," and what are the misconceptions and stereotypes to avoid?

In the course of the preceding chapters and the current chapter I have set out to answer these questions primarily through the study of key sources from theological, historical, sociological, and psychological research relevant to couple relationships, along with insights from the lived experiences of ten long-term happily married couples and Christian virtue ethics. It is my hope that this small contribution to the field will be of help to some who may be searching.

APPENDIX A

Sample Standard Interview Questionnaire

[Names]
Date: [ ]
Venue: [Home address]

Question (Qn): Are you each happy with the marriage? If you could do so all over again, would you marry the same person?

Qn: Your respective ages?

Qn: Number of years you have been married?

Qn: Do you have any children?

Qn: Occupation or (if retired) previous occupation?

Qn: Are either/both of you Christians? If so, which denomination, and do you attend church regularly?

Qn: Any other beliefs/cultural practices?

Qn: Your ethnicity?

Qn: How did you meet?

Qn: How long did you date/court before marriage?

Qn: What were important criteria for you when you were dating? Why did you choose each other:
(i) To date?
(ii) For marriage?

Qn: What were your typical activities during dating/courtship? (For example: going to dances, movies, meals, and so on. Any exchange of letters/notes/cards/messages in any other form?)

Qn: Any aspects of compatibility/fit that you think have worked for you, from the experience of having been married now for these many years? Any changes from your criteria when you were dating?

Qn: Apologies in advance for two potentially quite sensitive and personal questions now. Please feel free to say if you would prefer not to answer.
(i) Were you physically intimate with each other (e.g., kissing, cuddling) before marriage?
(ii) Were you sexually intimate with each other before marriage?
(iii) Did you live together before marriage?

Qn: What do you consider your significant similarities/significant areas that you have in common? Which of those do you consider most important for helping you in your marriage/relationship with each other? (For example: shared interests, experiences, values, goals/concerns in life, and so on.)

Qn: What do you see as your differences? Which differences do you find helpful, and which do you find unhelpful in your relationship with each other? (For example: personality traits, strengths and weaknesses, and so on.)

APPENDIX A: SAMPLE STANDARD INTERVIEW QUESTIONNAIRE   287

Qn: What do you consider are key influences in formation of your traits, values, goals/motivations/concerns, and so on, and your attitude towards dating/courtship and marriage?—such as role models, community/friends, family, books, TV, and so on.

Qn: Is there any general advice you would give to younger couples? Any aspects of premarital/dating/courtship behavior and contexts that you consider are helpful generally towards a healthy marriage?

Qn: Do you think there are aspects of the above advice that are less (or more) applicable in today's context, as distinct from when you were dating? What may be the reasons for this?

Do you think there are significant differences between social expectations (particularly concerning premarital/dating behavior of couples) when you were dating and social expectations now? Please describe these and how you think such differences may (or may not) affect the advice you would give.

Qn: What personal qualities/virtues do you consider are important for a healthy marriage?

Qn: What other ingredients do you consider important for a happy healthy marriage?

Qn: Any other general advice on dating/courtship/choice of life partner?

<u>Four follow-up questions, please:</u>

If you described your views and approach towards courtship/dating in terms of numbers:

1. On a scale of 1 to 10

    (1 being most pragmatic/unromantic/functional in criteria—such as income, assets, skills—

10 being most romantic/non-pragmatic in criteria—such as romantic feelings, friendship—and

5 being a balance of both romantic and practical criteria),

your view/approach concerning criteria for choosing a life partner/marriage partner, <u>at the time you were dating/courting</u>, would be:

2. On a scale of 1 to 10

    (1 being most pragmatic/unromantic/functional in criteria—such as income, assets, skills—

    10 being most romantic/non-pragmatic in criteria—such as romantic feelings, friendship—and

    5 being a balance of both romantic and practical criteria),

    your view/approach concerning criteria for choosing a life partner/marriage partner <u>now</u> would be:

3. On a scale of 1 to 10

    (1 being most absolute/nonpermissive—such as no sexual involvement before marriage—

    10 being most permissive—such as "anything is fine, as long as both parties consent"—and

    5 being midway/flexible in allowing there could be some sexual activity prior to marriage, but that should be directly connected to commitment/engagement),

    your view/approach concerning practices in dating/courtship prior to marriage, <u>at the time you were dating/courting</u>, would be:

4. On a scale of 1 to 10

    (1 being most absolute/nonpermissive—such as no sexual involvement before marriage—

    10 being most permissive—such as "anything is fine, as long as both parties consent"—and

    5 being midway/flexible in allowing there could be some sexual activity prior to marriage, but that should be directly connected to commitment/engagement),

your view/approach concerning practices in dating/courtship prior to marriage, <u>now</u>, would be:

Thank you so much again for your time.

APPENDIX B

Compilation of Interviewees' Responses

Compilation of Interviewees' Responses to Questions relating to 5.2.2, 5.2.3, and 5.2.4

Note: Names have been changed to protect the privacy of individuals.

1. What were important criteria for you when you were dating? Why did you choose each other: (i) to date and (ii) for marriage?

Nicholas and Wilma:

Wilma: I liked the look of him.

Nicholas: I had known quite a few women. Wilma was different. I found her to be a very warm, open character, with no hidden foibles. Physical attractiveness was relevant, too, but that wasn't the primary consideration. I don't think either of us regard the other as "God's gift to the [other sex]" or "Mr. and Mrs. Universe."

Wilma: I liked the fact that he seemed very confident.

Nicholas: Despite working in a teaching hospital, she was quite naïve, coming from a female-sheltered household.

Nicholas and Wilma: We were both members of the scouting movement, with camping, outdoor life, and activities. Wilma was later a guide leader, and Nicholas was a scout leader at the time.

Edward and Sandra:

Edward: Physical attraction was certainly part of it. I never thought of it in terms of character traits. Just that we got on with each other.

Sandra: Edward was quite empathetic and kind when I was hurting. I had struggled with my relationship with my parents, particularly with my mother, as a teenager. I was a stroppy teenager. And I was a stroppy teenager who liked Edward. Yes, I liked his temperament. Like Edward said, we just found that we got on.

It was something intangible. Over time we just found that we really got on.

Rick and Cora:

Cora: I wouldn't know how to answer that.

Rick: I wouldn't know how to answer that either! It was just one of those things that happened!

Cora: And once the dog moved in, that was that. It's easier to move a person than a dog!

Rick: We got on alright. We got on well together.

Cora: We've had no trouble in talking with each other since, haven't we? [both chuckle]

You analyze these things when they don't work, don't you? But when they work, you just accept it, you don't think about it.

Stephen and Hannah:

Stephen: Physical attractiveness and intelligence.

Hannah: Stephen was really interesting, and he had a lot of knowledge of interesting things like music and so on. Physical attractiveness also. And optimism. Especially because my own family weren't very optimistic.

Qn: And for marriage too?

Hannah: That's where I hesitated a bit—about the marriage bit. I wasn't sure that Stephen would always be sensitive to my needs, having been an only child. We did consider others, dated other people. But eventually I decided on Stephen still, realizing that I couldn't live without him. Also,

Stephen being faithful and still sure of me, even when we broke up for awhile and I wasn't sure, that won me over. Stephen was more sure than me and eventually won me over.

Clare and Walter:

Clare: Physical attraction was definitely what it was to start with.

Walter: Physical attractiveness and your niceness. [*Both smile*]

Clare: Shared interests also. Walter was interested in sports cars and formula racing, car shows, and so on, various things to do with cars, and I was moderately interested.

Walter: And cinema and theater. I used to come and watch your drama productions.

Clare: Amateur dramatics was a big part of my life then. Both of us also enjoyed going to see films. *Star Wars* was out around that time. And Woody Allen.

Timothy and Natalie:

Shared interests, really. Village activities, countryside interests, rural interests. We both love rural activities, including dog walking and dog training. In the past, we kept dogs, but difficult to do that as we got older and needed to go away often.

Also, sense of humor. We have very much a shared sense of humor.

Shared values are also important, including regarding how we spend money. We are both very careful and selective about how we spend money, which is why we are quite affluent now in older age.

Both of us were brought up in a time of frugality, a time of rationing. Whereas the generations now are brought up in a time of waste and a lot more choice—including fast food and so on.

We are very supportive of charitable causes, but very selective of which causes—to make sure we know where the money goes.

Irene and Anthony:

Anthony: I think it was character traits.

Irene: Yes, you were so open about everything.

Anthony: Still am.

Irene: Yes, you still are, darling.

Anthony: One of the interesting things about our marriage is that we have never had a row.

Irene: Yes, we've never had a row. People don't believe us!

Anthony: When we first met, Irene had a fiery nature, because of how things were then. And we decided early on it was pointless arguing about things.

Irene: We don't see eye to eye in everything. In lots of ways we can differ from each other. But the important things we can always thresh out and sort out.

I've tempered down since being married to Anthony.

Anthony: Maybe it's because you're happy in the marriage.

Irene: Yes. [both smile]

Irene and Anthony: There's no point having a row over things. It's a waste of temper.

Our personalities, that's what drew us to each other.

Laura and Zachary:

Laura: Personality traits.

Zachary: I look at the whole package. If you weren't physically attractive to me, you wouldn't have been on my radar in the first place. We had good fun together. We enjoyed doing similar things, partying, dancing. Our common subject was probably the air force. Also music, theater, cinema, walking, skiing.

Zachary and Laura: We both had a core area of interests in common, and we each also had our own individual interests to pursue, so we also had our own space.

We also noticed various habits, such as being good at keeping house, when we were on holiday in Israel together and had to share a room because of budget.

Zachary: I wasn't looking for someone who would bring my slippers for me. I was looking for someone well rounded and well balanced, and I found that in Laura.

Laura: We just enjoyed each other's company, and were very relaxed with each other.

Zachary: We had a big group of social friends in the Air Force. But eventually realized that there's something special about this person, with qualities the others didn't have.

Laura: We also had discussions about religion. I didn't want to be Catholic. It mattered to me to be Protestant. And Zachary didn't mind.

George and Agnes:

George: It was Agnes's smile. It was her happy smile. She just smiled all night. It was very instant attraction.

Agnes: We were just drawn to each other. I liked the fact you were active, lively.

George: Our personalities were very different initially, but we've influenced each other over the years. We have a similar outlook on life, but different personalities.

Agnes: We are both "can-do" people.

George: We were very young. Agnes was eighteen, I was twenty. It was the attraction that drew us together. We didn't have a list of criteria. But obviously the compatibility between us kept us together.

Within three months of meeting each other, we were separated from each other. Agnes was posted to RAF L and I was posted to RAF C—about a couple of hundred miles apart from each other. If we weren't compatible, the relationship would have fallen apart. We had no cars, and there were no mobile phones then. We wrote a lot of letters.

Agnes: I've still kept them.

George: And we traveled by train to meet up on weekends. We also spoke on the phone.

We were both in company with lots of other eligible young people. So if we weren't compatible, we would not have carried on with the relationship.

The distance was a good test of our relationship. It was good preparation for our marriage, as we've had to be separated many times in our marriage because of work. We are both independent and adventurous. We both joined the RAF to see the world. We have a lot in common.

George and Agnes: The experience has helped us. We have been hundreds of miles away from family throughout most of our marriage. We've had to survive without much support from family.

Agnes's family did say she can come back, but if she had marriage problems it would be for her to work at that herself!

Resilience has been important for us. Agnes is not the sort of person to go running back to her parents if there's a problem. That also helped us in our common mindset together, to be independent.

Agnes: George's family didn't like the fact that I was a Protestant. They didn't like that I was not Catholic.

George: Yes, we spent a lot of time trying to sort things out with family about the wedding. In the end, it was a Church of England wedding. We got married in the church Agnes grew up in. And I told my family to attend if they wanted to. In the end they did, but they didn't come to the children's christening.

George and Agnes: That's why we say if we did it again, we would just elope! Or make it small and simple—just at a church on camp or something. Also, our families brought us up to be very independent. Agnes was the oldest child and very independent. George was the youngest child and ready to see the world.

Phyllis and Henry:

Henry: I thought she was very intelligent. I loved her. I loved everything about her, and I still do. I thought she was beautiful, and very intelligent.

You feel comfortable with the person. Or you also feel uncomfortable because you're afraid you'll lose her.

I knew definitely that this is someone I wanted in my life.

Phyllis: I thought he was very handsome. But at first I thought he joked too much, that he wasn't very serious. It took awhile to get to know him and find that he is trustworthy. He was very protective of me.

2. What were your typical activities during dating/courtship?

Phyllis and Henry:

Phyllis: We met in 1960, and got married in 1963. It was the coffee bar era. We went to the coffee bar a lot. Henry drank Coke floats, and I had Fanta Orange.

We went to the pictures a lot—watching people like Cliff Richard, Elvis Presley, other films also.

Yes, we wrote some letters. But we only lived eight to ten miles from each other.

We had quite a lot in common, in terms of living not far from each other.

Henry: I think I changed more towards Phyllis's view. My father was quite authoritarian.

Edward and Sandra:

Edward: Sandra used to come round to the flat, and we used to spend the evening on the living room floor, snuggled up and watching TV.

Sandra: Yes, we didn't go out a lot. Edward was training me to like curry. We just went and saw each other and talked.

We've never been a couple that have gone out for an evening very much or gone socializing with friends. We're both quite introverted in temperaments.

Edward: Yes, the only characteristic we share when we did Myers-Briggs is that we're both introverted, though other aspects changed over the years.

Sandra: I quickly get baffled by theoretical ideas and concepts. I'm glad he has a daughter (LSN) to talk to about that, because it's not something I really got the hang of. I'm closer in temperament to PSN.

Qn: Any other activities you were involved in?

Sandra and Edward: We did do some letter writing.

Edward: I did ask Sandra in a letter, "What are you reading?"

Sandra: The letter writing stopped when we got married. Technology has been changing so rapidly, and there are mobile phones these days, and so on. But we didn't have our first mobile phone until five years ago. So we've never been constantly on the phone with each other or texting each other the way our daughters do with their friends.

Rick and Cora:

Cora: Rick was a member of a Bowls Club, in fact, secretary. I watched him play sometimes and also helped with the teas.

Rick: We had dinner parties with friends.

Cora: We liked bird watching, butterfly hunting.

Rick: Had we started hill walking then?

Cora: Yes. Because you took me to the Lake District before you took me to meet your family.

Timothy and Natalie:

Concerts and theater. Occasional dances, but not much.

Walking miles across fields, usually with a dog or dogs, good conversation, lots of walking.

Also, keen interest in bird watching (ornithology). We could see the progress of the nests and the young coming out. We were both excited about that.

Countryside/rural activities.

Exchange of letters—we can't quite remember how many, but there were definitely some.

Clare and Walter:

Clare: Definitely the cinema, and occasionally the theater. Also meeting friends.

Walter: And a fair amount of drinking in the pub, going to the pub with colleagues. We were working in London in a bank, and that was part of the culture.

Clare: But not much eating out. That was quite expensive in those days. But going to the pub, yes. And meeting up with friends together.

Walter: Yes, meeting up with friends as a couple, rather than as individuals.

Clare: And we also went to a few car shows.

Walter: And motor racing occasionally as well.

Clare: At that point we were both living in South London, so it was easier to get to car racing shows.

Qn: Any letters or notes?

Clare: I don't remember much of that. Probably just birthday cards, that sort of thing. We were actually working in the same office, so we didn't really need to write to each other.

Walter: Yes, we were working in close proximity, and saw each other everyday.

Clare: We never worked in the same section as each other, but once senior management realized we were in a relationship, they moved me to a different floor.

Walter: To prevent fraud, collusion, that sort of thing.

Nicholas and Wilma:

Nicholas: I used to sing in an operatic society, and Wilma came to watch us.

Also, social activities of the scouting movement. I used to run scout campfires.

Nicholas and Wilma: We liked the open air, visiting places, walking, we went camping sometimes. We both liked the outdoors.

We also liked socializing with other couples. And that has continued since we've been married.

Wilma: I didn't use to go to church that much at that time. Nursing training doesn't give you that much time away. I was a member of the youth club at church.

We also had some letter writing, yes.

Nicholas: In those days, it was very difficult to communicate on the telephone, because Wilma was working at the hospital, and living at the nurses' home, with one phone for a floor of about sixteen to seventeen nurses. No private phone.

Stephen and Hannah:

Mainly student life—parties, Christian Union meetings and activities, walks, get-togethers.

Also going to church together sometimes, but a lot of the time we were at different churches.

Also letters, especially during holidays.

Laura and Zachary:

As friends, we had similar social circles, parties, dancing. When we were dating, we would go for a drink and a walk. Sometimes going for a pub lunch and a walk in the afternoon.

And we both enjoyed the theater in London and cinema.

Also sending letters and cards. We did that quite a lot.

Laura: I still keep all his letters. He even recorded cassettes for me.

Even now when we're married, if either of us is away, we'll leave a note for each other.

Irene and Anthony:

Anthony: We went to the pub a fair amount of times.

Irene: He had his own darts team when he was landlord of the pub.

We used to walk quite a lot when you had your dog.

Anthony: We got married on the dole.

Irene: We were both on the dole when we got married.

Anthony: She was made redundant before our marriage.

Irene: And you were out of work then.

It was a bit of a worry financially. We had to keep two cars going. For supply teaching for Irene, and seasonal work for Anthony.

<u>Anthony</u>: We did things that didn't cost money, because we didn't have any money.

Didn't really write letters to each other.

<u>Irene</u>: We didn't need to. We either were already arranged, or we picked up the phone.

George and Agnes:

The first three months we were together. After that we were two hundred miles apart. Every Friday, we would get onto trains, and the trains would meet at a common destination. We spent weekends and leaves together—we went out walking, spending time together then. Also dances, movies, meals. Generally spending time together. Also letters and phone calls.

<u>George</u>: After that, in our marriage, we were still letter writing, as I was away quite a lot—for about three to six weeks at a time, for about six months of a year. I was with the frontline squadron of the RAF.

<u>George and Agnes</u>: Also all the wars—Falklands, Kosovo, Iraq, Afghanistan—when George was away for five to six months at a time.

<u>Agnes</u>: And that was harder, as it was when communication could be quite difficult. Sometimes they would close down communication links.

<u>George and Agnes</u>: For Kosovo and Iraq, it was telephone calls once a week. For Afghanistan, it was emails. For Iraq and Afghanistan, we couldn't switch on mobile phones, as the enemy would detect them.

<u>Agnes</u>: We would also send letters and comfort packages.

3. **Any aspects of compatibility/fit that you think have worked for you, from experience of having been married now for these many years? Any changes from your criteria when you were dating?**

George and Agnes:

Resilience, independence, similar outlook on life.

<u>George</u>: We are both outward looking, ready to give things a go.

We are both outward looking, we both have the same worldview. Every time I want to try something new, Agnes says go for it.

There are other people, no matter how nice and beautiful, because they don't have the same outlook, it would have been a strain, and I couldn't get on with them. For Agnes it's the same.

<u>Agnes</u>: We are both big-picture people. We see the whole thing, and we don't concentrate so much on the detail.

We've also found that when one is down, the other is there to support. That helps.

It's also remembering why we fell in love with each other, what brought us together in the first place.

<u>George</u>: We also temper each other. Agnes puts in a few more details on my ideas, to temper what I do. And I pull her out of her comfort zone.

<u>Agnes</u>: That's right, because I can be a bit timid.

<u>George</u>: And I know Agnes's there to help put more details on my ideas, fill in some gaps and things.

Also, now with experience and years of marriage, we can also detect when the other person needs support. The more you get to know each other, through the years, the more we can support each other.

Nothing has changed for me, from the moment I said I want to be with Agnes. We've just got closer and closer through the years.

<u>Agnes</u>: Yes. We continue to love each other. In some ways, I still see in George the young man I fell in love with.

<u>George</u>: You very quickly realize when you go away a lot, that you have to adjust to each other, and understand what each has been through.

Edward and Sandra:

We're both homebodies, introverted. Not that keen on going out too much.

We both love books.

<u>Sandra</u>: Edward is more interested in politics than I am. I'm more interested in social history, genealogy.

<u>Qn</u>: Shared values that are important to you?

Edward and Sandra: Yes, social concern.

Edward: Sometimes we have common concerns, but we don't completely overlap.

Sandra: Over time, Edward has been involved in various groups—Christian Solidarity Worldwide, Amnesty International. I support him being in that, although I've not been as involved. I've been involved in other aspects of social concern such as the food bank. Mine tends to be more local.

Also communication, learning to talk to each other. Over the years, we've learned to talk to each other. And having had some misunderstandings, we've tried to stop and talk more. It has got easier as the girls got older.

Edward: Yes, and sometimes I listen to audio or video, and Sandra doesn't do that.

Sandra: We tolerate each other's need to be on our own. There is space and difference. But we would happily be in the same space. We like to know the other one is around.

Sandra and Edward: And books. We both like books. We have books everywhere in the house.

Timothy and Natalie:

What we said earlier (on criteria for dating, choosing each other). And also being easygoing, being not easily fussed nor flustered over small things or when things go wrong.

Timothy: I think we have almost identical likes and dislikes! I know I do get on Natalie's nerves, sometimes. [smiles]

Natalie: We both like the same sort of music.

Timothy: And same sort of cultural issues.

Natalie: For holidays we want to do the same thing—history and culture. Neither of us want to go lying on a beach somewhere.

And locally we're interested in culture and history.

Timothy: [nods] Though we also have our separate activities. I have football and cricket, and Natalie has tennis.

Natalie: Timothy was very involved in local government, he was a district councillor. I was chairman's lady and accompanied him on lots of civic activities.

Timothy: Even now, we are still very involved in community activities—including for the village memorial hall.

Natalie and Timothy: Not pulling in opposite directions, but each of us also has space for our own activities.

Hannah and Stephen:

Hannah: The fact that we talk quite a lot, and we're both intelligent people, we always have interesting conversations.

Stephen: Yes, intelligent conversation.

Hannah: In terms of character traits, I tend towards the depressive, worrying, seeing how things can go wrong, whilst Stephen has always been optimistic—though not always seeing when things might go wrong. Both are important, I think.

In terms of values, we are quite well agreed—including on how to spend money.

Hannah and Stephen: We have learned over the years to give each other space to pursue our own activities, whilst also having shared interests such as music. Stephen has tennis and cadets, and Hannah has book club activities.

Hannah: Also, loyalty and trust are important. Over the years, Stephen has always been very loyal, and I have always been able to trust him.

Nicholas and Wilma:

Nicholas: Yes, Wilma is extremely tolerant, patient. That helps a lot. I can be very impatient. That is one of my biggest problems, impatience.

Wilma: But he has improved. He's good at making decisions, and I'm not.

Nicholas: Most of the decisions to move, five to six times, were mainly my decision. My work dictated where I lived, largely. And it was not really a matter of discussion. Wilma was very tolerant of that.

Wilma: I worked until we had our first child, and I didn't work after that for twelve years. I did manage to go back to nursing work after the twelve years.

Nicholas and Wilma: We grew together in the marriage and adapted to each other.

Wilma: We still love the outdoors and walking. And concerts.

Nicholas: We both like music.

Wilma: Nicholas introduced me to classical music.

We've rubbed the corners off each other as we faced challenges.

Nicholas: I was away from home quite a lot for the first ten to fifteen years (1968 to 1980s) of our marriage, because of my work as a civil engineer.

Wilma just had to keep the home going. And it was very difficult for her at times.

Wilma: I enjoyed having the home and children to myself.

Nicholas: Wilma is very maternal. She managed the home and the children very well. I did the practical things.

Wilma: We had clear roles.

Nicholas: I always dealt with the practical things and the finances.

Wilma: And he sorted things that needed to be attended to in the big house we lived in for thirty-one years.

Rick and Cora:

Cora: I suppose, it's that we're prepared to be interested in each other's interests. I'm not interested in bowls, but I go along to them because Rick's interested. And Rick's not so interested in history, but he comes along to talks that I go to.

And if I want to go somewhere, he'll come with me. And I'll go to a model engine exhibition with him.

Qn: So you take an interest in each other's interests?

Cora and Rick: Yes.

Rick: Yes. A bit of give-and-take.

Cora: Yes. But we also don't do everything together. We don't live in each other's pockets.

Qn: So you do some things together, but you also have your own space?

Cora and Rick: Yes.

Rick: You have your space upstairs, and I have my workshop.

Cora: The other thing is that Rick is a lot more patient than me.

Qn: So, some differences in personality?

Cora and Rick: Yes.

Qn: Any changes from when you were dating?

Cora: I suppose we take each other for granted more now, isn't it? When you're dating, you're a bit more careful.

Irene and Anthony:

Anthony: Basically it's the honesty. We are always honest with each other. And we try to discuss everything before we jump in.

Qn: Is that the same for Irene?

Irene: Oh yes. As I said, it was his openness that appealed to me. You always knew where you were with Anthony.

We don't pry into the past. It doesn't concern us.

Clare and Walter:

Walter: I think what has changed is the fact that we both became Christians about thirty years ago. I think that's a very important aspect of where we are now.

Qn: How did you become Christians?

Clare: My parents were Christians, and had a born-again experience. I had been brought up to go to church. My mum died before we got married. And it caused me to question things, want to find out about things more. It made me want to find out the difference between being a church-goer and being a Christian.

So I went to the local church where we had moved to, and meeting up with the vicar/curate there helped.

Walter: I had quite a different experience.

Clare: Walter was brought up in a Catholic family.

Walter: Catholic mother. My father was non-Catholic, but we had to be brought up Catholic. But it was quite meaningless to me.

Qn: When did it start becoming meaningful for you?

Walter: When Clare started going to our local church where we moved to, and I started to go along to that. Listening to preaching, various speakers, and other events.

Definitely influenced by Clare going to church then. That's where it came from. She drew me along.

Qn: So that has become your shared interest?

Clare and Walter: Yes. And we've continued with some of the other interests—such as the cars, but not so much the drama anymore.

Qn: Any other aspects of compatibility that have worked for you? Such as shared values?

Clare: Yes. I think that ties in with our faith. Shared values in our faith.

Clare: I've also spent quite a lot of time working with the church, and that took me away from home sometimes, and Walter was supportive of that. He did not resent that it took me away from cooking the meals and doing the housework during those times. So that is an aspect of compatibility. Whereas we know of some couples where the husbands resent the wives even going to church on Sundays.

Walter: Yes, we had friends who really struggled with that.

Qn: So, compatibility in terms of pulling in the same direction, supporting and understanding each other?

Clare and Walter: Yes.

Clare: I guess, parenting, as well, has been a major part of our marriage, and by and large, we've agreed on that.

Walter: And, to an extent, we're still parenting them now!

Clare: It's a privilege that they still want us in their lives.

Walter: Yes, thinking about when we were their age, both of us didn't really have our parents around.

Clare: Both my parents had died when I was thirty.

Walter: Both my parents had died by the time I was in my 40s.

Clare: There's the sadness that the children didn't really have grandparents to be involved with. Walter's father lived quite far away. Walter's mother appreciated seeing them, but didn't really parent them.

But we're delighted that we can still enjoy our children now. And grandchildren now too.

Qn: So in terms of parenting, you're quite agreed and have compatibility there as well?

Clare and Walter: Yes, in terms of parenting, we've not really fallen out over things. We're both quite hands-on parents.

Walter: Yes, and in a sense, breaking the cycle of historic parenting. I was brought up in a culture/generation where children were not really enjoyed.

Qn: Was that the same for you, Clare?

Clare: No, my parents were quite involved, and would have been super grandparents, and I feel a sadness that they didn't get to enjoy their grandchildren. I did get to see my grandparents quite often. It was a bit more remote than what people are used to nowadays, but no, they weren't remote. They were quite involved. So in that sense, quite a different experience from Walter.

Laura and Zachary:

Laura: Good sense of humor. Some shared interests, but also some different interests.

Sometimes it's good to have your own space and feel secure that having your own space, you have no worries.

Zachary: I still think that physical attraction is important. I think it's also important to be able to sit down together in the evenings and be comfortable together.

Laura: Yes, to be able to say anything, and then know that we can still get on.

Zachary: Yes, to know that we can still get on. We don't have to agree on everything.

To feel comfortable to be yourselves and accepted for who you are.

Phyllis and Henry:

Henry: My mother was intelligent, more intelligent than my father. And that worked. I didn't realize it at the time, but over the years I realize that I was looking for somebody who was like my mother—intelligent. I was close to my mother.

Qn: Describe other qualities of your mother?

Henry: My mother was intelligent and worked very hard. After the war, the women were always looking for jobs. My father was in the army.

Phyllis: Yes, money was short. My family was very similar. Both my father and mother worked on a farm.

Qn: So you both came from quite similar economic backgrounds, with a strong work ethic, valuing hard work and resilience, and with a strong sense of shared values?

Henry: Yes. She's like my mother. For me, that came from my mother.

Qn: Other aspects of compatibility?

Phyllis: After we each converted, becoming Christians.

We also had good supportive parents, especially my parents who helped look after me and the children, especially as Henry was traveling a lot. I also have two sisters.

Henry: Yes, I had good supportive in-laws. And I hope my mother-in-law loved her as much as I loved her.

I traveled a lot throughout the marriage, until retirement at age sixty-four. What helped keep our marriage together was a strong work ethic and strong values, resilience and perseverance, and supportive family (Phyllis's family).

For a start, I found it difficult—traveling so much and being away from family, but you have to harden yourself to that. I had to work hard and earn money for the family.

Also, intelligence. I genuinely think that I couldn't live without my wife. I think that we are compatible. I can't imagine being without her.

Phyllis: We like different things, but we also like a lot of the same things—looking in antique shops, walking, nice walks, drives, and exploring. We also like reading, we like to read together.

Henry: Walking is very good, and it stretches you.

Phyllis: Yes, and we've gone blackberry picking.

Henry: We're working-class people. And we like gardening.

BIBLIOGRAPHY

Acevedo, Bianca, et al. "Neural Correlates of Long-Term Intense Romantic Love." *Social Cognitive and Affective Neuroscience* 7 (2012) 145–59.
Angell, Roger. "This Old Man: Life in the Nineties." *New Yorker Magazine*, Feb. 9, 2014. https://www.newyorker.com/magazine/2014/02/17/old-man-3.
Anscombe, G. E. M. "Modern Moral Philosophy." *Philosophy* 33 (1958) 1–19.
Aquinas, Thomas. *Providence: Part II*. Edited and translated by Vernon J. Bourke. Book Three of *Summa Contra Gentiles*. Notre Dame, IN: University of Notre Dame Press, 1956. Kindle.
———. *Summa Theologica*. Translated by Fathers of the English Dominican Province. 10 vols. 2nd ed. London: Burns, Oates & Washbourne, 1920–22. Kindle.
Aristotle. *Nicomachean Ethics*. Translated by Terence Irwin. 2nd ed. Indianapolis: Hackett, 1999. Kindle.
Armstrong, Elizabeth, et al. "Is Hooking Up Bad for Women?" In *Family in Transition*, edited by Arlene S. Skolnick and Jerome K. Skolnick. 17th ed. New York: Pearson, 2014. Kindle.
Aron, Arthur, and Jennifer Tomlinson. "Love as Expansion of the Self." In *The New Psychology of Love*, edited by Robert J. Sternberg and Karin Sternberg. 2nd ed. Cambridge: Cambridge University Press, 2019. Kindle.
Augustine. *City of God*. Translated by Marcus Dods. In *The Nicene and Post-Nicene Fathers*, ser. 1, edited by Philip Schaff, vol. 2, locs. 206249–223729 of 661649. London: Catholic Way, 2014. Kindle.
———. *Confessions*. Translated by Henry Chadwick. Oxford World's Classics. New York: Oxford University Press, 1992. Kindle.
———. "On Christian Doctrine (Book 1)." Translated by J. F. Shaw. In *The Nicene and Post-Nicene Fathers*, ser. 1, edited by Philip Schaff, vol. 2, locs. 223736–226437 of 661649. London: Catholic Way, 2014. Kindle.
———. "On Marriage and Concupiscence." Translated by Dr. Holmes. In *The Nicene and Post-Nicene Fathers*, ser. 1, edited by Philip Schaff, vol. 5, locs. 272307–273958 of 661649. London: Catholic Way, 2014. Kindle.
———. "On the Good of Marriage." Translated by C. L. Cornish. In *The Nicene and Post-Nicene Fathers*, ser. 1, edited by Philip Schaff, vol. 3, locs. 238733–239261 of 661649. London: Catholic Way, 2014. Kindle.

———. "On the Morals of the Catholic Church." Translated by Richard Stothert. In *The Nicene and Post-Nicene Fathers*, ser. 1, edited by Philip Schaff, vol. 2, locs. 244273–245052 of 661649. London: Catholic Way, 2014. Kindle.

Austen, Jane. *The Complete Novels*. N.p.: Book House, 2016. Kindle.

Ayres, Lewis, and Medi Ann Volpe, eds. *The Oxford Handbook of Catholic Theology*. Oxford Handbooks. Oxford: Oxford University Press, 2019. Kindle.

Bailey, Beth L. *From Front Porch to Back Seat: Courtship in Twentieth-Century America*. Baltimore: Johns Hopkins University Press, 1989. Kindle.

Banner, Michael. *The Ethics of Everyday Life: Moral Theology, Social Anthropology, and the Imagination of the Human*. Oxford: Oxford University Press, 2014.

Barbour, Ian G. *When Science Meets Religion: Enemies, Strangers, or Partners?* New York: HarperCollins, 2000. Kindle.

Barclay, John M. G. *Paul and the Gift*. Grand Rapids: Eerdmans, 2015. Kindle.

Barker, Chris, and Bessie Moore. *My Dear Bessie: A Love Story in Letters*. Edited by Simon Garfield. Edinburgh: Canongate, 2015. Kindle.

Barth, Karl. *The Doctrine of Creation*. Edited by G. W. Bromiley and T. F. Torrance. Translated by J. W. Edwards et al. Vol. 3.1 of *Church Dogmatics*. Edinburgh: T&T Clark, 1958.

Barton, John. "Virtue in the Bible." *Studies in Christian Ethics* 12 (1999) 12–22.

Bauman, Zygmunt. *Liquid Love: On the Frailty of Human Bonds*. Cambridge: Polity, 2003. Kindle.

BBC. "Cohabiting Couples Warned of 'Common Law Marriage' Myths." BBC, Nov. 27, 2017. http://www.bbc.co.uk/news/uk-42134722.

Bell, Charlie. *Queer Redemption: How Queerness Changes Everything We Thought We Knew About Christianity*. London: Darton, Longman and Todd, 2024.

Beste, Jennifer. *College Hookup Culture and Christian Ethics: The Lives and Longings of Emerging Adults*. New York: Oxford University Press, 2018. Kindle.

———. "Hookups, Happiness, and Human Flourishing." *Sex, Love, and Families: Catholic Perspectives*, edited by Jason King and Julie Hanlon Rubio. Collegeville, MN: Liturgical, 2020. Kindle.

Biermann, Joel D., ed. *A Case for Character: Towards a Lutheran Virtue Ethics*. Minneapolis: Fortress, 2014. Kindle.

Birds, John. *Birds' Modern Insurance Law*. 10th ed. London: Sweet & Maxwell, 2016. Kindle.

Bix, Brian H. *Jurisprudence: Theory and Context*. 8th ed. London: Sweet & Maxwell, 2019. Kindle.

Blakemore, Sarah-Jayne. *Inventing Ourselves: The Secret Life of the Teenage Brain*. London: Transworld, 2018. Kindle.

Blomberg, Craig L. *1 Corinthians*. NIV Application Commentary. Grand Rapids: Zondervan, 1994. Kindle.

———. *Matthew*. NAC. Nashville: B&H, 1992. Kindle.

Boethius. *Treatise Against Eutyches and Nestorius*. Logos Library, n.d. Translated by H. F. Stewart and E. K. Rand. https://www.logoslibrary.org/boethius/eutyches/index.html.

Brain World. "Sex, Love, and Attachment: An Interview with Dr. Helen Fisher." *Brain World*, Feb. 14, 2019. https://brainworldmagazine.com/sex-love-and-attachment-an-interview-with-dr-helen-fisher/.

Brebner, Samuel. "Are Christian Guys Not Taking Dating Seriously? Five Reasons Why They're Not Dating." *Relevant*, July 18, 2017. https://relevantmagazine.com/life5/career-money/are-christian-guys-not-taking-dating-seriously/.

Bretherton, Luke. *Christ and the Common Life: Political Theology and the Case for Democracy*. Grand Rapids: Eerdmans, 2019. Kindle.

———. *A Primer in Christian Ethics: Christ and the Struggle to Live Well*. Cambridge: Cambridge University Press, 2023. Kindle.

Briggs, Richard S. *The Virtuous Reader: Old Testament Narrative and Interpretive Virtue*. STI. Grand Rapids: Baker Academic, 2010. Kindle.

Brown, Peter. *The Body and Society: Men, Women and Sexual Renunciation in Early Christianity*. New York: Columbia University Press, 1988.

Bryan, Jocelyn. *Human Being: Insights from Psychology and the Christian Faith*. London: SCM, 2016.

Bryman, Alan. *Social Research Methods*. 5th ed. Oxford: Oxford University Press, 2016.

Buber, Martin. *I and Thou*. Translated by Ronald Gregor Smith. Bloomsbury Revelations. London: Bloomsbury Academic, 2013. Kindle.

Buss, David M. "The Evolution of Love in Humans." In *The New Psychology of Love*, edited by Robert J. Sternberg and Karin Sternberg. 2nd ed. Cambridge: Cambridge University Press, 2019. Kindle.

———. *Evolutionary Psychology: The New Science of the Mind*. 6th ed. New York: Routledge, 2019. Kindle.

———. "Sex Differences in Human Mate Preferences: Evolutionary Hypotheses Tested in 37 Cultures." *Behavioral and Brain Sciences* 12 (1989) 1–49.

Cacioppo, John T., et al. "Marital Satisfaction and Break-Ups Differ Across On-Line and Off-Line Meeting Venues." *Proceedings of the National Academy of Sciences* 110 (2013) 10135–40. https://doi.org/10.1073/pnas.1222447110.

Cahill, Lisa Sowle. *Sex, Gender, and Christian Ethics*. New Studies in Christian Ethics. New York: Cambridge University Press, 1996.

Canetto, S. S., and D. Lester. "Love and Achievement Motives in Women's and Men's Suicide Notes." *Journal of Psychology* 136 (2002) 573–76.

Carr, Alan. *Positive Psychology: The Science of Happiness and Human Strengths*. 2nd ed. New York: Routledge, 2011. Kindle.

Cavanaugh, William T. *Being Consumed: Economics and Christian Desire*. Grand Rapids: Eerdmans, 2008. Kindle.

Chapman, Gary. *The 5 Love Languages*. Chicago: Northfield, 1995. Kindle.

———. *Things I Wish I'd Known Before We Got Married*. Love Language Resource. Chicago: Northfield, 2010. Kindle.

Cherlin, Andrew. "American Marriage in the Early Twenty-First Century." In *Family in Transition*, edited by Arlene S. Skolnick and Jerome K. Skolnick. 17th ed. New York: Pearson, 2014. Kindle.

———. *The Marriage-Go-Round: The State of Marriage and the Family in America Today*. New York: Random House, 2009. Kindle.

Choi, Edmund, et al. "The Association Between Smartphone Dating Applications and College Students' Casual Sex Encounters and Condom Use." *Sexual and Reproductive Healthcare* 9 (2016) 38–41.

Church of England. *Living in Love and Faith: Christian Teaching and Learning About Identity: Sexuality, Relationships and Marriage*. London: Church House, 2020.

Clapp, Rodney. *Naming Neoliberalism: Exposing the Spirit of the Age*. Minneapolis: Fortress, 2021.

Clark, Russell, and Elaine Hatfield. "Gender Differences in Receptivity to Sexual Offers." *Journal of Psychology and Human Sexuality* 2 (1989) 39–55.

Clemens, Chris, et al. "The Influence of Biological and Personality Traits on Gratifications Obtained Through Online Dating Websites." *Computers in Human Behavior* 49 (2015) 120–29.

Cloud, Henry, and John Townsend. *Boundaries in Dating: How Healthy Choices Grow Healthy Relationships*. Grand Rapids: Zondervan, 2000. Kindle.

Clough, David L. *On Animals*. Vol. 1 of *Systematic Theology*. T&T Clark Theology. London: T&T Clark, 2012. Kindle.

Cloutier, David, ed. *Leaving and Coming Home: New Wineskins for Catholic Sexual Ethics*. Eugene, OR: Cascade, 2010. Kindle.

———. "Marriage and Sexuality." In *The Oxford Handbook of Catholic Theology*, edited by Lewis Ayres and Medi Volpe. Oxford Handbooks. Oxford: Oxford University Press, 2019. Kindle.

Coakley, Sarah. *God, Sexuality, and the Self: An Essay 'On the Trinity'*. Cambridge: Cambridge University Press, 2013. Kindle.

Cochran, Elizabeth Agnew. *Protestant Virtue and Stoic Ethics*. T&T Clark Enquiries in Theological Ethics. London: Bloomsbury T&T Clark, 2018. Kindle.

Collicutt, Joanna. *The Psychology of Christian Character Formation*. London: SCM, 2015. Kindle.

Conley, Terri D., et al. "Backlash from the Bedroom: Stigma Mediates Gender Differences in Acceptance of Casual Sex Offers." *Psychology of Women Quarterly* 37 (2013) 392–407.

Cook, Christopher C. H., et al., eds. *Spirituality and Narrative in Psychiatric Practice: Stories of Mind and Soul*. London: RCPsych, 2016. Kindle.

Cook, Hera. *The Long Sexual Revolution: English Women, Sex, and Contraception 1800–1975*. Oxford: Oxford University Press, 2004. Kindle.

Coontz, Stephanie. *Marriage, a History: From Obedience to Intimacy or How Love Conquered Marriage*. London: Viking Penguin, 2005. Kindle.

Cooper, Marianne. *Cut Adrift: Families in Insecure Times*. Oakland: University of California Press, 2014. Kindle.

Cornwall, Susannah. *Theology and Sexuality*. SCM Core Text. London: SCM, 2013.

Cortez, Marc. *Theological Anthropology: A Guide for the Perplexed*. Guides for the Perplexed. London: T&T Clark, 2010.

Cortez, Marc, and Michael P. Jensen, eds. *T&T Clark Reader in Theological Anthropology*. London: Bloomsbury, 2018.

Dargie, Emma, et al. "Go Long! Predictors of Positive Relationship Outcomes in Long-Distance Dating Relationships." *Journal of Sex & Marital Therapy* 41 (2015) 181–202.

Davies, Brian, and Eleonore Stump, eds. *The Oxford Handbook of Aquinas*. Oxford Handbooks. New York: Oxford University Press, 2012. Kindle.

Davies, Charlotte Aull. *Reflexive Ethnography: A Guide to Researching Selves and Others*. 2nd ed. ASA Research Methods. New York: Routledge, 2008. Kindle.

De Botton, Alain. "Why You Will Marry the Wrong Person." YouTube, Aug. 13, 2017. https://youtu.be/-EvvPZFdjyk?si=whO4QT_xznOuZ9pD.

Demography Team. "Families and Households in the UK: 2023." Office for National Statistics, May 8, 2024. https://www.ons.gov.uk/peoplepopulationandcommunity/birthsdeathsandmarriages/families/bulletins/familiesandhouseholds/2023.

———. "Marriages in England and Wales: 2021 and 2022." Office for National Statistics, June 20, 2024. https://www.ons.gov.uk/peoplepopulationandcommunity/birthsdeathsandmarriages/marriagecohabitationandcivilpartnerships/bulletins/marriagesinenglandandwalesprovisional/2021and2022.

Diduck, Alison, and Felicity Kaganas. *Family Law, Gender and the State: Text, Cases and Materials*. 3rd ed. Oxford: Hart, 2012. Kindle.

Dobransky, Paul, with L. A. Stamford. *The Secret Psychology of How We Fall in Love: Dr. Paul's 9 Proven Steps to Lasting Love*. New York: Penguin, 2007. Kindle.

Doherty, Sean. *The Only Way Is Ethics; Quiltbag: Jesus and Sexuality*. Milton Keynes, UK: Authentic, 2015.

Dolan, Paul. *Happy Ever After: A Radical New Approach to Living Well*. UK: Penguin, 2019. Kindle.

Dominian, Jack. *Passionate and Compassionate Love: A Vision for Christian Marriage*. London: Darton, Longman and Todd, 1991.

Dormor, Duncan. *Just Cohabiting? The Church, Sex and Getting Married*. London: Darton, Longman and Todd, 2004.

Durheim, Benjamin. "The Human as Encounter: Karl Barth's Theological Anthropology and a Barthian Vision of the Common Good." *Lumen et Vita* 1 (2011). https://doi.org/10.6017/lv.v1i1.1696.

Eliot, George. *Middlemarch*. Richmond, UK: Alma Classics, 2017.

Ellison, Marvin M. *Making Love Just: Sexual Ethics for Perplexing Times*. Minneapolis: Fortress, 2012.

Emmons, Robert A., and Michael E. McCullough, eds. *The Psychology of Gratitude*. New York: Oxford University Press, 2004. Kindle.

Farley, Margaret. *Just Love: A Framework for Christian Sexual Ethics*. London: Bloomsbury, 2006.

Fergusson, David. "Humans Created According to the *Imago Dei*: An Alternative Proposal." *Zygon* 48 (2013) 439–53.

Fein, Ellen, and Sherrie Schneider. *The Complete Book of Rules: Time-Tested Secrets for Capturing the Heart of Mr. Right*. Expanded ed. London: HarperCollins, 2000. Kindle.

Felker Jones, Beth. *Faithful: A Theology of Sex*. Grand Rapids: Zondervan, 2015. Kindle.

Finkel, Eli J. *The All-or-Nothing Marriage: How the Best Marriages Work*. New York: Penguin Random House, 2017.

Finkel, Eli J., and Roy F. Baumeister, eds. *Advanced Social Psychology: The State of the Science*. 2nd ed. New York: Oxford University Press, 2019. Kindle.

Fisher, Helen. *Anatomy of Love*. New York: Norton & Company, 2016. Kindle.

———. "The Drive to Love: The Neural Mechanism for Mate Selection." In *The New Psychology of Love*, edited by Robert J. Sternberg and Karin Weis. New Haven, CT: Yale University Press, 2006.

———. *Why Him? Why Her? Finding Real Love By Understanding Your Personality Type*. London: Oneworld, 2009.

———. *Why We Love: The Nature and Chemistry of Romantic Love*. New York: St. Martin's, 2004.

Fisher, Kate. *Birth Control, Sex, and Marriage in Britain 1918–1960*. Oxford: Oxford University Press, 2006.
Fitzsimons, G. M., and J. Y. Shah. "How Goal Instrumentality Shapes Relationship Evaluations." *Journal of Personality and Social Psychology* 95 (2008) 319–37.
Foot, Philippa. *Virtues and Vices: And Other Essays in Moral Philosophy*. New York: Oxford University Press, 2002. Kindle.
Francis, Pope. *Amoris Laetitia: On Love in the Family*. Vatican City: Vaticana, 2016.
Freeman-Powell, Shamaan. "Could Love Island Hold the Key to Lasting Happiness?" BBC, July 27, 2018. https://www.bbc.co.uk/news/education-44966931.
Freitas, Donna. *The End of Sex: How Hookup Culture Is Leaving a Generation Unhappy, Sexually Unfulfilled, and Confused About Intimacy*. New York: Basic, 2013. Kindle.
———. *The Happiness Effect: How Social Media Is Driving a Generation to Appear Perfect at Any Cost*. New York: Oxford University Press, 2017. Kindle.
———. *Sex and the Soul: Juggling Sexuality, Spirituality, Romance, and Religion on America's College Campuses*. New York: Oxford University Press, 2008. Kindle.
Freitas, Donna, and Jason King. *Save the Date: A Spirituality of Dating, Love, Dinner, and the Divine* New York: Crossroad, 2003.
French, Juliana, et al. "The Implications of Sociosexuality for Marital Satisfaction and Dissolution." *Psychological Science* 30 (2019) 1460–72.
Gabb, Jacqui. "About *Enduring Love?*" Brook, n.d. https://www.brook.org.uk/your-life/about-enduring-love.
Gabb, Jacqui, and Janet Fink. *Couple Relationships in the 21st Century: Research, Policy, Practice*. Cham, Switz.: Palgrave Macmillan, 2018. Kindle.
Garcia-Moreno, Claudia, et al. "Prevalence of Intimate Partner Violence: Findings from the WHO Multi-Country Study on Women's Health and Domestic Violence." *Lancet*, 368 (2006) 1260–69.
Gardner, Christine. *Making Chastity Sexy: The Rhetoric of Evangelical Abstinence Campaigns*. Berkeley: University of California Press, 2011. Kindle.
George, Ivy, and Margaret Masson. *An Uncommon Correspondence: An East-West Conversation on Friendship, Intimacy and Love*. New Jersey: Paulist, 1998.
Ghosh, Kanak. "Marriages in England and Wales: 2017." Office for National Statistics, Apr. 14, 2020. https://www.ons.gov.uk/peoplepopulationandcommunity/birthsdeathsandmarriages/marriagecohabitationandcivilpartnerships/bulletins/marriagesinenglandandwalesprovisional/2017.
———. "Marriages in England and Wales: 2018." Office for National Statistics, Aug. 10, 2021. https://www.ons.gov.uk/peoplepopulationandcommunity/birthsdeathsandmarriages/marriagecohabitationandcivilpartnerships/bulletins/marriagesinenglandandwalesprovisional/2018.
Giddens, Anthony. "The Global Revolution in Family and Personal Life." In *Family in Transition*, edited by Arlene S. Skolnick and Jerome K. Skolnick. 17th ed. New York: Pearson, 2014. Kindle.
———. *The Transformation of Intimacy: Sexuality, Love & Eroticism in Modern Societies*. Cambridge: Polity, 1992. Kindle.
Gill, Robin, ed. *The Cambridge Companion to Christian Ethics*. 2nd ed. Cambridge Companions to Religion. New York: Cambridge University Press, 2012. Kindle.
Golombok, Susan. *Modern Families: Parents and Children in New Family Forms*. Cambridge: Cambridge University Press, 2015. Kindle.

Goody, Jack. *The Development of the Family and Marriage in Europe*. Past and Present Publications. Cambridge: Cambridge University Press, 1983.

Gottman, John, with Nan Silver. *Why Marriages Succeed or Fail: And How You Can Make Yours Last*. London: Bloomsbury, 2007. Kindle.

Gould, Rose Mary. "What Is Ghosting?" Very Well Mind, updated Nov. 2, 2023. https://www.verywellmind.com/what-is-ghosting-5071864.

Goundrey-Smith, Stephen. *Transhumanism, Ethics and the Therapeutic Revolution: Agents of Change*. Routledge New Critical Thinking in Religion, Theology and Biblical Studies. New York: Routledge, 2023.

Gowing, Laura. *Gender Relations in Early Modern England*. Seminar Studies. New York: Routledge, 2012. Kindle.

Grant, Jonathan. *Divine Sex: A Compelling Vision for Christian Relationships in a Hypersexualized Age*. Grand Rapids: Brazos Press, 2015. Kindle.

Grenz, Stanley. *The Social God and the Relational Self: A Trinitarian Theology of the Imago Dei*. Louisville: Westminster John Knox, 2001.

Guest, Mathew. *Neoliberal Religion: Faith and Power in the Twenty-First Century*. London: Bloomsbury, 2022.

Gurrentz, Benjamin. "Cohabiting Partners Older, More Racially Diverse, More Educated, Higher Earners." United States Census Bureau, Sept. 23, 2019. https://www.census.gov/library/stories/2019/09/unmarried-partners-more-diverse-than-20-years-ago.html.

———. "Living with an Unmarried Partner Now Common for Young Adults." United States Census Bureau, Nov. 15, 2018. https://www.census.gov/library/stories/2018/11/cohabitation-is-up-marriage-is-down-for-young-adults.html.

Gray, John. *Beyond Mars and Venus: Relationship Skills for Today's Complex World*. Dallas: BenBella, 2017. Kindle.

Gushee, David P., and Reggie L. Williams, eds. *Justice and the Way of Jesus: Christian Ethics and the Incarnational Discipleship of Glen Stassen*. New York: Orbis, 2020. Kindle.

Hall, Lesley. *Sex, Gender and Social Change in Britain Since 1880*. 2nd ed. Hampshire, UK: Palgrave Macmillan, 2013.

Hardy, Thomas. *Far from the Madding Crowd*. Ware, UK: Wordsworth, 1993.

Hargaden, Kevin. *Theological Ethics in a Neoliberal Age: Confronting the Christian Problem with Wealth*. Theopolitical Visions. Eugene, OR: Cascade, 2018.

Harper, Demetrios. *The Analogy of Love: St. Maximus the Confessor and the Foundations of Ethics*. Scholarly Monographs. New York: St. Vladimir's Seminary Press, 2018. Kindle.

Harper, Kyle. *From Shame to Sin: The Christian Transformation of Sexual Morality in Late Antiquity*. Revealing Antiquity. Cambridge, MA: Harvard University Press, 2013. Kindle.

Harris, Joshua. *Boy Meets Girl: Say Hello to Courtship*. Sisters, OR: Multnomah, 2005. Kindle.

———. *I Kissed Dating Goodbye*. Colorado Springs: Multnomah, 2003.

———. *Sex Is Not the Problem (Lust Is)*. Colorado Springs: Multnomah, 2003. Kindle.

———. "A Statement on *I Kissed Dating Goodbye*." Josh Harris, 2018. https://joshharris.com/a-statement-on/.

Harrison, Peter, ed. *The Cambridge Companion to Science and Religion*. Cambridge Companions to Religion. New York: Cambridge University Press, 2010. Kindle.

Harvey, David. *A Brief History of Neoliberalism*. Oxford: Oxford University Press, 2005. Kindle.

Hatfield, Elaine, and Richard Rapson. *Love and Sex: Cross-Cultural Perspectives*. Lanham, MD: University Press of America, 2005.

Hatfield, Elaine, et al. *What's Next in Love and Sex: Psychological and Cultural Perspectives*. New York: Oxford University Press, 2020. Kindle.

Hauerwas, Stanley. *A Community of Character: Toward a Constructive Christian Social Ethic*. Notre Dame, IN: University of Notre Dame Press, 1981. Kindle.

———. *Hannah's Child: A Theologian's Memoir*. Grand Rapids: Eerdmans, 2012. Kindle.

———. *The Hauerwas Reader*. Edited by John Berkman and Michael Cartwright. Durham: Duke University Press, 2001. Kindle.

———. *The Peaceable Kingdom*. Notre Dame, IN: University of Notre Dame Press, 1983.

———. "Sex and Politics: Bertrand Russell and 'Human Sexuality.'" *Christian Century* (Apr. 19, 1978) 417–22. https://www.religion-online.org/article/sex-and-politics-bertrand-russell-and-human-sexuality/.

Hauerwas, Stanley, and Charles Pinches. *Christians Among the Virtues: Theological Conversations with Ancient and Modern Ethics*. Notre Dame, IN: University of Notre Dame Press, 1997.

Hays, Richard B. *First Corinthians*. IBC. Louisville: Westminster John Knox, 2011. Kindle.

———. *The Moral Vision of the New Testament*. New York: HarperCollins, 1996. Kindle.

Herdt, Jennifer A. "Augustine on Grace and Worship in Virtue Formation." In *Faith and Virtue Formation: Christian Philosophy in Aid of Becoming Good*, edited by Adam C. Pelser and W. Scott Cleveland. Oxford: Oxford University Press, 2021.

———. *Putting on Virtue: The Legacy of the Splendid Vices*. Chicago: University of Chicago Press, 2008.

———. "Varieties of Contemporary Christian Virtue Ethics." In *The Routledge Companion to Virtue Ethics*, edited by Lorraine Besser-Jones and Michael Slote. Routledge Philosophy Companions. New York: Routledge, 2015. Kindle.

Herring, Jonathan. *Family Law*. 9th ed. Longman Law. Harlow, UK: Pearson, 2019. Kindle.

Hill, Daniel. "Population Estimates for Marital Status and Living Arrangements, England and Wales: 2020." Office for National Statistics, Dec. 16, 2021. https://www.ons.gov.uk/peoplepopulationandcommunity/populationandmigration/populationestimates/bulletins/populationestimatesbymaritalstatusandlivingarrangements/2020.

Hirsch, Jennifer S. *A Courtship After Marriage: Sexuality and Love in Mexican Transnational Families*. Berkeley: University of California Press, 2003. Kindle.

Hodgson, Nichi. *The Curious History of Dating: From Jane Austen to Tinder*. London: Robinson, 2017. Kindle.

Hollinger, Dennis P. *The Meaning of Sex: Christian Ethics and the Moral Life*. Grand Rapids: Baker Academic, 2009. Kindle.

Horowitz, Juliana Menasce, et al. "Marriage and Cohabitation in the U.S." Pew Research Center, Nov. 6, 2019. https://www.pewresearch.org/social-trends/2019/11/06/marriage-and-cohabitation-in-the-u-s/.

House of Bishops. *Issues in Human Sexuality: A Statement by the House of Bishops of the General Synod of the Church of England*. London: Church House, 1991. Kindle.

Hughes, John A., et al. *Understanding Classical Sociology: Marx, Weber, Durkheim*. 2nd ed. London: Sage, 2003. Kindle.

Hunt, Elle. "We've 'Gamified' Dating." *Guardian*, Sept. 25, 2024.

Hursthouse, Rosalind, and Glen Pettigrove. "Virtue Ethics." *Stanford Encyclopedia of Philosophy*, July 18, 2003; rev. Oct. 11, 2022. Edited by Edward N. Zalta. http://plato.stanford.edu/entries/ethics-virtue/.

John, Oliver P., et al., eds. *Handbook of Personality: Theory and Research*. 3rd ed. New York: Guilford, 2008.

Johnson, Eric L., ed. *Psychology and Christianity: Five Views*. 2nd ed. Downers Grove, IL: IVP Academic, 2010. Kindle.

Kadandara, Nyasaha. "Sex and the Sugar Daddy." BBC, Aug. 2018. https://bbc.in/2MzrygK.

Kallenberg, Brad. "Virtue Ethics." In *Christian Ethics: Four Views*, edited by Steve Wilkens. Downers Grove, IL: InterVarsity, 2017. Kindle.

Kamel, Onsi Aaron, et al., eds. *Protestant Social Teaching: An Introduction*. Landrum, SC: Davenant, 2022. Kindle.

Keenan, James F. "Linking Human Dignity, Vulnerability and Virtue Ethics." *Interdisciplinary Journal for Religion and Transformation in Contemporary Society* 6 (2020) 56–73.

———. *The Moral Life: Eight Lectures*. Martin J. D'Arcy, SJ Memorial Lectures. Washington, DC: Georgetown University Press, 2023.

———. "Virtue Ethics and Sexual Ethics." *Louvain Studies* 30 (2005) 180–97.

Keller, Timothy, with Kathy Keller. *The Meaning of Marriage: Facing the Complexities of Commitment with the Wisdom of God*. London: Hodder & Stoughton, 2011. Kindle.

Kelsey, David H. *Eccentric Existence: A Theological Anthropology*. 2 vols. Louisville: Westminster John Knox, 2009.

———. *Proving Doctrine: The Uses of Scripture in Modern Theology*. Harrisburg, PA: Trinity, 1999.

King, Helen. *Immaculate Forms: A History of the Female Body in Four Parts*. London: Profile, 2024. Kindle.

King, Jason. *Faith with Benefits: Hookup Culture on Catholic Campuses*. New York: Oxford University Press, 2017. Kindle.

King, Jason, and Donna Freitas. *Sex, Time, and Meaning: A Theology of Dating*. Hor 30 (2003) 25–40.

King, Jason, and Julie Hanlon Rubio, eds. *Sex, Love, and Families: Catholic Perspectives*. Collegeville, MN: Liturgical, 2020. Kindle.

Langhamer, Claire. *The English in Love: The Intimate Story of an Emotional Revolution*. Oxford: Oxford University Press, 2013.

Lawler, Michael, and Todd Salzman. "People Beginning Sexual Experience." *The Oxford Handbook of Theology, Sexuality, and Gender*, edited by Adrian Thatcher. Oxford Handbooks. Oxford: Oxford University Press, 2015. Kindle.

Lawrence, E. M., et al. "Marital Happiness, Marital Status, Health, and Longevity." *Journal of Happiness Studies* 20 (2019) 1539–61.

Leary, Mark R., et al. "Emotional Responses to Interpersonal Rejection." In *Interpersonal Rejection*, edited by Mark R. Leary. Oxford: Oxford University Press, 2001. Kindle.

Leong, Rebecca. "Divorce and Remarriage After Abuse: Conservative Protestant Responses." *Theology* 121 (2018) 323–31.

———. "The *Imago Dei*, a Redemptive-Movement Hermeneutic and Protestant Virtue Ethics." Paper presented at the Society for the Study of Christian Ethics, online conference, Sept. 11, 2020.
Lewis, C. S. *The Four Loves*. London: Collins, 2010.
———. *Perelandra*. London: HarperCollins, 2013.
Loader, William. *Sexuality in the New Testament: Understanding the Key Texts*. London: SPCK, 2010. Kindle.
Luther, Martin. *The Large Catechism* (1530). In *The Life and Works of Martin Luther*, vol. 1, locs. 1409–1552 of 5511. Christian Classics Treasury. Burlington, Can.: Classic Christian Ebooks, n.d. Kindle.
MacCulloch, Diarmaid. *Lower Than the Angels: A History of Sex and Christianity*. UK: Penguin Random House, 2024.
MacFadyen, Alistair. "Redeeming the Image." *International Journal for the Study of the Christian Church* 16 (2016) 108–25.
MacIntyre, Alasdair. *After Virtue: A Study in Moral Theory*. 3rd ed. Notre Dame, IN: University of Notre Dame Press, 2007. Kindle.
Mann, Jim. "British Sex Survey 2014: The Nation Has Lost Some of Its Sexual Swagger." *Guardian*, Sept. 28, 2014. https://www.theguardian.com/lifeandstyle/2014/sep/28/british-sex-survey-2014-nation-lost-sexual-swagger?CMP=share_btn_link.
Martikainen, Tuomas, and François Gauthier, eds. *Religion in the Neoliberal Age: Political Economy and Modes of Governance*. AHRC/ESRC Religion and Society. New York: Routledge, 2016. Kindle.
Mazo Karras, Ruth. *Unmarriages: Women, Men, and Sexual Unions in the Middle Ages*. Philadelphia: University of Pennsylvania Press, 2012. Kindle.
McAdams, Dan P. *The Art and Science of Personality Development*. New York: Guildford, 2015.
McCabe, Megan. "Relationships Instead of Hooking Up? Justice in Dating." In *Sex, Love, and Families: Catholic Perspectives*, edited by Jason King and Julie Hanlon Rubio. Collegeville, MN: Liturgical, 2020. Kindle.
McEwan, Ian. *On Chesil Beach*. London: Vintage, 2008. Kindle.
Meconi, David Vincent, and Eleonore Stump, eds. *The Cambridge Companion to Augustine*. 2nd ed. Cambridge Companions to Philosophy. Cambridge: Cambridge University Press, 2014. Kindle.
Meilaender, Gilbert C. *The Theory and Practice of Virtue*. Notre Dame, IN: University of Notre Dame Press, 1984.
———. "Time for Love: The Place of Marriage and Children in the Thought of Stanley Hauerwas." *JRE* 40 (2012) 250–61.
Mental Health Foundation. "What Is Wellbeing, How Can We Measure It?" Mental Health Foundation, July 20, 2015. https://www.mentalhealth.org.uk/blog/what-wellbeing-how-can-we-measure-it-and-how-can-we-support-people-improve-it. Link discontinued.
Messer, Neil. *Science in Theology: Encounters Between Science and the Christian Tradition*. London: T&T Clark, 2020. Kindle.
Metaxas, Eric. *Bonhoeffer: Pastor, Martyr, Prophet, Spy*. Nashville: Nelson, 2010.
Middleton, J. Richard. "The Liberating Image? Interpreting the *Imago Dei* in context." *Christian Scholars Review* 24 (1994) 8–25.
———. *The Liberating Image: The Imago Dei in Genesis 1*. Grand Rapids: Brazos, 2005. Kindle.

Migliore, Daniel L. *Faith Seeking Understanding: An Introduction to Christian Theology.* 3rd ed. Grand Rapids: Eerdmans, 2014. Kindle.

Moberly, Jennifer. *The Virtue of Bonhoeffer's Ethics: A Study of Dietrich Bonhoeffer's "Ethics" in Relation to Virtue Ethics.* Princeton Theological Monograph. Eugene, OR: Pickwick, 2013. Kindle.

Moltmann, Jürgen. *God in Creation: An Ecological Doctrine of Creation.* Gifford Lectures. London: SCM, 1985.

Monroe, S. M., et al. "Life Events and Depression in Adolescence: Relationship Loss as a Prospective Risk Factor for First Onset of Major Depressive Disorder." *Journal of Abnormal Psychology* 108 (1999) 606–14.

Murphy, Nancey, et al., eds. *Virtues and Practices in the Christian Tradition: Christian Ethics after MacIntyre.* Notre Dame, IN: University of Notre Dame Press, 2003.

Ngien, Dennis, ed. *The Interface of Science, Theology, and Religion: Essays in Honor of Alister E. McGrath.* Eugene, OR: Wipf and Stock, 2019.

Niebuhr, H. Richard. *Christ and Culture.* New York: Harper & Row, 1951.

Nolan, Kirk J. *Reformed Virtue After Barth: Developing Moral Virtue Ethics in the Reformed Tradition.* Columbia Series in Reformed Theology. Louisville: Westminster John Knox, 2014. Kindle.

Norman, Jesse. *Edmund Burke: The Visionary Who Invented Modern Politics.* London: Collins, 2013. Kindle.

Nygren, Anders. *Agape and Eros.* Translated by Philip S. Watson. Philadelphia: Westminster, 1939.

O'Donovan, Oliver. *Resurrection and Moral Order: An Outline for Evangelical Ethics.* 2nd ed. Grand Rapids: Eerdmans, 1994.

Ogolsky, Brian G., et al. *The Developmental Course of Romantic Relationships.* New York: Routledge, 2013. Kindle.

———. "Pathways of Commitment to Wed: The Development and Dissolution of Romantic Relationships." *Journal of Marriage and Family* 78 (2016) 293–10.

O'Rourke, Norm, et al. "Personality Trait Levels Within Older Couples and Between-Spouse Trait Differences as Predictors of Marital Satisfaction." *Aging & Mental Health* 15 (2011) 344–53.

Osborne, Grant R. *Matthew.* Zondervan Exegetical Commentary Series on the New Testament. Edited by Clinton E. Arnold. Grand Rapids: Zondervan, 2010. Kindle.

Pannenberg, Wolfhart. *Systematic Theology.* Translated by Geoffrey W. Bromiley. 3 vols. Grand Rapids: Eerdmans, 1994. Kindle.

Papadopoulos, Linda. *Whose Life Is It Anyway: Living Life on Your Own Terms.* London: Piatkus, 2014. Kindle.

Paul VI, Pope. "*Humanae Vitae*: On the Regulation of Birth." Vatican, July 25, 1968. https://www.vatican.va/content/paul-vi/en/encyclicals/documents/hf_p-vi_enc_25071968_humanae-vitae.html.

Perel, Esther. *The State of Affairs.* London: Hodder & Stoughton, 2017. Kindle.

Peterson, Christopher, and Martin E. P. Seligman. *Character Strengths and Virtues: A Handbook and Classification.* New York: Oxford University Press, 2004. Kindle.

Peterson-Iyer, Karen. *Re-Envisioning Sexual Ethics: A Feminist Christian Account.* Washington, DC: Georgetown University Press, 2022. Kindle.

Pieper, Josef. *Faith, Hope, Love.* San Francisco: Ignatius, 1997. Kindle.

———. *The Four Cardinal Virtues: Prudence, Justice, Fortitude, Temperance.* Notre Dame, IN: University of Notre Dame Press, 1965. Kindle.

———. *Guide to Thomas Aquinas*. Translated by Richard Winston and Clara Winston. San Francisco: Ignatius, 1991. Kindle.
Pinches, Charles. "Virtue." In *The Oxford Companion to Christian Thought*, edited by Adrian Hastings. Oxford Companions. Oxford: Oxford University Press, 2000.
Pinckaers, Servais. *The Sources of Christian Ethics*. Translated by Mary Thomas Noble. Washington, DC: Catholic University of America Press, 1995.
Pines, Ayala Malach. *Falling in Love: Why We Choose the Lovers We Choose*. 2nd ed. New York: Routledge, 2005. Kindle.
Pinsent, Andrew. "The Gifts and Fruits of the Holy Spirit." In *The Oxford Handbook of Aquinas*, edited by Brian Davies and Eleonore Stump. Oxford Handbooks. New York: Oxford University Press, 2012. Kindle.
Plant, Stephen. "When Karl Met Lollo: The Origins and Consequences of Karl Barth's Relationship with Charlotte von Kirschbaum." *SJT* 72 (2019) 127–45.
Plato. *The Republic*. Translated by Benjamin Jowett. N.p.: N.p., n.d. Kindle.
Ployd, Adam. "Inseparable Virtue and the *Imago Dei* in Augustine: A Speculative Interpretation of *De Trinitate* 6.4." *SJT* 72 (2019) 146–65.
Porter, Jean. *The Recovery of Virtue: The Relevance of Aquinas for Christian Ethics*. Louisville: Westminster John Knox, 1990.
———. "Virtues and Vices." In *The Oxford Handbook of Aquinas*, edited by Brian Davies and Eleonore Stump. Oxford Handbooks. New York: Oxford University Press, 2012. Kindle.
———. "Virtue Ethics." In *The Cambridge Companion to Christian Ethics*, edited by Robin Gill. 2nd ed. Cambridge Companions to Religion. New York: Cambridge University Press, 2012. Kindle.
Prior, Matthew T. *Confronting Technology: The Theology of Jacques Ellul*. Princeton Theological Monograph Series. Eugene, OR: Wipf and Stock, 2020. Kindle.
Radin, Sara. "With Little Luck on Dating Apps, Some Singles Shift to Pitch Decks." *New York Times*, Oct. 3, 2024.
Ramsey, Paul. *Basic Christian Ethics*. New York: Scribner's Sons, 1950.
Ravizza, Bridget Burke and Julie Donovan Massey. *Project Holiness: Marriage as a Workshop for Everyday Saints—Real Wisdom from Real Married Couples*. Collegeville, Minnesota: Liturgical Press, 2015. Kindle.
Regnerus, Mark. *Cheap Sex: The Transformation of Men, Marriage, and Monogamy*. New York: Oxford University Press, 2017. Kindle.
———. *Forbidden Fruit: Sex and Religion in the Lives of American Teenagers*. New York: Oxford University Press, 2007. Kindle.
Regnerus, Mark, and Jeremy Uecker. *Premarital Sex in America: How Young Americans Meet, Mate, and Think About Marrying*. New York: Oxford University Press, 2011.
Relate. "How to Find Someone." Relate, n.d. https://www.relate.org.uk/relationship-help/help-relationships/being-single-and-dating/how-do-you-find-love.
Relate and eHarmony. *The Way We Are Now 2021: Singles and Couples in the UK Today*. Relate, 2021. https://www.relate.org.uk/sites /default/files/2022-08/relate_eharmony_twwan21_report_final.pdf.
Richardson, Herbert. *Nun, Witch, Playmate*. New York: Harper & Row, 1971.
Rivers, Julian. "Could Marriage Be Disestablished?" *TynBul* 68 (2017) 121–51.
Roberts, Robert C. *Spiritual Emotions: A Psychology of Christian Virtues*. Grand Rapids: Eerdmans, 2007. Kindle.

Rodrigues, David, and Diniz Lopes. "Sociosexuality, Commitment, and Sexual Desire for an Attractive Person." *Archives of Sexual Behavior* 46 (2017) 775–88.

Rogers, Eugene F., Jr., ed. *Theology and Sexuality: Classic and Contemporary Readings.* Blackwell Readings in Modern Theology. Malden, MA: Blackwell, 2002.

Ruether, Rosemary Radford. *Christianity and the Making of the Modern Family.* London: SCM, 2001.

Russell, Scarlett, and Dean Kissick. "Is Tinder Really Creating a 'Dating Apocalypse'?" *Guardian*, Aug. 16, 2015.

Ryan, Christopher, and Cacilda Jetha. *Sex at Dawn: How We Mate, Why We Stray, and What it Means for Modern Relationships.* New York: HarperCollins, 2010. Kindle.

Ryken, Leland. *Worldly Saints: The Puritans as They Really Were.* Grand Rapids: Zondervan, 1986. Kindle.

Saggino, Aristide, et al. "Compatibility Quotient, and Its Relationship with Marital Satisfaction and Personality Traits in Italian Married Couples." *Sexual and Relationship Therapy* 31 (2016) 83–94.

Sales, Nancy Jo. "Tinder and the Dawn of the Dating Apocalypse." *Vanity Fair*, Aug. 6, 2015. https://www.google.com/amp/s/www.vanityfair.com/culture/2015/08/tinder-hook-up-culture-end-of-dating/amp.

Salzman, Todd A., and Michael G. Lawler. *Sexual Ethics: A Theological Introduction.* Washington, DC: Georgetown University Press, 2012.

———. *The Sexual Person: Toward a Renewed Catholic Anthropology.* Washington, DC: Georgetown University Press, 2008.

Sharfman, Amanda, and Pamela Cobb. "Families and Households in the UK: 2021." Office for National Statistics, Mar. 9, 2022. https://www.ons.gov.uk/peoplepopulationandcommunity/birthsdeathsandmarriages/families/bulletins/familiesandhouseholds/2021.

———. "Population Estimates for Marital Status and Living Arrangements, England and Wales: 2022." Office for National Statistics, Jan. 25, 2024. https://www.ons.gov.uk/peoplepopulationandcommunity/populationandmigration/populationestimates/bulletins/populationestimatesbymaritalstatusandlivingarrangements/2022.

Shults, F. LeRon. *Reforming Theological Anthropology: After the Philosophical Turn to Relationality.* Grand Rapids: Eerdmans, 2003. Kindle.

Silva, Jennifer M. *Coming Up Short: Working-Class Adulthood in An Age of Uncertainty.* New York: Oxford University Press, 2013. Kindle.

Skolnick, Arlene S., and Jerome K. Skolnick, eds. *Family in Transition.* 17th ed. New York: Pearson, 2014. Kindle.

Slater, Dan. *A Million First Dates: Solving the Puzzle of Online Dating.* New York: Penguin, 2014. Kindle.

Smedes, Lewis B. *Sex for Christians: The Limits and Liberties of Sexual Living.* Rev. ed. Grand Rapids: Eerdmans, 1994.

Smit, Laura A. *Loves Me, Loves Me Not: The Ethics of Unrequited Love.* Grand Rapids: Baker Academic, 2005.

Smith, Hollie. "'Sugar Baby' Students Sell Their Company to Fund Studies." BBC, Mar. 29, 2018. http://www.bbc.co.uk/news/uk-wales-43416627.

Song, Robert. "Creator, Christ, and Sexuality." In *The Routledge Companion to Christian Ethics*, edited by D. Stephen Long and Rebekah L. Miles. Routledge Religion Companions. New York: Routledge, 2023.

Spaemann, Robert. *Persons: The Difference between 'Someone' and 'Something'*. Translated by Oliver O'Donovan. Oxford: Oxford University Press, 1996, 2006.

Stanley, Scott. "Is Cohabitation Still Linked to Greater Odds of Divorce?" Institute for Family Studies, Jan. 12, 2021. https://ifstudies.org/blog/is-cohabitation-still-linked-to-greater-odds-of-divorce.

Stassen, Glen H. *A Thicker Jesus: Incarnational Discipleship in a Secular Age*. Louisville: Westminster John Knox, 2012. Kindle.

Stassen, Glen H., and David P. Gushee. *Kingdom Ethics: Following Jesus in Contemporary Context*. Downers Grove, IL: InterVarsity, 2003. Kindle.

Statista. "Estimated Median Age of Americans at Their First Wedding in the United States from 1998 to 2022, by Sex." Statista, Sept. 2023. https://www.statista.com/statistics/371933/median-age-of-us-americans-at-their-first-wedding/.

Stephenson, Lisa. "Directed, Ordered and Related: The Male and Female Interpersonal Relation in Karl Barth's *Church Dogmatics*." *SJT* 61 (2008) 435–49.

Sternberg, Robert J. "A Triangular Theory of Love." *Psychological Review* 93 (1986) 119–35.

Sternberg, Robert J., and Karin Sternberg, eds. *The New Psychology of Love*. 2nd ed. Cambridge: Cambridge University Press, 2019. Kindle.

Sternberg, Robert J., and Karin Weis, eds. *The New Psychology of Love*. New Haven, CT: Yale University Press, 2006.

Stodart, Leah, and Miller Kern. "The Best Dating Sites for Finding a Boo Before Spring." Mashable, Apr. 10, 2023. https://mashable.com/roundup/best-dating-sites.

Stodart, Leah, et al. "The Best Dating Sites to Help You Find a Connection." Mashable, Sept. 11, 2024. https://mashable.com/uk/roundup/best-dating-sites-uk.

Stone, Lawrence. *The Family, Sex and Marriage in England 1500–1800*. New York: Harper & Row, 1977. Kindle.

Strauss, Mark E., and Paul E. Engle, eds. *Remarriage After Divorce in Today's Church: Three Views*. Grand Rapids: Zondervan, 2006. Kindle.

Stuart, Elizabeth. "The Theological Study of Sexuality." In *The Oxford Handbook of Theology, Sexuality, and Gender*, edited by Adrian Thatcher. Oxford Handbooks. Oxford: Oxford University Press, 2015. Kindle.

Stump, Eleonore. *Wandering in Darkness: Narrative and the Problem of Suffering*. Oxford: Oxford University Press, 2010. Kindle.

Sumter, Sindy R., et al. "Love Me Tinder: Untangling Emerging Adults' Motivations for Using the Dating Application Tinder." *Telematics and Informatics* 34 (2017) 67–78.

Swinton, John, and Harriet Mowat. *Practical Theology and Qualitative Research*. London: SCM, 2016. Kindle.

Szreter, Simon, and Kate Fisher. *Sex Before the Sexual Revolution: Intimate Life in England 1918–1963*. Cambridge Social and Cultural Histories 16. New York: Cambridge University Press, 2010. Kindle.

Tennov, Dorothy. *Love and Limerence*. Lanham: Scarborough, 1979. Kindle.

Thatcher, Adrian. *God, Sex, and Gender: An Introduction*. Chichester, UK: Wiley-Blackwell, 2011. Kindle.

———. *Living Together and Christian Ethics*. New Studies in Christian Ethics 21. Cambridge: Cambridge University Press, 2002. Kindle.

———. *Making Sense of Sex*. Modern Church. London: SPCK, 2012. Kindle.

———. "Marriage, the New Testament, and Pastoral Ministry." *Theology* 124 (2021) 420–27.

———, ed. *The Oxford Handbook of Theology, Sexuality, and Gender*. Oxford Handbooks. Oxford: Oxford University Press, 2015. Kindle.
———. *Redeeming Gender*. Oxford: Oxford University Press, 2016. Kindle.
———. *Vile Bodies: The Body in Christian Teaching, Faith and Practice*. London: SCM, 2023. Kindle.
Thomas, Gabrielle. *The Image of God in the Theology of Gregory of Nazianzus*. Cambridge: Cambridge University Press, 2019. Kindle.
Tietz, Christiane. *Theologian of Resistance: The Life and Thought of Dietrich Bonhoeffer*. Translated by Victoria J. Barnett. Minneapolis: Fortress, 2016. Kindle.
Timmermans, Elisabeth, and Elien De Caluwé. "To Tinder or Not to Tinder, That's the Question: An Individual Differences Perspective to Tinder Use and Motives." *Personality and Individual Differences* 110 (2017) 74–79.
United States Census Bureau. "Number, Timing and Duration of Marriages and Divorces." United States Census Bureau, Apr. 22, 2021. Press release CB21-TPS.46. https://www.census.gov/newsroom/press-releases/2021/marriages-and-divorces.html.
Van Der Wyngaard, Jessica, dir. *I Survived "I Kissed Dating Goodbye."* N.p.: DOCSology, 2018.
Van Huyssteen, J. Wentzel. *Alone in the World? Human Uniqueness in Science and Theology*. Gifford Lectures. Grand Rapids: Eerdmans, 2006.
Van Nieuwenhove, Rik. *An Introduction to Medieval Theology*. Introduction to Religion. New York: Cambridge University Press, 2012. Kindle.
Van Ouytsel, Joris, et al. "Exploring the Role of Social Networking Sites Within Adolescent Romantic Relationships and Dating Experiences." *Computers in Human Behavior* 55 (2016) 76–86.
Van Thiel, Edwin. "Big Five Personality Traits." 123 Test, updated June 21, 2024. http://www.123test.com/big-five-personality-theory/.
Vilhauer, Jennice. "What to Do When You've Been Ghosted." American Psychological Association, Feb. 2020. *Speaking of Psychology*, episode 100. https://www.apa.org/news/podcasts/speaking-of-psychology/ghosting.
Vos, Pieter. *Longing for the Good Life: Virtue Ethics After Protestantism*. T&T Clark Enquiries in Theological Ethics. London: Bloomsbury T&T Clark, 2020. Kindle.
Wade, Lisa. *American Hookup: The New Culture of Sex on Campus*. New York: Norton, 2017. Kindle.
Waite, Linda J., and Maggie Gallagher. *The Case for Marriage: Why Married People Are Happier, Healthier, and Better Off Financially*. New York: Random House, 2000. Kindle.
Ward, Pete, and Knut Tveitereid. *The Wiley Blackwell Companion to Theology and Qualitative Research*. Wiley Blackwell Companions to Religion. Oxford: Wiley Blackwell, 2022. Kindle.
Watts, Fraser. "Psychology and Theology." In *The Cambridge Companion to Science and Religion*, edited by Peter Harrison. Cambridge Companions to Religion. New York: Cambridge University Press, 2010. Kindle.
———. *Psychology, Religion, and Spirituality: Concepts and Applications*. Cambridge Studies in Religion, Philosophy, and Society. Cambridge: Cambridge University Press, 2017. Kindle.

Webb, William J. "A Redemptive-Movement Model." In *Four Views on Moving Beyond the Bible to Theology*, edited by Stanley N. Gundry and Gary T. Meadors. Counterpoints: Bible and Theology. Grand Rapids: Zondervan, 2009. Kindle.

———. *Slaves, Women & Homosexuals: Exploring the Hermeneutics of Cultural Analysis*. Hermeneutics. Downers Grove, IL: IVP Academic, 2001.

Weber, Max. *Methodology of Social Sciences*. Edited and translated by Edward A. Shils and Henry A. Finch. Abingdon, UK: Routledge, 2017. Kindle.

Welcher, Rachel Joy. *Talking Back to Purity Culture: Rediscovering Faithful Christian Sexuality*. Downers Grove, IL: IVP, 2020. Kindle.

Wellings, Kaye, et al. *Sexual Behaviour in Britain: The National Survey of Sexual Attitudes and Lifestyles*. London: Penguin, 1994.

Wenham, Gordon. *Genesis 1–15*. WBC 1. Grand Rapids: Zondervan, 1987. Kindle.

Wetzel, James. *Augustine: A Guide for the Perplexed*. Guides for the Perplexed. London: Bloomsbury, 2010. Kindle.

———. "Splendid Vices and Secular Virtues: Variations on Milbank's Augustine." *JRE* 32 (2004) 271–300.

Whipp, Margaret. *Pastoral Theology*. SCM Studyguide. London: SCM, 2013. Kindle.

White, Lynn, Jr. "The Historical Roots of Our Ecologic Crisis." *Science* 155 (1967) 1203–7.

Wilcox, Brad, and Lyman Stone. "Too Risky to Wed in Your 20s? Not If You Avoid Cohabiting First." *Wall Street Journal*, Feb. 5, 2022. https://www.wsj.com/articles/too-risky-to-wed-in-your-20s-not-if-you-avoid-cohabiting-first-11644037261.

Williams, Rowan. "The Body's Grace." In *Theology and Sexuality: Classic and Contemporary Readings*, edited by Eugene F. Rogers Jr. Blackwell Readings in Modern Theology. Malden, MA: Blackwell, 2002.

———. *On Augustine*. London: Bloomsbury, 2016. Kindle.

Wilson, Glenn, and Jon Cousins. "Partner Similarity and Relationship Satisfaction: Development of a Compatibility Quotient." *Sexual and Relationship Therapy* 18 (2003) 161–70.

Winner, Lauren. *Real Sex: The Naked Truth About Chastity*. Grand Rapids: Brazos, 2005. Kindle.

Witte, John, Jr. *From Sacrament to Contract: Marriage, Religion, and Law in the Western Tradition*. 2nd ed. Louisville: Westminster John Knox, 2012. Kindle.

———. "Sex and Marriage in the Protestant Tradition, 1500–1900." In *The Oxford Handbook of Theology, Sexuality, and Gender*, edited by Adrian Thatcher. Oxford Handbooks. Oxford: Oxford University Press, 2015. Kindle.

Witte, John, Jr., and Robert M. Kingdon. *Courtship, Engagement, and Marriage*. Vol. 1 of *Sex, Marriage, and Family in John Calvin's Geneva*. Religion, Marriage and Family. Grand Rapids: Eerdmans, 2005. Kindle.

Wolterstorff, Nicholas. *Educating for Shalom: Essays on Christian Higher Education*. Edited by Clarence W. Joldersma and Gloria Goris Stronks. Grand Rapids: Eerdmans, 2004. Kindle.

Wood, James. "Introduction." In *The Book of Common Prayer*. 350th anniv. ed. Penguin Classics Deluxe. London: Penguin, 2012. Kindle.

Wright, N. T. *The Challenge of Jesus*. London: SPCK, 2000.

———. "Faith, Virtue, Justification, and the Journey to Freedom." In *The Word Leaps the Gap: Essays on Scripture and Theology in Honor of Richard B. Hays*, edited by J. Ross Wagner et al. Grand Rapids: Eerdmans, 2008. Kindle.

———. *Paul and the Faithfulness of God*. London: SPCK, 2012.

———. *Scripture and the Authority of God*. London: SPCK, 2005.

Wright, Tom. *Broken Signposts: How Christianity Makes Sense of the World*. London: SPCK, 2020.

———. *Justification: God's Plan and Paul's Vision*. London: SPCK, 2009.

———. *Virtue Reborn*. London: SPCK, 2010.

———. *What Saint Paul Really Said: Was Paul of Tarsus the Real Founder of Christianity?* Oxford: Lion Hudson, 1997.

Young, Ben, and Samuel Adams. *The Ten Commandments of Dating*. Nashville: Nelson, 1999. Kindle.

Zahl, David. *Seculosity: How Career, Parenting, Technology, Food, Politics, and Romance Became Our New Religion and What to Do About It*. Minneapolis: Fortress, 2019. Kindle.

Zimmerman, Kari-Shane Davis. "Hooking Up: Sex, Theology, and Today's 'Unhooked' Dating Practices." *Hor* 37 (2010) 72–91.